REMEDIAL CHRISTIANITY

REMEDIAL CHRISTIANITY

What Every Believer Should Know
about the Faith,
but Probably Doesn't

PAUL ALAN LAUGHLIN

with Glenna S. Jackson

Polebridge Press

Remedial Christianity: What Every Believer Should Know about the Faith, but Probably Doesn't

Unless otherwise noted, quotations from the gospels are taken from Scholars Version translation in *The Complete Gospels*, copyright 1992, 1994 by Polebridge Press. Used by permission. All rights reserved. Other biblical quotations are from the New Revised Standard Version Bible, copyright 1989, Division of Christian Education of the National Council of the Churches of Christ in the United States of America. Used by permission. All rights reserved.

Design and illustrations by Ron Cox

Library of Congress Cataloging-in-Publication Data

Laughlin, Paul A., 1946–
    Remedial Christianity : what every believer should know about the faith but probably doesn't / Paul Alan Laughlin ; with Glenna S. Jackson.
        p. cm.
    Includes bibliographical references and index.
    ISBN 0-944344-77-1
    1. Christianity I. Jackson, Glenna S. II. Title.

    BR121.2 .L29 1999
    230-- dc21

                                                            00-049452

CONTENTS

Foreword   vii

Introduction   1

Chapter 1
The Bible in Historical Perspective   9

Chapter 2
Christian Theism and Its Alternatives   39

Chapter 3
Jesus of Nazareth and the Origins of Christianity   73

Chapter 4
The Christ of Faith in the History of Christianity   107

Chapter 5
Sin and Human Nature in the Christian Tradition   139

Chapter 6
Grace and Salvation in the Christian Tradition   171

Chapter 7
The Church and the Churches from Pentecost
to the Parousia   201

Chapter 8
Alternative Christian Views, the World's Religions,
and the Future of the Faith   229

Conclusion   257

Glossary   259

Index   277

FOREWORD

I tagged onto this work initially as a new faculty member teaching the required sophomore religion course at Otterbein College. After several quarters of frustration in an unsuccessful attempt to find an appropriate textbook, Paul Laughlin (my colleague and departmental Chairperson) casually suggested that I take a look at a text entitled *Remedial Christianity*, which he had created for the same course some years earlier. It fit my syllabus and agenda perfectly and I have been using versions of it ever since with excellent results. During this time, students have reacted to *Remedial Christianity* passionately—either for or against, with not many in between those extremes. Most of those who reject the ideas, approach, and attitude presented in the book are the very ones whom Paul Laughlin identifies as Fundamentalists; others find the book refreshing and humorous; all find it thought-provoking and educational.

One of my missions in teaching—from my years as a Director of Christian Education to my present tenure as college professor and Fellow of the Jesus Seminar interested in re-educating adults, youth, and children about the historical Jesus and related issues—has always been to place the Christian tradition in its proper context, that is, as a product of communities of faith. I have always believed it to be essential for students to become adept at identifying the raw materials of these communities and to explore the role of their faith in the Christian past and present. *Remedial Christianity* helps students in that task by introducing them to some of the methods and many of the results of historical-critical scholarship in biblical and religious studies.

As a biblical scholar, I appreciate the fact that *Remedial Christianity* begins with the Bible, thereby reflecting Dr. Laughlin's belief (and mine) that central to any serious study of Christianity—whether it be in a college classroom, in a church school setting, or in the privacy of one's home—is placing the scriptural heart of the faith in its true historical context. That means, first of all, recognizing the Bible both as a product of reflection upon God and the divine-human relationship and as a source of further thought on these important matters. But, as the opening chapter of *Remedial Christianity* makes clear, the Bible as a product of reflection does not begin to exhibit a uniformity of belief on any topic, including the character and role of Jesus; and as a source for further thought the Bible has always been open to a wide range of interpretations even within the Christian fold, and remains so today. Moreover, as Dr. Laughlin points out, the Bible is only one among many other such sources, including reason, experience, tradition, and even other scriptures, religions, and philosophies.

But *Remedial Christianity* doesn't stop with the Bible. For those who assume, as many of my incoming students do, that one either believes in God or does not, chapter 2 provides a variety of theologies (that is, ways of viewing God). And for those Christians who naïvely assume that what they know about Jesus is historically correct or sound, and that the Christian tradition is based primarily on what Jesus allegedly said and did, *Remedial Christianity* helps to correct this state of religious illiteracy with separate chapters on the Jesus of history and the Christ of faith, which together clarify the crucial distinction between the actual person and the orthodox Christian tradition's image (or images) of him. The book then proceeds to identify and focus upon the mainstream Western Christian tradition that begins with St. Paul, then adds to the discussion other less influential currents (for example, Gnosticism, mysticism, Eastern orthodoxy, and Liberalism), thus demonstrating how much variety there really is within Christianity—doctrinal, spiritual, and denominational. For those (probably the majority) who assume (innocently but incorrectly) that the Church (Roman Catholic, Protestant, or otherwise) and all of its teachings have their origins in the Bible, Laughlin presents factual information about both the first century of the Common Era and the religious traditions preceding and succeeding that time, all of which paints a much more complicated, but also more accurate picture of how Christianity as we know it, in all of its diversity, came to be.

One of the real bonuses of *Remedial Christianity* is the author's interest and expertise in Eastern religious traditions, particularly Hinduism, Buddhism, and Taoism. His deep familiarity with and appreciation for these faiths allow him to use them to illuminate Christianity in an excitingly fresh way. The resulting connections that he makes are a lively part of virtually every chapter, and are sure to fuel the thought and discussion that are bound to arise from this book.

It has been my experience that *Remedial Christianity*, with all else that it does, is also instrumental in helping its readers gain critical and analytic skills that will improve rational thinking and problem-solving, and in assisting them to form judgments and make decisions about religious matters. I know from experience that thought and discussion stemming from this text will open minds, enhance religious tolerance, and make religion relevant.

Remedial Christianity was originally designed for use in the college classroom, but has evolved into a work that can be most useful for both formal Christian education and for individuals seeking independent intellectual edification and spiritual growth. To Dr. Laughlin, for writing this book, and to all Otterbein students in our "Human Nature in the Christian Tradition" classes over the years who have contributed to its production through their participation, evaluations, and suggestions, I express my sincere gratitude and continued enthusiasm.

Glenna S. Jackson
Otterbein College
December, 1998

INTRODUCTION

"...writing books involves endless hard work...."

—Ecclesiastes 12:12 *(New Jerusalem Bible)*

"Of making many books there is no end...."

—Ecclesiastes 12:12 *(New Revised Standard Version)*

Whether either of these translations comes close to the real meaning of this biblical proverb is anybody's guess, given the utter ambiguity of the original Hebrew text. But the fact is that both assertions are profoundly true: the writing of books is certainly laborious *and* more and more of them are published every day, despite the seeming glut of existing titles. A fair question, then, is why anyone would go to the enormous trouble of adding yet another volume to an already flooded market—particularly in the field of religion, in which the proliferation of new titles seems especially relentless.

This book arose, quite simply, from my own perception of a need for an introduction to the Christian faith directed primarily to those who profess it, and informed by academic religious studies. That perception, in turn, is based on my nearly quarter century as both a teacher of religious studies at the collegiate and seminary levels and an ordained Christian minister who has taught classes and led seminars on various topics in many local churches of a variety of denominations. What has impressed me most about this experience is the lack of basic knowledge that my students typically have brought to the subject—not just about this or that distinctive denominational doctrine, but of the basic contents of the Christian message itself.

Not only have my incoming students exhibited little sense of what it means to assert that Christians are historically monotheists (as opposed, say, to deists, pantheists, or monists), but their initial comments about God, Christ, and the Holy Spirit (much less the Trinity) have been so vague and superficial (and often purely sentimental) as to reflect little real understanding. Even such distinctive and indeed axial Christian doctrines as Sin, Grace, Incarnation, and Atonement are at worst barely recognized and at best completely unexamined, dimly grasped, and unrelated to one another in any consistent way. Consequently, any profession of faith that my students might make or notion of salvation that they might harbor is groundless, free-floating, and without context—theological, existential, psychological, or sociological.

If my thousands of students over the years are at all representative of the larger population, and I believe that they are, I must conclude that the vast majority of Christians today simply don't know nearly as much about their professed religion as they should; or, to put it more strongly, they are pervasively and persistently ignorant about the very faith they claim to embrace. Indeed, it is not uncommon for students in one of my college courses, after weeks of exposure to information about the scripture, theology, and historical development of Christianity, to wonder silently and sometimes inquire aloud why no one has ever told them this important "stuff" before.

To be sure, some of my students may lack knowledge about their faith because they belong to denominations and sects of Christianity that do not require their ministers or other church leaders to be formally educated, and that even discourage it on the dubious grounds that knowledge and faith, intellect and piety are somehow mutually inimical. But in truth, most of my students were born and reared in mainline (which is to say, "standard-brand") Protestant and Roman Catholic churches, both of which traditions profess an appreciation for higher education and require graduate-professional education for their clergy. These students have attended Sunday School or catechism classes or their equivalents for much of their lives. Most would classify themselves as sincere and informed Christians. Yet nearly all of the facts about the faith that they encounter in my college courses or weekend workshops are literally *news* to them.

One explanation for this strange and sad situation may be that most Christian churches entrust religious education to sincere and well-meaning—and perhaps even spiritual and pious—lay persons who are nevertheless untrained and ill-prepared as educators. On the whole, lay religious education in nearly all Christian denominations is abysmally deficient. In fact, to call it "education" at all is often a generous assessment. It is an abiding irony that for the instruction of grammar school students in the three Rs, general science, or physical education we insist on well-educated, supervised, certified, and experienced professional teachers; but we then assign the religious, spiritual, and theological edification of these same children— and indeed of all age groups—to any volunteers who will devote enough time and effort to stay a page or two ahead of their students in the church school lesson book, and who will show up consistently and on time for class. With responsibility for Christian education left largely to amateurs, it is no wonder that ignorance of the faith among the faithful is rampant.

In all fairness, it must be said that a considerable share of the blame for this sad situation belongs to the clergy, most of whom—at least in the mainstream denominations—are well-schooled in the history and doctrines of Christianity and thus are fully aware of some of the faith's inconsistencies, contradictions, and other potentially troubling aspects. Once they find themselves in their parish assignments, however, many if not most ministers and priests have the unfortunate but understandable tendency to let other important concerns and activities get in the way of the education of their parishioners. But the real problem is more likely their fear of shaking the faith of their flock (and thereby perhaps jeopardizing their own job security and professional advancement) by challenging long-held, but naïve and mistaken religious notions. Sometimes it is just easier and safer to allow parishioners the comfort of their ignorance—to let sleeping dogmas lie, as it were.

My students' reactions over the years have persuaded me that ignorance of the Christian faith among its followers is the rule rather than the exception. Indeed, I came to realize quite early on that I was really teaching what my old grade school teachers would have called a "remedial" course, designed for students who for some reason didn't know nearly as much about a particular subject as they should, given their ages and backgrounds.

On the positive side, my teaching experience has also convinced me that Christians, once primed with and piqued by a little real information about their faith, are eager to learn more about it, including the points at which incongruities and uncertainties present themselves. It has also become clear to me that many believers have secretly harbored questions and doubts, sometimes for many years, but have kept silent about them out of fear or guilt. I continue to be especially touched by the relief expressed by the middle-aged and elderly folks in my classes and seminars who have just learned that a belief or doctrine that has perplexed or discomforted them for decades—the Trinity, the Virgin Birth, the divinity of Christ, or the verbal inerrancy of the Bible, for example—not only is problematical on rational or historical grounds or both, but has troubled professional theologians for centuries. These students are much relieved to find that teachings they had always believed to be essential are neither necessarily true nor truly necessary to the faith; and they are pleasantly surprised and gratefully reassured to be told that to have healthy doubts about such things is not sinful, but sensible.

Almost as disturbing to me as the pervasive ignorance among my incoming students has been the poor quality of the introductory books on Christianity currently available—all of which I examined, many of which I tried in my courses, and none of which proved effective or satisfactory. The purpose of this book from its inception, then, has been to inform Christian believers about their faith tradition in a clear and compelling way, and in so doing to free them to inquire and think about it intentionally and seriously. To that end, in the pages that follow I shall discuss in historical context the very scriptures, beliefs, and doctrines that have characterized Western Christianity, by which I mean Roman Catholicism and Protestantism, and that have distinguished it from other world religions. Indeed, whenever this book mentions and describes "traditional" or "orthodox" Christian belief, unless otherwise noted (for example, by capitalizing the "O" to indicate Eastern Orthodoxy), it will be referring to the teachings that most Christian denominations in the Western world share—at least historically and officially—despite the sometimes profound doctrinal discrepancies among them.

In the process, I shall be largely ignoring two important components of Christianity. First, for most of the book I shall be paying little attention to Eastern Orthodox Christianity, not because of any lack of appreciation on my part for that venerable tradition's history or views, but for the simple reason that it is far more common in certain parts of Europe and Asia than it is in the Americas, where its impact on the culture and popular piety (mostly in its Greek and Russian forms) has been relatively small. The distinctiveness and nobility of Eastern Orthodoxy will, however, be recognized and treated appreciatively in the book's final chapter. Second, I shall be paying very little attention to specific *practices* and how these vary from one Christian denomination to another, but will concentrate instead on *doctrines*. That focus is a concession to space and to my own interest, and should not be taken as a disparagement of the important role of the practical dimensions (for example, ritual and ethics) in religion generally or Christianity in particular.

This book is topically arranged. Chapter 1 begins with the Bible, and examines its nature, structure, and history, as well as the sticky issues of inspiration and authority. Chapter 2 turns attention to theology proper, and defines the monotheistic view of God that makes Christianity similar to some world religions and very different from others. Chapter 3 focuses upon the historical Jesus, in order to see how much (or little) we can really know about the man who became the foundation of the faith. Chapter 4 also deals with Jesus, but specifically as he has been identified and venerated through the ages—particularly in beliefs, doctrines, and theologies—as the Christ of faith. Chapters 5 and 6 address the pivotal and interrelated issues of sin and salvation respectively, and explain why traditional Western Christianity promotes what is arguably the most negative view of human nature among the world's religions—or, to put it another way, the most radical view of sin; and why, not coincidentally, it also claims for its founder the most dramatic and drastic act of redemption. Chapter 6 also explains why, when traditional Christianity envisions eternal life, it does so sometimes in terms of immortality of the soul, and sometimes in terms of resurrection of the body. Chapter 7 then covers in broad strokes the place of the Church in the life of the faith, and attempts to make sense of two curious phenomena: the extraordinary and sometimes contentious denominational variety within Christianity and the persistent and occasionally intense expectation of the Second Coming of Christ. The book's final chapter looks at historical and contemporary Christian departures from the mainstream tradition, as well as at

Christianity's place among other world religions, and suggests certain directions that the Christian faith might productively explore in its third millennium.

I know from experience that an excursion through topics like these is sometimes hard, confusing, slow-going, discomforting, threatening, and even downright scary for the uninitiated; and that exposure to this kind of remedial knowledge in an historical perspective often causes some consternation and pain on the part of the learner, especially at first. It is difficult for anyone to have long-standing and cherished assumptions questioned, challenged, or destroyed. Like all effective education, however, real Christian education sometimes requires dispelling entrenched misinformation and shaking and even shattering some treasured biases and beliefs. In religious studies as well as most other worthwhile pursuits, it really is often a matter of "No pain, no gain."

Let me therefore issue a word of assurance, again based upon my experience with students: if at first you feel deeply intimidated or downright assaulted by the new facts and perspectives contained in this book, simply hang in there and press on! The Christian faith itself and the faithful who embrace it can not only withstand the kind of inquiry that I undertake and information that I impart in the present volume, but will at last be edified and strengthened by it.

While I am certainly not a complete rationalist in matters of faith and theology, I have no doubt whatsoever that it is far better to apply our intellects to the faith than to disengage them from it. I am also certain that ignorance of the faith on the part of the faithful is detrimental not only to their faith, but to the faith itself. I would even argue that the very survival of the message and mission of Christianity and the Church in their third millennium depends in large part on the creation and cultivation of a laity thoroughly educated in their own religious heritage and at least conversant with alternative views presented by other faiths and philosophies, not to mention the natural sciences.

Catholic and mainline Protestant clergy who are seminary graduates will find little new or controversial in this book, although they may not always agree with my interpretations or emphases. In fact, for the majority of them, both the approach and most of the subject matter contained here will probably seem old hat—a mere recapitulation of the formal education for ministry to which they have been exposed. As far as they (and their college and seminary professors of religious studies) are concerned, therefore, I am not breaking new ground or unearthing new truths in the pages that follow, though they might find an original interpretation or two to consider, especially in the later chapters. But the book was not written for them. It is intended to be a guide for inquisitive laypersons, both convinced believers and committed seekers, into what for most of them will be new territory, areas previously entered and inhabited (and sometimes, unfortunately, guarded) almost exclusively by paid professionals like me.

My hope is that this book will both convey to lay readers the kind of information and ideas and stimulate the sort of curiosity and independent thinking that will lead to intellectual and spiritual growth among convinced believers and committed seekers. Thus I intend it not as the end of a journey, but as a beginning. I sincerely hope that no one will take anything that I or anyone may say about any aspect of the Christian faith or any other religion at face value or as the last word, but will be driven by what he or she reads and hears to thoughtful consideration, as well as to libraries and bookstores, in order to test any and all claims.

To that end, I have provided at the end of each chapter not only a set of questions for further thought and discussion, but also a list of suggested works that I believe will help the reader who wishes to pursue the topic further. The authors of these recommended books are by no means of one mind, but rather represent a variety of perspectives on each particular topic. The one thing that they have in common is that they accept, as I do, the presuppositions and methods of modern historical-critical scholarship. What this means, to put it simply, is that we all agree that *careful, contextual, and comparative* biblical and theological study is a truly effective and appropriate route to religious and spiritual truth.

Though I am solely responsible for the contents of *Remedial Christianity*, and especially for any shortcomings therein, I would be both untruthful and ungrateful to claim the book as solely my own. I am indebted first of all to the many Otterbein College students who have been required to work (and sometimes suffer) through early drafts of this book over the last decade or so, and particularly to the many of them who have made helpful suggestions and corrections. Chief among these is Ms. Penelope Morgan, a former student and steadfast friend, who for the better part of a decade has been gently badgering me to publish this book. I am deeply grateful as well to my good friend, spiritual adviser, and perspicacious reviser, Dr. C. Grey Austin, whose careful readings and emendations have made this a far more substantial and readable book than it otherwise would have been—and to his wife, Barb, who frequently got both of us unstuck with just the right word or phrase. I owe a great deal as well to Dr. Robert W. Funk, founder of both the Jesus Seminar and the Westar Institute, for his interest in and enthusiasm for the book, as well as for his wise criticisms and helpful suggestions for improving it. My sincere thanks extend as well to Ms. Char Matejovsky and the fine editorial staff at Polebridge Press for their excellent work, and especially to Mr. Tom Hall, whose meticulous, thoughtful, and good-humored editing of style and substance clarified, enhanced, smoothed, and polished the text throughout; and to Mr. Ron Cox, whose great artistic talent and considerable graphic expertise have added much style and charm to this book.

A very special and heartfelt word of gratitude is owed to my esteemed departmental colleague and valued friend, Dr. Glenna Jackson, who modestly describes her work on this book as "tagging on." The fact that this book exists at all in its present form is largely through her encouragement and efforts. Having used and tested early drafts of *Remedial Christianity* in the classroom more than anyone, including myself, she has been an avid witness to its effectiveness and a staunch advocate of its publication for years, even after my own teaching responsibilities had led me to other academic interests and research projects. It was she who brought the working manuscript that we had been using in the classroom to the attention of Dr. Funk and Polebridge Press. As an active Fellow of the Jesus Seminar, she then worked diligently and patiently with me to bring the book up to speed on current New Testament scholarship, and then served as a true, tireless, and cheerful collaborator in molding the entire book into its final form. Readers of this book and I are deeply in her debt.

Last but certainly not least of all, I am grateful to my dear wife Randy, who not only supported me morally and spiritually through the demanding process of multiple revisions and deadlines, but gave me a strong indication of the book's potential by marrying me not long after reading an early draft of it in its unpolished entirety. I lovingly dedicate *Remedial Christianity* to her.

Paul Alan Laughlin
Otterbein College
Advent, 1998

THE BIBLE
IN HISTORICAL
PERSPECTIVE

Objectives of this chapter:

- to present the Bible as a rich library, representing a delightful variety of authors, viewpoints, and discrepancies

- to introduce higher criticism as a valuable tool of modern biblical scholarship

- to show the structure of the Bible and the literary types represented in its two Testaments

- to provide an overview of the historical evolution of the Bible, including the place of oral tradition, manuscripts, copying, translation, and canonization—and the books that were left out

- to examine the important and interrelated issues of inspiration and authority, with special attention to how Fundamentalism and Liberalism deal with them

*T*he centrality of the Bible in the Christian faith is undeniable and appropriate. After all, it contains valuable evidence for the background and origins of Christianity, including some of the earliest and—however incomplete and biased—the most detailed information about Jesus available. It further serves as the basis for all the major beliefs, doctrines, and creeds associated with Christianity, and, despite widely varying views and interpretations of its contents and meaning, it provides the touchstone for faith and practice for every denomination of Christianity.

Ironically, however, no aspect of Christianity is more misunderstood and misused by Christians themselves than the Bible. The common description of it as "The Good Book," for example, obscures a central but often ignored fact about it: it is not a book at all, but a collection of individual writings. Indeed, the very title "Bible" comes from the Greek *ta biblia*, meaning "the books." Taken from a much larger number of ancient Hebrew and Christian writings, these books underwent a long and complicated process of selection and compilation in accordance with various criteria reflecting a host of perceived needs. They speak, therefore, out of different contexts, with distinctive voices, and from divergent viewpoints. Yet, again and again we are either led to believe or told outright that the Bible is the product of a single mind; that it is thus completely coherent and consistent, infallible and inerrant; that its contents therefore admit of only one possible interpretation; and that to deny or even to question any of these premises is to negate not only the importance of "God's Word," but the validity of the faith itself.

The truth of the matter is, however, that the Bible is a treasure trove of literature exhibiting wide variety in genre, style, vocabulary, theology, and quality; that, in its present form, it has a definite structure that "houses" that variety; that it has a long and complicated history; that its contents, as well as its inspiration and authority, are open to more than one understanding; and that it not only invites but withstands a wide range of interpretation. Thus Christians and non-Christians may well disagree about *whether* the Bible is "the Word of God," while Christians may differ among themselves concerning *how* the Bible is "the Word of God."

This chapter explores the Bible from an historical perspective. It examines that body of religious literature with respect to its nature, structure, and history, as well as with regard to the related issues of its inspiration and authority. The underlying conviction in this exercise is that every Christian should know what the Bible really is; for only then will it be truly useful as a religious standard and spiritual guide.

The Nature of the Bible

The fundamental fact about the Bible is that it did not one day "drop out of heaven" like some divine telegram, or get carried down from some mountaintop by a fortunate recipient. It is a collection of largely separate writings, a kind of library of ancient literature, which gradually came together over many centuries in response to real human needs and desires, eventually gained widespread acceptance, and finally evolved into the literary monument (at the very least) that it is today. The Bible is, in short, the product of a process, one that left its indelible marks.

Variety and Inconsistency in the Bible

The Bible exhibits the same kind of variety that one would expect to find in any anthology, with one important exception: all or nearly all of its books were written by men. Indeed, one unfortunate shortcoming of the Bible from a modern perspective is its androcentricity, that is, its male-centeredness. Some modern biblical scholars have suggested that women may have written some books or portions thereof—most notably, Mark, John, Hebrews, and one of the documentary sources of the first five books of the so-called Old Testament; and it is certainly the case that women play prominent and often crucial roles in the Bible: Eve, Sarah, Ruth, Esther, several Marys, Prisca, Phoebe, and Hulda, for example. But the fact is that most of the language and imagery—not to mention the fundamental orientation and perspective of the Bible, beginning with its dominant images of God as "Lord" and "King"—is androcentric, reflecting the ancient patriarchal societies in which it was written. The result is that women are often portrayed in and relegated to subservient roles, while the relatively few important women and gems of feminine imagery for God and God's Wisdom (Sophia) are overshadowed, and thus easily overlooked or downplayed—an injustice that modern biblical interpretation is working very hard to redress.

Be that as it may, the Bible has many authors, some named, some claimed, and some simply anonymous. Its books come from different periods of ancient history, and arose from divergent situations and cultural, social, and political contexts to meet disparate needs. The writings are of various literary types (or genres) and lengths, they exhibit a wide range of styles, and they reflect a diversity of viewpoints, even with respect to theology.

The biblical writings, in fact, exhibit the same kind of inconsistencies and downright contradictions that one would expect when many authors are involved. These are too numerous to catalogue here, but let two important examples illustrate the point. In the first place, there are not one but two creation stories in Genesis (1:1–2:4a and 2:4b–2:25), written at least three centuries apart and contradictory in many, if not most respects. The first (which is actually the more recent) is the seven-day account, in which God commands the universe into existence one portion at a time and climaxes the entire work on the sixth day by creating male and female humankind in a *single* act and *after* the production of all vegetation and animals. The second (but older) implies a single day of creation in which God works more as an artisan, horticulturalist, and husbandman, creating first a man, then vegetation, then animal life, and finally—either to cure an oversight or to provide the *pièce de résistance*—woman.

A second important place that one finds incredible variations and contradictions is in the New Testament gospels. Matthew, Mark and Luke tend to be in general though hardly total agreement, with John almost invariably going his own distinctive way. The first three, for example, have Jesus speaking in short epigrams and parables about the kingdom of God (or God's domain, reign, or imperial rule), and making hardly any claims for himself at all. John has Jesus speaking in long, convoluted, and sometimes abstruse discourses, seldom mentioning the kingdom, and constantly calling attention to himself. (The seven familiar "I am" assertions—for example, "I am the Way, the Truth, and the Life" and "I am the Vine"—all come from John). Matthew, Mark, and Luke have Jesus conducting a ministry that could not have lasted more than a year and making only one career-ending trip to Jerusalem; John has Jesus making three Passover trips to Jerusalem during his ministry, which must therefore have lasted more than two years and perhaps three. John also reports the last supper as a common meal prior to Passover, while the others make it a specifically paschal meal during Passover. And so on.

The reason for the relative consistency between the first three gospels is that both Matthew and Luke almost certainly used the earlier Gospel of Mark as one of their sources. (Thus they are commonly called the "*Synoptic* Gospels," since they can be "viewed together" or "look alike.") Yet Matthew and Luke often adapted, altered, and rearranged Mark's contents, then added materials of their own to suit their own purposes. (See figure 1.1.) Indeed, the freedom with which they changed the content and order of their predecessor's work itself suggests anything but a literalistic approach to scripture on their part; and the many resulting variations in the three gospels make it obvious that even the Synoptic writers disagreed among themselves on minor and major points.

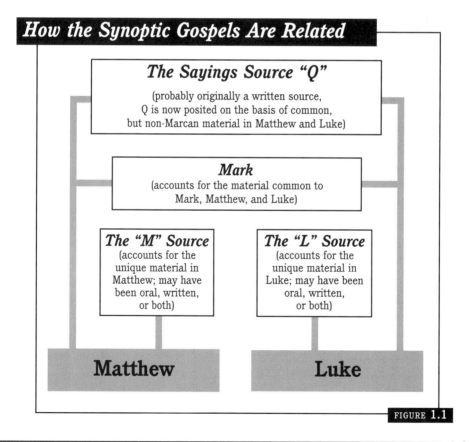

How the Synoptic Gospels Are Related

The Sayings Source "Q"

(probably originally a written source,
Q is now posited on the basis of common,
but non-Marcan material in Matthew and Luke)

Mark

(accounts for the material common to
Mark, Matthew, and Luke)

The "M" Source

(accounts for the
unique material in
Matthew; may have
been oral, written,
or both)

The "L" Source

(accounts for the
unique material in
Luke; may have been
oral, written,
or both)

Matthew

Luke

FIGURE 1.1

13

For example, in their accounts of the resurrection of Jesus and its after-math, Matthew, Mark, and Luke disagree about the names of the women who approached the tomb on Sunday morning, about whether it was before or after dawn, about what (or whom) they experienced and found there, about what instructions they were given, and about what they did as a result. Most incredibly, none of the three tells of the moving incident reported by John (almost certainly the latest of the four gospel writers), in which Mary Magdalene meets Jesus and mistakes him for a gardener, an incident so memorable that surely the earlier synoptic authors would have reported it had they known about it—unless, of course, they were purposely writing Mary out of the story.

Divine Authority and Inspiration

Despite the plethora of such obvious inconsistencies and contradictions, and irrespective of all of the undeniable variety in form and content within the Bible, some conservative Christian groups—particularly those known as "Fundamentalists"—assert a single, divine authorship for the books of the Bible. It is interesting that this claim is made despite the fact that not one of the books of the Bible claims to have been written by God. In fact, when-ever the books of the Bible speak to the issue at all, they claim (or at least imply) human authorship. Many of the books of the Old and New Testa-ments, for example, bear the names of their respective (or purported) authors. Even if these are late ascriptions, they bear a relatively early con-viction of human authorship on the part of those who most treasured them.

The Gospel according to Luke goes a significant step further. It not only claims human authorship by its very title, but in its preface states as clearly as possible a very practical human motivation and decision to write:

> Since so many have undertaken to compile an orderly narrative of the events that have run their course among us, just as the original eye-witnesses and ministers of the word transmitted them to us, it seemed good that I, too, after thoroughly researching everything from the beginning, should set them systematically in writing for you, Theophilus, so that your Excellency may realize the reliability of the teachings in which you have been instructed (Luke 1:1–4).

The absence of any mention of any sort of divine inspiration here is note-worthy in light of persistent, but finally unbiblical, claims and assumptions of God's authorship made on behalf of this and the other books of the Bible. That is not to say, of course, that Luke was not inspired. Inspiration is an important but complicated issue and will be discussed in detail later in the chapter. For now, let it suffice to say that, whatever inspiration Luke may have experienced then (or may exhibit now), it did not move him to give credit for authorship to God. In other words, Luke appears to have had no sense of being a "Holy Ghost-Writer"!

Over against such compelling biblical testimony to human authorship, the strongest and most often cited scriptural argument for divine authorship is

2 Timothy 3:16: "All scripture is inspired by God and is useful for teaching, for reproof, for correction, and for training in righteousness, so that everyone who belongs to God may be proficient, equipped for every good work." The word for "scripture" here refers to the "sacred writings" mentioned in the preceding verse, and probably meant the Hebrew scriptures, later called by Christians "the Old Testament." Taken at face value and literally, though, it could be seen as referring to all scripture of every religious tradition that existed in the world at that time—or now, for that matter! But when it was written, it certainly could not have referred to the New Testament, which did not yet exist as a body of scriptures, and would not for several centuries. In fact, some of the books eventually included in the New Testament were probably not yet widely known or even written when this verse was penned. So to use this verse to refer to the Bible as we know it is anachronistic at best, and to use it as the basis of a theory of inspiration appears to be a desperate effort to impose upon the biblical writings a non-scriptural idea of divine authorship. Indeed, the original Greek wording itself is ambiguous, and may well mean "Every God-inspired scripture is profitable. . . ." This would leave completely open to question which scriptures were and were not thus inspired. In any case, the verse is an insubstantial foundation for a general theory of biblical inspiration.

Higher Criticism and Real Bible Study

Recognition of the nature of the Bible as a diverse collection of human writings has led modern scholars of the Old and New Testaments to employ what is called "higher criticism" or the "historical-critical" method. This is a very complicated process, but what it boils down to is focusing on a single biblical writing in its own context, and asking such tough questions as these: (1) Who wrote this? (2) When and where was it written and what was going on then and there? (3) What kinds of sources (and precisely which ones) did this author (or these authors) use, and how did these affect the final product? (4) To what audience was the writing addressed, and what was the dynamic between it and the author? (5) What was the writer's purpose? These and similar questions attempt to examine the scriptures on their own terms and to avoid imposing modern or individual presuppositions on them.

Such an approach is "critical" not in the sense of being negative about the Bible—though that is often the fear and the charge of people who do not understand the process—but in the same way that a good movie critic is critical in reviewing a film: he or she may produce a glowing, positive review or a scathing, negative one, but in either case with sound judgment derived from a wealth of knowledge about cinematic history and technique. (The words "critic" and "critical," in fact, come from the Greek *kritikos*, which means "skilled in judging.") In the same way, a good biblical scholar may like or dislike a particular book of the Bible or a specific idea or concept in it, but in either case endeavors to use the accepted scholarly methods and standards in order to understand that piece of literature on its own terms. That means that he or she is attempting to determine what a text meant to its writer and first readers—the only real protection against a modern reader's unconscious (and usually anachronistic) preconceptions and subjective interpretations.

Some Protestant denominations and sects—many of them the same ones that require no specialized education for their clergy—disparage the use of higher criticism of the Bible, preferring to read it uncritically. These groups often found "Bible colleges," whose doctrinal constraints do not permit the freedom and scope of inquiry generally accepted in both secular and church-affiliated liberal arts colleges and universities. By contrast, most Catholic and mainstream Protestant clergy are trained in the historical-critical method of biblical study in seminary and probably use it in their own Bible study and in the preparation of their weekly sermons. Unfortunately, however, most laypeople are generally exposed to only a fraction of the results of their pastors' labors with scripture, are little acquainted with the process itself or its more daunting implications, and thus have few guidelines to follow in their own attempts to encounter the scriptures in a meaningful way.

One result of the widespread ignorance among lay people of the methods of quality biblical scholarship is that much of what passes for "Bible study" among Christians amounts to a mere sharing of impressions by well-intentioned, but woefully uninformed people. Typically such exercises treat a biblical book, or passage, or single verse simply as a message for us and our day—a kind of timeless telegram from God—with little concern for the context in which it was written or the intent of its author. Often the only credential that the leader of such a group can claim is that he or she has read the Bible "x" number of times.

By such reasoning one could claim expertise in the American legal system after reading the Constitution repeatedly, or in medicine simply through successive perusals of clinical textbooks! Such so-called "Bible studies" are perhaps best recognized and accepted for what they are: devotional readings of the scriptures intended for the edification rather than the education of the believer. Still, one has to wonder whether even devotional interests would be better served by consulting the critical results of professional Bible scholars and by discovering the original meanings of the texts in question.

The sections that follow attempt to afford lay people some guidance on approaching the Bible the way that the "pros" do, and the list of sources at the end of the chapter will provide a good start for anyone who wants to develop a fuller appreciation of the Bible's contents. Like this book, all of the works cited attempt to see the Bible in all of its richness and variety, and to read it for what it says on its own terms—contradictions and all; and most of the authors share with me the conviction that both the Bible and Christian faith can not only survive such scrutiny and the information that it yields, but may in fact be enhanced by it.

The Structure of the Bible

The most obvious structural feature of the Bible is its division into two Testaments, the Old and the New. These very designations, however, obscure an important point: what Christians call "Old Testament" was and is a body of spiritual writings, a scripture in its own right that in the eyes of the people who have held it most dear is not a mere preamble for, and has not been superseded by, some "New" (and presumably improved) writing. A recognition of the implicit disparagement couched in the phrase "Old Testament" has led an increasing number of Christians to refer to that body of writings as "The Hebrew Scriptures" or "The Hebrew Bible." Jews, of course, simply refer to it as "The Bible."

The Hebrew Bible (or Tripartite Tanakh)

What Christians call their "Old Testament" is really a collection of Hebrew literature, all of which was written before the time of Jesus. (See figure 1.2.) Most of these writings were originally separate pieces representing a variety of authors, genres, and periods; and except for a few chapters of one book (Daniel) in Aramaic, the spoken language of Jesus, all were written in the Hebrew language. These writings gradually became an authorized body of sacred writings (or "canon") called the *Tanakh* or Hebrew Bible—though there was some disagreement among various ancient Judean (proto-Jewish) communities about the number of books that should be included.

Most Christians probably don't know that, as a result of this ancient disagreement, their so-called Old Testament has different tables of contents for Roman Catholic, Eastern Orthodox, and Protestant believers. Catholics generally recognize forty-six books (although eight of these are sometimes paired to reduce that number to forty-two), as well as some additions to three others. The Catholic canon (that is, "official scripture") reflects the books accepted as canonical by ancient Greek-speaking Jews outside of

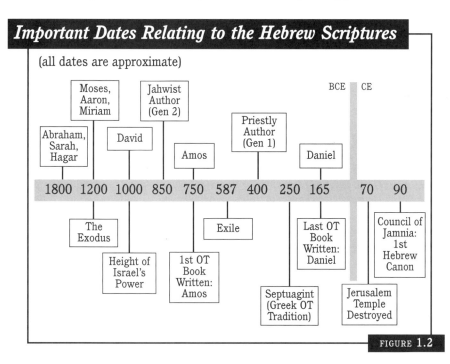

Important Dates Relating to the Hebrew Scriptures

(all dates are approximate)

| | | | | | | | | BCE | CE |

- Abraham, Sarah, Hagar
- Moses, Aaron, Miriam
- David
- Jahwist Author (Gen 2)
- Amos
- Priestly Author (Gen 1)
- Daniel

| 1800 | 1200 | 1000 | 850 | 750 | 587 | 400 | 250 | 165 | 70 | 90 |

- The Exodus
- Height of Israel's Power
- 1st OT Book Written: Amos
- Exile
- Septuagint (Greek OT Tradition)
- Last OT Book Written: Daniel
- Jerusalem Temple Destroyed
- Council of Jamnia: 1st Hebrew Canon

FIGURE 1.2

Palestine and included in the Septuagint, a pre-Christian Greek translation of the Hebrew scriptures. Eastern Orthodox Christians reduce that larger number to forty-three, while Protestants generally follow the lead of six-teenth-century reformer Martin Luther (the founder of Protestantism) and accept only the thirty-nine books regarded as canonical by first-century rab-bis of Palestine, who agreed upon that number at the Council of Jamnia in 90 CE. Protestants often refer to the remaining books of their Old Testament (that is, those included by Roman Catholicism and Eastern Orthodoxy) as "The Apocrypha."

Various Christian groups have ordered and categorized the Hebrew scrip-tures in their own distinctive patterns. One common schema, for example, divides the so-called Old Testament into Law, History, Poetry, Major Prophets, and Minor Prophets. Jews, however, have long divided their Bible into three parts: Law, Prophets, and Writings. (See figure 1.3.)

The Law (or Torah or Pentateuch) consists of the first five books (Gene-sis, Exodus, Leviticus, Numbers, and Deuteronomy), which contain some of the most familiar and beloved (if not always well understood) biblical sto-ries. Its authorship was traditionally attributed to Moses, a view maintained today only in the most conservative Jewish and Christian circles. Modern biblical scholarship in both traditions has determined beyond reasonable doubt—on the basis of vocabulary, style, and content—that Moses could not possibly have written these books as they now stand. In fact, scholars have detected the work of at least four different authors intermixed within these books, and perhaps the hand of a compiler-editor as well. Whatever their number, these writers were actually relating and correlating very ancient stories derived from the oral (that is, word-of-mouth) traditions of their Semitic predecessors. Nevertheless, the Torah remains the most sacred of scripture for religious Jews, as well as an important part of the Christian canon.

The second traditional division of the Hebrew canon is designated "the Prophets." This category is usually associated with the great prophets of the eighth century and later—the likes of Isaiah, Jeremiah, Ezekiel, Daniel, Amos, and Hosea. But it also includes earlier Hebrew writings—Joshua, Judges, 1 and 2 Samuel, and 1 and 2 Kings—that were really histories writ-ten from a prophetic perspective about a period in which the prophetic office had not yet fully emerged in its classic expression. But at no time in the his-tory of ancient Judaism were prophets prognosticators or "future tellers" in the way often perceived and portrayed. They are better understood as social critics who adopted a religious perspective and claimed divine sanction; who observed the behavior of their fellow citizens of Israel or Judah; and who warned them in the name of God that because they were breaking the his-toric covenant with God that had been in effect since the days of Abraham, they would certainly suffer dire consequences. In light of the number of mil-itant superpowers surrounding the Hebrew people and ready to overrun them in those days, it did not take a crystal ball, tea leaves, or even a sixth sense for a prophet to issue such a warning—any more than it does today for an ecologist to alert us to the cataclysmic environmental effects of fluorocarbon hairsprays or acid rain.

The Tanakh (Hebrew Bible)

Law (Torah)	Prophets (Nevi'im)	Writings (Khetuvim)
Genesis	Joshua	Psalms
Exodus	Judges	Proverbs
Leviticus	Samuel**	Job
Numbers	Kings**	Song of Songs
Deuteronomy	Isaiah	Ruth
	*Jeremiah	Lamentations
	Ezekiel	Ecclesiastes
		*Esther
		*Daniel
	["The Twelve"]	*Ezra
		Nehemiah
	Hosea Nahum	Chronicles**
	Joel Habukkuk	
	Amos Zephaniah	
	Obadiah Haggai	
	Jonah Zechariah	
	Micah Malachi	

1

The Bible
in Historical
Perspective

*Parts of these books were included in the Greek translation of the Tanakh called "Septuagint," and are included in the Roman Catholic Bible, but not in the Protestant Bible. Also included in the Septuagint (and the Catholic Bible) are: Tobit, Judith, Additions to Esther, Wisdom of Solomon, Ecclesiasticus, Baruch, The Letter of Jeremiah, Additions to the Book of Daniel (The Prayer of Azariah and the Song of the Three Jews, Susanna, and Bel and the Dragon), and 1 & 2 Maccabees.

**The division of Samuel, Kings, and Chronicles into two volumes each was a Christian innovation not adopted by Jews.

FIGURE 1.3

It is true, however, that some of the prophets (especially those who wrote after the Babylonian sack of Jerusalem in 587 BCE and the deportation of its people into exile) occasionally employed the kind of highly visionary and symbolic discourse usually associated today with the New Testament book of Revelation. These writers envisioned, often in fantastic and even outlandish terms, an end to the present age, accompanied by cataclysmic, cosmic events, violent and grotesque animal imagery, number symbolism, and mythical beings. (The best examples of this sort of writing in the Old Testament are found in the book of Daniel, which in the Hebrew Bible is not numbered among the Prophets at all, but in the eclectic category of "Writings.") This sort of writing, relatively rare among the prophets, is designated as "apocalyptic" rather than "prophetic" by biblical scholars.

The Prophets—that is, the books by the prophets—have sometimes been designated "former" or "latter," depending on when they were written; or divided into "major" and "minor," on the basis, not of their importance, but of their relative lengths. The writings of the minor prophets were short enough to fit together on one scroll, which Jews traditionally regarded as a single book, "The Book of the Twelve." The term "minor," though, is extremely misleading, for some of the prophets who were minor in terms of the length of their works were major in importance—for example, Amos and Hosea. (If that distinction seems confusing, just wait until we get to the epistles and apostles of the New Testament!)

The third group of books in the Hebrew Bible is known simply as "The Writings," and, as that designation suggests, is a kind of literary miscellany. Among this diverse collection are fiction (Job, Ruth), pastoral poetry (Psalms), erotic poetry (Song of Songs), epigrammatic sayings (Proverbs), and the closest thing to philosophy in the entire Bible (Ecclesiastes). The most interesting thing about this collection is the marginal relevance of some of its works to either religion or theology. Indeed, two of the books— Esther and Song of Songs (or Song of Solomon)—never mention the name of God. In fact, once such apparently secular writings became a part of the canon (that is, official scriptures), both Jewish and Christian interpreters took great pains to spiritualize or allegorize these works in order to make them seem more religious. Hence, the explicit eroticism of the lovers in the Song of Songs became a representation of the love of God for Israel or of Christ for the Church. Such a reading was at best anachronistic; at worst, it subverted the intent and compromised the integrity of the writing itself. Besides, it nearly ruined a good erotic poem!

The New Testament

The New Testament is a distinctively Christian collection with some unique literary forms. The gospels, for example, provide stories of the conception, birth, ministry, trial, death, and resurrection of Jesus Christ— though not all of them mention all of these events, nor are they very consistent in the ones that they do treat. The gospel narratives, far from being objective accounts or biographies, are testimonies by believers concerning the life of one who has changed their lives. Written to teach the faithful, to win converts, and to silence critics, the gospels are by nature biased accounts. They are also quite selective, providing only brief vignettes of small portions of the life of Jesus. Laid end-to-end, they would account for at most a few weeks out of a life of some thirty years.

The four canonical gospels almost certainly were not written by any of the original twelve disciples (later apostles) of Jesus, despite the fact that Matthew, Mark, and John have traditionally been identified with members of that august group. For one thing, these names were not attached to the books until the second century at the earliest. For another, these were very common names in ancient Palestine. Third, it was a common practice in the ancient world for disciples—or disciples of disciples—to honor forerunners by writing in their names, and presumably their spirits. Most telling of all, however, is the fact that most modern biblical scholars place these three gospels at dates so late in the first century as to make it highly unlikely that any of the original twelve would have been alive, much less in any shape to remember and record details of Jesus' life and ministry.

In addition to the gospels, the New Testament contains three other kinds of literature. (See figure 1.4.) Like the gospels, the epistles (letters) have no parallel in the Hebrew scriptures. The Acts of the Apostles, however, is similar to books like Kings and Chronicles in that it purports to document historic events in the life of a God-oriented people. Likewise, the book of Revelation is an apocalyptic work not unlike certain parts of the book of Daniel.

More attention will be given to these writings shortly. Suffice it now to say that over the course of some three and a half centuries following the

The New Testament Canon

*Gospels	**Church "History"	Epistles	Apocalyptic Literature
Mark	Acts		Revelation
Matthew			
Luke			
John			

*Pauline	***Pseudo-Pauline	Non-Pauline
1 Thessalonians	2 Thessalonians?	Hebrews
1 Corinthians	Colossians	James
2 Corinthians	Ephesians	1 Peter
Philippians	1 Timothy	2 Peter
Philemon	2 Timothy	1 John
Galatians	Titus	2 John
Romans		3 John
		Jude

* The gospels and Pauline letters are listed here in probable chronological order. (All of Paul's authentic letters predate all of the gospels.)

** While chronicling the early years of the Church after Jesus and being useful as an historical source, the book of Acts—like the gospels—is not a history in the modern sense because of its obvious theological bias.

*** The pseudo-Pauline epistles are those that bore the name of the self-designated Apostle from ancient times but that, because of marked differences in vocabulary, style, and/or theology, almost certainly were written by other people, perhaps by disciples of Paul. 2 Thessalonians is still in dispute on this score.

FIGURE 1.4

death of Jesus, these 27 books gradually emerged from a veritable sea of treasured Christian writings that were being circulated and preserved among the faithful throughout the Mediterranean basin. Early accorded a position of prominence, they came gradually over several centuries to earn general acceptance (together with the Hebrew scriptures) as the authoritative Christian canon. Unlike the Hebrew writings, however, the New Testament was never canonized *officially*, but merely recognized in time *by tradition*. Nevertheless, in order to bolster the ultimate status of these quasi-canonical writings, many if not most of the other Christian writings were suppressed, lost, forgotten, or destroyed.

The Canonical and "Other" Gospels

Mark, the shortest and earliest of the canonical gospels (usually dated around 70 CE), completely ignores Jesus' early years, including his conception and birth, and begins with his baptism. John, the latest of the gospels (probably written around 100 CE), goes to the other extreme and begins his gospel at the beginning of time, with the divine Word that was actively present in the world's creation and that ultimately became incarnate (enfleshed) in Jesus. But he, too, ignores the conception and birth stories, and jumps from his assertion that "the divine word and wisdom became human" (1:14) to John the Baptist's testimony to Jesus, though he does not report an actual baptism of Jesus (1:29–31).

Matthew and Luke (both written around 90 CE) give different accounts of Jesus' conception and birth, and of his infancy and childhood they report only a few incidents—also widely divergent. Matthew alone tells of a visit by wise men and of an escape of the infant Jesus with his parents into Egypt to avoid the "slaughter of the innocents" under King Herod. Only Luke relates the famous incident when the youthful Jesus, visiting Jerusalem with his parents, gets separated from them and is found astounding the Temple elders with his wisdom; and Luke brackets this account with two short references to Jesus' growth and increasing wisdom (2:40–52), but says nothing else about his childhood, adolescence, or early adulthood. It is almost certain that these infancy narratives were the last part of the gospel tradition to develop, that is, the accounts of Jesus' conception and birth were added to Matthew and Luke in order to correspond to other fantastic infancy stories of contemporary heroes.

After these few and brief accounts, Matthew and Luke jump nearly two decades or more in Jesus' life to his baptism and the beginning of his ministry. As Matthew, Mark, and Luke have it, that ministry must have been about a year in length; but John's narrative requires over two years, and perhaps three. In any case, it is clear that each of the gospels was written with a particular agenda and audience in mind. Most modern biblical scholars agree that these writers attributed to Jesus words and deeds that he very likely never spoke or performed, and that they did so in order to suit their own theological and political purposes or those of the early churches that they represented. It should be noted, however, that these scholars are rarely in complete agreement about which words and deeds were authentically those of Jesus himself.

In any case, all four evangelists (gospel writers) provide only the barest of episodic sketches of Jesus' ministry, while spending a disproportionate amount of time detailing the final, tragic-triumphant week. In this way they indicate what was most important to them, and no doubt to the early Christian communities in which they were participants: the death and resurrection of Jesus.

Most Christians don't know that in addition to the four gospels in the New Testament there were more than fifty others that simply were excluded from the New Testament by the gradual consensus that produced the final, definitive list of books. Nor do they have any idea that some of these still exist in whole or in part today. Among these so-called pseudepigrapha were a Gospel according to the Twelve Apostles, a Gospel of Andrew, a Gospel of Thomas, a Gospel of Peter, and a Gospel according to the Hebrews—to name but a few. These are particularly interesting because some of them "fill in the gaps" about the infancy and childhood of Jesus, though sometimes in ways that would not be particularly agreeable to most Christians.

For example, the Infancy Gospel of Thomas (not to be confused with the Gospel of Thomas) tells of several people being healed by the infant Jesus' bath water (In Thom 2:1–2) and also of Jesus' making of clay sparrows that come to life when he claps his hands (In Thom 2:3–7), of his stretching boards to the length needed by his carpenter father (In Thom 13), and of his striking dead a little boy who has bumped into him—not to mention blinding a crowd who faults him for doing that! (In Thom 4). No doubt this last incident alone would have been enough to keep this particular gospel out of the New Testament; but its exclusion should lead us to wonder what kinds of presuppositions about Jesus determined which books were and were not made a part of the Christian Bible. We do know from early lists of Christian writings that some communities valued and even preferred books now regarded as non-canonical. Nonetheless, by the end of the second century (around 185 CE) the four gospels regarded as canonical today, along with the letters of Paul, were widely favored above the other Christian writings in most Christian communities.

What is certain is that the gospel-selection process itself served to define normative or "orthodox" Christian belief for many centuries to come. Virtually excluded, for example, was the early Gnostic Christian viewpoint that accepted divinity (rather than sin) as a natural and inherent human quality, and reincarnation as a fact of spiritual life. Such notions would have made Christianity not only less preoccupied with human depravity, but also more compatible with the spiritual teachings of Hinduism and Buddhism, which were already well established in India and elsewhere in Asia in the first century CE. Because gospels (and other writings) that depicted Jesus as teaching such things were rejected, these Gnostic ideas became "heterodox" or "heretical," and Christians espousing them through the ages have risked censure and punishment.

Acts, Epistles and the Revelation of John

The Acts of the Apostles easily made "the cut" for inclusion in the New Testament. Apparently written by Luke as a sequel to his gospel, it tells of the events immediately following the ascension of Christ into heaven. Beginning with Pentecost (a Jewish holiday co-opted by Christianity as the "birth" of the Church), it goes on to narrate the earliest missions and struggles of the apostles. It is, therefore, the first church history, and records, among other important events and trends, the deliberate extension of the gospel to non-Jews, largely at the insistence and through the effort of the apostle Paul (d. circa 64 CE). These early days were hardly idyllic, however: there was considerable tension, dissension, strife and conflict among the first apostles. Indeed, any modern church that has experienced internal disagreements and hard feelings should find a great deal of comfort in Acts.

The third group of writings in the New Testament consists of the epistles (letters). Literally, "epistle" means "sent document" and has the same Greek root as "apostle"—a "sent person." But there is no other necessary connection between epistles and apostles, despite the fact that the New Testament epistles traditionally have been attributed to apostles, and notwithstanding the likelihood that some apostles sent epistles that were either lost or intentionally excluded. One didn't have to be an apostle to send an epistle. (Any literate person could do that.) Nor did one have to send an epistle to be an apostle. (I warned you that this wouldn't be easy!)

In any case, it is the epistles of the apostle Paul (especially Romans, Corinthians, Galatians, and Thessalonians) that have been the most influential of all the letters on Christian theology. One reason for this is that despite their placement after the gospels, his letters are the earliest writings of the New Testament—most having been written in the 50s CE, and thus some ten or twenty years before the earliest gospel and at least twenty years after the death of Jesus. (For the historical relationship of the gospels, epistles, and other New Testament writings, see figure 1.5.) So important, in fact, are the Pauline letters, that the rest of the New Testament epistles are usually designated as non-Pauline (those not claiming to have been written by Paul) and pseudo-Pauline (those claiming Pauline authorship, but judged in terms of their style, vocabulary and content, as almost certainly reflecting the work of a different author). Regardless of authorship, however, all of the epistles are important for their glimpses of early Christian belief, practice, and diversity in a period during which a young Christianity was struggling to realize its identity, often in the face of internal uncertainties and external opposition.

The technical term for the fourth type of literature in the New Testament is "apocalyptic," and only the book of Revelation (singular!) in that collection is representative in its entirety of this genre. (In fact, Revelation's Greek title, *Apokalupsis*, gives the genre its name.) As already suggested, the Hebrew scripture also has at least one example of apocalyptic literature (specifically, chapters 5–12 of Daniel); and certain portions of the gospels and epistles seem to fit the pattern as well (for example, Mark 13 and 1 Thess 4:13–5:2). Like all literature of this type, Revelation uses highly dramatic and symbolic imagery and thus delivers a message that to the modern reader is inevitably obscure, if not downright opaque.

More attention will be paid to this writing in a later chapter, but for now suffice it to say (1) that Revelation was written around 96 CE by a Christian

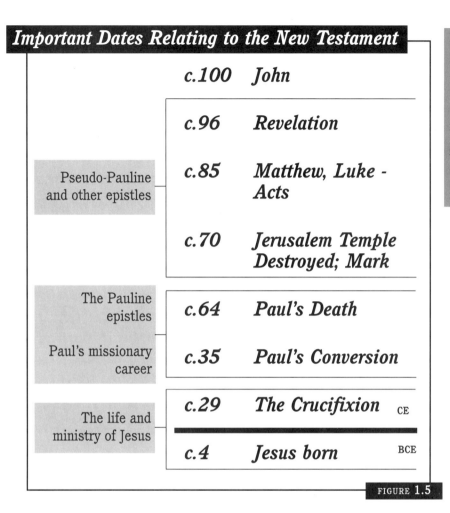

Important Dates Relating to the New Testament

	c.100	*John*
	c.96	*Revelation*
Pseudo-Pauline and other epistles	*c.85*	*Matthew, Luke - Acts*
	c.70	*Jerusalem Temple Destroyed; Mark*
The Pauline epistles	*c.64*	*Paul's Death*
Paul's missionary career	*c.35*	*Paul's Conversion*
The life and ministry of Jesus	*c.29*	*The Crucifixion* CE
	c.4	*Jesus born* BCE

FIGURE 1.5

named John who, though later made a saint, was almost certainly *not* the disciple of that name, *nor* the writer of the fourth gospel, *nor* the author of the New Testament epistles that bear that name; and (2) that this "other" John wrote it for contemporary Christians living under the very real threat— or the stark reality—of persecution at the hands of the Roman authorities. That it is written in a kind of esoteric "code," therefore, should not surprise us. Nor, by the way, should it tempt us to search the contemporary world for the meaning of its many strange symbols. But more about that in a later chapter.

The History of the Bible

In what passes for religious education for lay people today, the idea that the Bible might have a history is seldom even considered. On the contrary, people tend to treat it as a finished artifact, which one day floated down from heaven and landed gently—gold-leafed, red-lettered, leather-bound, and in seventeenth-century English, no doubt—on some ancient coffee table.

The truth is, however, that the Bible as we know it came to be through a long and demonstrably human process. That process had various stages: original compositions were often dependent on oral traditions, and were followed in every case by a complicated succession of copies, translations, and ultimately either formal or informal canonization. (For a graphic representation of this process as it relates to the New Testament, see figure 1.6.) An historical perspective requires the modern reader to recognize from the outset that the biblical authors themselves had no sense of contributing to any later collection of scriptures, much less to what we know as the Christian Bible. They were working as individual authors (and sometimes editors), and would undoubtedly be surprised to learn the part that their literature plays today in the collection we call the Bible.

How the New Testament Came to Be

29 –70CE		70 – 100CE	100 –1500CE	1500 – present
Stage 1	**Stage 2**	**Stage 3**	**Stage 4**	**Stage 5**
Oral Tradition (the word-of-mouth transmission, especially of the words and deeds of Jesus that were later recounted in the gospels.)	*Pre-gospel writings* (the letters of Paul and others; but also possible sources used by gospel writers, especially Matthew and Luke, e.g., Q and perhaps M and L.)	*Gospel and later NT writings* (the original Greek manuscripts of each of the various books; there is no "New Testament" during this period, only the makings.)	*Copying, translating, and canonization* (original manuscripts copied, recopied and translated into many ancient languages, e.g., Latin, Coptic; 27 books, first grouped in late 4th century, slowly emerge as a canon.)	*Translations currently in use* (scholars work with the best available manuscripts and try to render their meanings in the vernacular—e.g., in English: KJV, NRSV, NJB, REB, and SV.)
Problem: inherent untrustworthiness of hearsay	*Problem:* whether Q, M and/or L were in fact written, or merely another level of hearsay	*Problem:* no way to verify the accuracy of even our best manuscripts	*Problem:* mere translation introduces new meanings; copyists make mistakes and selection process excludes disagreeable ancient writings and views	*Problem:* more recent manuscript discoveries and better scholarship render beloved older versions like the KJV obsolete

FIGURE 1.6

REMEDIAL CHRISTIANITY

Oral Tradition and the Original Manuscripts

Behind many of the books of the Old and New Testaments lies a stage of oral tradition. That means that some or much of the material that finally appeared in writing first circulated by word of mouth, perhaps for generations, before being consigned to the written page. This is obviously not true of literary products like the epistles, which presumably came into existence when the correspondent, or his scribe, put quill to parchment. It is true, however, for such important scriptural works as Genesis in the Old Testament and the gospels in the New (to mention only two of the most notable). Thus, much of what we now find recorded in literary form undoubtedly originated as stories and sayings shared in conversation and only later recorded for posterity.

There is good news and bad news in this process. The bad news is that oral communication is inevitably altered in the process of transmission. Many of us have played the popular parlor game variously called "gossip" or "party line," in which one person in a circle is whispered a simple sentence and told to pass it on, only to find it inevitably unrecognizable and often humorously mangled by the time it returns to the originator. How much more, we might wonder, would this alteration process be exacerbated by religious folks sharing stories about such great (and remote) events as divine interventions, charismatic religious figures, and the events surrounding them? We can only speculate about the extent, but to conclude that some such elaborations must have occurred among faithful yet fallible human beings seems unavoidable, and no doubt helps to explain at least some of the variations we get from book to book (and sometimes within books) in the biblical descriptions of certain events and the reports of specific utterances.

The good news about this oral process is that people in non-literate or largely illiterate societies have been shown to have better memories than literate folks. One of the trade-offs in our learning to write is that our writing becomes a mental crutch, a substitute for a good memory. (God forbid, for example, a college student's losing lecture notes before a final exam!) But in preliterate societies, stories are passed with far more care and far less elaboration. Evidence of this fact presented itself in Alex Haley's popular book and TV movie, *Roots*, which recounted the author's tracing of his heritage back seven generations to a single member of an obscure African tribe on the basis of the stories told to him in childhood by his illiterate grandmother. We would like to believe (but can really only surmise and hope) that this sort of accuracy prevailed among the people who transmitted what we have in the biblical accounts of Moses and Jesus (among others). Still, we cannot but wonder what elaborations and omissions crept in, both intentionally and inadvertently, and how these have affected our perception of those pivotal periods and the key figures involved.

All of the writings of the Bible, of course, achieved literary form at some point in time as manuscripts. The original manuscripts are called "autographs," which means that they were written by the authors themselves or by scribes under the authors' direction. It would be wonderful to be able to view and study these historic documents, but unfortunately all are lost, and no one seriously expects a curious Palestinian shepherd boy (or anyone else, for that matter) to unearth them. The earliest fragment that we have of any New Testament book is a small corner of one page, containing a few partial lines from chapter 18 of the Gospel according to John, and dating to sometime around 125 CE. The earliest complete manuscripts are much later than that.

That we have biblical texts at all is the result of a long and fortunate but complicated and confusing copying process. Indeed, much of what we know about the contents of the Bible is derived from the study of the many copies that exist of each of its books. A regrettable fact, often obscured by pretensions of biblical certainty, is that (1) most of the extant manuscripts available to scholars and translators are relatively late, and amount to copies of copies of copies, at best; and (2) of the thousands of biblical manuscripts we have dating from the fourth to the eighteenth centuries, no two of them agree in every detail. Indeed, variations are astronomical in number, and by their nature reveal a great many accidental errors and much conscious editing. These variations range from misspellings, to discrepancies in words and phrases, to obvious omissions and additions; and these inconsistencies persisted until the invention of the printing press in the fifteenth century, from which time we begin to see at least the beginnings of standardization in biblical texts. The many thousands of variations among even the most ancient of biblical manuscripts present an enormous challenge to the biblical scholar trying to translate and interpret the scriptures: how can one hope to know which one of these conflicting manuscripts comes closest to the original?

Troublesome Texts and Translations

Scholars use a variety of rules-of-thumb in order to ferret out the reading of any given text that is closest to the original, and generally do this on a verse-by-verse basis. One such rule is that all other things being equal (and they rarely are), the oldest existing manuscript is the most reliable, simply because the multi-generational copying process can only deviate further and further from the original. Some of these deviations were obviously intentional efforts by copyists to clarify; thus another working assumption is that the more difficult the reading of a passage in any given manuscript, the more likely it is to be closer to the original, since the tendency would be for later copyists to "improve" the text rather than to obfuscate it.

The modern scholarly task is still further complicated by the many translations that began to appear even in ancient times. These have given rise to yet another scholarly rule-of-thumb: a manuscript in the original language is generally to be preferred to one in translation. But scholars sometimes have to choose between an ancient manuscript of a New Testament book in the original Greek, for example, and a translation of that book (in Latin, Coptic, Aramaic, or Syriac) that is older and thus closer in time to the lost original. Or—worst case—they will have to choose between an older manuscript that is not only closer in time to the original *and* clearer in meaning and a more recent one whose reading is more difficult but somehow seems more authentic precisely because of its unpolished quality. So much for "all things being equal"!

The fact of the textual variations in the biblical manuscript tradition poses an even greater problem for those who would maintain the inerrancy of the Bible. If the Bible has no errors, exactly which one of the many manuscripts of a given book is the error-free one? Some Fundamentalists have argued that the original autographs were error-free, but since these are all lost, that claim is unverifiable and therefore specious. One also wonders why a deity so concerned with verbal inerrancy would have abandoned the process so abruptly and let so much variation creep in, instead of blessing the copyists with infallibility as well—or inspiring them to invent the photocopy machine!

Further complicating the process of translating and interpreting the biblical texts are linguistic problems that sometimes make it difficult to know what a text means even when we are pretty sure what it says. Ancient Hebrew, for instance, had no vowels, and one particular configuration of consonants could represent many different words, depending on the context. It would be like running across the English phrase "th pnt n th wll." That could mean "the paint on the wall," "the point in the will," or "the pint in the well," among other things! Old Testament scholars have to weigh just these sorts of options in the Hebrew text again and again. Ancient Greek manuscripts pose a different, but no less sticky problem: it had vowels, but no distinction between upper and lower case letters, no punctuation, and, worst of all, no division between words!

Imagine in English running across the phrase "godisnowhere." That could mean "God is now here," "God is nowhere," or "God, I snow here." The last reading we could probably reject as nonsense, but that would still leave us with two plausible but very different options. We might even find that, with proper punctuation, we actually have fragments of two different sentences here. Or, to use another example: "womanwithouthermanisnothing." We might fairly easily decide that the words there are "Woman without her man is nothing." But punctuated that could mean "Woman, without her man, is nothing" or "Woman! Without her, man is nothing!"—the exact opposite in meaning. Many existing texts in the original Hebrew and Greek manuscripts of the biblical books are equally ambiguous if not more so.

In light of these and other similarly frustrating problems, it is no wonder that modern biblical scholars weigh (and sometimes argue) at length not only which manuscript's version of a given passage is closest to the original, but also which of a number of possible variant readings of a problematic text in a given manuscript might be the correct one. Only when those problems are resolved can the scholar begin to talk—and argue—about what the author's intent really was.

Our most popular English biblical translations, of course, are the result of the work of such scholars, and represent a rather late stage in the history of the Bible. The most famous, of course, is the King James Version. (The KJV, as far as I can determine, is the only biblical translation named after a homosexual, a fact that is relevant only for the irony that fundamentalist Christians often insist on this version in their literalistic scriptural refutation and condemnation of homosexuality.) The translation was not the idea of the seventeenth-century monarch whose name it bears, but of Puritan Christians in England who were concerned to have an authorized (meaning "officially sanctioned") English version of the Bible, and who therefore pressured the king to commission one. The result was to become one of the monuments of English literature, influential beyond estimation and unsurpassed to this day in beauty and majesty of expression.

The KJV has been eclipsed, however, in at least three important ways by such twentieth-century translations as the (New) Revised Standard Version, the (New) Jerusalem Bible, the New/Revised English Bible, the Scholars Version, and others. (*The Living Bible*, marketed under a variety of titles, is a paraphrase, not a true translation.) First, all of these modern translations were motivated and informed by some important manuscript discoveries made long after the KJV was completed, and for that reason in some important cases come closer to the original words and intent of the biblical authors. Second, modern biblical translators—by virtue of nearly four hundred years of scholarship—have a far better understanding of the grammar and vocabularies of the biblical languages than did their seventeenth-century counterparts. Third, the KJV uses many seventeenth-century English words that today mean nothing at all or something very different from what they did in Jacobean England. The KJV admonition of Jesus to "suffer the little children," for example, has nothing to do with what we call "suffering"—though you can bet that many sermons on child-abuse have mistaken it that way! In fact, "suffer" there means "let," while elsewhere in the KJV "let" means "hinder," and "prevent" means "precede."

If accuracy and understanding are important considerations, therefore, all of the modern translations are probably preferable to the KJV—assuming, of course, that definitive Hebrew and Greek editions are inaccessible to the reader. Muslims typically insist that their holy Qur'an's true meaning can be found only in the original Arabic. Shouldn't especially fundamentalist Christian literalists likewise want to turn to the original languages of their own scripture, not only to see and hear the pure word of God for themselves, but also to minimize the distortion of it that translation invariably introduces? Why do they seem so content with a translation, and more often than not with such an old and faulty one as the KJV at that?

Canons—Consensus and Controversy

Separate from this copying and translating process was the issue of canonicity, that is, the determination of which books would comprise the two Testaments. This process had two distinct, but parallel and chronologically overlapping phases, each with two stages: (1a) The Old Testament writings (or, more properly, the Hebrew scriptures) were all completed, widely circulated, and highly regarded (though not formally canonized) at least one hundred years before Jesus, and portions of them served as his Bible. (1b) At the Jewish Council of Jamnia in 90 CE the Hebrew canon was set at twenty-four books (which Christians later divided into thirty-nine), though that decision was not universally accepted among the Judeans (later called Jews) for at least several centuries; and, as noted earlier, Greek-speaking Hebrew congregations continued to recognize seven additional ones and eventually included them in their Greek translation of the Hebrew scripture, the Septuagint. (2a) The New Testament writings circulated individually, gaining more or less wide acceptance and authority among the various Christian communities. (2b) Twenty-seven of these writings achieved canonical or quasi-canonical status, though not until some four or five centuries after Jesus' life, and perhaps much later than that. Indeed, the first list of the twenty-seven New Testament books now recognized as canonical appeared in 367 CE, but not until many centuries later was there a general consensus among Christians as to what Christian writings actually comprised the New Testament.

The processes that gave rise to the two Christian Testaments were quite similar because both canons arose in response to the perceived need to preserve the respective traditions for future generations in the face of crises, and in recognition of the value of writing in guaranteeing permanence and precision for these records. For a time, however, it was not at all certain whether these two separately formed canons would be combined by Christians into a single body of scripture or Bible. Some early Christians (like Marcion in the late second century) did not believe that the Old Testament should be included because of its non-Christian origins and what he perceived to be its rather severe, vindictive, punitive, and anthropomorphic view of God, who seemed hardly to resemble the loving, merciful, gracious, and spiritual "Father" of Jesus Christ. Furthermore, Marcion accepted only the Gospel of Luke and the epistles of Paul as valid scripture. That his position did not prevail is obvious, though in all fairness to him it might be said that a conscientious modern reader of the two Testaments might reasonably conclude from the many differences between them in style and substance that his argument about the Hebrew scriptures had some merit.

Well prior to and probably for some time after the fixing of the New Testament canon, whenever that finally occurred, there was also a great deal of disagreement between the various Christian communities scattered throughout the Roman Empire about the relative virtues of many Christian writings. We have little clear evidence about how the final decision was made, or whether it was more of a consensus than a formal decision, much less how generally accepted this decision or consensus was; but we can safely infer from the historical data that there were compromises between different Christian communities, each holding out for its own favorite books and, in return, conceding places for the preferred scriptures of their counterparts.

What we do know for certain is that, for whatever reasons, some early Christian writings of comparable antiquity to the ones selected were excluded. Some of these are still extant, being classified as either "patristic writings" or "pseudepigrapha," depending on the prestige accorded them. All of these writings help, however, to shed light on the formative period of Christian history, and especially on the diversity of perspectives and practices that existed even in the earliest Church.

The fact that it took at least three and a half centuries for the New Testament as we know it to begin to be defined, and even longer for it to be recognized as authoritative, should be enough to indicate that Christianity itself was a long time gaining self-definition. Indeed, the process of canonization was part of a much larger (and moving!) picture in the development of the faith, as we shall see in chapter 4. For now, it is enough to note that the history of the Bible suggests the fluidity and dynamism of a people struggling to understand their relation to God and the place of Jesus in the divine plan and human history. It does not bespeak a fixed rigidity of revealed truth delivered once-and-for-all, to which believers had merely to assent and acquiesce. Some have argued convincingly that it may be high time to reopen the Christian canon, so as to include such important ancient writings as the Gospel of Thomas.

The Inspiration and Authority of the Bible

The term "inspiration" is ambiguous. It does not necessarily carry the connotation of divine authorship, as is often assumed, although some do construe it that way. (For a spectrum of representative views on the inspiration and authority of scripture, see figure 1.7.) Conservative Christian groups, particularly Protestant Fundamentalists, often equate inspiration with divine authorship, and thus with verbal (that is, word-for-word) inerrancy. For them, the Bible is the Word of God in the sense of being God's

---

Typical Positions on Inspiration and Authority

Most Inspiration & Authority	**Divine Authorship**	
	Fundamentalist Christian	Bible as literally the Word of God, with every word inspired, authoritative, true and binding
	Evangelical Christian	Bible as truly the Word of God, inerrant in matters essential to faith and practice; the concepts are inspired
	Human Authorship	
	Liberal Christian	Bible as "Word of God" in that God can speak with power through its inspired but human and flawed words
	Secular Humanist	Bible as literary treasure, a great monument to the human spirit and imagination, thus "inspired"
	Secular Historicist	Bible as a valuable source of information about a bygone historical era; "interesting"
Least Inspiration & Authority	**Dogmatic Atheist**	Bible as a tired old book with no value, perpetuating ignorance; "incapacitating"

FIGURE 1.7

very words: God is the author, having employed the human writers as scribes or secretaries, speaking to their minds, hearts, or spirits in order to convey the precise, divinely-intended content.

One influential nineteenth-century advocate of biblical literalism promulgated just such a "dictation theory" of divine inspiration to explain this process. For him, as well as for those who still maintain his strict view of inspiration, the Bible is thus authoritative in an unequivocal sense: God wrote it. The Bible is therefore to be read and understood in its most literal sense, and believed and obeyed absolutely. Or, as a popular bumper sticker puts it: "God wrote it. I believe it. That settles it!"

That really does not settle it, of course, for there are insurmountable problems with this viewpoint. The challenge posed by the manuscript variations and other textual difficulties has been mentioned already, and it is formidable: it is simply impossible to determine which, if any, of the many manuscripts of the various books might be the one thus inspired. Beyond this problem is the obvious variety of viewpoints (including theologies) in the Bible, as well as the undeniable contradictions at the factual level, a few of which we have already noted and more of which we shall identify in due time. Third, Fundamentalism tends to demand that one embrace an ancient worldview (that is, view of reality), including an earth-centered universe inhabited by spirits and demons—a perspective that is ultimately incompatible with the prevailing scientific worldview by which most rational people today understand the world and direct their lives. Finally, it is difficult if not impossible to find a Fundamentalist who is literalistic about all parts of the Bible.

For example, most Fundamentalists worship on Sunday rather than the true Jewish Sabbath (in direct contradiction of the fourth commandment in Exodus 20:8); they allow women to pray with uncovered heads or to speak in church and to teach men in church school (in defiance of clear prohibitions in 1 Cor 11:4–8 and 1 Tim 2:11–12); and they would not think of advocating capital punishment for adultery or even homosexuality (though it is expressly prescribed for both "offenses" in Leviticus 18 and 20), much less of requiring an unmarried rape victim to marry her assailant (as required by Deut 22:28–29). And these are but a few examples. In short, Fundamentalists generally tend to be literalistic about what *they choose* to consider "fundamental" to the faith—which usually appears to be whatever censures beliefs and behaviors of which they disapprove.

The Strange Appeal of Fundamentalism

Despite its shortcomings, however, the fundamentalist position is enormously attractive to those who want their religion to be neat, unambiguous, and replete with black-and-white answers. And, it must be admitted, advocates of this point of view have, on the surface at least, a very appealing position from which to make their assertions. For it is only natural for people to want clear, concise, and compelling solutions to life's questions; and Fundamentalists appear to provide precisely this kind of assurance, usually in the form of selected Bible verses often called "proof texts."

Examined a bit more closely, however, this approach to scripture really subverts, subtly but substantively, the very source of authority that it claims to value and defend; for it employs an undisclosed (and perhaps even unexamined) interpretive system for choosing certain verses over others as well as for correlating them, irrespective of their original contexts and intentions. One of Fundamentalists' favorite catch-phrases, for example, is the familiar assertion that "The Bible says. . . . " Those three words surely have the ring of authority to them and are bound to grab the attention of a listener; but they obscure both the rich variety of individual viewpoints and the discrepancies of the biblical writings by implying (falsely) that the Bible speaks with one voice. At the same time, they also give the impression that whatever is about to be quoted is unassailable, absolute, and final. Ironically, however, the very claim that appears to accord the scriptures such authority commonly introduces either a single verse lifted completely out of context or a succession of individual verses pulled from various books of the Bible and juxtaposed with no regard for their original contexts. Such a practice—which resembles nothing so much as the reading of fortune cookies drawn at random from a basket—demeans the very Bible that it purports to hold so dear.

What really has precedence for Fundamentalists is not the Bible, but their idiosyncratic system of selecting and correlating verses. This system, in turn, is based on an unspoken and perhaps even unconscious and unexamined set of presuppositions derived from a method of scriptural interpretation that is no more than a hundred years old and totally out of touch with modern historical-critical biblical scholarship. This method, in effect, amounts to a hidden agenda, one that ironically leads those who claim to esteem the Bible the most to do enormous violence to it, precisely by ignoring its original contexts and meanings and imposing an interpretative framework that is all the more insidious because it is transparent—that is, merely assumed rather than acknowledged. The selective use of scripture that results calls to mind the folks at sports events and parades who hold up huge placards citing single scripture verses. My fantasy is that one day I'll see someone displaying a sign that says, not "John 3:16," but "Read the Bible contextually!" I'm not holding my breath.

The Mixed Blessing of Liberalism

Fundamentalists also like to leave the impression that theirs is the only really "Christian" way to read the Bible. But there is an alternative approach that is equally Christian. It is usually termed "liberal," which historically has described any position willing to test and validate (or invalidate!) faith claims rationally. More recently, the term has come to denote any approach to biblical study that is open to modern historical-critical methods and findings.

A typical liberal stance on the Bible asserts that although inspired, it nonetheless has multiple human authorship, and that it therefore exhibits the same variety of genre, style, period, and viewpoint that you would find in any good library—along with the errors, editings, biases, contradictions, and all of the other imprints that human beings leave on their literature. Yet for the Liberal none of these discrepancies would be grounds for denying that the Bible is inspired; for the word "inspiration" itself allows for a number of interpretations. It is commonly used to describe outstanding works of human genius—creations that need not be religious, much less perfect, in order to merit that adjective. That very usage of the word "inspiration" suggests that the scriptures may well be both inspired and human in authorship, both inspired and flawed.

To say that the books of the Bible are of human authorship is not, as some suggest, to demean them. Liberal Christians do not typically deny the importance or the validity of scripture; they simply conceive of its importance and validity in terms very different from those of the Fundamentalist. The Bible can still be enormously helpful and even inspirational as a record of the grapplings of human beings with their understanding of God and their relationship to God; and it can still remain a rich compendium of diverse and divergent faith journeys and faith struggles unified by the conviction that there is a God who cares for humanity and who acts in history. It may also be seen as a treasury of divine truth presented in mythical or even fictional settings, and thus demanding figurative rather than literal interpretation. Thus Liberals can affirm that God speaks through these human writings—not in the simple, literalistic way that Fundamentalists purport, but in a more subtle and yet all the more powerful manner.

Liberal Christians are therefore neither surprised nor chagrined by contradictions in scripture, for the variety of viewpoints is part of the richness of the literature. Such variety is actually beneficial to the reader because it has the ability to open him or her up to that mind-boggling, category-shattering reality that most Westerners call "God." In this way, many Liberals like to assert, the whole Bible is best understood in light of the model that Jesus himself laid down in his teachings (at least in the synoptic gospels): the open-ended, metaphorical, often confusing parable, which "gets at" the truth through fictional stories that "talk around it" rather than "nailing it down." The Bible, say liberal Christians, should certainly be informative for our own lives' travels and travails, though probably not as an "easy-answer book." By treating it in such a simplistic way, they argue, Fundamentalism looks a lot like the fastidious and legalistic scripture-quoting of the gospels' Pharisees who opposed and hassled Jesus. In response to them, he was always ready to offer broader and more relaxed interpretations, ones that appealed to the *spirit* rather than the letter of the texts.

The main weakness of Liberalism is that it gives the impression of being vague, uncertain, and even wishy-washy, especially in comparison to the inflexible pronouncements of Fundamentalists. The principal pitfall of the liberal interpreter is to find in scripture only what tends to support his or her prior assumptions and agendas. As we have already seen with respect to fundamentalist proof-texting, this is not a danger only for Liberals; nor is it a necessary consequence of a liberal perspective. A Liberal can, for example, discover in the stories and sayings of Jesus a standard that calls into serious question, if not outright judgment, his or her own values and lifestyle.

The primary strength of the liberal position, of course, is that it does not require one to ignore the obvious facts about the nature and development of the Bible or to reject the prevailing modern worldview. And, paradoxically, it demands a stronger stance of faith than does Fundamentalism, since it does not present God as pinned-down in absolute formulas, but perceives divinity as miraculously conveyed in the "earthen vessels" of scripture, just as Christian doctrine has always maintained that it was manifested in the fragile humanity of Jesus of Nazareth.

Conclusion

The most important thing that Christians should know about the Bible, but probably do not, is how excitingly diverse and inexhaustibly rich a resource it really is—and, as a corollary, how these qualities derive from its complicated history. To be sure, it does exhibit coherence in a central unifying theme: the gracious presence and redemptive activity of God in human history. Beyond that, however, the wonderful variety of its contents, the imaginative eloquence of its authors, and even the discrepancies and contradictions that it contains afford Christians not only motivation and direction in their own spiritual formation, but freedom and encouragement as well.

What the Bible speaks to, above all, is the religious *experience* of the authors and characters. More than anything else, then, it puts the reader in touch with her or his own spirituality on the experiential level; and this, one might say, is the fundamental dynamic and true value of the Christian—or any—faith. Had the Bible been single-minded, definitive, and utterly consistent, it might have stifled spiritual searching and growth. As it is, however, it calls and challenges the reader to forge a living, growing, active, and uniquely personal faith. At the same time, it comforts the reverent seeker with the examples of the biblical authors, whose words fashioned not a flawless vessel to contain God, but a window that provides salutary glimpses of divinity, despite its surface imperfections.

DISCUSSION QUESTIONS & EXERCISES

A. Write down in your own words what the following texts say literally: Matthew 5:43–48; 7:1–5; Mark 10:2–10, 17–22. For the fun of it, compare Matthew 19:3–9 to Mark 10:2–10, noting the difference. If you are (or were) a literalist, which text do (or would) you take literally? Why? Then ask these questions of each passage: Do we or Christians we know live this text literally? Should we? Could we? Why or why not?

B. Find the humor in an English translation of Matthew 21:1–7.

C. Read Mark 14:33–36, 50–52; 15:34–37 and John 18:4–11; 19:28–30 and answer the following questions:

1. Who falls to the ground?
2. Does Jesus want to drink or not?
3. Do the disciples appear to be acting of their own accord or at Jesus' admonition in the various things that they do?
4. Is the offering of something to drink mockery on the soldiers' part or Jesus' idea and command?
5. Did Jesus die willingly or reluctantly?

D. Look at or listen to any item from the news and answer these questions about it:

1. What is the medium?
2. What is the source?
3. What is the form?
4. What is the motivation of the author?
5. What is the purpose of the editor?
6. Compare the same news item in two or more newspapers (including one that is international, if possible). How does such a process of inquiry affect your final assessment of that story? How might such questions affect your reading of biblical texts?

E. Find the story of the Empty Tomb, preferably in a Gospel Parallels (Mark 16:1–8//Matt 28:1–10//Luke 24:1–12//John 20:1–18) and note the similarities and differences. What do you make of these?

F. How much authority should the Bible have? Why? Should it be added to or subtracted from or merely left alone? Why?

G. What is at stake in biblical scholarship? How is it the same or different from other disciplines? How might biblical scholarship interfere with faith? How might it strengthen faith?

RECOMMENDED READING

Elisabeth Schüssler-Fiorenza, *Sharing Her Words: Feminist Biblical Interpretation in Context*. Boston: Beacon Press, 1998.
— argues that feminist biblical interpretation can make a difference in the struggle against structures of injustice and exploitation.

Frank S. Frick, *A Journey Through the Hebrew Scriptures*. Orlando, FL: Harcourt Brace, 1997.
— an excellent introduction to the Hebrew scriptures from a Jewish perspective.

Richard Elliott Friedman, *Who Wrote the Bible?*. San Francisco: HarperSanFrancisco, 1997.
— an examination of the first five books of the Hebrew Bible by a well-respected scholar writing for a popular audience, in an effort to identify the authors of these crucial books in light of archaeological evidence.

Stephen L. Harris, *The New Testament: A Student's Introduction*. Mountainview, CA/London/Toronto: Mayfield Publishing Co., 1995.
— a concise and extremely readable introduction to the entire Christian canon, based on current biblical scholarship

Lee Martin McDonald, *The Formation of the Christian Canon*. Revised ed. Peabody, MA: Hendrickson Publishers, Inc., 1995.
— a fascinating historical account of how the Bible came to be, and of how much time and effort it took.

Burton L. Mack, *Who Wrote the New Testament?: The Making of the Christian Myth*. San Francisco: HarperSanFrancisco, 1996.
— an excellent introduction to both the New Testament and modern biblical scholarship and a critical account of the mutual formation of myth and society.

Robert J. Miller, ed., *The Complete Gospels: Annotated Scholars Version*.
(Revised and Expanded Edition with Foreword by Robert W. Funk). San Francisco: HarperSanFrancisco, 1992.
— new translations of the four canonical gospels as well as what remains of some sixteen others, including the complete Gospel of Thomas.

Elaine Pagels, *The Gnostic Gospels*. New York: Vintage Books, 1981/1989.
— a now classic examination of early Christian Gnosticism based on an important Egyptian manuscript discovery in the 1940s, and of the vastly different Christianity that might have been, had this strain not been suppressed.

John Shelby Spong, *Rescuing the Bible from Fundamentalism: A Bishop Rethinks the Meaning of Scripture*. San Francisco: HarperSanFrancisco, 1991.
— a uniting of contemporary biblical scholarship with modern scientific insights to challenge the literal interpretations of scripture that have supported outmoded prejudices and cultural biases.

CHRISTIAN THEISM AND ITS ALTERNATIVES

Objectives of this chapter:

- to define and clarify the ideas of transcendence and immanence as the building blocks of all theologies

- to present and explain theism as the dominant theological model for the Western religions of Judaism, Christianity, and Islam in comparison with other historic theological types

- to identify at least three key points at which Christianity appears to hedge on its claim to be monotheistic

- to explore deism as a revision of the monotheistic model, one that has great historical significance for Americans

- to examine pantheism and monism as more Eastern ways of conceiving of Ultimate Reality than monotheism, and panentheism as a kind of theological compromise that is commanding some widespread theological attention in the West

- to examine evil and suffering as daunting challenges to the monotheistic model and to religious practices based upon it

- to examine the timely issue of the gender of God and the serious questions about God-language that it triggers

There is a commonly-held view of God in popular Christianity that is, if a little vague, at least consistent in its general characteristics. God exists as a "Supreme Being" or "Higher Power" in some "supernatural" sense, is personal and masculine in gender, is responsible for Creation, cares providentially for the world and its inhabitants (or at least for those who are "on His side"), even to the point of making provisions for their "salvation." This God is good, fatherly, merciful, loving, but not above being jealous, wrathful, punitive, or even vengeful when necessary. This God bears a unique relationship to Jesus Christ, sent him to the world as Savior, and continues to make His own presence felt as the Holy Spirit.

This popular, tacitly-accepted, generic view of God is not without its problems, however. For one thing, it is based on a particular theological model that is only one of several possible ways of picturing a deity or an ultimate reality. The theism—or, more specifically, the monotheism—reflected in the description above pervades the scriptures and doctrines of traditional Christianity as well as those of Judaism and Islam. But it is not by any means a universal way of conceptualizing God or The Absolute. Other possibilities include deism, monism, pantheism, and panentheism; and these alternatives have proven attractive, not only for other religions, but for a minority of Christian believers and theologians who have found the more traditional monotheism implausible or otherwise untenable.

In addition to its theistic structure, the popular Christian idea of God has other conceptual problems, which usually go unnoticed until they are brought to light by some crisis—such as a personal tragedy or a required college religion course. (Some of my students would say that these amount to the same thing!) The most common such catalytic experiences are unexpected or untimely disasters, illnesses, sufferings, or deaths for which no reason can be found or fairness discerned. They can be as varied in magnitude as the undiagnosed brain tumor that kills a bright, lovely, and popular coed a few days before her graduation and the Holocaust that exterminated millions of innocent victims under Hitler. Both situations, however, raise profound questions about the justness, the goodness, and even the existence of a providential God; and for some they may lead to atheism (utter disbelief in the existence of God), or agnosticism (uncertainty about either the existence of God itself or particular beliefs concerning God). But far less catastrophic or negative stimuli may also prompt a reevaluation of the standard images and attributes of the deity, and thus call into question some of popular Christianity's comfortable theological assumptions.

Transcendence and Immanence

The two most fundamental concepts at stake in all theological modeling are the diametrically opposed ideas of *transcendence* and *immanence*. Indeed, every theology (that is, a formal way of conceptualizing God) is a balancing of these two key ideas achieved by assigning different weights and different spins to those terms. Said another way: the notions of transcendence and immanence are the building blocks for all formal views of God.

"Otherness," "Withinness," and Combinations Thereof

The term "transcendence" derives from a Latin word meaning "to go beyond," and in theological terms is the quality of being somehow "prior to," "above," "beyond," or "other than." To declare that God is *transcendent*—in the strongest application of that adjective—is to affirm a God who is not identical to the universe and its constituents, but some sort of "Other Being" that has some kind of priority with respect to the created order. Such priority may be temporal, in the sense that God is pictured as having existed before the cosmos was created; or it may be what philosophers call "ontological," which in this context is a fancy way of saying "of a different and higher order of being"; or it may be both of these. Such a transcendent Being, then, tends to be "above it all" in some substantial way (sometimes but not necessarily spatially), and perhaps even aloof or remote.

Just to make things interesting—not to mention confusing—"transcendence" has a second, weaker sense, one that refers not to the *being* of God, but to the *accessibility* of God to the senses, the mind, or both and to the limits of human awareness and apprehension. One may say, for example, that God is "transcendent," and mean merely that this deity is beyond humanity's perceptual or conceptual powers, without taking a stand on God's actual (ontological) relationship to nature or human nature. Of course, a God who is *really* (ontologically) transcendent (in the strong sense) may very well be—indeed is likely to be—more or less transcendent in the weaker sense as well, the extent depending on how accessible the Divine One is and how limited human faculties are. But the reverse is not necessarily true: a deity that is transcendent simply to human sight and knowledge may not be transcendent in character (being) at all, as we shall soon see in the case of the Transcendentalists.

The word "immanence" also derives from Latin, but conveys the polar opposite sense of "indwelling" or the quality of "within-ness." Understood in the strongest sense, an *immanent* God (or Ultimate Reality by whatever name) is a deity that is somehow in its essence substantially and intimately related to the universe, for example, as its very inner depth, reality, or soul. This kind of divinity, therefore, is not above but within the cosmos, perhaps even one with it in some profound sense. Examples of theologies of immanence would be views of God as the inner Soul, Spirit, Consciousness, Mind, or Life Force of the universe, and, conversely, the Universe as the body, nervous system, or physical expression or extension (versus creation) of God.

But "immanence," too, has a weaker meaning; for God may be "in" the world only in the sense of being *active* in its affairs. Such a God might actually be transcendent in *being*, but impact the world and natural and human history. This sort of God might even exert some kind of occasional or ongoing Divine Presence—for example, as a Holy Spirit—moving things and people in mundane or miraculous ways. But as long as this God is thought to dwell elsewhere *and* to maintain an essential "Otherness" with respect to nature and human nature, this is a *basically* transcendent and only an *incidentally* immanent deity.

The Misnamed Transcendentalists

In a perfect world, one might expect the Transcendentalist movement in nineteenth-century America, represented by such notables as Emerson and Thoreau, to have been grounded in the notion of a transcendent "Other" God. But in fact, precisely because the terms "transcendence" and "immanence" are equivocal, Transcendentalist belief was based on just the opposite: the idea of God as an Immanent Spirit within nature, albeit One beyond our everyday awareness. In other words, strictly speaking and from a theological perspective, one must say that the Transcendentalists were really and truly Immanentalists! They merely recognized that the Indwelling One more often than not escaped our perception, leaving the world to appear merely natural.

Even taken in their purest and strictest senses, however, both transcendence and immanence can manifest themselves in a wide variety of forms. It is important, therefore, to investigate the particular kind of transcendence or immanence that any religion or theology embodies and intends. Still, the terms "transcendence" and "immanence" always suggest ideological types that stand at opposite ends of a conceptual spectrum. Thus two religions that start with a basically transcendent view of The Absolute (for example, orthodox Judaism and mainstream Islam) will always be more similar to one another theologically than to one based on a model of immanence (for example, philosophical and mystical Taoism). Yet nearly all theologies embody both of these concepts in various mixtures, with virtually none being a pure representative of one or the other. Even a unitive power and presence like the *Tao*, which Chinese philosophy locates as *really* and *truly* immanent within all of nature and human nature, is not always obviously so. Its very hiddenness makes it "transcendent" to (that is, beyond) our apprehension, but in a comparatively weak sense of that word.

Historically, transcendence and immanence have combined in their respective strong and weak senses to produce four principal theological models: theism, deism, pantheism (or monism), and panentheism. (See figure 2.1.) Henotheism and polytheism are really variations on theism, the former paying devotion to only one among many gods of the theistic type, and the latter encouraging attention to more than one or all such gods. Let us examine the "Big Four" in turn, starting with a closer look at the one that has dominated Western religions.

The Theistic Model for God

Theism, the basic theological model of traditional Christianity (as well as of Judaism and Islam), is built upon a particular blending of transcendence and immanence. Of these two qualities, transcendence is the more fundamental to theism, which begins by saying, "Whatever God is, God is not to be confused with the universe or any of its constituents, including the world, nature, and humanity." What theism teaches, therefore, is both transcendence of being—whereby God is not the universe and the universe is not

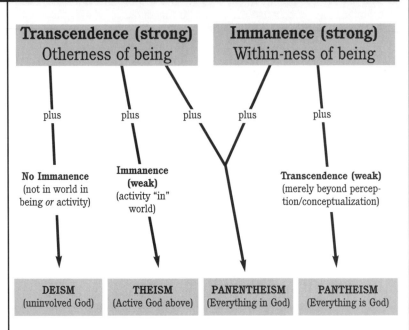

How Transcendence and Immanence Mix to Produce Classic Theologies

Transcendence (strong) Otherness of being	**Immanence (strong)** Within-ness of being

plus   plus   plus   plus   plus

No Immanence (not in world in being *or* activity)

Immanence (weak) (activity "in" world)

Transcendence (weak) (merely beyond perception/conceptualization)

DEISM (uninvolved God)	**THEISM** (Active God above)	**PANENTHEISM** (Everything in God)	**PANTHEISM** (Everything is God)

The qualities of transcendence and immanence are the basic building blocks of all theologies. What is often confusing about them is that both terms are used in imprecise and equivocal ways. The strong sense of both is the ontological, which refers to the being or essence of God. The weak sense of "immanence" is "activity." The weak meaning of "transcendence" is something close to "elusive." (The God of the Transcendentalists was precisely that: nature's immanent but elusive Spiritual Essence.)

FIGURE 2.1

God—*and* immanence of activity, which keeps God involved in the workings of the world.

Strong Transcendence, Qualified Immanence, and An Exceptional Incarnation

In technical terms, philosophers would call the type of transcendence found in theism "ontological," which simply means that God's *essence* or very *being* is involved. Some theologians have referred to this kind of transcendence of being as "ontological discontinuity," which suggests that two distinct orders or sorts of being are being posited, one divine and one natural, with a clear boundary between them. In fact, the very term "supernatural," which is often used in connection with the God of traditional Christianity, implies a theistic transcendence, for it connotes a dualistic distinction between the "natural" (that is, the physical universe) and that which is "above" it (that is, God).

Even if this transcendent God is portrayed as Creator, and however much the created order and its various creatures may reflect the handiwork or even bear the deity's "image and likeness," there can be no confusion between the two fundamental realities: God is not the universe and the universe is not God. Indeed, to mistake anything in the universe for God is idolatry, a very serious offense in the transcendence-heavy monotheistic faiths of Christianity, Judaism, and Islam. It is for this reason that these three religions cannot be classified as "nature religions," or their followers as "nature-worshippers." Their God is above nature . . . above it all!

Theism does not stop with the assertion of the ontological transcendence of God, however. In an important but qualified way, it asserts God's immanence as well. The theistic God is immanent in the sense of being divinely *present* and *active* in the universe and the world, and especially in human events and history. Though the God of theism never *becomes* the creation or any part of it—with the notable exception of Jesus Christ in traditional orthodox Christianity—this God is involved in its affairs in an ongoing way, which is precisely the meaning of "divine providence." Only in such a limited though very important way is God "within" the world, according to the theism model.

Of course the New Testament talks about the Holy Spirit of God as being "in" or "within" Christians. But when it does so, its language never suggests that those individuals thereby *become* divine. On the contrary, the language suggests that the Spirit works in much the same way as breath: in fact, the Greek New Testament word for "spirit" and "Spirit," *pneuma*, means "breath" as well. That provides a telling image, for it implies that, as the intake and presence of breath maintains vitality, but does not really change the nature or essence of the person, so do the "invasion" and indwelling of the Spirit bring spiritual life and its benefits, but without blurring the fundamental distinction between the human recipient and God. Philosophers and theologians might say here that an "ontological distinction or discontinuity" between humanity and God is maintained even in the case of the indwelling presence of the Holy Spirit. Thus both God's transcendence of being and the theism model itself, though apparently threatened by "indwelling spirit" language, are preserved.

The point at which mainstream Christianity really *does* compromise theism (the "one notable exception" mentioned above) is in the doctrine of the Incarnation, which—together with Atonement, Trinity, and Original Sin—is one of several teachings that distinguish Christianity from all of the other world religions. The very word "incarnation" means "enfleshment"; and the doctrine that bears that name affirms that in one person, and one person *only*—the man Jesus—God was embodied in such a way that there were two complete and united natures, one human and one divine. Thus, in a very real sense, he *was* God: there was no ontological distinction or "boundary of being" between him and God. This human, says traditional Christianity, *was* divine—and uniquely so.

From a Jewish or Muslim perspective, both of which are very strictly theistic, the Christian doctrine of the Incarnation is a clear violation of the profound distinction that *should* be maintained in a true, monotheistic religion. By contrast, for reasons that we shall see below, non-theistic Hindus would say that the Christian view of the Incarnation doesn't go nearly far enough.

Monotheism (More or Less)

The specific type of theism embraced by Christianity is monotheism, which is nothing other than belief in only one God of the theistic type. (Belief in more than one such god is polytheism, which has prevailed in many of the world's historical religions, from ancient Greece to tribal Africa to modern India.) The Hebrews are commonly credited with "inventing" monotheism, and if Judaism can be said to have a creed at all, it is probably contained in Deuteronomy 6:4, the so-called *Shema*: "Hear, O Israel: the LORD our God, the LORD is one."(NIV) Taken at face value, that assertion would appear to be one of strict monotheism; and the Jewish faith has taken it that way for well over two millennia.

There is some evidence, however, that sometime in their past (and perhaps even into so-called Old Testament times), the Israelites had held polytheistic beliefs. Indeed, one of the names for God in the Hebrew Scriptures is *Elohim*, which is a plural noun. That might account for God's curious declaration in Genesis 1: "Let *us* make humankind in *our* image." Also, many of the episodes in Exodus suggest that the people of Israel escaping from Egypt were only *henotheistic*, which means that although they were devoted to one God (Jahweh, sometimes spelled and always pronounced "Yahweh"), with whom they understood themselves to have a covenant or pact, they did not deny the existence of other gods. In fact, the wandering Israelites occasionally turned their affections to one or another of these—to Moses' great dismay. But by the eighth century BCE, at least, the Jews appear firmly monotheistic, and have remained so ever since.

As one consequence of its strict monotheism, mainstream Judaism (like Islam) for most of its history has viewed Satan as a minor figure. Indeed, a "satan" (Hebrew for "adversary") appears only four times in the entire Hebrew Bible ("Old Testament"): in Psalms 109:6 and Zechariah 3:1–2 as an accuser; in I Chronicles 21:1 as an instigator; and in Job 1 and 2 as one of God's heavenly court, an observer and tester on behalf of Jahweh. Only in this last instance is Satan a real persona and name; and even in this, his starring role, he disappears from the plot after the seventh verse of the second chapter. In none of these appearances, moreover, is this satan or Satan an adversary against Jahweh, but in every case is employed by the deity as a kind of provocateur or prosecutor. The reason for such a small and subordinate role is clear: Jews had become so completely monotheistic that they preferred to attribute evil and human suffering (like Job's) to God rather than to envision a second power or divinity to account for it.

Despite its otherwise strict monotheism, for a brief period of time following their sixth-century BCE exile into Babylonian captivity, Jews changed "the satan" (the adversary) into Satan (the personification of evil). This change was due, no doubt, to the influence of Persian Zoroastrians, who recognized a god of goodness and light and a god of evil and darkness (or perhaps a single God with profoundly opposing spirits) locked in an eternal struggle. Whether Jesus was affected by this brief detour in Jewish thought and believed in a powerful Devil-Satan is unclear. What is certain is that early on Christians reconceived Satan, further elevated his status, and gave him a major role, turning him into the Devil. From a Jewish and Muslim perspective, that amounts to further evidence of Christianity's watering-down of monotheism.

To be sure, Christianity has never called Satan a "god." Yet it clearly adopted and developed a view of Satan as a counter-force of evil to God's power of good—in effect, "a bad god." Throughout the synoptic gospels especially, beginning with the temptation of Jesus at the start of his ministry, Satan is an Evil Power out to thwart Jesus' mission and God's divine, redemptive plan for humanity. Indeed, the book of Revelation closes the New Testament with God and the legions of light lined up to do battle with Satan and his army of darkness on the plain of Maggedo (Armageddon), a scene that resembles nothing so much as a titanic confrontation of competing divinities. For all intents and purposes, then, Christianity's Satan is a god.

In addition to its doctrine of the Incarnation and its view of Satan, a third point at which Christianity appears to have compromised monotheism was its doctrine of the Trinity. The word "trinity" appears nowhere in the New Testament, but was coined by a Christian theologian, Tertullian, in the early third century to account for the New Testament's occasional references to "Father," "Son," and "Spirit." As early as the end of the first century CE, as we shall see in the following chapter, Christians were equating Jesus with God, a merging of identities that became official doctrine by the early fourth century. Eventually, a place was made for the Holy Spirit as well, and the orthodox view of the Trinity was formulated. It maintained something that few Christians today are aware of or understand: that God has three different, distinct, and coeternal Persons—not personalities, not roles, not aspects, not functions, not modes, but Persons. To be sure, all Three are of the same divine "substance" or "essence"—a philosophical (not biblical) way of saying that there was no "boundary of being" between the Three. Still, such an assertion of three distinct, divine Persons, if taken at all as any kind of statement of truth (rather than, say, poetry or metaphor) appears at least to qualify the strict monotheism that Christianity has historically claimed.

That is certainly the way Muslims view Christianity: as a monotheistic religion gone awry. Their faith, Islam, is strictly and uncompromisingly monotheistic. The First Pillar of their faith is their creed, the *Shahadah*, the first line of which closely resembles the Jewish *Shema*: "There is no God but Allah, and Muhammad is Allah's messenger." "Allah" means "The God," and the creed affirms not only this God's uniqueness, but Islam's founder's subordinate status: Muhammad is not "God" or even "Son of God," for either of these titles would threaten Islam's monotheism; he is merely a human messenger—the last and greatest of God's spokespersons, and divinely inspired, certainly, but still a human being.

This unrelenting monotheism is a major point of superiority that Islam claims over her sister religions, Judaism and Christianity. According to Muslims, Jews at least had *claimed* the exclusive oneness of God in their *Shema*; in practice, however, as the Old Testament shows, Jews fell into the worship of other deities, and were chastised and punished for it. Christianity, however, strayed much more quickly and profoundly, when its early theologians found and identified in the New Testament itself what amounts to three gods, and built an official doctrine to that effect.

A Muted But Mighty Monotheism

Despite Christianity's rather glaring compromises of theism (see figure 2.2.), the theistic model largely prevails. That is not to say that concepts of God do not differ within the Old Testament literature, or from the Old to the New Testament, or in extra-canonical Jewish and Christian writings; but it *is* to say that whatever theological variations do take place, the theistic pattern remains at least relatively intact.

Thus, from the moment of Creation as described in Genesis 1 and 2, God and the world are distinct entities. From that point forward, God continually gets involved in the history of the world, and particularly in human history by expelling Adam and Eve, cleansing the world in the days of Noah, calling Abraham to be the progenitor of a chosen people, leading the children of Israel out of Egyptian captivity, speaking through the prophets, and so forth. For traditional Christians, God also sent an "only begotten Son," worked miracles through him, sent the Holy Spirit, established and inspired the Church, and continues to answer prayers—but always as an entity distinct

Monotheism, More or Less

Strict	Not so strict
Islam's Creed *(Shahadah)*: "There is no god but God, and Muhammad is God's Messenger."	**Christianity's Compromises:** 1. Trinity: one Godhead, three Persons
	2. Incarnation: Jesus Christ as God-in-the-flesh, "very God of very God"
Judaism's Creed *(Shema)*: "Hear, O Israel, the Lord your God, the Lord is One."	3. Satan: the Devil, a god-like power of evil

FIGURE 2.2

from ordinary humanity and from a heavenly dwelling place beyond the natural world.

This theistic model is also reflected in the way Christians generally perceive their relation to God. This God is "on high" in some sense. Indeed, mention of this deity is often accompanied by a pointing upward. It is from that lofty position that (depending upon your theology) God is seen either to send blessings, or to inflict sufferings, temptations, and perhaps "trials and tribulations," or to do both sorts of things. To this God Christians render worship and prayer, and in both of these activities they communicate with One who may or may not respond, but who in either case always remains a distinct Other, which is to say, "transcendent."

Theism is so much a part of the "baggage" of traditional orthodox Christianity that it provides the background for virtually every doctrine central to Christian belief, and persists as an unspoken assumption behind nearly all that Christians think, say, and do about God. It is especially important as the foundation upon which Christian views of sin and salvation have been formulated. For the affirmation of the ontological transcendence (that is, "essential otherness") of God and the resulting dualism prepare the way for, and perhaps lead inevitably to, the radical view of human sin and alienation from God that is so distinctive of Christian teachings from Paul on (as we shall see in chapter 5). Likewise, the idea of a uniquely divine Savior "sent down" from "on high" reflects the theistic view of God (as we shall see in chapter 6). Had Christianity started with a theology other than theism, not only the human condition and the nature of salvation, but the person and significance of Jesus might well have been understood and formulated very differently.

Until very recently, theism has so dominated Christian theology that often what is termed "atheism" in the Western world is in reality only a repudiation of this particular theological stance. Finding the theistic model in some way unpalatable, some simply decide to deny the existence of God altogether, unaware that there are alternative ways of conceptualizing a deity. Of course, there have always been thoughtful, informed atheists who have rejected the idea of any God in principle, irrespective of how that God may be conceived. But the more specific a-theism appears increasingly attractive in the modern age of experimental science, whose preference for empirical reality makes it increasingly difficult to relate to a God conceived as being somehow "up there" or "out there" or "wholly other," as Christianity has traditionally taught.

Alternative Theologies

Other possible theological models have emerged in the history of the world's religions, however, each in its own way as plausible—or implausible, perhaps—as the theistic God of Christianity. One is deism, a distinctly Western invention and, indeed, a conscious and deliberate departure from Christian theism. A second, pantheism, is more common in Eastern religions, especially in its philosophical form, monism. The third is panentheism, a modern western blend of theism and pantheism.

Enlightenment Deism

Deism grew out of the Enlightenment of the seventeenth and eighteenth centuries, a philosophical and scientific movement whose emphasis on rationalism (that is, the necessity of applying reason to all truth claims, including the religious) and empiricism (that is, the reliance on sensory data) produced our own prevailing modern scientific worldview. Associated with such European philosophers as Lord Herbert of Cherbury, John Tillotson, John Toland, and Voltaire, deism found its most famous American representative in none other than Thomas Jefferson.

Deism accepted the existence of God as a perfectly rational—in fact the most reasonable—explanation for the empirical fact and apparent orderliness of the universe. The God of deism was above all the Creator God, conceived in the image of the Great Clockmaker. This God had been wise and skillful enough to build both natural law and moral law into creation in such a way that further intervention would be unnecessary. For God to have intervened after creation to interrupt the natural order, therefore, would have amounted to a divine admission of a faulty initial design that required adjustment or repair. Furthermore, the deists saw no unambiguous, empirical evidence of such divine intervention in the world around them. Hence, they concluded that God neither worked miracles nor answered prayers. In other words, like the theistic God, the deistic God was transcendent in being, but, except for the moment of Creation itself, was not immanent even in the limited, weaker sense of being active in the world or its history.

Like many of the leading lights of the American Revolution, Thomas Jefferson was a thoroughgoing deist. In fact, he even edited the New Testament gospels in light of his deistic beliefs, removing all miraculous works and events, and especially resurrection accounts, because they were violations of natural law and human reason. His so-called "Jefferson Bible" retained such teachings as the Sermon on the Mount, since they were eloquent expressions of the moral law that the Creator had "programmed into" the universe. For the same reason, Jefferson had no problem with the Ten Commandments in the Old Testament. But the idea that Moses had received them on tablets from God on a mountain top—or that Jesus had fed an audience of five thousand with a few loaves and fishes—was to him absurd.

Jefferson's radical deism, of course, sheds historical light on the original meaning of his famous words in the Declaration of Independence: "We are endowed by our Creator with certain unalienable rights . . . " meant that the Creator God had infused such principles as "life, liberty, and the pursuit of happiness" into the very fabric of the world. For Jefferson, however, the extended prayer-request in the beloved hymn "God Bless America" would have been a pointless petition, since there could be no intervention without a divine admission of a design flaw in the Creation. Only an inept God would have to step in to fix a faulty world.

According to Jefferson, God had given humanity moral principles, consciences by which to know them, and intellects to help in their application and even in the construction of a government around them. God had there-

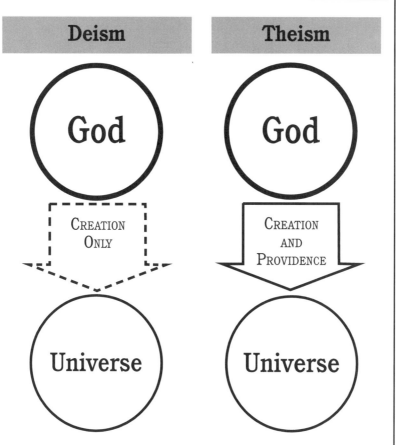

Theological Models Dominated by Transcendence

Deism

God

CREATION
ONLY

Universe

Theism

God

CREATION
AND
PROVIDENCE

Universe

The strong (ontological) transcendence that dominates these two models is here represented in each case, as it might be in set theory in mathematics, by two circles: the one representing God, and the other representing the universe and everything in it (including the world and humanity, nature and human nature). In each case the message of ontological transcendence is that *God is not the universe and the universe is not God*. The arrows represent the kind of immanence found in both models, namely, *divine activity that impacts the universe*. In the case of deism, that immanence is limited to creation and the natural and moral law "programmed into" the universe at that time—hence the broken arrow. In theism, the immanence of activity is much stronger because it continues in an ongoing fashion after creation as intervention in nature, history, and everyday life.

FIGURE 2.3

fore blessed America (along with all humanity) sufficiently already! What more of a blessing could the people of America possibly want in that prayer-song? For God to "stand beside her" and to "guide her" would have implied the very kind of divine intervention in human history that the deists found both implausible and unnecessary. For this reason alone, Jefferson would have been a staunch opponent of prayer in public schools. For, aside from weakening the "high wall of separation" between church and state that he thought essential to a true democracy, such an exercise would simply be a waste of time, since the God of deism answers no prayers. With its God-given mental capacity and moral compass, humanity has all it needs to ameliorate the difficulties it faces.

Such historical information about the views of our nation's founders, of course, renders many of the standard annual sermons around the Fourth of July ridiculous. Preachers who implore us to "return to the faith of our founding fathers" are really asking us (unwittingly, I suspect) to stop praying and expecting miracles, and to cease going to church! For thoroughgoing deists, the proper worship of God was simply the leading of a moral life: ritual of any kind was, at best, a waste of time. (Jefferson himself, it seems, was inconsistent at this point, for as President he regularly attended Sunday services—but apparently only to set a good example for non-deists.) It was in ethical living, not ceremony, that one paid due honor to the Creator of it all, but not in anticipation of any pay-off in the form of special acts of blessing or gifts of bliss, since the God thus honored was not one to intervene, much less to reward. The God of deism had made a world precisely as it was supposed to be, and it functioned very nicely without divine intervention.

Pantheism and Monism

At the other extreme on the transcendence-immanence spectrum is pantheism, yet another alternative to the theism of traditional Christianity. The term "pantheism" itself derives from the Greek words for "all" and "God," and means either that everything is literally God, or that everything is essentially God. This view has surfaced occasionally in Western religion and philosophy. Its clearest and most famous representative was probably the seventeenth-century Jewish philosopher Spinoza. But the Christian mystic Meister Eckhart had already been accused of it in the fourteenth century, just as existentialist Christian theologian Paul Tillich would be in the twentieth.

The purest forms of pantheism, however, appear in Eastern religions like Hinduism and Taoism, though there it is more accurate to speak of this form of immanence as a specific kind of "monism," that is, the belief in an indwelling and pervasive One rather than a God within. (See figure 2.4.) For if Eastern religions talk about gods—and some do so rather off-handedly if at all—it is usually in the plural; and the gods themselves are relative and subject to a more profound universal Power or Principle, which, though maintaining the same status as the Ultimate Reality claimed by the Christian God, is not itself a "god."

Pantheism or Monism?

There is room for confusion between the models of pantheism and monism, for the two are quite similar. The basic difference is that pantheism is a theology, while monism connotes a philosophy.

Monism is the philosophical view that all of reality consists of one thing or one kind of thing. The possible candidates for this fundamental "stuff" are nearly always matter, spirit (or consciousness), or some mysterious third thing. Those who opt for the first of these are called "monistic materialists," those who choose the second are known as "monistic idealists," and those who advocate the third are dubbed "neutral monists."

If a monist speaks in "God" terms, as some philosophers do, then they may well be said to be "pantheists," since they are likely saying that the one thing of which everything consists is God. While it is possible for a monistic materialist to be a pantheist by maintaining that God is the physical cosmos, it is far more likely and common for pantheists to be of either the idealistic monist (God is Spirit or Mind) or the neutral monist (God is Mystery) variety.

In any case, the distinction between a pantheist and a monist may be slight and essentially semantic, hinging on whether or not "God" language is employed for the Ultimate Reality. As a rule, pantheists are more common in the West, where religious thought tends to produce theologies; and monists are more common in the East, where the Ultimate Reality is seldom called "God," and where spirituality therefore tends to yield philosophies rather than theologies.

FIGURE 2.4

Hinduism, for example, has literally millions of gods, each with his or her individual characteristics and domain. The most popular of these today are Shiva and Vishnu, but they are but two among legions of deities. Greater than all of them in importance and stature is *Brahman*, the Eternal One, the cosmic Unity, the "great sea of all souls." But unlike the gods of monotheistic religions (such as Jahweh in Judaism or Allah in Islam) Brahman is conceived of more as a non-personal force or principle—Being-Itself, perhaps—than as an existing being. Thus, unlike the theistic Christian God (and Allah and Jahweh) Brahman does not think, or feel, or do anything; yet, without Brahman, there could be no thinking, feeling, or doing at all. Also, in contrast to all forms of theism, Brahman is in absolute ontological continuity with the physical order, which is to say that Brahman is completely immanent in the universe: infused and pervasive.

Hinduism teaches that each living thing, including human beings, has *atman*, which we may guardedly translate "soul" as long as we realize that it is not that in the Western or Christian sense. For atman is impersonal; and indeed atman is Brahman, a "drop in the great sea of all souls." Even the gods are but manifestations of one or another or several of the infinitely numerous aspects of Brahman.

This thoroughgoing immanence of Hinduism is typical of Eastern religions. That is, there is at least a formal similarity between what the Hindus call "Brahman," the Taoists call "Tao," and the Buddhists call "Shunyata"; and all three religions variously assert the final oneness of the inner self of the person and this Ultimate Reality. This framework explains why mysticism (the spirituality of inwardness) has always had a stronger foothold in the Eastern than in the Western religious traditions: a much more intimate relationship, an essential continuity or identity, in fact, exists naturally between the worshipper and the object of worship from the outset. This continuity can be realized and experienced (with the proper techniques) through contemplative introspection ("looking inward").

By contrast, communication with the Other of theism (for example, in prayer) involves two separate and distinct parties: the religious person and the object of her or his devotion. Furthermore, these two parties sometimes require a mediator. Thus, the God of Western theism is by definition more remote than the Ultimate Reality of Eastern religions. The sort of "oneness" that Christian mystics have claimed to have achieved has almost always been an intimacy of *relationship* rather than an absorption of identity, to which their Eastern counterparts have aspired.

Another important consequence of the immanence of divinity in the Eastern religions is that sin plays very little part in their view of the human predicament. As already pointed out, Christianity's view of God as transcendent leads quite naturally to the radical and thoroughgoing view of sin that Christianity teaches. For if a religion begins with the notion that the divine and human are in a situation of "otherness," a state of alienation is far more likely and profound than if there is presupposed an essential oneness, as is the case of Brahman-atman in Hinduism. Hindus see the basic problem for humanity not as sin or alienation, therefore, but as *ignorance* of their own essential divinity. Likewise, they have defined "salvation" not as a mere reconciliation with the Ultimate One, as in classic Christianity, but as a realization of an unambiguous oneness with this Reality, which is none other than one's own true Self.

Panentheism, Process, and Popular Piety

The starkness of this scenario of alienation, radical sin, and salvation, which seem almost unavoidable in theism, coupled with the existence of plausible alternative theological models available in other religions, has led some Christian theologians to explore some different ways of conceptualizing God, especially those that emphasize immanence. In the forefront of these revisionists for several decades have been so-called "process theologians" like John Cobb and Charles Hartshorne, most of whom have attempted to reinterpret the Christian message from a panentheistic viewpoint. In this conception God is not only profoundly immanent in the cosmos, but indeed evolving with it, as it were, "from within." Yet process theologians see God as transcending the world in some important sense—hence, pan-en-theism: everything is in God and is also infused with and permeated by God.

Panentheism is like pantheism in that for both theologies God is the inner spiritual reality of the universe and nature. The difference is that for panentheists, God is more than just the inner spirituality of this universe: "God is

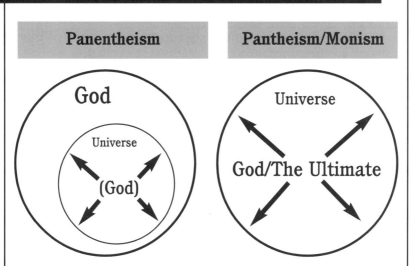

Theological Models Dominated by Immanence

Panentheism

God

Universe

(God)

Pantheism/Monism

Universe

God/The Ultimate

The strong (ontological) immanence that dominates these two models is here represented by the arrows, which indicate that God (in the case of a Western theology) or The Ultimate (in the case of an Eastern philosophy) is an inner Presence and Power that *permeates*, *saturates*, or *infuses* the universe and everything in it (including the world and humanity, nature and human nature) *from within*. The fact that there is only one circle in pantheism/monism underscores that God/The Ultimate is not a Reality separate from the universe, but is instead its very spiritual Essence. The larger circle containing the smaller one in panentheism indicates that in this model God contains the universe but (according to the parenthetical name and the arrows) in such a way that God also infuses the universe and everything in it, exactly as in the case of pantheism/monism. The difference is that in panentheism, there is some of God "left over"—that is, God has an ontologically transcendent aspect that is untouched by (and unrelated to) the universe. To put this subtle but important distinction another way: *in pantheism, God/The Ultimate is the inner spiritual essence of everything, while in panentheism, God/The Ultimate is that and then some.*"

FIGURE 2.5

the inner Spirit of the cosmos, and then some." (Pantheists would omit the last three words.) For the process thinkers, God and the universe are intimately one in being (that is, ontologically), rather than two, as dualistic theism holds. Indeed, God is undeniably immanent. Yet there is also something of God—an aspect or dimension, perhaps—that is beyond the universe: God and the universe are not (to use a spatial image) coextensive. Just as a drop of ink in a glass of water can be commingled with the water, yet with some clear water surrounding and untouched, so there is a part (aspect? dimension?) of the God who saturates the universe that is nevertheless "beyond" it, transcendent with respect to it.

Besides such philosophically-oriented and academy-based thinkers as the process theologians, other Christian thinkers have adopted and advocated the panentheistic model for a popular audience. In fact, if there is a popular theological bandwagon whose music is celebrating the beginning of a new millennium, its name is "Panentheism." The first to bring this model to the attention of the general public was probably Anglican Bishop John A. T. Robinson in his controversial book, *Honest to God*, published in 1963. Panentheism was further popularized by Roman Catholic priest Matthew Fox in his signal work, *Original Blessing* (1993), which presented a "Creation Spirituality" that eventually got him defrocked. More recently, Marcus Borg has endorsed and expounded panentheism in a most accessible way in his popular volume, *The God We Never Knew* (1997). Some modern scientists are also exploring the panentheistic model in their dialogue with religion and its spokespersons.

Still other Christians have been looking to Eastern religions like Hinduism and Taoism for possible theological correctives to Christianity's stark theism. Some of them have found that a monistic theology that posits God *within* the cosmos rather than above or beyond it, as theism likes to do, is more in keeping with the modern scientific worldview, which tends to treat the universe (and our world within it) as an organic whole or closed system, *and* more in resonance with their own experience of divinity. Some of these people have even looked to the Christian mystical tradition (especially the medieval) for examples of deeply spiritual individuals who found God not above, but within—and who were often accused of pantheism by astute guardians of orthodox theism. Some have even argued that Jesus' reported claims that "God's imperial rule is in you" (throughout the synoptics) and "And those who see me see the one who sent me" (John 12:45) portray him challenging the dualism of his Jewish heritage in favor of a God who is immanent (or incarnate) — not just in himself, but in everyone else.

While professional theologians develop and debate just such abstract and difficult ideas, and at least toy with Eastern-type images for God, at the popular level, many inheritors and advocates of Christianity appear to be drifting in the opposite direction, by exhibiting what amounts to a "practical deism." Polls show that the vast majority of Americans believe in the existence of God, and the number one reason they give is the fact of the universe itself, for which there "had to be" a Creator. But those same polls show that even among the self-consciously religious there is little or no sense of divine intervention in everyday life. In other words, although most everyone is sure that there is a God (of some sort, somewhere), they are not sure what that God does besides account for the existence and design of the universe.

That belief-with-reservation amounts to deism; and it is a direct result, no doubt, of the pervasiveness of the modern scientific worldview in the Western world. Mere belief in God takes more mental energy today than ever before, requiring some kind of empirical evidence, serious rational deliberation, and an intentional conclusion on the subject. What is more, even when God's existence is assured to the satisfaction of reason, those thus convinced continue to lead largely self-sufficient lives, hardly ever requiring recourse to any spiritual realm and rarely seeking divine intervention. For the universe and human life seem to proceed on automatic pilot, subject to natural law rather than divine providence, and amenable to the powers of reason, science, and technology rather than to those of revelation, prayer, or miracle. Thus, when appliances don't work, we call repairpersons, and when our health fails, we call a physician—in both cases because we trust those with knowledge and skill in manipulating the lawful workings of the natural, material world. Conversely, when we hear any claim of miracles, even the sincerely religious among us are skeptical; and we look upon those parents who treat their sick children with spiritual rather than medical means as abusive or negligent. Thus most twentieth century folk—believers and non-believers alike—appear to be proceeding largely "under their own steam." The deistic faith of our precursor Jefferson seems to have caught up with us!

Evil, Monotheism, and the Justness of God

The remoteness of the theistic God of traditional Christianity relative to the world and humanity probably made the utter aloofness of the deistic God of Jefferson all but inevitable. For a God who is "up there" or "out there" at some distance is but a step removed from irrelevancy. But the fact that the Christian faith is monotheistic raises some conceptual problems that in many ways are even more troublesome than the unemployed God of deism. The most serious of these by far is the question of the goodness or justness of God. Simply put, the sticky question is this: if there is only one God, and if this one God is both Creator of and Ongoing Provider for the world—in other words, is really in charge of it all—how is it possible to account for the existence of evil in the first place, much less its persistence? To make matters worse, how can we explain the fact that evil befalls the undeserving and helpless, bringing unmerited and often unremitting suffering.

A Persistent Problem, Some Suggested Solutions

As I write this paragraph, for example, the newspaper and TV headlines are filled with the news of a devastating volcanic eruption and resulting mudslide in South America that have killed over twenty thousand people in a few minutes; of a little girl killed at play by a drunken driver; of a prominent young businessman's sudden death in his mid-thirties caused by an

Transcendent and Immanent Gods

The basic building blocks of theology, *transcendence* and *immanence*, as well as the four classic theological models they combine to produce – theism, deism, pantheism and panentheism – can best be understood by analogy. For the more athletically inclined, these concepts may be viewed in the context of sports. For those of a more artistic inclination, some comparisons with music might be more helpful.

The God of theism, for example, is like the manager of a baseball team. Though not a part of the line-up as a player (transcendence), the manager is very much in the game (immanence), not only by virtue of his prior coaching, but also by determining the starting line-up and directing the actions of batters, base-runners, pitchers, and fielders. The manager is also free to replace players, adjust the line-up, send in pinch-hitters, and so forth. In other words, though not in the game physically, the manager plays a very active part in its action and outcome.

Deism

Now that's the way Abner Doubleday meant for baseball to be played!

I've never heard Mozart performed better!

God is a transcendent power of a very different and higher order, remote, but still indirectly affecting the action.

Similarly, the conductor of a symphony orchestra, though generally not one of the instrumentalists in a performance, is nevertheless crucial to its quality and success, controlling the tempo, phrasing, dynamics, and so forth.

Deism's God would be very much like the inventor of a sport, who – though probably long-deceased – still influences the play and outcome of the game enormously by the original layout of the playing field and the initial formulation of the rules. Likewise, the deistic God would be comparable to a classical composer who – despite being a century or more dead – still continues to shape the performance by the character of his or her composition.

The pantheistic God is like the innate talent and motivation (immanence) one sees in an uncoached pick-up basketball game, especially if the players are extremely gifted. They razzle and they dazzle, not because

Theism

Anything you say Coach Lombardi!

I'll play it just the way you want it, Mr. Bernstein!

God is a transcendent power of a very different and higher order, active and directly controlling the action.

anyone has told them how or is calling in plays and moves from the sideline, but simply because they have it "in their bones." There is no coach or manager (no transcendence), nor is one needed. In a similar vein, the pantheistic God would be like the emergent musical talent of a group of untutored street musicians that composes and performs complicated tunes or creates impromptu improvisations with no formal instruction whatsoever.

The panentheistic God, then, would be like the internal ability and drive of other naturally talented and uncoached athletes (immanence), but taken by a remarkable team or individual with astounding skills to an extraordinary and unprecedented level (transcendence). Or the panentheistic God might be analogous to a prodigious, young, unschooled musical group that is so moving or inspiring that one uses words like "heavenly" and "celestial" to describe it.

Pantheism

Those kids playing basketball on the playground sure are talented!

Not a single member of that excellent barbershop quartet can read a note of music!

God, (or the Ultimate) is a natural, immanent power (an inner dimension of the ordinary), utterly unaffected by any external, transcendent power or authority.

Panentheism

The members of that team are so talented, they're out of this world.

No one in that jazz ensemble has had a single music lesson, but their music is divine!

God, (or the Ultimate) is a natural, immanent power (an inner dimension of the ordinary), yet suggestive of a quality that somehow transcends the ordinary.

It is important to note that in these analogies, the gods of theism and deism are both represented by a *uniquely authoritative individual*, while the gods of pantheism and panentheism are both represented by a *collectively shared attribute*. In fact, though it may press the analogy a bit, to be absolutely true to the "pan-" ("all") in the latter two models, the attribute – be it athletic ability or musical talent – would have to be shared to *some* degree or extent by everyone if not everything. Also, the difference between the two "pan-" models is very subtle – a matter only of degree. The element of divine transcendence in panentheism is *not* like that in theism or deism, for it is not really *active*: it does not impinge upon or affect the inhabitants of ordinary reality, but is only inferred from what they do or experience.

FIGURE **2.6**

undiagnosed congenital heart defect. The same news reports also tell of a convicted murderer getting paroled early from prison, a hardened criminal avoiding prosecution on a technicality, and a well-known leader in organized crime living in prosperity, luxury, and health into his twilight years. Where is there justice in a world in which a child suffers and dies of an accident or a disease while a deliberate and persistent purveyor of evil lives long and luxuriously? Indeed, the most difficult thing for us to understand or accept about evil is the seeming injustice of its distribution. If for some unexplained reason there has to be evil, why does it seem to afflict so many apparently innocent people with so much seemingly undeserved suffering?

Human suffering occurs at any number of levels. Individual suffering is difficult, especially if a loved one is involved. Congenital disease and deformity as well as terminal childhood diseases are particularly hard to explain because the victims are so young. So are incurable diseases of all kinds, which appear to strike at random. Chance victims of street crimes, not to mention casualties of terrorist-caused airplane crashes or building collapses or bombed busses, make us very sad indeed. On a much wider, almost mind-numbing scale, statistics tell us that over forty thousand of our world's people are dying daily of starvation and hunger-related diseases. That amounts to more than fourteen million yearly, the vast majority of whom perish through circumstances beyond their control—most of them, children. Where is God while all of this is happening?

Classical monotheism, it would seem, must almost necessarily make God somehow ultimately responsible for evil and suffering. If something goes awry in the One Creator's universe, after all, where else can the "buck" stop? Thus it is that in Muslim-dominant countries a favorite saying is: "Allah wills it." Likewise, in the Jewish tradition, evil is attributed to Jahweh: "I am the Lord, and there is none else . . . I make peace, and create evil." (Isa 45:6–7, KJV) And create evil God does! He (masculine only because the dominant imagery for God in the Hebrew Bible is anthropomorphic and male) sends a great flood in the time of Noah to drown the human race, presumably including many innocent babies and children (Genesis 7). He dispatches the death angel across Egypt to kill, not the intransigent Pharaoh and his supporters, but all of the first-born children (Exodus 12). He issues orders through Moses to the people of Israel to take the land of the Midianites and slaughter even the women and children—except, of course, for the virginal females, whom the Israelite soldiers are allowed to keep for themselves (Numbers 31). He gives his agent, Satan, permission to wipe out Job's children, servants, cattle, sheep, house, and health, all to prove the point that the man is truly righteous (Job 1). Were we to find out that an American general had done such things in wartime, we'd have him imprisoned and tried, then hospitalized or shot.

Of course, the ancient Jews saw clearly the dilemma: to attribute these things not to God, but to some other force or being, is to threaten not only the sovereignty of God but monotheism itself, by positing, in effect, an evil power of divine status. And they were far more willing to yield on the goodness of God than on their fundamental faith in God's oneness. That is why (as we noted earlier and shall see in detail in chapter 5) Satan is not an evil force in the Hebrew Scriptures at all, but a minor agent of God—a wielder of God's woe and a tester of humanity's faith.

Of all of the world's religions, monistic Hinduism (and its derivatives) may have propounded the most satisfying solution to this eternal puzzle in its doctrine of *karma*. Hinduism begins with an impersonal Ultimate that cannot rightly be said to "do" anything. Brahman is simply powerless either to cause or alleviate evil. Evil is simply taken to be a part of *samsara*, which means both everyday reality and the ceaseless and eternal cycles of birth, life, death, rebirth in which all human beings are caught up. The law of *karma* says that you reap what you sow—if not in this life, then in the next or the next. Hence, a seemingly innocent victim of an untimely, perhaps painful death, is really paying the price of evil-doing in a past life. Thus, the Hindu view is that the universe and its underlying eternal principle, Brahman, provide justice after all, at least in the long run—not intentionally, but as a matter of cosmic routine.

Christianity's Complication and Challenge

Christianity not only has no such "neat" system for explaining evil, it has a view of God that makes an affirmation of the fairness of life and the justness of God difficult to explain, much less defend. Christian theism has usually assigned to God some traditional attributes that, though probably deriving more from Greek philosophy than from biblical theology, have nevertheless impressed themselves on the commonly held concept of "God." Thus it is that God is simply assumed to be *omnipotent* (all powerful), able to do anything at will. This God is also *omnipresent* (or, as theologians like to say, "ubiquitous"), which means that God is everywhere, not being spatially limited. God is also presumably possessed of *omniscience*, that is, knowledge of everything that is or that happens. This usually includes prescience, or "foreknowledge" of future events as well. On top of all of these impressive traits, God is *omnibenevolent*, that is, favorably disposed toward the created order and, in particular, humanity. That means that from the human perspective, God is completely and utterly good—the very personification of love.

Each of these attributes is rationally problematic in its own right. Omnipotence, for example, raises this classic conundrum: "If God can do anything, can He make a rock so big that not even He can lift it?" (It was this very question, posed to me by a playmate when I was seven, that set me on the path to become a theologian.) Medieval Christian theologians tackled and resolved that, at least to their satisfaction, by admitting that God could not do the illogical, the self-contradictory, or anything that would violate God's own character or attributes. Violations of the natural order, of course, were another matter, for without them miracles would have been impossible; and these theologians certainly wanted to retain the possibility of miracles.

But the real challenge for Christian theologians was to claim for God all of the traditional "omni-" attributes simultaneously and still be able to explain evil and suffering in the world. They had some challenging questions to confront. For example, where did evil come from in the first place? Did

God as Creator invent it or at least allow for its possibility? If so, why? Could not this omniscient God have foreseen evil's future effects and prevented them? Why, then, are there so many natural disasters—catastrophic floods, fires, tornadoes, earthquakes and the like? Why is there so much moral evil at the human level—murder, rape, war, repression, dishonesty, thievery, terrorism, genocide, and so on? Given such evil, why does an all-good, all-powerful, all-knowing God, who could (because of those very attributes) alleviate or even eliminate it, permit it to continue—and on such a grand scale? For that matter, why doesn't such a God wipe out dreaded diseases and turn the drought-ridden regions of the world into vegetable gardens or fruit groves?

The matter of intercessory and petitionary prayer arises at this point. Why do Christians have to request God's assistance for themselves or others in the face of evil and human suffering? Does God really withhold blessings and refuse to remedy the effects of disease and disaster until enough people sway the divine will with their pleadings? What kind of "Father," being aware of the plight of "his" suffering children and able to come to their aid, waits until the cries are loud enough or long enough or numerous enough before "He" acts? Why do we have to beg for mercy and aid? Why does God not intervene with healing and help (if not prevention and protection) as a matter of heavenly routine, without our having to plead for it? Could God be merely inattentive to or unaware of such suffering? If so, that God is not omniscient. And, finally, why is the suffering sometimes not alleviated at all, no matter how much pleading is done by many sincere and spiritual people?

To answer such questions is not any easy matter. Indeed, the attempt to justify God in the face of evil (called "theodicy" from the Greek words for "God" and "justice") has been one of the great challenges of Christian theology through the centuries. Simply put, the question is how an omniscient (all-knowing), omnipotent (all-powerful), and merciful (utterly loving and kind) God can let evil and suffering exist and continue to afflict human beings, especially the apparently undeserving—the very young and old, the very poor and powerless. For if God can do something and doesn't, then God appears not to be completely merciful; and if God would like to do something, but can't, then God is not really all-powerful after all. Another possibility, of course, is that God is both willing and able, but the evil and suffering have somehow escaped the divine notice, in which case God is not all-knowing.

Strategies for Salvaging God's Reputation

The classic solutions to this dilemma have been numerous and largely unsatisfying. Some have argued, for example, that evil is somehow necessary for goodness and freedom to exist. For (so the argument runs) without evil as a standard of reference we would not be able to appreciate the good; nor would we have true moral choices without evil as an option. But such arguments for the necessity of evil to make life more interesting or goodness more meaningful crumble before the idea of an omnipotent God; for certainly a God who could do anything could produce a Creation in which there were an infinite number of wonderful possibilities at every level, all of them good, and all of them enjoyable and satisfying as such without the existence of evil. If I go to a fine cafeteria, there doesn't have to be a pot of poison or a photo of a starving child at the end of the line for me to appreciate all of the excellent choices of delicious food. Nor does the fact that burglary is a vocational option make my choice of a respectable and fulfilling profession any more satisfying.

A second attempt at theodicy argues that evil is an illusion resulting from the fact that we humans are short-sighted, limited in intellect and perspective, and thus unable to see the whole picture. Had we God's divine viewpoint, evil would not appear so bad, especially in light of the eventual rewards awaiting us "beyond this vale of tears," in comparison to which what we regard as evil here and now will seem, at worst, an inconvenience. Perhaps, as the old hymn goes, "we'll understand it better by and by" (that is, in heaven). But why would a merciful and good God keep us waiting and guessing? Why would such a God perpetuate an illusion that makes so many so undeservedly miserable and unhappy? Can we really in good conscience comfort the grieving Ethiopian mother of a child who has just starved to death, or the devastated American father of a young daughter who has just been run over by a drunken driver, with the glib assurance that "It's not as bad as it seems"?

A third strategy of theodicy takes the didactic approach: evil and suffering are valuable in teaching us how to love and to be humane and merciful ourselves. They are, in other words, opportunities for us to exercise responsibility. Such an argument makes little sense, however. Suppose, for example, that I alone had seen a neighbor's child fall and hurt herself seriously and, knowing the situation and being able to do something about it (not to mention being a decent human being and a good neighbor), I had nevertheless decided to do nothing on the grounds that she or her parents and neighbors would learn an important lesson from her prolonged, unrelieved suffering. If you found me out, you would probably look for some way to send me to jail, or a mental institution, and properly so; for normal, responsible people are more merciful than that. Yet, some seriously try to maintain that God allows millions of impoverished and drought-stricken people all over the world to starve in order to teach prosperous and well-fed Americans to be more charitable!

A fourth approach to theodicy holds that evil is a force or power opposed to God, perhaps the result of some heavenly revolt and personified in the Devil (or Satan in the New Testament sense), and perhaps with the unwitting cooperation of human beings (usually in the form of the primordial pair in Paradise). This inimical power holds sway now, and all evil and suffering can be blamed on it, but eventually it is to be neutralized or utterly defeated. Such a solution appears at first to absolve God of any part in evil by attributing its inception to another being. But if the source of evil was some creature (like a rebellious angel or curious human), then who created the possibility of evil as an option in the first place, if not the Creator? And who designed this creature so "flawed" that it would be inclined or even able to choose that option? And could not an omniscient God, foreseeing that this (or some other) creature would deviate from the good, have made provisions to forestall such an event? Finally, having permitted the revolt to occur, why would God allow its effects to persist—and particularly the unmerited suffering it has inflicted?

It is this last scenario that raises the specter of two divinities, one good and one evil, with offsetting or countervailing powers. But monotheistic Christianity will not refer to Satan as a god, and so winds up fumbling for an explanation of the apparent and persistent inability of the capable, cognizant, and caring God to overcome the evil enemy. Another possibility, sometimes entertained in college Philosophy of Religion classes but seldom explored in Christian circles, is that evil, undeserved suffering, or simple misfortune is God's doing or an aspect of God's nature. In this view, God evinces a personality not unlike our own: a mixture of good and bad, able to bless and to curse. Oddly enough, such a notion is reflected in commonplace statements about God. For example, whenever someone suffers an untimely death, there is always someone around to declare that "God took him" or "it was God's will." Indeed, damaging and deadly natural disasters—such as floods, earthquakes, hurricanes, and the like—are legally classified as "acts of God." Even the attestation of survivors that "God spared us" implies that the deity wasn't so gracious to the casualties.

Current Christian Thinking About Evil

The willingness of traditional Judaism to deny God's omnibenevolence in order to preserve its monotheism might suggest a reexamination of the other traditional attributes, particularly omniscience and omnipotence. Indeed, we have already seen that the deists gave up omniscience, leaving at least the impression that God was not attentive to what went on in human history, having provided for it quite adequately at the moment of Creation. To be sure, that is one possible solution to the challenge of theodicy: God may be both omnibenevolent and omnipotent, but preoccupied with other things, and thus unaware of the need to become involved. Intercessory and petitionary prayer would then make sense as a way of attracting the distracted divine attention.

A final possibility, of course, is that God is aware of and affected by human suffering, but is unable to do anything about it, having limited powers. This is the conclusion reached by some modern Jewish theologians in the wake of the Holocaust, in which six million of "God's chosen people" were systematically exterminated. That awful event dramatically forced the issue of God's relation to evil and suffering. Some concluded that God no longer existed, or never really had existed. Others surmised that God existed, but was not really omniscient, and had been unaware of what was happening; or was not really omnibenevolent, and simply let it happen through lack of compassion. The majority, however, preferred to believe that God was not really omnipotent, and thus had simply been powerless to save his chosen people.

Likewise, modern Christian theologians who have struggled with the problem of theodicy have been far more willing to yield on God's omnipotence than on the quality of divine goodness. Among these are the process theologians already mentioned, who from a variety of perspectives have concluded that God is best understood not according to the theistic model, but as immanent in the evolutionary processes of nature and the universe: God is not yet what God will be, and so lacks (among other things) omnipotence. From this perspective, natural and human evil and suffering can be explained in terms of God's inability—at the present point in history, at least—to do anything about it.

Some would say that, in order for humanity to have the free will that we appear to possess, there simply have to be bad consequences to suffer as a result of wrong decisions. Otherwise, how could we appreciate and enjoy the benefits and blessings of life? But why, then, is it so often the innocent and righteous and undeserving—that is, those who tend to make good decisions—who suffer, while many seemingly unrighteous folks prosper? Again, if the Creator God is and was truly omnipotent, omniscient, and omnibenevolent, could not a universe have been created with an infinite number of choices, all of them good and enjoyable and fulfilling? If God could not have created such a universe, then God is not omnipotent. Also, if that God could not have foreseen that humanity's free will would introduce evil and suffering, does that not reflect either a lack of foresight (omniscience) on God's part—reflected in an unintended design flaw—or a lack of concern (omnibenevolence) for the hapless creatures?

The truth is that there is nothing inherent in the concept of God that demands any of the traditional attributes, whether omnipotence, omniscience, or thoroughgoing benevolence. Indeed, the Old Testament God appears less than omniscient as early as the Garden of Eden story (Genesis 3), when Jahweh seems to arrive at Adam's whereabouts and transgressions by probing questions and common sense rather than clairvoyance. The Hebraic God is called "Almighty," but to the ancient Israelite mind that probably meant little more than "much more powerful than we or other gods are." Omnipotence is an idea of perfection drawn from Greek philosophy rather than from the Bible, and, like the other "omni-" attributes, is an abstraction that may be more problematic than it is worth, and perhaps even misleading.

Gender and Language Issues

A more recent and equally valid question about traditional attributes of God has been expressed by feminist theologians, who have called into serious question the common assumption that God is of the male gender, and have challenged the seemingly automatic use of male pronouns (He, Him, His) when referring to the deity. (Have you, too, been startled and amused by the tee-shirt or bumper sticker that asserts, "When God created man, She was only kidding"?) They have rightly pointed out that such an assumption is not only problematic but downright harmful on theological, biblical, and practical grounds.

Theologically, to assign maleness to God seems to limit "Him" in unwholesome ways, depriving "Him" of some very positive qualities traditionally associated with women (such as motherly nurture, tenderness, sensitivity, and intuition). Feminists are also certain that envisioning God in this way has had an enormously negative effect on the role and status of women in both Church and society by reinforcing their subordination to males in both blatant and subtle ways. As one Roman Catholic priest has put it: "If God is male, then male is God." Surely enough, studies at the University of Chicago have indicated that men imprisoned for abuse toward women use this slogan, at least subconsciously, as part of their behavioral defense and rationalization. Other sociological studies have shown a much higher than average incidence of wife abuse among conservative Christians who take literally the biblical injunctions supporting submission of women to their husbands.

Early (and Eclipsed) Feminine Images

This commonplace association of God with masculinity has not always been so automatic. There is a great deal of evidence from archaeology and mythology—though much of it is inferential—that ancient peoples before about 3000 BCE used more feminine images of God. People in the Neolithic era or "New Stone Age" in particular seem to have envisioned God as Mother Earth, perhaps because their society was based on agriculture and women more closely and clearly emulated both the cycles and the fertility of nature than did men. Thus in Egypt the goddess Isis reigned before Osiris or Ra; in Mesopotamia, Ishtar before Marduk or Mazda; and in Greece, Gaia before Zeus. Indeed, this primordial, archetypal female deity has been found with remarkably little variation from the Near and Middle East to ancient India, China, Africa, and even Australia. Among her many names have been Anat, Anahita, Asherah (who appears in the Hebrew Bible), Ashtart, Ashtoreth, Attoret, Attar, Au Set, Hathor, Inanna, Innin, Ishara, Nana, and Nut. In every case, God was a Mother and a "She."

So what happened to the goddess? One theory derives from the recurring mythological pattern of the primordial goddess who takes on a male consort, who in turn eventually becomes a warrior god. In the end, he forcibly appropriates the goddess's birthing capabilities and assumes the role of dominant deity, who can do all things without assistance from the goddess. As it pertains to Judaism, Christianity, and Islam, the theory proposes that the roots of these religions are historically grounded, not in an agricultural context, but in the life of the nomadic herding people called Hebrews, whose God Jahweh was not tied to the soil. He traveled with them, detaching "Himself" and "His" people from any real connection with Mother Earth.

Christianity was perhaps further "masculinized" because it emerged in a Roman Empire that was dominated by Greek culture, whose dominant images of God by the time of Jesus were either Jupiter, or Zeus, or the male emperor, who had come to be called "god." It was only natural, then, that the male sky God who wielded his monarchical power throughout the Hebrew Bible and Hellenistic mythology became the God of Christianity. Images of God, after all, tend to be more or less anthropomorphic, since our principal point of spiritual reference is our own humanity. But these images also tend to be culturally influenced; and since the theological imagery of Judaeo-Christianity sprang up in a thoroughly patriarchal (that is, male-dominated) first-century Middle Eastern society, and propagated itself in subsequent androcentric cultures, including our own, it is no wonder that our conceptions of and references to God tend to be infused with masculine nouns, pronouns, and adjectives; or that the Holy Trinity winds up two-thirds male, with the other third generally being treated as either completely neuter (for example, a mighty wind) or a bird of indeterminate gender. Nor is it surprising that the dominant images in Christian discourse and hymnody about God are patriarchal ("Father"), militaristic ("Power," "Might"), and hierarchical ("Lord," "King").

In practice, attributing exclusive maleness to God has had many repercussions. It has reinforced, for example, the use of male language to refer to humanity both in biblical translations and in worship. Hence Christian hymns have God sending Jesus to set "men" free and congregants singing "Rise Up, O Men of God," when in each case "humanity" or "people" would be more to the point. The use of exclusive male language also serves to legitimize the patriarchy of both society and church, and thus to keep women in many Christian denominations out of such positions of power and authority as the ordained ministry, priesthood, or episcopacy. The inherently shaky arguments are that men are allegedly more like God and thus more competent to do "His" work, and that Jesus and his disciples were all males.

The Feminist Fix for a High-Testosterone God

That male images of God permeate the Bible cannot be denied. The writings of the Bible, after all, were produced largely, if not exclusively, by males in patriarchal societies. Yet, as feminist scholars point out, there are passages that attribute motherliness and other "feminine" traits and imagery to God. Indeed, even in the first chapter of the Old Testament, humanity is created in the image of God "male and female" (Gen 1:27). This declaration even led some ancient rabbis to conclude that Adam had originally been created androgynous, that is, male-female; and that he-she was only later separated into two genders, an event figuratively rendered in the "rib" story, in which the first person or "earth-creature" (Hebrew, *ha-adham*) becomes woman (*ishshah*) and man (*ish*).

The solution to the problems posed by male-dominated theology offered by feminist theologians is to use such scriptural evidence, however sparse, as a basis for reconceiving God, although they vary greatly on the question of how that reconception should be carried out. Some have come to the conclusion that the Judaeo-Christian tradition is hopelessly sexist, and have given up on it to search elsewhere (for example, paganism or Wicca) for more agreeable spiritual imagery (for example, Mother Earth). Others have remained optimistic about and devoted to the Christian tradition, but determined to move it theologically in the direction of some kind of androgyny, that is, to recognize God as both fatherly and motherly, both strong and sensitive, both powerful and passionate, and so forth. The result, they assert, would be a more wholesome image of God that would add cherished characteristics to our necessarily limited theological vocabulary.

An important effect of such a change of imagery would be a more wholesome view of humanity as the "image and likeness" of God. This shift would free men and women alike to embrace all God-like qualities, which until now we have tended to classify as either "male" or "female" and to emphasize the former while we devalued the latter. Thus, as God would become more fully conceived and in a sense more "godly," we would become more fully human, able to experience and express our full range of innate, but often suppressed, capabilities. In the process, Church and society would take one giant step toward true equality for men and women.

Limitations of Language

The feminist critique of thought and language about God should alert us to the fact that all human discourse about Ultimate Reality is necessarily tentative and imperfect, especially in the present day and age. Speak about God we must; yet, words always somehow seem to fail.

There are at least three reasons that it is so difficult to speak meaningfully about God in the modern era. First, the very idea of such an Ultimate Reality is mind-boggling and category-shattering. To expect human beings to be able to understand the vast universe, much less to conceptualize the creative Power, Principle, or Person beyond or within it, is a little like expecting an insect to make sense of nuclear physics. Second, human language itself is extremely limited, especially when we are faced with the task of speaking meaningfully about any abstract entity, let alone Ultimate Reality. Third, the picture of our universe being painted by scientific theorists seems much more amenable to a God abiding within the cosmos and its processes—a God who is more immanent than transcendent, and therefore more compatible with the view of divinity found in the ancient religions of India and the Far East. It is perhaps this last reason that most threatens to render archaic and obsolete all traditional Christian language and imagery that depicts a deity above or beyond our world.

Addressing the problem of speaking about The Ultimate at all, some medieval theologians employed what they called the *via negativa*, which meant that they dared to indicate only what God was not, since the very assertion of attributes was to limit and disparage the deity. If, for example, both a pizza and a football play can be described as "great," then to call God "great" seems to damn the deity with faint praise. Their mystic contemporaries were also suspicious of direct language about God, and elected to express their own ineffable experience of the Divine, if at all, only in imaginative, poetic strains. When they did so, oddly enough, their words often bespoke an immanent divine reality not unlike that attested half a world away by Hindu yogis and Zen masters. Perhaps it is time for us to take a cue from both groups, the theologians and the mystics, and to become more modest and metaphorical in our language about God.

A Return to Metaphor and Mother Nature

It is becoming increasingly clear that any language presuming to speak meaningfully and humbly about God must be metaphorical and poetic rather than literal and prosaic. It is no accident that the most beloved scriptures in all of the world's religions are poetic: the *Bhagavad Gita*, the *Tao Te Ching*, and the *Qur'an*, to name only a few. Can it be merely coincidental that the most beloved of all scriptures among Christians are the Psalms of the Hebrew Bible? It is as though people know intuitively that the freer and more open-ended the expressions about God, the more likely they are to provide the "windows to divinity" mentioned in the conclusion of chapter 1. In fact, here is a good rule of thumb: "The best religious language is always closer to poetry than to prose." Mystics and old-style Quakers would add a *caveat*: "But the real language of the spirit is silence."

For Christians, the best clue to proper God-language might well be the parables of Jesus. These at the very least suggest that speaking of God in images and likenesses is eminently more evocative than analytic assertions about God's nature, God's will, and God's activities. Christianity will probably be at its best theologically when it has attempted to speak of God, not in philosophical abstractions, but in the kind of creative images used by its Master, who drew his material from the concrete realities of everyday life, yet opened up his audiences to the inexpressible wonder of God.

Metaphorical language has that ability precisely because it doesn't claim finality for itself: in offering an image or scenario, it says that God is *like* this-or-that, and thereby offers a truth—but not *the* truth—about God. Being metaphorical, however, it admits that God is also *not like* whatever has been specified, and invites us to supplement the analogy with others so that we may get a fuller picture. The images used for God may be many and even mixed. After all, the Bible itself refers to God as a rock, a stream, a fortress, an eagle, a shepherd, a powerful king, a merciful father, a womb, and a midwife, among other things. The reason for such diversity is the no doubt intuitive recognition that no one image can encapsulate the deity. Thus, the richer and more varied the images the better.

Still, the more timely and contemporary the image, the better it will communicate to its audience. Thus, in a modern urban and democratic society, the once rich metaphors of king and shepherd may carry few connotations, or even misleading ones. And, as pointed out in the previous section, using exclusively male images for God will no longer do. Those reasons alone will increasingly compel us to employ more effective images, even if they are not strictly biblical.

Once it is acknowledged that meaningful language about God will have to be metaphorical, that the metaphors will be mixed, and sometimes even non-biblical, there still remains the important issue of what kind of image will be most appropriate. My own sense is that the best images for God will prove to be both natural and dynamic. They will be natural because images drawn from nature are universal rather than culturally specific: regardless of socio-economic status or political milieu, nearly everyone in the world has experienced sunshine, flowing streams, and the changing of the seasons. Of course, we have also experienced rocks, but that static image, however biblical, would seem to have limited dynamism for a people increasingly aware of the universe and life as a process, and evermore attuned to the idea of God as a dynamic presence within the cosmos.

Conclusion

In view of other religions' alternative concepts, in the face of undeniable injustice and suffering in the world, in light of a rising consciousness and appreciation of feminist concerns, and in recognition of theology as an essentially metaphorical enterprise, what every Christian believer should know about God is that the traditional answers about God's nature and character (much less will and purpose) are no longer as convincing as they once seemed. Our theistic assumptions about God's "otherness" and providential control over the affairs of this world "from above" may reflect some important truths about God, but they have made God seem remote, alien, and even irrelevant to modern-day people and their world. Our further insistence that God must be completely in charge has forced us again and again to question God's sensitivity to, and even responsibility for, human misery of unspeakable variety and magnitude. Our retention of primarily masculine and monarchical imagery for God has given us an outdated, unbalanced, and unhealthy view of both the deity and ourselves. And our inclination toward literal and prosaic language about God has given us at once a false sense of certainty and a constricting theology.

To say that much of the traditional thought and language about God is no longer very meaningful and may even be detrimental does not mean that either the Christian faith or its theological enterprise is pointless or beyond remedy. It does mean, however, that we should more carefully consider the implications of our theological assumptions and attributions, and be more open to the insights of other religious traditions. As we shall see in a later chapter, much of twentieth-century theology has tended (1) to recognize all statements about God as poetic and metaphorical rather than factual and literal; (2) to delve for divine images in women's experience, in nature, and in Asia's great non-theistic religions; and thus (3) to emphasize God's immanence, intimacy, and dynamic relationship to the universe, rather than the traditional theistic attributes of transcendence, remoteness, and static perfection. With the increasing dialogue between the great religious traditions of the Occident and Orient, these trends will almost certainly continue.

Christian lay people will also continue to see the language of their worship changing in response to these trends. More and more of them will come to recognize their traditional and biblical views of God as historically and culturally conditioned, and thus relative rather than absolute. The ever-increasing interest in Eastern religions—particularly monistic Hinduism, Buddhism, and Taoism—will almost certainly continue to expand and deepen, and their images of Ultimacy may well provide a salutary supplement and balance to the Western theistic model and its imagery.

Such a trend will merely acknowledge what should have been obvious all along: that in trying to comprehend and relate to the Ultimate One of the universe with our limited and finite intellects, experiences, and perspectives, we humans would be foolish to restrict ourselves to the viewpoints and interpretations of a single religious tradition, however attached or committed to it we may be. In relating to the Eternal, we mere mortals need all of the help that we can get.

DISCUSSION QUESTIONS & EXERCISES

A. Check out variations in God-language by looking in the Hebrew Bible for metaphors for God. The following is a list of examples that utilize male, neutral, and female imagery:

1. Exodus 15:3; Deuteronomy 32:6; Psalm 23:1–3; Psalm 82:1; Isaiah 42:13; Exodus 3:2; Exodus 19:19;
2. Exodus 40:38; Isaiah 5:2; Jeremiah 2:13; Deuteronomy 32:18; Ruth 2:12; Psalm 22:9;
3. Isaiah 42:14; Hosea 13:7–8.

B. Identify the implications of the following three scripture texts for God-imagery: Genesis 1:27, Exodus 20:4–5a, and Deuteronomy 4:15–16.

C. List the metaphors and images for God in hymns and liturgies with which you are familiar. How does God-language affect the theology that is implicit there?

RECOMMENDED READING

Karen Armstrong, *A History of God: The 4,000-Year Quest of Judaism, Christianity and Islam*. New York: Alfred A. Knopf, 1993.
—a highly readable study of the historical development of monotheism in the three great Western religious traditions from the time of Abraham to the present, with an eye toward their mutual influence

Marcus Borg, *The God We Never Knew: Beyond Dogmatic Religion to a More Authentic Contemporary Faith*. San Francisco: HarperSanFrancisco, 1997.
—a fascinating exposition in layperson's language of theological systems and how we image the divine, coupled with a compelling presentation of and argument for panentheism

Charles Hartshorne, *Omnipotence and Other Theological Mistakes*. Albany: The State University of New York, 1983.
—a brief foray against traditional theism by one of the century's leading exponents of panentheistic process theology

John Hick, *God Has Many Names*. Philadelphia: Westminster Press, 1982.
—the classic treatment of the very idea of God by the premier philosopher of religion of the twentieth century

Harold Kushner, *When Bad Things Happen to Good People*. New York: Avon Books, 1994 (reissue).
—the best-selling, extremely compelling and readable treatment of the perennially difficult human problem of undeserved suffering, by a Rabbi with reason to know whereof he speaks

Jack Miles, *God: A Biography*. New York: Alfred A. Knopf, 1995.
—a fascinating, Pulitzer Prize-winning literary exploration of the unfolding of the character of God in the Hebrew Bible

John C. Polkinghorne, *Belief in God in an Age of Science*. New Haven, CT: Yale University Press, 1998.

2

Christian
Theism
and Its
Alternatives

—an assertion of the similarities in the methods of theologians and scientists by an Anglican priest and theoretical physicist in the quest for truth, with a suggestion of future possibilities for the cooperation of religion and science

Carl A. Raschke and Susan Doughty Raschke, *The Engendering God: Male and Female Faces of God.* Louisville, KY: Westminster John Knox Press, 1995.
   —a tracing of the self-revelation of God as both male and female through the entire Christian canon, in support of human gender equality

Rosemary Radford Ruether, *Gaia & God: An Ecofeminist Theology of Earth Healing.* San Francisco: HarperSanFrancisco, 1994.
   —a sweeping new theology that strongly condemns the Western theistic tradition and seeks instead a theology that heals relationships at every level: male-female, humanity-earth, humanity-humanity, humanity-divinity, and divinity-earth

Howard W. Stone and James O. Duke, *How to Think Theologically.* Philadelphia: Fortress Press, 1996.
   —a short and clearly-written introduction to theology as an important vocational skill, not just for academics, but for all Christians

JESUS OF NAZARETH AND THE ORIGINS OF CHRISTIANITY

Objectives of this chapter:

- to review the historical sources for the life of Jesus: secular, canonical, and extra-canonical

- to reveal Jesus' real name, as well as his mother's

- to establish the historical and cultural context out of which Jesus emerged and in which he conducted his ministry

- to examine the doctrine of the Virgin Birth, its possible origins, its problems, and its place among the teachings of the world's religions

- to review the "Lost Years" of the youth of Jesus, including an Indian tradition about where he was and what he was doing

- to examine the ministry and message of Jesus, and how these revolved around the central idea of the domain or reign of God

- to survey the self-image of Jesus and the titles that he claimed, as well as the ones that were applied to him later

- to note and assess the discrepancies in the canonical gospel accounts of the death and resurrection of Jesus

- to see whether Jesus really intended to found a religion like Christianity or an institution like the Church, or expected to return

3

Jesus of
Nazareth
and the
Origins of
Christianity

N o historical figure has generated more commentary and controversy than Jesus of Nazareth. Such attention is extraordinary in light of the fact that his career lasted at most only a few years and his activities were confined to his own homeland and ethnic group. Yet, the brief life and narrowly focused ministry of this first-century Palestinian Jew became the basis for what is now a religion of universal appeal with the largest number of followers in the world.

One of the many things that have made Jesus so intriguing and the subject of so much discussion and debate is that he was and is such a man of mystery—a person who is barely visible, and only in soft focus. He left no writings, apparently spoke and taught in an oblique and ambiguous style that puzzled even his closest followers, and—despite later claims to the contrary—founded no institution and left no clear agenda or program to be followed in his name. Complicating the situation is the fact that most of what we know about Jesus is based on New Testament writings that were composed long after the fact, are very sketchy and often contradictory, and are already biased by several layers of Christian belief, interpretation, and intent.

It is no wonder, then, that successive generations have remembered this man in a variety of ways, refashioning him time and again in their own images. He has been portrayed as everything from a simple rabbi to a deluded religious fanatic to a revolutionary zealot to the redeemer of all humanity. He has been reconceived in every culture and age according to its own standards and values, hopes and aspirations, and by countless individuals in light of their own predispositions, preferences, and prejudices. Historians of Christianity and Christian thought have shown again and again how views of and beliefs about Jesus have grown, developed, changed, and been codified (and sometimes condemned) in doctrines and dogmas over the centuries.

New Testament scholars have spent a great deal of time and effort, especially in the past two centuries, attempting to recover the flesh-and-blood historical person concealed behind the scriptural accounts. In the process, they have frequently made an important distinction—not widely known among Christian laypersons—between the *historical Jesus* (that is, the human being who lived in first-century Palestine) and the *Christ of faith* (that is, the object of religious devotion for subsequent generations of Christians). This distinction recognizes the fact that the Jesus portrayed in the writings of the New Testament is already the object of veneration if not outright worship, and that his portrait there is largely the product of a generation or more of interpretation, and thus is quite different from the actual person who trod the dusty roads of Palestine two millennia ago.

Some biblical scholars have despaired of ever recovering an accurate picture of the historical person who, even in the earliest scriptural sources, is hidden beneath layers of tradition and belief. Others are more optimistic that, given certain precautions and specific scholarly strategies, at least a glimpse of the historical Jesus is possible. In this chapter we shall attempt to sketch both what we know and what we don't know about the man Jesus, saving for the following chapter an investigation of the object of devotion and doctrinal definition that he became in the earliest days of Christianity and the later Church.

Historical Sources and Context

Despite some utterly skeptical claims to the contrary, we have enough references to Jesus from non-Christian Roman writers of the first century CE to verify that such a man most probably did live, died on a cross, and generated a following that persisted. Far more numerous and substantial, though still hardly complete or entirely trustworthy, are the Christian references, both those in the New Testament and those regarded as "extra-canonical" or "non-canonical." It is from these Christian sources that we glean most of what we know—or think we know—about the historical Jesus.

The Letters of Paul and the Gospels

Since Jesus apparently wrote nothing, and nothing that may have been written about him during his lifetime has survived, the earliest extant canonical Christian writings are the letters of Paul, which are generally dated in the 50s CE—more than a decade before the earliest of the four canonical gospels. Thus Paul is potentially a very valuable source, indeed. The problem is that his writings evince very little interest in the historical Jesus and provide only a few scattered and sketchy references to events in his "Lord's" life.

The only biographical material Paul offers for Jesus is that he was born a Jew (Gal 3:16), was born of a woman (Gal 4:4), was a descendant of David (Rom 1:3), directed a ministry toward the people of Israel and gentiles (Rom 15:8), forbade divorce (1 Cor 7:10–11), celebrated what became known as the Last Supper on the night of his betrayal (1 Cor 11:23–25), and died by crucifixion (Gal 2:20, 3:1; 1 Cor 1:23; Phil 2:8), rose from the dead and appeared to Peter, the twelve, over five hundred others, James, "all the apostles," and finally Paul himself (1 Cor 15:4–8, 9:1; Gal 1:12,16). That is a grand total of twenty-one verses devoted to the entire life of Jesus, eight of which are really post-mortem resurrection appearances! The reasons for this dearth of biographical detail are two: first, Paul had not known the earthly Jesus "in the flesh"; and second, he was much more interested in the death of Jesus and its atoning effects than in the events of Jesus' life or his teachings. (Not coincidentally, so has been the Christian faith that Paul helped to define.)

The canonical gospels—Matthew, Mark, Luke, and John—provide far more details than Paul does, but these are later compositions (70 to 100 CE), quite short, based on memory and hearsay, and clearly persuasive in intent. They make no pretense of being biographies, and obviously reflect both the faith of the early (post-Easter) Church and the particular agendas and theologies of their authors. Of these four, the Gospel of John is widely agreed among New Testament scholars to be relatively late and extremely developed and stylized theologically. Thus they generally regard it as less trustworthy historically than Matthew, Mark, and Luke. But even these three pose a formidable challenge to scholars who dig through the layers of written and oral tradition in order to recover authentic traces of the historical figure still hidden there.

There are other gospel accounts, extant today either whole or as fragments, that didn't make it into the New Testament, despite the fact that many ancient Christian congregations valued, used, and preserved them. Called the "non-canonical gospels," these include the Gospel of the Ebionites, the Gospel of the Egyptians, the Gospel of the Hebrews, the Gospel of Peter, the Gospel of Thomas, the Gospel of Mary, several "infancy narratives," and a recently discovered fragment now titled the "Gospel of the Savior." Most of these are of later dates than the canonical gospels, and most of their accounts and reports have long been regarded as too fanciful and legendary to be trusted much as historical sources. Yet, as the recent work of scholars of this literature has shown, all of these non-canonical sources can help to flesh out our picture of the historical context of Jesus and his earliest followers. At the very least, the mere existence of so many gospels is an indication that from the earliest days of the faith there were many views of Jesus and his work.

Jeshua and the Galileans

As fond as many Christians are of "calling upon the name of Jesus," the first step in coming to terms with the historical person of Jesus is the recognition that his name wasn't Jesus. "Jesus" is the English equivalent of the Latin version of the Greek rendering of his original Aramaic name, which was Jeheshua, or Jeshua, and was probably pronounced (and may actually be spelled) "Yeshua." It is the exact equivalent of the name of the Old Testament prophet Joshua (which we've also Anglicized, but differently). What this means is that no one ever called Jesus "Jesus" in his lifetime, and if they had done so, he would not have responded. It simply wasn't his name. (While we are at it, his mother's name wasn't Mary, either, but Miriam.)

What the seemingly trivial recovery of the Aramaic name of Jesus accomplishes is to remind us of his decided foreignness to us, not because of his alleged heavenly origins or purported divine nature, but simply by virtue of his having been born two thousand years ago, half a world away, and into a culture and worldview to which we can relate only with the greatest stretch of the imagination. Many modern Christians like to make "Jesus" into a nice, congenial, middle-class, twentieth-century American—albeit one who probably dressed a bit strangely and looked a tad odd by modern western standards. Remembering that the reported founder of Christianity was really Jeshua at least forces us to begin to take him on his own terms rather than ours. In other words, recognizing the real name of Jesus helps prevent the simplistic and false contemporizing and familiarizing of this important historical person. Modern Jesus scholarship has been of great assistance in this regard, because it doggedly insists on placing Jesus and his message in their own historical setting and context, however unfamiliar that seems to make Jesus and regardless of how uncomfortable that makes Christian believers.

This man we know as "Jesus," then, was born sometime between 7 and 4 BCE in Palestine, the "boondocks" of the Roman Empire, during the reign of the Jewish "puppet," King Herod the Great. The reason for this obvious anomaly in dates, which has Jesus being born some years "before Christ," is that the earliest framers of the Christocentric calendar misfigured. In any case, Jesus was apparently reared in Galilee, a beautiful region north of Judea and Samaria relatively remote from the provincial capital of Jerusalem.

Galileans were considered uncultured, semi-pagan, of mixed blood, and open to foreign influence. They had developed the reputation, probably justified, of fostering revolutionary anti-Roman sentiment and activity; for all of the Jews of Palestine were painfully aware of having been defeated and dominated over the previous six centuries by the Babylonians, the Assyrians, the Ptolemaic Egyptians, and the Seleucid Syrians. They were now under the control of the Romans, and they did not like their situation one bit. Religiously, the Galileans were a patchwork of competing sects: there were the fiercely traditionalist, priestly Sadducees; the "liberal" lay, reformist and often self-righteous Pharisees; the radically ascetic, priestly, and perfectionist Essenes; and the politically revolutionary Zealots. At the popular level, religious hope tended to be either *messianic* or *apocalyptic*. Messianism involved expectation of a Messiah, a worldly political and military successor to David, the greatest of all of Israel's kings, who would restore the nation of Israel to its millennium-past position of power and prosperity. Apocalypticism, by contrast, looked for a heavenly Son of Man who would bring peace and prosperity to all nations.

Thus Jesus brought a message and ministry to a people with conflicting agendas and expectations. It should come as little surprise, therefore, that he did not completely satisfy any of these parties. Many have tried, with more or less plausible results, to link Jesus and one or more of his followers with the Essenes and the Zealots, an interesting endeavor since the one group practiced withdrawal from the world and its affairs, while the other advocated active engagement! Yet he seems to have fit neatly into neither of these groups—or any other.

The Virgin Birth

The Virgin Birth of Jesus is surely one of the most difficult doctrines for Christians to explain or for non-Christians to understand. To begin with, the doctrine is probably misnamed, since the alleged miracle was the conception rather than the birth itself—at least until theologians got hold of the idea. In any case, the doctrine is used by most modern Christians as evidence of Jesus' divinity, despite the fact that (1) there is no necessary correlation between a miraculous birth and divinity; (2) the virginal birth served a very different purpose for those who first reported it; and (3) the accounts of the miraculous conception are fraught with historical problems.

Most Christians assume that the original point of the virginal birth story was to prove Jesus divine, as though there were some logical or other necessary connection between maternal chastity and the quality of deity. But in the ancient world, all sorts of people were believed to have been virgin-born, whether or not divinity was attributed to them. Before Jesus, for example, many Mediterranean people believed that the Macedonian conqueror

Alexander the Great had been virgin-born, as well as the philosopher Plato. In the Far East, Hindus taught the same about Lord Krishna, Buddhists about Siddhartha Gautama (the Buddha), and Taoists about Lao Tse. Six centuries after Jesus, Muslims asserted that their founder, Muhammad, had been born of a virgin. Yet, not even the followers who made such claims concluded that their leaders or masters were therefore divine, much less God incarnate. They were simply, in a word, "extraordinary." Indeed, Muslims have always asserted that Jesus was virgin-born on the basis of their *Qur'an*; but they have concluded from that claimed miracle only that, like their own virgin-born Muhammad, he was a great prophet.

Erratic Evidence

One unsettling fact for many Christians is the scant scriptural evidence for the miraculous conception of Jesus. Jesus never mentions it, nor do Mary, Peter, or any others of the Twelve. Paul, whose writings are the earliest in the New Testament and who had perhaps the most exalted view of Jesus in his day, never even alludes to it. His only comment about the natal event was that Jesus had been "born of a woman" (Gal 4:4), a description that suggests no awareness whatsoever of a miraculous motherhood.

Of the four canonical gospels—indeed of all of the New Testament writings—only Matthew and Luke mention a virginal conception. The earliest Evangelist, Mark, appears to have no knowledge of it at all. Oddly enough, neither does the latest, John, who has the most developed view of incarnation and the most divinized image of Jesus of all the gospels. Even Luke, who does report it in his first chapter, seems to have forgotten it by chapter 2, in which he treats Joseph as Mary's husband and the natural father of the newborn Christ-child. By chapter 3, he is even tracing Jesus' lineage back to Adam through Joseph! Likewise Matthew, who also reports the miraculous conception in his own first chapter, does so after delineating Jesus' ancestry back to Abraham through Joseph.

In relating their very different stories about Mary's virginal conception of Jesus, Matthew and Luke seem to be showing not that Jesus was God or divine, but that he fulfilled Old Testament prophecy. But even in this regard, these two authors may have tried to declare too much, all on the basis of a mistranslation. For Isaiah had said, "Behold, an *almah* shall conceive, and bear a son. . . . " Now the Hebrew word *almah* means simply "young woman." But Matthew and Luke were likely using the third-century BCE Greek translation of the Hebrew Scriptures called the *Septuagint*, which rendered *almah* as the Greek word *parthenos*, which also originally meant "young woman." By the first-century CE, however, *parthenos* had come to mean "virgin," the most famous being the goddess Athena, whose grand temple in Athens is still called the "Parthenon." Utterly convinced that Jesus was the fulfillment of Isaiah's Messianic prophecy, then, Matthew and Luke would have been certain that Jesus' mother *must* have been a *parthenos*, which they simply assumed to mean "virgin."

So they composed stories (or retold tales already circulating as oral tradition) that depicted how the virginal birth that they *thought* had been prophesied might have been accomplished. But what they were actually showing

3

Jesus of Nazareth and the Origins of Christianity

in their respective miracle-laden narratives was Jesus fulfilling not the Hebrew scripture, but their own mistaken reading of the Greek version of that scripture. It is also possible that the evangelists were consciously writing for a partly gentile audience for whom most heroes were believed to have been conceived by a human female and a male god, and to whom a miraculous birth-story would have added some credibility to the person of Jesus. But for them, ironically, Jesus' virginal birth—even if convincing—would simply have made him a hero, not a god.

Possible Paternity

There are various theories about the actual paternity of Jesus, some of which stretch credulity more than others. Some interpreters have followed the ancient tradition reported in the Talmud that the father of Jesus was a Roman centurion named Panthera. Others have argued that there is subtle, but compelling scriptural evidence that the father was one Alpheus (or Cleophas), Joseph's brother, whom the gospels strangely identify as the father of one James (Mark 3:18), the brother of Jesus (Mark 6:3); and that this was ostensibly the same James whose mother's name was Mary, mentioned as the only Mary besides Magdalene present at Jesus' crucifixion and burial (Mark 15:40), and therefore very possibly none other than the mother of Jesus. If this James' mother Mary was Jesus' mother as well, then Jesus and James might well have shared the paternity of Alpheus, too.

Some interpreters have even suggested that Luke himself provides the basis for an intriguing alternative theory concerning the virgin birth when he reports that, after being informed by an angel that she is to bear this special child, Mary (Miriam) left her home and went to live with her cousin Elizabeth, whose husband, Zechariah, just happened to be a priest of God. So, it is argued, old Zechariah may have done his "priestly duty" and acted as God's agent in fathering the promised child. In this scenario, Joseph apparently could not have done this for God because he didn't hold the proper credentials. Luke further reports that Mary stayed in the priest's house for three months, the time it would have taken in those days to be sure that a woman was pregnant, at which point she returned home (Luke 1:39–56).

Of course, one could never prove that Mary was not a virgin at the time of Jesus' conception and birth, or for that matter, that she was not a virgin in perpetuity, as a later Catholic doctrine holds—despite the fact that the New Testament itself says that Joseph did not "know" his wife "until she had given birth to a son" (Matt 1:25) and refers (by name) to Jesus' three brothers and to some unnumbered and unnamed sisters (in Mark 6:3 SV, though the NSRV names *four* brothers). One can only point out that the evidence is very thin and note the obvious: that Matthew's and Luke's accounts of the matter at least stretch our modern notions about how the world works.

The "bottom line" on the alleged virginal birth of Jesus seems to be that if one wants to maintain the traditional doctrine, he or she is left with the perplexing prospect that if the miraculous conception of Jesus was historically true, it was not important enough for either Jesus or the earliest New Testament writer (Paul) or earliest gospel author (Mark) to mention, and thus probably is not essential to the Christian faith. On the other hand, the notion of virginal birth has been such an enduring one, not just in Christianity but in the world's mythology as a whole, that one might wonder whether it expresses some important archetypal image residing (in good Jungian fashion) in the collective human unconscious. If so, it may have some basis in reality if not in history, and may well serve some psychological or spiritual function despite its lack of historicity.

Other Oddities

Bringing to light some of the commonly overlooked (or ignored) aspects of the stories of Jesus' birth always makes me feel like the "Grinch Who Stole Christmas." But it also makes me wonder why so few Christians have seemed to notice.

Recasting the Christmas Story

First of all, only half of the canonical gospels even have a "Christmas" story, namely, Matthew and Luke, the same ones that report a miraculous conception. Neither Mark, written nearest in time to the events being reported, nor John, the last-written and most theological of the gospels, has a nativity account or even mentions Jesus' birth. Mark begins his gospel with Jesus' baptism, while John says merely that the eternal Word of God "was made flesh" (1:14). We are left, then, with three possible explanations for the omission by Mark and John: (a) they didn't know anything about the nativity of Jesus, or (b) they knew about it, but didn't think it important enough to report, or (c) they both had heard one or more stories about the birth of Jesus, but didn't believe them.

Second, the two gospels that do report the Christmas story have very different versions of it. Matthew describes traveling astrologers ("wise men," perhaps, but not kings!) and a star, but says nothing about the heavenly host, shepherds, an inn, or a manger. Luke tells about heavenly hosts, shepherds, an inn, and a manger, but doesn't mention astrologers or a star. Modern nativity scenes, Christmas cards, and Yuletide carols present a pretty but wholly artificial blending of these two very different accounts. (See figure 3.1.) Moreover, Matthew, who alone reports astrologers, never says that there were three of them, much less give us names for them. He says only that there were three gifts (or *kinds* of gifts), which presumably could have been borne and delivered by two or twenty! Nor does he say that the astrologers showed up at a manger, much less a stable. (Even Luke fails to mention a stable.) In fact, Matthew says that the star led them to a "house" where they found Jesus and his mother—but with no mention of the presence, upon their arrival, of Joseph, shepherds, or anyone else.

There is also the distinct possibility that—Luke's colorful and memorable story (2:1–7) notwithstanding—Jesus was not born in Bethlehem at all. The stated reason for the journey of Joseph and Mary from Nazareth to Bethlehem was a Roman census. But there is no historical evidence that a census was conducted in Palestine within ten years of Jesus' estimated birthdate, or that Romans were foolish enough to require people to return to their ancestral birthplaces for censuses anyway. As if they cared or wanted to create a logistical nightmare!

Unbiblical Christmas Carols

Of the four canonical gospels, only Matthew and Luke have Nativity narratives, and they are very different. Matthew's involves a star, wise seekers from the East finding Mary and Jesus in a house and presenting them with three kinds of gifts. Luke's has a census trip to Bethlehem, angelic hosts, shepherds, an inn with no vacancy, a manger, and all three members of the Holy Family. The only things that Matthew and Luke seem to agree upon is the appearance of an announcing angel to one of the parents—though Matthew says to Joseph and Luke says to Mary—and the involvement of Mary and Jesus in the story. Our modern Nativity scenes, therefore, are composites of the two stories, with a few new elements thrown in—an indication, perhaps, that popular theology originates in large part in the collective human imagination. Christmas carols are often hybrids, too.

Angels We Have Heard on High and *O Little Town of Bethlehem* are clearly based on Luke's account alone. So is "Away in a Manger," but where did those "lowing cattle" come from? (Shouldn't those be bleating sheep, if anything?!) And so is *"Silent Night,"* but where in scripture are the "radiant beams" from the baby Jesus' "holy face"?

We Three Kings is based on Matthew, but is on shaky ground indeed. Luke's account has only shepherds; Matthew's has "wise men from the East"; but neither has "kings." Matthew never says that there were three wise men, only that they brought gifts of three substances, which could have been in the form of any number of objects and carried by any number of wise people. Also, the song says that Jesus was "Born a King on Bethlehem's plain," but Matthew never says that the Eastern seekers went to Bethlehem. In fact, with no mention whatsoever of Bethlehem in Matthew, one might assume that the house (not stable) where they find the mother and child (but not Joseph) in his account was in Nazareth.

In the Bleak Midwinter says that "frosty winds made moan" and that "earth stood hard as iron." *"Gesu Bambino"* begins with "When blossoms flower e'er 'mid the snow." The only problem is that neither gospel account says anything about winter.

Of all the popular carols, *The First Noel* probably conflates the two accounts the most. Its second verse says that the shepherds from the first verse "looked up and saw a star shining in the East, beyond them far" that gave "great light" to the earth "both day and night." But the shepherds are Luke's, and in his account they look up and see angels, not a star (which is Matthew's—though even he doesn't indicate the daytime stellar visibility that the carol claims). The third verse brings in Matthew's wise men, but specifically three in number, which Matthew never quite says; and they are then drawn by the star to Luke's Bethlehem, where they offer Matthew's gold, frankincense, and myrrh, thereby rounding out the fusion of the stories.

Infant Holy, Infant Lowly adds "oxen lowing, little knowing" from who knows where, and says that Jesus has "for his bed a cattle stall." *O Come Little Children* is an invitation to that "stall." But not even Luke, who has a manger, specifies that it was in a stall or stable. It could have been out in the open air for all we know.

And don't get me started about that *Little Drummer Boy*!

FIGURE 3.1

REMEDIAL CHRISTIANITY

The reports that Jesus was born in Bethlehem may have come from the same impulse on the part of Matthew and Luke seen earlier with reference to the virginal birth: to have him fulfill the ancient Hebrew prophecies that the Messiah would be born in the city of David, that is, Bethlehem. Here, again, the earliest gospel writer, Mark, appears to know of no such tradition and consistently calls Jesus a Nazarene, which is to say a native of Nazareth (Mark 1:24; 10:47; 14:67; 16:6). In fact, Mark never even mentions Bethlehem—which would be a curious oversight—and Matthew treats it as the hometown of Mary and Joseph at that point in their life, rather than an ancestral place to which they had to travel to be taxed.

Finally, there is an ancient belief (usually identified with the ancient Syrian Christian community) that Jesus had a twin brother, none other than "doubting" Thomas, whom the gospels regularly refer to as Didymos, "The Twin." If so, the burning issue would seem to be not whether to have a crèche at Christmastime, or whether to include Matthew's star and astrologers with Luke's angels and shepherds—but how many babies to put in the manger!

The Lost Youth of Jesus

It is really quite amazing how little we know of most of the life of such a key figure as Jesus, and downright astonishing how little most Christians seem to notice this glaring gap. Only one canonical gospel relates an incident from his infancy: the flight to Egypt with his parents to escape the "slaughter of the innocents" by fearful King Herod (Matt 2:13–15). Another tells of one event in his childhood: his getting separated from his parents in Jerusalem and being found "about his Father's business," astounding the elders with his questions (Luke 2:40–52). Other than those two episodes, we have no reports about Jesus' childhood, adolescence, or early adulthood. He simply "shows up" at about age thirty to inaugurate his ministry. In short, the lack of information in the canonical Gospels about Jesus' teens and twenties leaves us with the remarkable prospect that for two decades he did little that was memorable.

By contrast, the non-canonical gospel accounts—the ancient narratives about Jesus that were excluded from the New Testament—do report some interesting details about his childhood. The Infancy Gospel of Thomas, for example, tells of Jesus at age five fashioning twelve sparrows from clay on the Sabbath and, having been chastised by Joseph for his impiety, making the birds come to life and fly away. It also reports that Jesus struck a little boy dead for bumping into him, and rendered blind those who found fault with his behavior. According to the same account, he resurrected another boy, a playmate who had died of a fall from a roof in his presence—though only because he needed the victim to exonerate him in the matter. He also reportedly helped Joseph in his carpentry by stretching to their proper length boards that were too short. Clearly we must be skeptical about such accounts—wherever we find them. Why they were excluded from the canonical scriptures is not altogether clear, but it cannot have been because they involved purported miracles. After all, a man who could walk on water as an adult conceivably could have stretched a board as a child!

3

Jesus of
Nazareth
and the
Origins of
Christianity

Some have inferred from the gaps in the canonical record that Jesus was married during adolescence, as Jewish Law would have demanded for a healthy male, and that his wife was none other than Mary Magdalene. This might help explain her extraordinary prominence throughout the synoptic gospels. Some have even suggested that the actions of Jesus and his mother at the wedding at Cana (John 2:1–11) are explicable only if he happened to be the bridegroom and she, the hostess!

Another intriguing possibility (though one for which the evidence is admittedly sparse) is that during these years he was simply nowhere near his homeland. Indeed, there is an ancient tradition among the gurus of India, still widely believed there today, that Jesus (or St. Isu, as they call him) traveled to that country during his youth and studied with all of the great spiritual Masters—probably Hindu and Buddhist—and then returned to his homeland via Persia, where he spent time among the spiritualist-philosophers or astrologers called Magi. The fact that Judea was then on a major trade route to the East and that it would have been relatively easy for a young man to join a caravan going in that direction makes this legend at least plausible historically.

Whatever one thinks of such traditions, they would at least help to explain why Jesus appears so suddenly in his late twenties (in all the synoptics), and why (according to Luke) he so abruptly announces the inauguration of his ministry in his hometown of Nazareth and so profoundly offends the very people with whom he has supposedly lived his whole life that they try to kill him. The extreme annoyance of the townspeople in that account might make more sense if they saw him as someone who had deserted them as a youth and returned later from God-knows-where with a lot of newfangled (perhaps exotic?) ideas.

A youthful period of study in India might also account for the tenor of some of Jesus' teachings. (See figure 3.2.) John's report that he claimed to be one with "the Father" echoes the Hindu teaching that everyone is spiritually one with "The Supreme Ultimate," Brahman. Likewise, when he claimed that the "kingdom" (better translated now "domain" or "reign") of God was "within" his hearers, it certainly sounds like an affirmation of an Eastern-style *immanence* of divinity. And when he says to Nicodemus that he must be "born again," any Hindu or Buddhist would respond: "Of course! Reincarnation!"

Story's Wobbly? So What?

All of these seemingly outlandish possibilities have been explored extensively in scholarly discussions and publications for the better part of a century, and materials for further exploration can be found in any good library. Yet, for most Christians these possibilities have never been raised, much less considered and refuted.

My own experience from years of teaching college courses that deal with Christian origins is that people are often disconcerted, alarmed, and threatened at the prospects that Jeshua's mother Miriam may not have been biologically a virgin, and that Jesus may have had a human father, a twin brother, and perhaps even a wife. But a better question might be whether

(all rendered from the King James Version, and all at least 500 years later than the parallel Eastern ideas)

The Canonical Jesus	Eastern Religions
"I and my Father are one." *Jn 10:30*	It is a fundamental belief of Vedantic (philosophical) Hinduism that the human soul is essentially one with the Ultimate Supreme Spirit, *Brahman*. That key spiritual conviction is nicely expressed in the Sanskrit affirmation: *aham Brahmasmi* ("I am Brahman.").
"Ye must be born again." *Jn 3:7*	A basic belief of Hinduism as well as Buddhism is *samsara*, which is reincarnation or transmigration of the eternal, indestructible soul.
"Consider the lilies of the field, how they toil not, neither do they spin; yet . . . even Solomon in all his glory was not arrayed like one of these." *Lk 12:27*	Especially in its early stages, the Taoist faith of China extolled a "less is more" philosophy. "The Tao (Way) does nothing," says the *Tao Te Ching*, "yet nothing is left undone."
"The kingdom of God is within you." *Lk 17:21*	The Hindu *Upanishads* tell us that our body is a castle, at the center of which dwells the Supreme Spirit, Brahman, in the form of *atman*, our own eternal spiritual energy-essence.
"Take my yoke upon you . . . and ye shall find rest for your souls." *Mt 11:29–30*	The Sanskrit word *yoga* connotes a spiritual discipline. Its root meaning, however, is "yoke." Students of Hinduism often speak of "taking on" a *yoga*.
"I am the Way, the Truth, and the Life . . . " *Jn 14:6*	The Supreme Reality in Taoism is *Tao* or the "Way." The *Dharma* in Buddhism is the eternal Truth. The most valued principle in Jainism is *Ahimsa*, Life in all Its inherent sacredness. The proper name of God in Hebrew, *Jahweh*, means "I am."

3

Jesus of Nazareth and the Origins of Christianity

FIGURE **3.2**

any or all of these things, even if true, would necessarily detract from Jesus' importance or mission. In fact, it could be argued that natural human origins and normal family life, both of which we say we value highly, would make the incarnation of God all the more real, profound, miraculous, and relevant to us and our lives.

The Ministry and Message of Jesus

However and wherever Jesus spent his "lost years," it is clear that he began his ministry rather abruptly around 26–28 CE when he was thirty or so. As the author of the Gospel of John asserted in so many words at the end of his own account, so many and varied were Jesus' reported sayings and doings that it would be impossible to do justice to them here. We can, however, look at the main theme and some of the major highlights of the life of this man of mystery.

Jesus and John the Baptizer—and Beyond

All four gospels indicate that Jesus began his ministry by seeking baptism from John "the Baptizer," who represented a religious position and personal style very different from that which Jesus would adopt. John had chosen the traditional prophetic life of the desert ascetic. That means that he followed a very austere regimen of self-denial in the isolation of the Jordan wilderness. Dressing strangely and subsisting on locusts and wild honey, he sought to purify and prepare himself for what he expected to be God's impending, decisive action.

Yet, at the beginning of Mark's gospel, and early in the others, John appears practicing a baptism of ritual washing to cleanse would-be followers of their sins and thus prepare them as well for God's expected intervention in history to establish a "kingdom" (domain, reign, or rule). It is to this decidedly charismatic prophet that Jesus reportedly presents himself for baptism (Mark 1:2–11). This incident raises, at the very least, a curiosity: why would the one whom Christians have long regarded as "the sinless Son of God" seek out a "baptism of repentance for the forgiveness of sins"?

The actual relationship between the ministries of Jesus and John the Baptizer has been, and continues to be, a matter of much scholarly interest and debate. Initially, Jesus was probably a disciple of John, and at the very least he seems to have deferred to his predecessor by not beginning his own ministry in earnest until John had been arrested and soon afterward executed by Herod Agrippa. But even during John's lifetime, Jesus did not choose John's ascetic style for himself or his followers. This difference in style may account for his being labeled (in comparison to John) "a glutton and a drunk" (Matt 11:19//Luke 7:34), and may also lie at the root of tensions that scholars detect in the gospels between the disciples of John and those of Jesus— a kind of party loyalty. Finally, Jesus apparently never performed baptisms himself, though he is later recorded as admonishing his disciples to do so.

It is also important to note that John the Baptizer, in consonance with his austere life and theology, preached a message of dire warning and doom-and-gloom. His preaching was apocalyptic, meaning that he proclaimed a radical contrast between the wicked present and the bright future in which

God would act decisively to establish righteousness. He called upon people to reform their lives or suffer terrible consequences (Mark 1:4; Matt 3:2 Luke 3:3). Jesus, as we shall see, went his own way here, as well.

With John's execution, according to the gospel stories, Jesus became the uncontested leader of the "kingdom" movement among his fellow Jews, and, becoming an itinerant sage, gathered an odd assortment of followers to be his disciples (Mark 1:16–20; compare the very different version in John 1:35–42, which includes some of John the Baptizer's disciples). The historicity of the stories about his calling disciples is highly debatable. Similar stories can be found in the Hebrew Bible (for example, Elijah's recruitment of Elisha in 1 Kgs 19:19–21). The gospel writers may have once again been "proving" Jesus on the basis of Hebrew prophecy, with the number twelve co-opted to connect Jesus symbolically to the twelve tribes of Israel. There is no reason to doubt, however, that Jesus did in fact attract followers who accompanied him on his teaching tours.

Having gathered some followers, as the story goes, Jesus began his ministry either with synagogue teaching and miracles, as Mark 1 and Matthew 4 would have us believe, or with a startling announcement to his hometown congregation, as Luke 4 relates, or with a miracle producing 176 gallons of wine to keep a wedding party going, as John 2 tells it. The length of his ministry is unclear, since the gospel accounts are episodic, compressed, stylized, and contradictory. The synoptics, for example, have him exclusively in Galilee and probably for not more than a year until his one final trip to Jerusalem in Judea; John (the Evangelist, not the Baptizer) has him bouncing back and forth between Galilee and Judea, with several trips to Jerusalem over the course of three or four years.

In any case, all of the gospel episodes compressed together would cover at most a few weeks of Jesus' life. John explicitly acknowledges how abbreviated is his own account in comparison with the action-packed ministry of Jesus with this parting observation: "Jesus of course did many other things. If they were all to be recorded in detail, I doubt that the entire world would hold the books that would have to be written" (21:25). One has to wonder, however, whether John's selected recollections or those of the other gospel accounts did justice to Jesus' person or accomplishments. Certainly none would satisfy modern historical standards—or, for that matter, be recognizable to Jesus himself.

A Distinctive and Disarming Style

In any event, we have enough glimpses of Jesus' ministry to know that he combined elements of the traditional roles of prophet and rabbi, though he departed from the usual patterns of both. As a prophet (Mark 8:28; Matt 21:11, 46, etc.), for example, he abandoned the practice of presenting credentials and employing formulas like "Thus saith the Lord" in favor of speaking on his own authority. Likewise, as a rabbi (Mark 9:5; 10:51; 11:21, etc.), he seldom followed the usual routine of commenting and expounding on scripture in the synagogue, preferring to base his messages on everyday life and to deliver them outdoors and mostly in casual conversations or impromptu utterances. In fact, when he did quote the Hebrew scriptures, more often than not it was to contradict them. His typical pattern was: "As you know, our ancestors were told, . . . but I tell you. . . " (Matt 5:21–22, 38–41, 43–44). Jesus relied less on scripture than on shared experiences as the basis of his teachings, building quotable proverbs and memorable parables upon these vignettes. In short, he was a master of the saying and the story.

Everyone knows that Jesus taught in parables, right? Everyone, that is, except the author of the Gospel of John! Jesus does indeed teach in parables as well as aphorisms in the earlier synoptic gospels; but not one does he utter in John. Instead, he delivers long discourses—yet another instance of the fourth gospel going its own way. Still, it might be argued that because of its idealized Jesus, the Gospel of John in effect *becomes* a parable—a spiritual story with Jesus as the main character.

One might assume that with teachings based on the everyday experiences of his listeners and a presentation using sayings and stories, Jesus' message would have been simple and easily grasped. In fact, it was not. Apparently, his closest disciples were frequently confused about his message. Mark even quotes Jesus to the effect that he intended his parables to be confusing to the uninitiated: " . . . to those outside everything is presented in parables, so that they may look with eyes wide open but never quite see, and may listen with ears attuned but never quite understand, otherwise they might turn around and find forgiveness!" (Mark 4:11–12). Modern New Testament scholarship has determined that Jesus probably didn't actually say those words, and that they instead reflect Mark's view of Jesus' intent. But even that is not quite clear in this passage. Is Mark's Jesus being ironical or sarcastic here, or indeed admitting to his inner circle that he was deliberately trying to confound his larger audience and keep them from God's mercy? At the very least, we are certain of Mark's conviction that Jesus was not necessarily telling parables in order to clarify things.

The Heart of the Matter

Christians have heard all of their lives that the purpose of Jesus' life, ministry, and message was to send souls to heaven, and that their own Christian faith was primarily about getting to heaven themselves. But if the synoptic gospels are to be believed, not only is that inaccurate, but the very opposite is true. Despite his often confusing sayings, it is quite clear that Jesus' fundamental message was that God's ultimate goal was to bring heaven down to earth in the form of the kingdom—domain, reign, or imperial rule—of God.

Until recently mainstream New Testament scholarship was fairly certain that Jesus had adopted the same eschatological (that is, end-time-oriented) theme that John had employed before him and that Paul would develop later; though to be sure some had long recognized a unique "already-but-not-yet" quality about it. Current historical Jesus research, however, indicates that while Jesus undoubtedly preached God's kingdom or imperial rule, it is doubtful that he proclaimed that "God's imperial rule is closing in," as Mark (1:15) said he had and John the Baptizer indeed had. The heart of Jesus' message and his ministry, the very basis of all that he allegedly said and did, was actually that God's rule is *immediate* in two senses: (1) it is *already* here, albeit in a veiled, unrecognized form; and (2) it is *unmediated* by rituals, rules, or authorities.

Jesus seems not to have separated God's present activity from God's future activity as the Baptizer had done. His vision of God's domain was such that the future and the present simply merged in a kind of "apocalypse now"! Thus he probably did not declare: "Repent! For the Kingdom is at hand!" as the gospel writers reported. They simply "remembered" John's call to repentance onto the lips of Jesus decades after the fact, most likely because Christians had adopted by then an eschatological (that is, future-oriented, end-time) attitude of their own, one similar to the Baptizer's.

The focus of the teachings and activities of Jesus, then, was his proclamation of the immediate presence of the reign of God in the here and now. Matthew, as a pious first-century Judean, calls this "Heaven's imperial rule" in order to avoid using God's holy name. Luke, probably a gentile, has no such compunction, and uses the phrase that Jesus himself, as one known for his liberal interpretation of the Law, almost certainly did: the domain of God.

Vexing Pronouncements and a "Voice Print"

Jesus' mission, then, was not to call people to repentance, but to proclaim the good news that God's immediate domain or reign was open to anyone and everyone. And, if the beatitudes and many of the parables and other reported Jesus-sayings are to be believed, he wanted to make it abundantly clear that God's domain included the meek, the poor, the hungry, the dispossessed, and those of ill-repute. Indeed, the poor may even have a special claim on it.

If the gospel accounts are any indication, Jesus had more to say about wealth and poverty than about any other single issue, including love. And Americans firmly committed to a capitalist economy may find it unsettling that he almost invariably spoke against the rich and the accumulation of wealth: "I swear to you, it is very difficult for the rich to enter Heaven's domain" (Matt 19:23), harder, in fact than getting a camel through a needle's eye (19:24); and "Don't acquire possessions here on earth! . . . You can't be enslaved to both God and a bank account!" (Matt 6:19, 24) And remember: he sent away a rich young man who wanted to be a disciple but could not bring himself to part with his wealth.

We contemporary capitalists might try to imagine that Jesus is, after all, one of us, and therefore couldn't possibly have meant any of these things literally; that what he *really* was saying was that it was all right to be rich, *if* one had the spirit of charity; and that one *could* lay up treasures, *if* one did not love them too much. Unfortunately, Jesus made no such equivocations. For us worldly, rich accumulators of "stuff" to follow such a demanding leader authentically would be difficult indeed—if we really paid attention to his hard sayings. (See figure 3.3.)

Other preachers, like John the Baptist, had already proclaimed God's imperial rule; and many rabbis had made many of the same pronouncements.

Eight Reported Sayings of Jesus That You'll Rarely Hear Preached

. . . and Never See Taken Seriously (Much Less Literally)
(all rendered in the King James Version preferred by Fundamentalists)

*"Lay not up for yourselves treasures on earth,. . . but
lay up for yourselves treasures in heaven . . ."* Mt 6:19–20
(There go the houses, cars, belongings, savings
accounts, stock portfolios, and retirement plans!)

*"Consider the lilies, how they grow: they toil not, they spin not; yet...
Solomon in all his glory was not arrayed like one of these."* Lk 12:27
(Not exactly a ringing endorsement of type-A personalities or
the Protestant work ethic, is it?)

*". . . sell all that thou hast, and distribute unto the poor, and thou
shalt have treasure in heaven: and come, follow me."* Lk 18:22
(Christians take to heart the thing Jesus said to one man about the need
to be born again, but ignore what he said to this other guy.
Why? Because it's cheaper to be born again!)

". . . woe unto you that are rich!" Lk 6:24
(This includes, not just the likes of Bill Gates, but the vast majority of
North Americans, whose per capita income makes even members of
the middle class the rich of the world.)

*"It is easier for a camel to go through the eye of a needle,
than for a rich man to enter into the kingdom of God."* Mk 10:25
(The old rationalizations about there being in the old Jerusalem gate a small
door called "the needle's eye," through which camels could
enter on their knees—as in prayer, get it?—is bogus.
Camels can't crawl to save their lives!)

*"Love your enemies, bless them that curse you,
do good to them that hate you, and pray for them
which despitefully use you, and persecute you."* Mt 5:44
(Good advice for expressway driving!)

*". . . resist not evil: but whosoever shall smite thee
on thy right cheek, turn to him the other also."* Mt 5:39
(This is never part of the team chaplain's pre-game
devotions prior to a football game!)

*". . . and him that taketh away thy cloak
forbid him not to take thy coat also."* Lk 6:29
("My money or my life? How about my money and my wife?!")

FIGURE 3.3

Hillel (d. 10 CE), for example, had condensed the Law into "Love God and your neighbor" at least a generation before Jesus did; and the Dead Sea Scrolls, discovered in 1947, indicate that a forerunner of Jesus had already delivered much of the Sermon on the Mount — facts that do not so much detract from the uniqueness of Jesus as underscore his continuity with the Jewish rabbinic tradition.

Several things, however, seem to have made Jesus' teaching unique. In general, he apparently projected an unusual kind of authority, although it is noteworthy that he seldom initiated dialogue or debate. Nor did he offer to perform healings—in some cases, in fact, he had to be talked into it. But when he did talk or heal, there was no hedging or equivocation, and his certainty and successes must have startled his audiences, especially those who belonged to the religious establishment.

The Jesus Seminar, which is on the cutting edge of New Testament scholarship today, has identified a distinctive "voice print" for Jesus: his sayings and parables cut against the social and religious grain; they surprised and shocked; they characteristically called for a reversal of roles or frustrated common expectations; they were often characterized by exaggeration, humor, and paradox. Jesus' images were concrete and vivid, and his pronouncements and stories went straight to the point, seldom accompanied by explanation or application.

Intimacy, Iconoclasm, and Incredible Incidents

When Jesus spoke of God, he did so with unusual familiarity, addressing the Almighty as "Abba," or "Dad," and he encouraged his followers to address God paternally as well: "You should pray like this: Our Father in the heavens . . ." (Matt 6:9). This was certainly a softening of the imposing "Lord" and "King" imagery of traditional Judaism. His sense of intimacy with God, some have suggested, may reflect his lack of an earthly father. (For whatever reason, Joseph drops out of the picture early on). That, of course, may be a bit of twentieth-century psychology being imposed upon first-century texts. A more apt theory is that Jesus was once again throwing a tradition in the face of Jewish religious leaders who regarded God's name as too sacred even to pronounce. Jesus' use of this intimate form of address may have been simply another indication that God and God's domain were immediate in the here-and-now, and "unbrokered" in that relating to God required no intermediaries.

Jesus' actions were at least as radical as his teachings. In short, he was a social deviant. He associated with all the wrong people—laborers, tax collectors, outcasts, sinners. Most scholars believe that women were in his "inner circle" of disciples, but were relegated to subordinate positions by the less "liberated" gospel authors, and certainly by many church leaders down to the present. Jesus also flouted religious tradition by refusing to be strict about observing Sabbath regulations and religious rituals. He also failed to be pious in a typically religious way. As a result, and as noted earlier in comparison to John the Baptizer, he developed a reputation among the religious authorities as a "party animal" and, what was worse, a religious renegade.

According to gospel reports, Jesus worked such miracles as restoring sight to the blind, mobility to the lame, and sanity to the mentally deranged—often by casting out demons. The gospel authors even claim that he defied natural laws by walking on water, successfully commanding a storm to abate, and restoring life to the dead. Thoughtful modern readers have problems with such accounts (and rightly so), and even believers often can be heard arguing the rationality of such events—often in a way that would seem to "salvage" the miracles by denying their miraculous character!

Without settling the matter of miracles, or even entering the debate over them, let us simply note two things: (1) miracles were compatible with the mythopoetic worldview of ancient Middle Eastern peoples, among whom miracle workers were comparatively commonplace, as the New Testament itself attests; and (2) Jesus was portrayed as using miracles not as a self-validation, but as evidence that God's domain was already present in the midst of the witnesses to these wondrous events. In these acts he pointed beyond himself and his powers to God and God's mighty acts.

Did Jesus Save?

In light of Jesus' dominant reign motif, it is necessary to set aside, as best we can, all of the presuppositions that Christian teaching and preaching have instilled in us, and to recognize that Jesus appears to have had no interest in saving souls and getting them to heaven. Christians ought to have suspected all along that the dawning domain of God rather than soul-saving was the focus of Jesus' teaching, if only because the first petition in the Lord's prayer is "Thy Kingdom come." The second petition follows hard upon it, and in fact restates it in what biblical scholars call a "synonymous parallel": "Thy will be done on earth, as it is in heaven." If only we had been paying closer attention when we prayed these things!

These clauses neatly capture Jesus' religious angle and agenda, as do his often quoted but rarely understood so-called beatitudes: "Congratulations you poor! God's domain belongs to you" (Luke 6:20). "Congratulations to the gentle! They will inherit the earth" (Matt 5:5). Why the earth? Why not heaven? Because heaven was coming to earth, the earth would thus be renewed, and anyone could own a share in it! Even the Eucharistic (or Holy Communion) rituals used by most Christian denominations quote Jesus at his last supper to the effect " . . . I certainly won't drink any of the fruit of the vine from now on until God's domain is established!" (Luke 22:18)

One reason that soul-saving was not an objective of Jesus was that, being a first-century Jew, he almost certainly did not believe in a separable human soul in the way that Greek philosophers did then and most modern Christians do today. In traditional (what is now called "Orthodox") Judaism, people are not understood as born with *something* called a "soul," but rather with the *potential* or *capacity* for developing soul. "Soul" in the Hebrew language is *nephesh*, which connotes vitality, personhood, character, selfhood—qualities that are not understood as immortal, much less eternal. Simply stated: you have "soul" while you are alive, and when you die, it dissipates.

All that is left is the body. Since Jesus' thinking was clearly shaped by traditional Judaism, soul-saving would have been inconceivable, for there simply would not have been anything there to save.

The mistaken impression that Jesus was trying to send souls to heaven is based in part upon the version of his ministry contained in the latest and least historical of the gospels, John. There, Jesus preaches, not God's domain, as he does in the earlier synoptics, but himself. It is here, and here alone, that we get the seven "I am" sayings of Jesus, all pointing to himself as the pre-existent, eternal, heavenly "Son of God" who has descended to Earth to do God's will (for example, 4:26; 6:48; 10:7, 14, 36; 11:25; 15:1–5). Virtually all of the Jesus-sayings construed to suggest eternal souls attaining heavenly homes come from John's gospel; and even these are noteworthy because of their ambiguity. For example, the dictum that "There are plenty of places to stay in my Father's house . . . I'm on my way to make a place ready for you . . ." (14:2) is undoubtedly an embellishment by the later Church (or John himself) of a metaphor used by Jesus to indicate simply that there was a place for everyone in God's domain—which was not heaven so much as heaven on earth.

Many incidents in the synoptic gospels have been twisted and stretched to suggest Jesus' belief in immortal souls, for example, his words to the thief crucified with him: "I swear to you, today you'll be with me in paradise" (Luke 23:43). First of all it is doubtful that Jesus actually said these words, since Luke alone reports them *and* the earlier Mark asserts that *both* of his fellow victims taunted him (15:32). But even if Jesus really did say such a thing, it could hardly be understood as a general endorsement for the survival of everyone's immortal soul. As a first-century Jewish teacher, the only thing he possibly could have meant by such a promise was a miraculous translation of the whole person to heaven, as reportedly had happened to Enoch and Elijah (and possibly Moses) in the Hebrew Bible. For good Jews like Jesus, that was the only way a person could go anywhere: physically and whole.

Jesus' Self-Image and Titles

What is especially interesting (or disturbing) about the message and ministry of Jesus, particularly in light of later developments in Christianity, is that he seems to have been much less explicit and definite about his own identity and role than later generations of Christians have been. Indeed, Jesus was very tight-lipped, vague, and even evasive about himself—except, of course, in John's late and embellished gospel. One reason for Jesus' equivocacy is that he did not make himself the center of attention, as St. Paul and the Church later would, but constantly directed attention instead to God, God's fatherhood, God's will, God's actions, and above all God's domain.

But it is still odd that Jesus wasn't clearer about his own role and identity; and his ambiguity in this regard has long raised the question—still widely debated among scholars—of just what his self-concept or self-image really was. This modern confusion should not surprise us; even his closest companions reportedly wondered and asked just who he was. But it is the more acute for us because our only sources, the Jesus-sayings in the gospels, undoubtedly reflect later Christian beliefs about him.

Further compounding the problem of Jesus' self-image is the fact that he seems to have avoided claiming any of the traditional titles that for his hearers might have clarified his role, a caution that the early Church abandoned. To begin with, Jesus never claimed to be God or divine or anything of the kind. Gospel passages that are used to show that he did so are few in number and almost invariably from the idiosyncratic John; and even those passages are quoted out of context and with no thought of simpler alternative explanations. When, for example, Jesus says, "I and the Father are one," the simplest and most likely meaning is that they are of one mind or one spirit—not in any metaphysical sense, but because Jesus is attuned to God's will.

But even if Jesus did intend that statement to be a metaphysical one, it is not clear that he saw *only* himself as essentially one with God. That is, he may have meant: "I, like all of you, am one with God." Likewise, when he says, "If you have seen me, you have seen the Father," the simplest explanation is that he is viewing his own activity as being in concert with God's will, not declaring that he himself is literally God. Yet, here again, he may have!

"Rabbi" and "Son of Man"

Bound up with the question of Jesus' self-image is the issue of the titles ascribed to him in the New Testament. The least problematic is "Rabbi," which is used by his disciples throughout the Synoptics without objection from Jesus. Jesus does object when one of his followers refers to him as "Good Rabbi," reminding the well-intentioned fellow—in proper Jewish fashion—that only God is truly good (Mark 10:17–18). But his objection was to the adjective, not to the title.

In Jesus' day, the title "Rabbi" was applied rather generally to anyone who appeared to have mastered the scriptures and today is better rendered as "teacher." It did not necessarily mean that the individual so designated had had any formal training or recognition from the religious establishment.

There is rather convincing evidence that Jesus may have applied the term "Son of Man" to himself. It is by far the most frequent title that he uses for himself in the synoptic gospels, and the mere fact that the Christian authors of the rest of the New Testament use it hardly at all—preferring instead honorifics like "Christ"—suggests that it was his own preferred self-designation, in contrast with the Church's more definitive and exalted terms.

But even the term "Son of Man" (literally, "Son of Adam") was ambiguous, and not necessarily a title at all. The Jews of Jesus' day used it in at least three senses: (1) as a creature insignificant in the presence of God (see Job 25:4–6); (2) as one a little lower than God, that is, next to God in the order of creation (see Psalm 8:3–6); and (3) as an apocalyptically "loaded" title for the expected heavenly redeemer who would come "on clouds of heaven" to inaugurate the final divine overthrow and judgment of the world (see Dan 7:13–14).

Oddly enough, however, whenever Jesus clearly is quoted using the phrase in this third sense, that is, as a definitive title, his references are in the third person: "Then they will see the Son of Man coming. . . . Then he will. . . . " (for example, Mark 13:26–27 NRSV). Such references suggest that he did not regard himself as this apocalyptic Son of Man. In other contexts, however, the gospel writings reflect the view of the later Christian community in identifying Jesus as the "Son of Man" (for example, Mark 2:10–28; 8:31; 9:31; Matt 8:20).

"Son of God" and "Christ"

Despite his frequent use of the phrase "Son of Man," Jesus never calls himself "Son of God" in the synoptics, and uses of that designation elsewhere are very infrequent as well. Indeed, Jesus calls himself "Son of God" only in John, the latest and most Christologically developed of the gospels; and the phrase really is commonplace only in the letters of Paul and other New Testament writings, such as Hebrews, which apply it to him. This leads most New Testament scholars to conclude that Jesus probably didn't apply the phrase "Son of God" to himself at all; or that, if he did, it was infrequently, and probably in a "loose" Hebraic way. (In the Old Testament, "Son of God" could mean an angelic being, a member of the heavenly court, the king, Israel itself, or anyone who morally reflected the character of God.) Precisely because of Judaism's strict monotheism, it would not have had in Jesus' mind the heavily metaphysical or exclusivist connotation that it later would develop in Christian piety and theology.

Nor was "Son of God" a designation for the expected Messiah, at least in Old Testament times. Gentiles in the Greek-influenced world used the phrase for monarchs, military heroes, philosophers, poets, wonder-workers, and diviners. This practice no doubt influenced the early Church to apply the term retroactively to their king, despite the fact that he himself had not embraced it.

It is also extremely doubtful that Jesus ever called himself "Messiah," or its Greek-derived equivalent "Christ," the English translation of which is "Anointed." Indeed, he never calls himself that in the gospels, and when others do—either in declarations or inquiries—his responses are vague, evasive, or ambiguous. In Mark, for example, when Peter allegedly declares at Caesarea Philippi: "You are the Anointed!", Jesus neither affirms or denies, but tells him and the other disciples not to tell that to anybody (8:27–30). Luke's version (9:18–22) is similar; but in Matthew 16:13–23, Jesus gives a different, much more affirmative response, which most modern scholars take to be that author's "retouching" of the original. Indeed, in the synoptics, and especially Mark, Jesus spends a great deal of time imploring his followers not to tell anyone that he is the Messiah.

Some scholars and preachers argue that Jesus knew himself to be the Messiah/Christ, but merely wanted the disciples to keep it a secret so as not to bring about his arrest prematurely. But after he has been arrested, and with no apparent motive for maintaining secrecy, he is still non-committal about the title. When, for example, he is asked by the Sanhedrin and Pilate if he is the Christ (or "King of the Jews"), his response amounts to "Your words, not mine." Only Mark reports that he told the Sanhedrin "I am." Matthew and Luke have him being far more ambiguous, probably for the simple reason that that is the way their sources remembered his response.

Most scholars conclude, therefore, that Jesus did not use the term "Messiah" for himself. He had good reason not to, for—as we have already seen—that title had a very precise connotation in those days: it referred to the longed-for successor to Israel's greatest king, David, a mighty national, political, and military leader who would restore the security and fortunes of Israel that had long since been shattered. In light of such an expectation, therefore, it is no wonder that Jesus himself avoided the term, since he evidently had no such aspirations. It is only when Christianity later moved into gentile circles that the title "Christ," now stripped of its original Jewish connotation, was applied retroactively to Jesus.

"Lord" and "Savior" and the Trouble with Titles

The same is also true of perhaps the two most popular modern titles for Jesus: "Lord" and "Savior." The former is used infrequently in the synoptics, and seems there to be nothing more than a polite form of address, probably the equivalent of "Rabbi" or "Teacher." It does become a common title for Jesus in the rest of the New Testament, but that reflects the usage of the post-Easter Church, in which "Lord" became the standard way of referring to Jesus, and "Jesus is Lord" the first Christian creed. By then, of course, the title was loaded with meanings and connotations from other Hellenistic religions. Likewise, the term "Savior" is usually reserved for God in the New Testament (for example, Luke 1:47 and 1 Tim 1:1), but is applied editorially to Jesus in a few places (for example, Luke 2:11, John 4:42, Acts 5:31). In short, Jesus appears never to have referred to himself as either "Lord" or "Savior."

None of this proves, of course, that Jesus was not the Lord, Savior, Messiah-Christ, apocalyptic Son of Adam, Son of God, or even God in person. Nor does it provide conclusive evidence that he didn't see himself as fitting one or more of these roles. It does, however, raise the curious question of why Jesus didn't call himself such things, and why such titles were applied to him only by others in retrospect. One possibility is that Jesus avoided all such titles because they were too restrictive, and defined too narrowly his person and mission. Perhaps he simply didn't want to be pigeon-holed. Above all, however, he wished to shatter human expectations and categories in order to divert attention from himself and focus it on what he thought to be far more important: God and God's immediate domain.

The Last Days of Jesus

Even if Jesus didn't adopt grandiose titles or make definitive claims about himself, surely there was plenty in his message and actions to offend the religious and political establishment—and to result in his death. And that is in fact what happened in or about the year 29 CE. Whatever the later generations of Christians made of that event, it is clear that the historical cause of Jesus' death was that his words and deeds alarmed the established religious and political authorities of his day.

Crucifixion Contradictions—and *Conspiracy?*

The circumstances of the arrest, trial, and execution of Jesus are confused, largely because two different kinds of authorities were involved: the Jewish Sanhedrin, a religious tribunal, and the Roman state, in the person of its procurator (or governor) Pontius Pilate. Since Jesus was executed by crucifixion rather than stoning, it is clear that the charge against him was sedition—that is, revolutionary activity against the Empire—rather than impiety or heresy. But it is no less clear that the religious authorities had a vested interest, and no doubt an important hand, in forcing that issue to its lethal conclusion.

The accounts of the end of Jesus' life are similar to those of his nativity in one important respect: no two of the gospel writers tell it the same way. In fact, their accounts are wildly at variance with one another. To begin with, the three synoptics predictably disagree with John on many points concerning Jesus' crucifixion, including such a basic detail as what day it occurred. But even the synoptics do not totally agree with one another on the facts of the matter. The result is that the modern image of the event is a mishmash of the four versions.

For example, the four gospels do not totally agree with each other about what Jesus' final words on the cross were. (See figure 3.4.) Mark, the earli-

The Seven Last Words of Christ

Mark & Matthew	*Luke*	*John*
"My God, my God, why did you abandon me?" (Mk 15:34, Mt 27:46)†	"Father, forgive them, for they don't know what they are doing." (23:34)*	"Woman, here is your son . . . . Here is your mother." (19:26a)
	" . . . today you'll be with me in paradise." (23:43)	"I'm thirsty." (19:28)
		"It's all over." (19:30)
	"Father, into your hands I entrust my spirit." (23:46)	

† In Mk 15:37 and Mtt 27:50, Jesus' last utterance is a great shout, either non-verbal or unintelligible.

* Luke 23:34 is in many ancient manuscripts of Luke's Gospel, but not in the most reliable. It was probably added later.

Now, precisely what was the last thing that Jesus said from the cross?

FIGURE **3.4**

est account, says that he "let out a great shout and breathed his last" (15:37). Matthew pretty much agrees (27:50), as one might expect, given his use of Mark as a source. But according to Luke, who also used Mark, Jesus' final words were "Father, into your hands I entrust my Spirit," at which point he died (23:46). John goes his own way as usual, making it very clear that that last thing that Jesus said before expiring was simply: "It's all over." (19:29)

John in fact gives a wholly unique impression of the entire crucifixion. The synoptics exhibit some real suffering on Jesus' part, while John—always stylizing—depicts Jesus as regally, even coolly in charge to the end. That probably explains the offhand comment of one of my theology professors in seminary about Bach's "St. John's Passion": "Hmph! There *is* no passion in St. John!" Only after a historical-critical study of John in a New Testament course did I fully understand and appreciate that remark.

Besides the variations in the accounts of the crucifixion, the death and burial stories also contain enough irregularities to have spawned a number of theories about what really happened. For example, attention has been called to the fact that Jesus was executed by the so-called short form of crucifixion, which had the victim standing on a small platform and thus required that the legs be broken in order for death by suffocation to follow. Yet we are told that Jesus' legs were not broken because he was already dead (but was he?). We are further told: (1) that at least one centurion involved expressed belief in Jesus' divine Sonship (a "closet" disciple?); (2) that Jesus was given a mixture of vinegar and "gall" (a sedative?) and almost immediately "gave up the spirit" (lapsed into a coma?); (3) that his side was pierced by a spear and yielded water and blood (a simple magician's trick for appearances?); (4) that he was removed from the cross, not by Roman soldiers, as would have been customary, but by two followers, Joseph and Nicodemus; (5) that his body was treated by these pious Jews not with contempt, as Jewish law demanded even of "innocent" criminals' corpses, but with respect; (6) that, also contrary to Jewish law, Jesus was buried in the tomb of a man who was not his relative—and who was a member of the conservative Sanhedrin at that; and, finally, (7) that Pilate accepted the report of Jesus' death with surprise at its swiftness and solely on the hearsay of one individual.

All of this has led to some speculation that Jesus in fact survived the ordeal because of a conspiracy, and that the truth behind his empty tomb and resurrection appearances is that he had not really died. According to one version of this explanation, the white-clad male figure (or figures) was (or were) representative of the Essene community, skilled in esoteric medical arts, and therefore capable of nursing the tortured and anesthetized Jesus back to health while hiding out in the borrowed tomb.

Resurrection Reconsidered

Many Christians grew up hearing and reciting the Apostles' Creed or the Nicene Creed, both of which affirm that Jesus arose from the dead on "the third day." If asked how long Jesus was in the tomb, they will invariably say,

"Three days," probably glaring in disbelief at the ignorance of the questioner. Asked how many hours that was, they will probably respond, "Why, seventy-two!" Imagine their surprise to learn that the real answer, based on scripture, is "A little over a day and a half, tops!" For if Jesus died at about 3 p.m. on Good Friday and if he was buried immediately, he was in the tomb a mere nine hours that day, and perhaps less. Add to that a full twenty-four hours for Saturday and between five and seven more until sunrise on Sunday, and we wind up with a total of thirty-eight to forty hours—a little over a day and a half, at most. In fact, we are only told that the women *discovered* the empty tomb on Sunday morning, having stayed away from the gravesite on Saturday because it was the Sabbath and unlawful to be there. Jesus might have arisen sometime on the Sabbath, then, shortening the time in the tomb even more!

Where, then, did we get those three days? Simply stated, it was from the way time was figured in Palestine in those days, according to which any part of a day *was* a day. Had Jesus been interred at one minute before midnight on Friday and arisen one minute after midnight on Sunday morning, he *still* would have been "dead and buried" for three days, despite having been entombed only twenty-four hours and two minutes. Of course, how many hours he was dead before arising matters little, if he really was dead and if he really did arise. But the fact that most Christians have never even noticed the apparent time discrepancy in this important account is a good indication of just how much has been taken for granted for so long—and how much insight a truly thoughtful reading of scripture might reveal about other matters, both great and small.

The skeptics' case about the resurrection is bolstered by the fact that the accounts of it in the four gospels are hopelessly contradictory on almost every count. They disagree about who went to the tomb on Easter Sunday morning, precisely what they found there, what they were told, and what they did afterward. Three of the reporters seem totally unaware of the tidbit reported only by John, that Mary Magdalene had an encounter and private chat with the risen Jesus there! All of this further suggests to many scholars—believers and unbelievers alike—that the whole resurrection story was a fabrication perpetrated by the first Christians in order to bolster their shaken faith and salvage their bereft Jesus movement.

As admittedly plausible as such theories may be, the gospel writers and countless generations of Christians have affirmed in their recitations of ancient creeds the fact of Jesus' death and resurrection—and have done so in a good Jewish way, with no reference to his having had a soul that survived the experience. Jesus "was crucified, dead, and buried," (Apostles' Creed) or "suffered and was buried" (Nicene Creed)—period. Likewise, traditional Christian belief has been that he came back to life, not as an immortal soul, but as a person who left an empty tomb behind him, and made physical appearances for as many as forty days before ascending bodily into heaven.

Paul, however, who provides the earliest testimony to Jesus' resurrection, does not mention the empty tomb; and despite his Jewish background, generally speaks of resurrected bodies as "spiritual." It seems odd, if not incredible, that this earliest of Christian writers could have known about an empty tomb and not thought it important enough to have reported it . . . just as if he could have known about a virginal birth and not reported that! One wonders whether these two "events" were concocted in the two decades or so between Paul's death (c. 64 CE) and the writings of Matthew and Luke (c. 85 CE).

Many alternative explanations for the resurrection have been offered even by believers. There is, of course, the literal: it really occurred as advertised. There is also the psychic explanation: that, whether Jesus had believed in a separable and survivable soul or not, he really had one (perhaps much to his own surprise), and that's what made appearances and impressions upon his forlorn disciples, who then created "empty tomb" stories to try to make sense of the experience. A third possible explanation is the psychological: the resurrection did in fact occur, but only in the hearts and minds of the disciples, who came to realize that the "spirit" of Jesus was still alive in them, and thus that their mission was still operative. Yet a fourth possibility (suggested with reference to the virginal birth earlier) is that "resurrection" is one of many archetypal images that are part and parcel of the human mind or what Carl Jung called "the collective unconscious"—an explanation reinforced by death-resurrection motifs that appear in other mythologies of the world, for example, Osiris in Egypt. In short, there is more than one way for Christians to affirm the resurrection of Jesus and still be "faithful."

The Founding of the Faith and the Future

It would seem reasonable for Christians to assume, as most probably do, that the founder of both their faith and the Church was Jesus of Nazareth. After all, Christianity does bear his name—or, more accurately, his ascribed title. And many books and articles still refer to Jesus matter-of-factly as "the founder of Christianity." But the truth of the matter is that Jesus never actually founded Christianity, nor did he even appear to have in mind a new religion at all. And it is unimaginable that he intended to found an institution anything like the Church as we know it today.

Founder or Foundation?

If Jesus did intend to start a religion, it is certainly curious (at the very least) that he gave it no name; for it is demonstrably true that he never used the words "Christian" or "Christianity." Acts 11:26 in fact, tells us that the term "Christian" was first used in the Syrian city of Antioch (one of the earliest "pockets" of Christianity in the Mediterranean area) after the death, resurrection, and ascension of Jesus; and the term "Christianity" did not appear until the early second century CE (and probably was not widely used until much later) to identify a distinctive type of religious belief and practice.

During Jesus' lifetime, what would become Christianity was much more informal: a movement, not an institution, based on the intimate relationship between a spiritual leader and his devoted followers. Moreover, the teachings of Jesus, as seemingly radical as they were, were still in sufficient continuity with his Jewish tradition to make his movement appear to his contemporaries as merely a sect within that religious tradition, rather than a separate faith or religion.

Jesus almost as certainly never used the term "church" (Greek *ekklesia*, more appropriately translated "congregation"). As extraordinary as this may seem, the word "church" does not appear on Jesus' lips anywhere in Mark, Luke, or John. Only in Matthew is Jesus depicted using the term, and only three times and in only two verses (16:18 and 18:17). The first of these happens to be one of the key verses that the Roman Catholic Church uses as the scriptural basis of the Papacy. But many New Testament authorities believe both of these verses to be anachronisms, that is, statements "remembered back onto the lips of Jesus" by Matthew, by whose day there certainly was such a thing as an institutional Church, however primitive. The argument runs as follows: first, if such a Church had been part of Jesus' agenda or vocabulary, the term would certainly have cropped up in all the gospels and much more frequently in Matthew; and second, the Church being as important as it was in the evangelists' time, the only thing that would have kept them from using the term in reporting the sayings of Jesus was the compelling fact that he had never actually used it himself.

We are left, then, with the high probability that what we know as "Christianity" and "the Church" were inventions, not of Jesus, but of his successors. Moreover, as we shall see in the next chapter, Christianity has always been not so much the religion *of* Jesus, but a religion *about* Jesus; and the Church was the institution that arose after Easter to perpetuate it. Thus Jesus was certainly the *foundation* of Christianity and the Church, but he himself was not the *founder*. He was a first-century Jew who for his entire life maintained his self-identity within that religious context.

Jesus' View of the Future

Many sermons have been preached and many books written and sold — largely in fundamentalist Protestant circles—that have claimed that Jesus is coming again, and very soon at that. Signs of the times are read and correlated with select scriptures, and dire warnings and threats of impending and imminent doom are issued with great urgency and passion. Ironically, several generations of ministers have spent their entire careers and built impressive and profitable (and enduring!) organizations on this inexplicably popular message. Its durability notwithstanding, however, Jesus' own expectations about a personal return are by no means clear.

Jesus' most definitive futuristic pronouncement is contained in Mark 13 and its synoptic parallels. There he appears to predict all sorts of cataclysmic events that will accompany the ruination of Herod's temple in Jerusalem, including wars, earthquakes, famines, and the stars falling from the heavens. It is in this connection that Mark has Jesus predicting the coming of the apocalyptic "Son of Man" discussed above and, more telling, has Jesus referring to this coming one in the third person, as though he envisions someone else altogether. In addition, he also warns his small audience that their generation will not pass away before these things happen, an apparently mistaken prognostication that modern end-time preachers always manage to ignore.

Other references to a "second coming" of Jesus in the gospels are rare, and most New Testament scholars agree that these reflect the faith of the early Church, which clearly expected Jesus to come again—as evidenced by the epistles of Paul and Peter and the book of Revelation. When, for example, Jesus reportedly promises (in John 14:3) that he "will return," it is in the same passage about "many rooms" in his "Father's house" that early Christians probably took out of context, and remembered and recorded in light of their own expectations rather than those of Jesus himself.

This is not to say, of course, that Jesus will not come again, but only that evidence from his words for such a claim is extremely meager. And even if his reported words on the subject are authentic, the projected event was at best peripheral to his central concern, God's immediate reign on earth, which preoccupied him and dominated his teaching. Modern Christian harbingers of doom, therefore, are preaching at best a mistaken digression of Jesus and an expectation of the earliest Christians that even they had abandoned within a generation or two.

Conclusion

As best we can reconstruct it, the life of Jesus reveals that much of what Christians are taught as a matter of fact is really uncertain. Christians are simply not told, as a rule, what New Testament scholars, historians of Christianity, and most seminary-trained clergy know: (1) that even the best sources about the life of Jesus are late, sketchy, contradictory, and differently slanted; (2) that the historical Jesus is best understood in his own first-century Palestinian historical context, rather than ours; (3) that the stories of his miraculous origins and destiny are problematic; (4) that we know nothing about most of Jesus' life, and only a little about the rest of it; (5) that Jesus talked most about God's present, unmediated domain and said nothing about souls being "saved" or going to heaven; (6) that in the most historically trustworthy sources he was extremely cryptic about himself, made no definitive claims about his own identity, and said little or nothing about expecting to return; (7) that his teachings on wealth and poverty, if taken seriously, would make the capitalism of "Christian" America impossible, and that his sayings about forgiveness and "enemy-loving" are incompatible with huge national defense budgets, not to mention the spirit of most contact sports; and (8) that we've been allowed to overlook or ignore such discrepancies and contradictions because Christianity and the Church that preserved and promoted it were not based on the teachings of Jesus, but on later beliefs about and faith in his having been the Christ.

Many would argue that to acknowledge the truth of any or all of these assertions would render Christian belief absurd and Christianity itself baseless. Yet, most of the scholars who have produced these findings, most seminary and college professors who have taught them, and most clergy who have learned them still identify themselves as Christians and remain fascinated with the historical person of Jesus. The seeming irony of this situation attests to the durability and no doubt the existential validity of the

Christian faith: there is something about it that allows it to stand up even to such rigorous, critical scrutiny.

That "something" may be the central miracle and mystery that has defined the Christian faith for nearly two millennia: the extraordinary idea that somehow God was radically present and active in the life, ministry, and destiny of this Jesus of Nazareth. That claim is underscored by a recognition, despite the questionable and problematic details, of the full humanity of Jesus. Something about this man Jesus led subsequent generations of believers to the conviction that he was Lord, Savior, Son of God, and even God Incarnate. In short, they transformed the man Jesus into the Christ of faith. It is to the historical development of that transformation that we turn next.

3

Jesus of
Nazareth
and the
Origins of
Christianity

A. Read the Passion Narratives in a) 1 Corinthians 15:1–11; b) Mark 15–16; c) Matthew 27–28; d) Luke 23–24; and e) John 18:28–21:25, and answer the following questions for each text:

What was Pilate's concern about the body of Jesus?
Who received the body of Jesus?
Who buried Jesus?
Who witnessed the burial?
What was the day and time?
Who took the body off the cross?
Who witnessed the actual resurrection?
Which women went to the tomb?
Who was at the tomb when they arrived?
What were the women told?
What was their response?
To which people did Jesus appear after his resurrection (list in chronological order)?
In what form did Jesus appear?
What instructions did Jesus leave? (Specifically, where did he say that he would meet them, and where did he?)
Name at least one unique issue that each account contains.
Name one general concern for each of the writers.
Identify and discuss one issue that surprises you.

B. Compare the nativity stories of Matthew 2:1–12 and Luke 2:1–20, noting for yourself the differences between them. What do you suppose each is trying to convey with his set of details? Which story do you think has made the bigger impression on the religious imagination of most Christians? Why do you think that is so?

C. Make a list of all of the claims made in this chapter about the historical Jesus that surprised you (whether you believe them or not). Which ones would you label as "greater" and "lesser" threats to Christian faith, were they to be proven absolutely true? Why? How important is the historical Jesus—his life, his teachings, and his miracles, especially—to Christian faith? Why? How do you suppose it is that many biblical scholars question such things and still remain professed and practicing Christians?

RECOMMENDED READING

Marcus Borg, *Meeting Jesus Again for the First Time: The Historical Jesus and the Heart of Contemporary Faith.* San Francisco: HarperSanFrancisco, 1995.
— a very personal, reassuring account of the author's search for an authentic,

mature, contemporary faith in light of his own participation in historical Jesus research and its shattering of confessional doctrines and popular images of Jesus

John Dominic Crossan, *Jesus: A Revolutionary Biography.* San Francisco: HarperSanFrancisco, 1994.

— a strikingly fresh portrait of Jesus as a Jewish peasant and radically egalitarian social revolutionary, based on anthropological, historical, and literary sources (a popularization of Crossan's *The Historical Jesus* [1992])

Robert W. Funk, *Honest to Jesus: Jesus for a New Millennium.* San Francisco: HarperSanFrancisco, 1996.

— an introduction to the exciting and ground-breaking, tradition-shattering work of The Jesus Seminar, its goals, methodologies, and surprising findings, including the image of Jesus as a revolutionary iconoclast upon which a new Christianity might be built

Robert W. Funk, *Parables and Presence: Forms of the New Testament Tradition.* Philadelphia: Fortress Press, 1982.

— examines the parables of Jesus and builds on the insight that they are the key to understanding Jesus' message

Robert W. Funk, Roy W. Hoover, and the Jesus Seminar, *The Five Gospels: The Search for the Authentic Words of Jesus.* New York: Macmillan, 1993.

— the results of the earlier work of The Jesus Seminar: a fresh translation of the words of Jesus in the Five Gospels (including Thomas), with color-coded text to indicate what Jesus probably said and what the Church likely attributed to him later

Robert W. Funk and the Jesus Seminar, *The Acts of Jesus: The Search for the Authentic Deeds of Jesus,* San Francisco: HarperSanFrancisco, 1998.

— a fresh, unorthodox new translation of the Gospels by the scholars of The Jesus Seminar, with color-coded text, exhaustive commentary, and helpful indices

Stephen Mitchell, *The Gospel According to Jesus: A New Translation and Guide to His Essential Teachings for Believers and Unbelievers.* New York: Harper Collins, 1991.

— a separation of the "essential" teachings of Jesus from those almost certainly added by the early Church, yielding a simplified (and freshly translated) version of the gospel, with added commentary, comparisons with Eastern spiritual teachings, and meditations

Marianne Sawicki, *Seeing the Lord: Resurrection and Early Christian Practices.* Philadelphia: Fortress Press, 1994.

— a combination of critical theology, sacramental liturgy and solidarity with the poor in order to understand Jesus' resurrection in its most profound sense

Jane Schaberg, *The Illegitimacy of Jesus: A Feminist Theological Interpretation of the Infancy Narratives.* San Francisco: Harper & Row, 1987.

— an exploration of the possibilities for Mary's pregnancy and their impact on the role of women in the Christian tradition

W. Barnes Tatum, *John the Baptist and Jesus: A Report of the Jesus Seminar.* Sonoma, CA: Polebridge Press, 1994.

— a consideration of all of the historical evidence related to John the Baptist found in ancient sources, with answers to major questions about his message and relationship to Jesus

THE CHRIST OF FAITH IN THE HISTORY OF CHRISTIANITY

Objectives of this chapter:

- to provide an overview of the four major periods of the history of Christianity

- to survey each of those periods briefly in order to discern its basic character and major figures and movements

- to examine the earliest "primitive" Christianity with an eye to the controversies within the Church about the person and work of Jesus Christ and the factions they produced

- to describe the subsequent ancient Christological debates and the councils and formal doctrines that they generated

- to explain in particular the Christological formula that insists on the full humanity and divinity for Jesus Christ

- to note the numerous and varied images of Jesus Christ that have emerged throughout Christian history

- to determine the place of Jesus Christ in modern popular piety with regard to what orthodoxy has held about him

- to explore two possible alternative views of Jesus as the Christ, one mythical and the other mystical

Any religion that has managed to survive more than a generation or two is bound to be a complex of traditions, that is, of beliefs and practices handed down and received, adopted and adapted, then handed on again. The history of such a religion will therefore necessarily be a record of its process and evolution. Thus, despite some claims to the contrary, not even in its most conservative or "orthodox" expression is any of the world's religions today what it was when it first emerged.

This is certainly true of Christianity. It consists of a certain core of beliefs and practices generated in the last two-thirds of the first century CE by what is generally called the "primitive" Church (the earliest Christian congregations), and elaborated and complicated ever thereafter by new doctrines, theologies, rituals, rules, spiritual and social expressions, and so forth. Like a snowball rolling down the hill of history, Christianity started small, fairly consistent, and relatively "clean," but grew and grew as it accumulated additional beliefs and practices, including a fair amount of foreign matter—some of which could only be described as debris—that became a part of the ever-growing composite. From time to time, the "snowball" has fragmented, producing various smaller entities (called "denominations" or "sects"), which have then proceeded to roll on their own paths and grow from their own accumulations. The end result is that today we have a veritable avalanche of Christian traditions, each a variegated composite surrounding fragments of the original core.

The primitive Church's simple faith and proclamation that Jesus was "Lord" and "Christ" and "Son of God" already differed from the key teachings of Jesus discussed in the previous chapter. The "snowball" effect then transformed that core Christian credo into a complex system of formulas, creeds, doctrines, and dogmas. As many interpreters of this process have put it, in the first couple of generations after Jesus, the reign of God became Christianity; and Christianity increasingly focused upon Jesus as the Christ. The task of defining just who this Christ was and is—the area of Christian theology called "Christology"—proved to be no simple matter. In fact, it occupied much of the attention of the earliest theorists of Christianity, who finally came to a hard-won consensus on the matter after a little over four centuries of sometimes bitter disagreement.

Thereafter—from the fifth century to the present—belief in Christ intensified and altered to produce a rich panoply of images of the God-human who was now the focus of the faith. It would be impossible in a volume like this to do justice to that historical development, and many excellent works that describe and document that process are readily available in libraries everywhere. But every Christian should know at least that the basic tenets of the Christian faith did not one day fall fully formed from heaven, nor did they issue forth from the lips of Jesus, nor are they even located in scripture (though the makings certainly are). Rather, they emerged slowly and evolved gradually in a process of thinking and rethinking, conflict and compromise that we shall be content merely to sketch in the following pages.

We shall begin with an overview of the history of Christianity, in order to provide a larger historical framework in which to view the development of

4

The Christ of Faith in the History of Christianity

the faith. We shall then focus upon the earliest, formative period of Christianity, and especially upon the views of Jesus as the Christ that gained definition in that period. Returning to the longer view, we shall see how images of Christ have evolved, multiplied, changed, and differed since they were originally formulated those many centuries ago. Finally, we shall reopen the question of just who Jesus Christ is for Christians today, and explore how he might be reconceived in light of the historic orthodox doctrines and creeds about him. Throughout, we shall try to keep as clear as possible this sometimes difficult distinction: when we talk about "Christ," "Jesus Christ," "Jesus the Christ," or "Jesus as the Christ," we are referring to the object of Christian belief and veneration, and not the historical Jesus.

Christianity Through the Ages

History doesn't *fall* into periods; historians *arrange* events into periods. They do this by recognizing that a particular cluster of decades or centuries has, at least in retrospect, a certain coherence—some common threads that seem to bind an era together and to distinguish it from those before and after it. Although historians often agree on these periods, including what to call them, they do not always see eye to eye on the exact threshold events or dates that signal the end or beginning of each. Indeed, historians love to quibble about such admittedly artificial demarcations; but out of such discussions a great deal of historical clarification and understanding often emerges.

Because of the dominance and power of the Church in Europe and the Americas, the periodization of the history of Christianity coincides, for all intents and purposes, with that of the history of Western civilization. Both historians of religion and those who analyze society, culture, politics, and economics tend to agree in recognizing four basic periods from the founding of Christianity to the present (though, as we shall see, secular historians extend the first of these back to pre-Christian times). They also generally agree in calling them, respectively, the Ancient Period, the Medieval Period, the Renaissance-Reformation Period, and the Modern Period. (See figure 4.1.) Each of these four basic periods has a particular "feel" about it in terms of what is going on in Christianity, religiously and spiritually, institutionally and theologically.

Definition and Dissemination

Historians of Western civilization generally mark the beginning of what they call "The Ancient Period" at five centuries or more BCE, so as to include classical Greece, Rome, and other pre-Christian ancient cultures, such as those of ancient Egypt and Mesopotamia. Historians of Christianity, by contrast, tend to define "The Ancient Period" more narrowly as comprising, roughly, the nearly five centuries from the death of Jesus around 29 CE to about 500 CE.

For Christianity, this Ancient Period is an "Age of Definition and Dissemination," during which the faith and its followers were transformed. Largely as a result of the conversion of the Roman Emperor Constantine, an informal and illegal new sect became a formal and legal religion in its own

Major Periods in the History of Christianity
(with representative people and events for each)

Ancient	Medieval (Middle Ages)	Renaissance/ Reformation	Modern
29ᴄᴇ 500ᴄᴇ	1400ᴄᴇ	1650ᴄᴇ	present
Age of Definition and Dissemination • missions and letters of Paul • persecution • *Apostolic Fathers; Apologists • *Irenaeus, Tertullian, Origen • Constantine and legalization • Councils and Creeds • Gnosticism & other "heresies" • theology of Augustine • rise of monasticism	**Age of Development and Dominance** • Charlemagne, first Holy Roman Emperor • split with Eastern Orthodoxy • rise and spread of Islam • Crusades • ongoing church-state clashes • *Anselm, Abelard,Catherine of Siena, Aquinas, etc. • Pope Innocent III: height of papal power • monastic orders: Franciscans, Dominicans, etc. • mystics: Bernard, Hildegard, Eckhart, etc. • Inquisitions against heresies	**Age of Dissent and Dissolution** • Copernicus • Michaelangelo • *Erasmus & humanism • *Luther, Calvin, etc. • Protestantism • Council of Trent • Anglicanism • Anabaptists *denotes representative theologians of each era	**Age of Diversity and Doubt** • proliferation of denominations • Enlightenment • Modern Science • historical-critical study of Bible • Liberalism & Fundamentalism • awareness of other religions • pluralism and relativism • *Barth, Bultmann, Tillich, Teilhard, Rahner, Küng, feminist, process, liberation, and creation theologies

FIGURE 4.1

right, replete with official doctrines, normalized practices, and other marks of a *bona fide* institution. It is during this period that Christianity grew from a largely localized Jewish phenomenon into a universal religion that left some mark on the entire known civilized world from England to Ethiopia, and from Iberia to India.

During these years an official, hierarchical clergy developed and ecclesiastical power in Western Europe began to be centralized in Rome as the Papacy became an institution not merely of prestige, but of real clout. It is also during this period that all of the key doctrines about what theologians call the "person of Christ" and the saving "work of Christ" were defined, as well as many other more peripheral Christological issues. (Keep in mind that

4

The Christ of Faith in the History of Christianity

the Christ of faith is not identical to the historical Jesus, and often seems to bear little connection to him.) Further, the basic theme of sin and redemption was set forth systematically and definitively by Augustine of Hippo and impressed itself indelibly upon the still young faith. All of this foundational doctrinal work was done in the context of an ever-expanding collection of abstract Greek (mostly Platonic) philosophical terms and categories that would have been utterly foreign to Jesus and his own pragmatic Jewish style of thought and teaching—and that are at least as far removed from our own conceptual patterns today.

Development and Domination

The next nine hundred years or so—from 500–1400 CE—are usually called "The Middle Ages" or "The Medieval Period." The first few centuries of this era used to be called "The Dark Ages," until historians finally realized that this era only seemed dark because of their lack of information about it. The more they found out, the brighter this period became. The Middle Ages as a whole were for European Christianity an "Age of Development and Domination," in which the Roman Catholic Church not only generated all of its distinctive religious institutions, beliefs, and practices, but also exercised enormous and increasing power and authority in every sphere of life, with an enforced but nonetheless effective unity. In many ways, European Christianity was "on a roll"!

But the Middle Ages was also a time of conflicting dynamics: authoritarianism and asceticism, cathedrals and Crusades, inquisitiveness and Inquisitions, mystics and monarchs, social upheaval and scholasticism. The Papacy, which had moved from a merely prestigious to a truly powerful position in the fifth century, steadily grew in authority and influence, reaching the peak of its power in the early 13th century. That power in the sacred realm spilled over into the secular—the distinction then was not at all clear—and often put it into conflict with the various European monarchs, who were themselves loosely organized into a Holy Roman Empire that melded church and state into an awkward and often uneasy alliance. Monasticism, which had begun in the Ancient Period as a response to Christianity's comfortable position after Emperor Constantine's conversion, became more defined and organized under the great religious "orders," such as the Benedictine, Cistercian, Franciscan, and Dominican. Theology continued to be articulated in Greek philosophical terms by scholastic theologians—the most notable being Anselm of Canterbury, Peter Abelard, and Thomas Aquinas—who argued issues as profound as atonement and as seemingly trivial as the size and shape of angels.

During this Medieval Period, the Roman Catholic Church launched a series of Crusades to protect itself from the palpable external threat of a rapidly spreading Islam. Though dismal failures and sometimes downright shameful debacles, these "holy wars" gave Europe access to long forgotten classical authors (like Aristotle) as well as to the Arabic number system. A more serious threat arose from within: numerous heresies (false beliefs) were identified, condemned, and turned over to various Inquisitions for extermination. A yet more subtle internal threat was posed by the great mystics who appeared in this period: by claiming direct, unmediated experiences of oneness with God, the likes of Julian of Norwich, Bernard of Clairvaux, Hildegard of Bingen, and Meister Eckhart undermined, however unintentionally, the Church's preferred role as mediator between humanity and God.

Though not monolithic, the European Church and society in this era did achieve a remarkable spiritual and political unity and coherence sometimes called the "Medieval Synthesis" or simply "Christendom." To be sure, there were numerous dissident individuals, groups, and movements during the Middle Ages; but the only major and lasting schism in this period occurred in the eleventh century with the official separation of the Eastern Orthodox Churches from Rome over a variety of issues, not the least of which was the ecclesiastical primacy and authority of the Pope.

Dissent and Disintegration

It was only with the rise of the Renaissance and the Reformation that there emerged individuals and issues that would eventually dissolve the relative cohesion and undermine the unity and security of European Christendom. The Renaissance-Reformation Period began around 1400 and ran through the sixteenth century, ending perhaps as late as 1650. This period was, from the standpoint of the Roman Catholic Church, an "Age of Dissent and Disintegration," in which the unity of European Christendom was shattered internally by the potent twin forces of humanistic individualism and religious dissent. (The image comes to mind of a very large ship being severely damaged, though by no means sunk, by two huge and unforeseen rocks.) This was happening at the very same time that Portuguese and Spanish explorations were revealing a much larger world of alternative cultures vastly different from anything Europe had ever known or even imagined.

The Renaissance was largely a secular movement of the fourteenth and fifteenth centuries, involving the arts, literature, and philosophy. It began sometime in the mid-1300s in Italy, and gradually spread northward to the rest of western Europe. The term "Renaissance," which is French for "rebirth," was coined during the period itself, and reflects the prevailing sense then that the previous thousand years or so had been a period of decline and decadence, and that something new was now happening. Ironically, much of that newness involved a rediscovery of the classical period of ancient Greece and Rome—roughly from the fifth century BCE to the fifth century CE. The art and architecture, the philosophy and literature of that time were studied with diligence and passion, under the banner-phrase—in Latin, of course—*Ad fontes* ("Back to the sources!").

One result of the Renaissance was a much more positive and optimistic view of humanity and human nature than had prevailed in the Middle Ages. During this earlier period, the Church had more or less successfully emphasized the sinfulness of humanity and its utter dependence upon God, and had generally maintained an other-worldly orientation, placing its hopes for human perfection in a heavenly afterlife. The new thought of the Renaissance, by contrast, emphasized human freedom, creativity, and potential in

4

The
Christ of
Faith in the
History of
Christianity

the here-and-now: humanity was now seen as basically good and capable of almost infinite improvement. Favorite themes were the dignity of human beings and humanity as "the measure of all things." A new term was even coined to describe this new attitude: "humanism." Much was made of reason, and optimism about the human intellect led Renaissance minds to reexamine everything anew, from the nature of the universe to the traditional teachings and practices of the Church—all the while revising or rejecting whatever failed to ring true.

Many Christians during the Renaissance—especially great scholars like William of Ockham, Nicholas of Cusa, and Lorenzo Valla—longed to ground their faith on reason, and to reform their Church in accordance with ancient norms. The lofty vision and ideals of such thinkers, and of their counterparts in the arts (for example, Michelangelo and Leonardo da Vinci) and literature (for example, Petrarch and Dante), contrasted markedly in character with the baser dreams and desires of the Renaissance Popes, who were largely men of political and material ambition rather than integrity or spirituality, and often corrupt, immoral, and ruthless as well. It was obvious to many that the Church was in need of reform, and several great leaders emerged in various parts of Europe—John Wycliffe in England, John Hus in Bohemia, Girolamo Savonarola in Italy—who pressed for change in the Church, and thus laid the foundation for the Reformation proper. And all the while the newly-invented printing press was making all of these ideas much more accessible.

The Reformation, which was a more specifically religious manifestation than the Renaissance, but closely intertwined with it, started a century or so later and overlapped its predecessor. Indeed, the Reformation was indebted to the spirit of the Renaissance in many ways, not the least of which was the urge to return to a Golden Age, though when the Reformers said that, they generally meant the Ancient Period of Christianity rather than Greek or Roman antiquity. In fact, there were two Reformations. The Catholic Reformation (sometimes mistakenly called a "Counter-Reformation") actually began first (in the late 1400s in Spain) and reached its culmination with the Council of Trent (1545–1563), which would define Catholic belief and practice for the next four hundred years. The Protestant Reformation began soon afterward with a succession of increasing radical and sweeping criticisms of Roman Catholic practices and doctrines by Martin Luther (1483–1546) and others, and distinguished itself by its uncompromising and finally divisive spirit.

The main reason for the disintegration of Christendom that resulted from the Protestant Reformation was Luther's radical appeal to scriptures as the norm for Christian belief and practice, and his insistence that the laity be able to read the Bible for themselves. Indeed, one of Luther's key Reformation projects was the translation of the Bible into his own German language. What happened thereafter is predictable, at least in retrospect: nearly everyone who read those supposedly normative scriptures interpreted them differently. Some found infant baptism there, some did not; some found two sacraments, some none at all; some found justification for an ordained clergy and ministerial hierarchy, others did not. On these issues and many

REMEDIAL CHRISTIANITY

others, dozens (and later hundreds) of new "Protestant" Christian sects emerged. And so it went, and so it still goes.

Diversity and Doubt

Everything after about 1650 falls under the category of "Modern" history, which may properly be called an "Age of Diversity and Doubt." Conflicting interpretations continued to spawn competing beliefs, practices, and institutions, a process that served to relativize religious doctrines and to place final authority in the hands of the individual. In addition, a whole new way of seeing and explaining the world arose to challenge the very worldview upon which the Christian scriptures were based. The Modern Age, then, is a time during which Christianity has had to respond creatively—and sometimes merely react defensively—to serious internal and external challenges to its authority and its integrity.

The foundations of the Modern Period are many, and their interactions complicated. Socially and economically, the late Middle Ages and the Renaissance-Reformation Periods saw the collapse of feudalism as a viable social structure, the rise of money-based (as opposed to land-based) economies, and the emergence of a recognizable "middle class" between peasants and nobility. Politically, the Modern Period saw the weakening and crumbling of European monarchies, as well as the end of the uneasy thousand-year alliance of ecclesiastical and secular power known as the Holy Roman Empire. The rapid growth of technology in the fifteenth century continued into the Modern Period, especially with regard to communications and travel, both of which effectively shrank the world and made people aware of other cultures' beliefs and viewpoints. This was the first step toward pluralism, that is, the relatively peaceful coexistence of various divergent opinions about life, human nature, Ultimate Reality, etc. Ironically, even Christian missionary efforts to "convert" the world made modern Christians much more aware of other faiths and much less absolutely certain that their own was the only right one. Finally, the gradual removal of education from control of the Church and the resulting rise of separate and independent spheres of learning and expertise—for example, science, humanities, medicine, and law, each with its own methodologies and claims to authority—contributed further to the general sense of uncertainty and malaise.

Perhaps the most important movement in shaping the Modern Period was the Enlightenment, for it produced the secularized (or de-sacralized) worldview that prevails today. In many ways, the Enlightenment was a seventeenth- and eighteenth-century continuation of the philosophical and scientific components of the Renaissance. Historians call these two centuries "the Age of Reason," for they were a time of intellectual revolution based on an extraordinary confidence in the powers of the human mind to understand reality and discern truth.

There were many contributors to this movement, but three deserve special mention. First, Sir Isaac Newton virtually created the modern science of physics with his view that the universe was as lawful and predictable as a machine. Francis Bacon established perhaps the cardinal principle of modern science when he insisted that real truth could only be obtained inductively, that is, by starting with data and a hypothesis, and working gradually "upward" through theses and theories. Finally, John Locke provided the classic formulation of the philosophy of empiricism—that "there is nothing in the mind that is not first in the senses," a view that dictated that the sort of evidence that was most trustworthy was that which could be experienced by the senses—which meant, of course, mostly matter and its "machinations."

What resulted from the work of these thinkers and their like was a *worldview*—a framework through which reality could be understood a bit at a time. That worldview was and is materialistic and mechanistic: it regards the universe as a machine in motion, operating with regularity and predictability, and as basically matter, its movements, and its effects. The task fell to other seminal theorists as successors of Newton, Bacon, and Locke to apply the revolution in thought to other fields: Hume in historiography, Marx in socio-econo-politics, Darwin in biology, and Freud in psychology. And apply them they did, with the result that virtually no aspect of learning or life remained untouched by this new way of seeing and understanding—including spirituality and religion.

What all of these great minds shared was a commitment to a secularized (that is, "this worldly") view of reality that was obviously challenging, if not out-and-out frightening, to Christianity. It was irrepressibly naturalistic: things formerly identified as "supernatural"—literally, "above nature"—were beyond the purview of the senses, thus not subject to empirical verification as "real" in any scientific sense, and therefore not trustworthy. That, of course, included such things as souls, spirits, angels, heaven, and—last but not least—God. The truths that the Church claimed about such things had not been derived inductively, but "from above," through revelation. They were therefore suspect. Finally, the mechanistic view of the universe seemed to belie Providence by leaving God nothing to do except perhaps to intervene now and then with a miracle. But even these interruptions of the natural processes were rendered much less credible in a worldview that had the universe operating "on automatic pilot," in accordance with rational principles that could be empirically verified, and in patterns that appeared regular and inviolable.

The most extreme Christian reactions to this new worldview were, in historical order, Liberalism and Fundamentalism. Liberalism (or Modernism) began in a formal sense in the nineteenth century. From the outset it largely accepted the methods and findings of the emerging worldview, and determined to interpret and rethink the doctrines and even the scriptures of the faith accordingly, adjusting or rejecting them whenever necessary. Fundamentalism, which emerged in earnest in the second and third decades of the twentieth century, took the opposite tack. Perceiving the new worldview as essentially incompatible with Christianity, it chose the Bible over science and faith over intellect. The vast majority of Christians, however, probably fell neatly into neither camp, but either ignored the dissonance between their modern worldview and that of their Bibles, or compartmentalized their religion and isolated it from their everyday view of the world and its processes.

Institutionally, the modern Church continued the disintegration begun in the Reformation—a trend now exacerbated by the post-Enlightenment intellectual divisions just mentioned. In chapter 7 some sense will be made of the plethora of Christian churches that resulted. Suffice it to say for now that the history of Christianity in modern times has shaken out into four largely distinct streams: Roman Catholicism, Ethnic Christianity (mainly the various brands of Eastern Orthodoxy), Protestantism, and Sectarianism. Not surprisingly, each of these has produced its own distinctive view of Jesus Christ, his person and purpose.

The Christological Era

Each of the periods of Christian history—Ancient, Medieval, Renaissance-Reformation, and Modern—is enormously interesting in its own right; and all of them have contributed to the ongoing process of Christianity's steady growth and evolution. But the Ancient Period was definitive in that it fixed the terms in which all other ages would see Jesus and define their faith in him as the Christ. This first era established the Christian core tradition to which every subsequent generation of believers has appealed, and upon which they have striven, with varying degrees of success, to build their beliefs. In particular, it is during this Ancient period that Christianity's "official" or "orthodox" view of Christ was formulated. This formative era, which we have already called an Age of Definition and Dissemination, and which we may now dub "The Christological Era," merits a much closer look.

The Christ "Cult" and an Active Apostle

For almost the first three centuries of its existence, Christianity was an illegal movement—seen as a renegade sect of Judaism at best, and at worst as what many today would dismiss as a "cult" (in the most negative sense of that word). Some of the charges against it were based on rumor and half-truths: Christians were called incest-mongers and cannibals, for example, because they loved their brothers and sisters and ritualistically ate flesh and drank blood. But mostly the Romans charged the earliest Christians with atheism because they would not acknowledge Caesar as divine, a refusal that besides being blasphemous was also unpatriotic and inherently seditious. Christians, however, were not uniformly prosecuted or persecuted during these years: emperors like Nero and Domitian in the middle and late first century were much worse than others. Many regional governors, in fact, adopted the policy of ignoring Christians unless they caused trouble—the ancient equivalent of "Don't ask, don't tell." Still, Christians had to remain "in the closet" for the most part, and congregations developed and grew slowly in small and relatively isolated communities around the Mediterranean.

The fact that there were Christian communities around the Mediterranean at all is due to the extraordinary missionary activities of the first

Christian apostles. (Remember, an "apostle" is simply a disciple commissioned to spread the good news.) The best known of these apostles, of course, was Paul of Tarsus, who flourished in the 40s and 50s CE and died in or about 64. He was important on two counts. First, he was the original theologian of Christianity, because in his epistles (letters) he provided the definitive explanations of both the human condition and Jesus' saving work that would become touchstones of the faith. Indeed, the doctrines of the Incarnation and the Atonement, which are the heart of the Christian religion (and both of which will be covered later), are traceable not to Jesus' teachings about the kingdom of God, but to the subsequent teachings of Paul about Jesus-as-the-Christ.

Perhaps of equally great importance was what Paul did to extend an emerging Christianity into the gentile world. Whereas Jesus never took his own ministry outside of his Palestinian homeland, Paul traveled all over the Mediterranean region, founding churches and nurturing and cultivating them through various crises by means of a pastoral correspondence, some of which survives in the New Testament as the "Pauline Epistles." As the book of Acts records, he also fought for "gentile rights" within the nascent Christian movement—for example, for the freedom of non-Jewish males to become Christian without first undergoing the Jewish ritual of circumcision.

Paul is such a towering figure on the landscape of these early years that it can be argued (as it was in chapter 3) that he is the true founder of Christianity as a religion about Jesus. The irony in this, of course, is that he not only had never been a follower of Jesus, he had never even seen him—except in an alleged resurrection appearance. In fact, he had actually been a persecutor of Christians on behalf of his own first-century Jewish community. But had it not been for Paul or someone very much like him, Christianity would undoubtedly have remained a localized Palestinian Jewish sect—and probably not for very long at that.

The type of organization that Paul founded and nurtured in the isolated communities of the primitive Church was what is often called "charismatic." This does not mean that everyone spoke in tongues or healed or prophesied—though many probably did—but that leadership and participation depended not on ordination or specialized training, but on whatever gifts the various members exhibited. In fact, there were no formal clerical offices at first. Some individuals were called "bishops" or "overseers," others were "presbyters" or "priests," and still others were "deacons" or "servers"; but these offices were not arranged into a hierarchy, nor were those who held them distinguished from laity as clergy.

Practices among the many congregations were understandably non-standardized under these circumstances, yet were remarkably similar. Baptism was widely practiced, and rather early on was done "in the name of the Father, the Son, and the Holy Spirit," though there was as yet no formulated doctrine of the Trinity. Shared meals were common and, though as yet not highly formalized or ritualized, always harkened back to Jesus' last meal with his disciples and recalled his words as recorded by Paul or one of the gospel writers. Christians built no buildings, and "church" still meant primarily "assembly" or "congregation" and connoted neither a special place of worship nor an institution. Even to call churches in this period "organizations" would be a stretch of that term.

The First Formulators and the Shifting Situation

The first theologians of Christianity (besides the writers of the New Testament) were the so-called Apostolic Fathers of the late first and early second centuries CE, eight of whose works survive, two of which (Clement of Rome and Barnabas) almost made it into the Christian canon. Though mostly concerned with practical matters like holiness, ethics, and church discipline, some of them dealt with such theological issues as Christ, resurrection, and the role of the Mosaic Law in the Christian life. One of them, Ignatius of Antioch, also fired the first salvos against Gnosticism and Docetism. Their successors were the Apologists (that is, "Defenders") of the mid-to-late second century, the greatest of them all being Justin Martyr, who died in 150 CE. These were essentially philosophers who were intent on explaining their beliefs to non-Christians in categories drawn from such Greek luminaries as Plato. In so doing, they established the pattern of blending, in effect, Jerusalem and Athens that would dominate Christian thought to modern times.

After the Apologists came a slew of "Greek and Latin Fathers," so called because of the languages in which they wrote. They were from all over the Mediterranean, but a disproportionately high number were African—especially Tunisian and Egyptian. For example, both Tertullian (c. 200 CE), who first coined the term "Trinity" and Augustine of Hippo (c. 400 CE), arguably the most influential theologian in the history of Christianity except for Paul, were residents of North Africa (and wrote in Latin). Equally influential early on were Tertullian's contemporaries, Clement and Origen, both of Alexandria (and both writers in Greek). The rest of the post-Apostolic Fathers were scattered around the Mediterranean and covered the full range of theological topics, but particularly issues surrounding Christology and the Trinity, and always in Greek philosophical terms.

Two things in this Ancient Period changed everything and ensured the survival of Christianity if not its health. The first was a "non-event": the failure of Jesus to return as Paul and probably most Christians of the first generation or two expected. This meant that steps had to be taken to guarantee that future generations would have access to the words and deeds of Jesus. It was undoubtedly this motivation that led to the composing of the canonical gospels in the last three decades of the first century, by which time there were few if any surviving eye-witnesses to Jesus, or even disciples of eye-witnesses. The non-occurrence of the *parousia* (that is, second coming) also led to the urge to define and protect the faith, so that it could be passed on to the future generations that apparently would be arising after all.

The second important "happening" in this period—and this really *was* an event—was the Edict of Toleration (or Edict of Milan) issued by the Emperor Constantine in 313 CE as a result of his own conversion to Christianity (which is itself an interesting story, but too long to relate here). This proclamation gave Christians the opportunity to come out of hiding, and to share and spread their gospel of salvation openly. Their efforts were helped,

4

of course, by the fact that Christianity was no longer a despised cult and membership no longer entailed the threat of persecution. Quite the contrary: now it was the Emperor's religion of choice, and thus not merely a safe option, but indeed a very attractive one.

Undoubtedly, after the legalization of the faith a great many people became Christians for all the wrong reasons. It was only natural, for example, for the emperor's religion of choice to be attractive and appealing for political reasons, and even trendy. In addition, as Christianity became more and more identified with the Roman Empire, and late in the fourth century was made its official religion, the faith became an integral part of the process of conquest as the Empire expanded and defeated the many tribes of Europe, such as the Goths, the Franks, and the Celts. Christianity now grew by leaps and bounds and spread throughout the empire as fast as the Roman army could conquer neighboring peoples. The challenge to "convert or die" added many more nominal "Christians" who only half-heartedly embraced the faith and, to make matters worse, only vaguely understood it.

It is no wonder, then, that some have called Constantine's conversion "a mixed blessing" for the Christian faith. With its ranks swollen by those who were becoming Christians either to curry favor with the Emperor or merely to escape the sword of the conquering Roman army, the Church obviously became watered down with less than devout adherents. To embrace the faith now no longer required real conviction or true commitment, much less courage in the face of persecution. (Not coincidentally, with the end of martyrdom came the rise of monasticism as a kind of voluntary reinstatement of rigor to the faith.) There was, however, a positive effect of the Edict of Toleration: it gave Christians the freedom and leisure to meet openly and to contact and convene with their brothers and sisters from other cities.

But even this benefit had its down side. For when Christians did move beyond their former enforced isolation, they found out just how much disagreement there was among them and began to dispute their differences. They found significant disagreement on many things, ranging from which scriptures were to be considered sacred to how Jesus Christ should best be understood. In order to settle these things, they met in the first great Ecumenical Councils—"Ecumenical" meaning here simply "including congregations from all over the Empire." These councils, and especially the Council of Nicea in 325 and the Council of Chalcedon in 451, produced the major decisions and the historic creeds that have shaped orthodox Christianity to the present day.

The Pauline Interpretation of Christianity

Among the first generations of Christians, beliefs were comparatively simple. The earliest, unofficial, yet widespread creed seems to have been "Jesus is Lord," with no apparent need to clarify exactly how that was the case or even what it meant. As we have seen, that declaration was already far more definitive about Jesus than he had been about himself, and went well beyond the titles that he bore during his lifetime: "rabbi" and "prophet."

A Message Perverted? A Man Promoted?

Now the Church clearly was surrendering the flesh-and-blood Jesus of history and casting its lot with the Christ of faith, that is, the object of Christian devotion and doctrine. The most obvious and serious ramification of this exchange is that the early Church thus turned the proclaimer of God's reign into the proclaimed redeemer: the iconoclast became an icon, the social deviant, a savior.

A clear indication of this change of focus is that both the early Church and the later Roman Catholic Church quite freely and easily applied to Jesus the very titles that he had avoided claiming for himself, and with some distinctive new spins. In addition to calling him "Lord," for example, they quite readily proclaimed him "Messiah" (or "Christ," the Greek equivalent), despite the fact that he had fulfilled neither the political nor the nationalistic expectations that had been basic to the job description for that office ever since the Jews had conceived it. Likewise, Christians called him "Son of God" in a unique and exclusive sense, despite the fact that he had taught that all people should see themselves as sons and daughters of their heavenly Father. Eventually they even came to call Jesus "God," a title that he not only never claimed, but—even as a radical Jew—would have avoided at all costs.

A number of scholars have detected and described a clear process by which the gospel writers retrospectively awarded Jesus successive promotions in divine rank. The earliest gospel, Mark, suggests that Jesus' sonship dated from his baptism, as a kind of adoption by God; a decade or so later, Matthew and Luke push it back to Jesus' conception; and later still, the Gospel of John begins by placing it before creation ("In the beginning there was the divine word and wisdom . . . " John 1:1). But whether or not Jesus was systematically elevated in the faith of his followers, it is certain that he was interpreted variously and finally defined in Greek philosophical terms that, as we have seen, he himself would neither have understood nor appreciated, much less endorsed.

Certainly the most influential person in the process of defining Jesus as the Christ was none other than Paul, who (as we observed in chapter 3) had never known the historical Jesus, and whose writings show little knowledge of, or for that matter interest in, either the life of Jesus or his message. Paul makes no mention of events in the ministry of Jesus and never cites his teachings, though some scholars believe they have found a few echoes of these in several of Paul's writings. But in the little he does say about Jesus' life, he reveals a disproportionate interest in its culmination: of the twenty-one verses from his writings cited in the previous chapter as referring to Jesus' life, more than three-quarters of them have to do with the events immediately surrounding his death and resurrection. Apparently these were the only reports about the earthly Jesus that interested Paul.

Jesus' focal reign of God theme and the parables and miracles that symbolized it simply disappear in the teachings of Paul. In their place, and forming the heart of Paul's message, is the resurrected, ascended, and exalted

"Lord Jesus Christ," who is "Son of God" in a unique sense. The terms that Paul and most of the early Church adopted during this period for defining Jesus as the Christ were—some would say "unfortunately"—derived from Greek culture rather than Jesus' own Semitic milieu. In large part, that shift probably reflects Paul's "turn to the gentiles" (Acts 13:46) in his missionary activities. But whatever the motive, it is certain that terms like "Christ" and "Lord" and "Son of God," drawn originally from a Jewish context, now took on new philosophical and religious connotations; and that, for better or for worse, these have survived in form if not in precise meaning into the modern era. The simple truth is that most modern Christians use those titles for Jesus Christ with no historical sense of or concern for their original meanings.

Conceiving a Christ, But Losing a Life

Two passages from the Pauline corpus reveal the character of Paul's Christology (his understanding or doctrine of Christ). The first is from the letter to the Colossians, which is widely regarded as pseudonymous, that is, written by one of his colleagues or followers, but made to sound authentic and probably reflective of Paul's views:

> He is the image of the invisible God, the first-born of all creation; for in him all things in heaven and on earth were created, things visible and invisible, whether thrones or dominions or rulers or powers— all things have been created through him and for him. He himself is before all things, and in him all things hold together. He is the head of the body, the church; he is the beginning, the first-born from the dead, so that he might come to have first place in everything. For in him all the fullness of God was pleased to dwell, and through him God was pleased to reconcile to himself all things, whether on earth or in heaven, by making peace through the blood of his cross (Col 1:15–20).

Here we see articulated by one of his followers two pillars of Paul's Christology. First, Paul regards Jesus as the image and embodiment of God's eternal fullness, in whom all things were created and through whom all creation "hangs together"—language and doctrine that is certainly resonant with the opening verses of the Gospel of John cited earlier. Elsewhere, Paul calls Christ "the image of God" (2 Cor 4:4). None of this, of course, resembles anything in the Synoptic teachings of Jesus that proclaim the reign of God. Second, with respect to what Jesus accomplished, Paul's answer is that his sacrificial death brought reconciliation and peace (a theme elaborated in Rom 3:24–26). Jesus' role as a teacher, it seems, was unimportant.

A second passage revealing Paul's "high"—some would say "ethereal" or "esoteric"—Christology is in his letter to the Philippians (which is regarded as authentically Paul's):

> Let the same mind be in you that was in Christ Jesus,
> who, though he was in the form of God,
> did not regard equality with God

as something to be exploited,
but emptied himself, taking the form of a slave,
being born in human likeness.
And being found in human form,
he humbled himself
and became obedient to the point of death—
even death on a cross.
Therefore God also highly exalted him
and gave him the name
that is above every name,
so that at the name of Jesus
every knee should bend,
in heaven and on earth and under the earth,
and every tongue should confess
that Jesus Christ is Lord,
to the glory of God the Father (2:5–11).

This passage is very revealing with respect to Paul's view of Christ. First of all, it is obvious that here again we are dealing with an eternal being "in the form of God," who "empties himself" in a process often referred to by the Greek term *kenosis* (literally, "self-emptying") in order to take on "human form" and to be "born in human likeness." Second, we see in this Christ not only an exalted object of worship but one of cosmic proportions.

Such language hardly suggests a real flesh-and-blood human being; nor was it meant to. Indeed, it implies the very same divine masquerade that the later Christological councils and creeds tried to avoid when they declared Jesus "truly human" (in Latin, *vere homo*). Thanks largely to Paul, that humanity has proven persistently elusive in traditional Christianity.

In these passages, and indeed throughout his letters, Paul makes it clear that he views Jesus Christ, not as an historical human being, but as a universal spiritual entity. Interestingly, Paul uses the title "Christ" in his letters far more than he uses the proper name of Jesus, perhaps further indicating his minimal interest in the historical person. Even more intriguing is the fact that in two passages (Rom 13:14 and Gal 3:27) Paul can even speak of Christians "putting on" Christ—the Greek verb literally means "to clothe"—which not only makes "Christ" sound like an impersonal quality, but actually seems to treat it as a kind of *costume*. Such imagery leaves us very far removed indeed from the flesh-and-blood sage of Galilee.

In any case, Paul seems to think that the whole point of Christ's having assumed human form was to make it possible for him to die, and thereupon to resume his divine status as a cosmic entity. It is for this reason that Paul can speak in rather strange terms of people being "one in Christ," in a way that no Roman would have ever imagined using with reference to, say, an emperor. ("We are one in Caesar Augustus"? Unthinkable!) It is also because of the dominance of the impersonal-eternal-cosmic Christ imagery that Paul can all but ignore whatever reports of Jesus' life and teachings that may have been available to him—and that the gospel writers take such pains to include.

4

The
Christ of
Faith in the
History of
Christianity

Paul's view of the person and redemptive "work" of Christ (to use the traditional term) made such an enormous impact upon early Christianity that it prevails today. Most Christians, for example, attend churches that use the ancient creeds—either the Apostles' or Nicene or both. Few of the faithful, I suspect, notice that these Creeds say virtually nothing about the ministry and teachings of Jesus. (See figure 4.2.) The Apostles' Creed says that Jesus was "conceived by the Holy Spirit, born of the Virgin Mary, suffered under Pontius Pilate, was crucified, dead, and buried." The Nicene Creed says that he "was made man, and was crucified also for us under Pontius Pilate; he suffered and was buried." Why is there no mention of Jesus' actual life? Why is there so sudden a leap from his miraculous birth to the events surrounding his death? Why is there no mention of his teaching and its central theme, the immediate domain of God, or of the miracles that for Jesus and the gospel writers signaled its presence?

A Life Lost?

Here is what the two most venerable and widely used Christian Creeds have to say about Jesus as the Christ:

From the Apostles' Creed (6th or 7th century CE)

I believe in . . . Jesus Christ his only Son our Lord: who was conceived by the Holy Ghost, born of the Virgin Mary; suffered under Pontius Pilate, was crucified, dead, and buried; he descended into hell; the third day he rose again from the dead; he ascended into heaven, and sitteth on the right hand of God the Father Almighty; from thence he shall come to judge the quick and the dead.

From The Nicene Creed (4th century CE)

I believe . . . in one Lord Jesus Christ, the only begotten Son of God: begotten of his Father before all worlds, God of God, Light of Light, very God of very God; begotten, not made, being of one substance with the Father; by whom all things were made: who for us men [sic] and for our salvation came down from heaven, and was incarnate by the Holy Ghost of the Virgin Mary, and was made man [sic]; and was crucified also for us under Pontius Pilate; He suffered and was buried; and the third day he rose again according to the Scriptures, and ascended into heaven, and sitteth at the right hand of the Father; and he shall come again with glory, to judge the quick and the dead; whose kingdom shall have no end.

Notice how quickly—instantaneously, in fact—both creeds move from the conception and birth of Jesus to his trial and death. Their apparent disinterest in earthly life of the pivotal person of the faith reflects Paul's own focus and, owing to Paul's enormous influence, that of the faith itself.

FIGURE 4.2

The answer is that these things simply didn't matter to Paul; and since they didn't matter to Paul, they haven't mattered to traditional Christianity either. Some would add: "And that's too bad." Some Christians might like to be in a congregation that affirmed their faith by saying "We believe in the reign of God, and in the love, equality, justice, and peace for which it stands; and in Jesus, who proclaimed, and enacted, and embodied its spirit, and taught us all to live as God's children, and to help the poor and helpless and hopeless; and who died because the world was not ready for his message." But those items, seemingly so germane to the message and person of Jesus, were not central to Paul's faith, and therefore have been marginal doctrinal concerns for most mainline Christian denominations—and presumably their members—ever since.

When the early Church set about the task of further defining Jesus as the Christ, it was in Paul's terms rather than those of Jesus himself. And, unlike Jesus, Paul had been intentional about reaching out beyond his own geographical homeland and ethnic group. Paul wanted to take his version of the gospel to the far-flung gentile world. Traditional Christianity quickly adopted this program, and thenceforth became increasingly Hellenized (that is, "Greekified"), and commensurably less Jewish, in its beliefs and doctrines.

Later Christological Debates and Doctrines

The increasing ethnic and doctrinal diversity fostered in the Christian community as a result of the missions of Paul and others was not a problem while the faith was illegal and fighting for its existence in relatively isolated, underground communities. Once liberated by Constantine's Edict of Toleration, however, the congregations were forced to recognize that not all of them viewed or practiced the faith in the same way. Thus, with the external threat removed, Christians found themselves vulnerable to internal dissension and compelled to clarify and unify their views over against what they perceived to be internal misrepresentations of faith in Christ. The results were doctrinal disputes, and eventually councils and creeds.

Perhaps the most crucial of the early controversies among Christians were Christological. The first concerned Jesus' identity with respect to God. The second focused on his personal constitution—that is, exactly what sort of entity he was. These two pivotal issues, though different, proved to be quite interrelated and complicated, and no small challenge to resolve.

Defining Divinity

The first bone of contention was Jesus' relation to God, or, more precisely, the Son of God's (or, in later Trinitarian language, God the Son's) relationship to God the Father. (There was no doctrine of the Trinity yet, so the place of the Holy Spirit in all of this was not yet an issue.) The debate was complicated, and it was framed in (what else?) Greek philosophical terms. But the issue finally came down to whether the Son was of the *same* divine "substance" or "essence" (Greek, *ousia*) as the Father, or of a merely *similar* substance. In Greek the debate hung on a single letter of the alphabet: *homoousios* versus *homoiousios*.

The matter was finally decided at the Council of Nicea in 325 CE, with the assertion that the Son was of the very *same* substance as the Father. That meant that Jesus, as the enfleshment of this fully and coequally divine Son, had in effect been God himself. As we have seen, that is something that far exceeds anything the historical Jesus would have claimed, accepted, or even understood.

Defending Divinity, Holding Onto Humanity

The second important Christological question that had to be addressed in this period was how this asserted divinity of Jesus related to his apparent humanity. On this issue there was wide divergence, producing a spectrum of subtly distinct views. Fortunately, all of them can be placed in two basic categories: those that emphasized the humanity of Jesus Christ, and those that stressed his divinity.

The early "Ebionite" Christians exhibit the classical expression of the first of these options. Since their background was Jewish, they were very down-to-earth, pragmatic thinkers, more comfortable with stories and proverbs, scriptural interpretation and ethics, than with lofty abstractions of the Greek metaphysical variety. Accordingly, they saw Jesus as so completely a human prophet, teacher, and moral example that "divinity," if they used the term at all, would have had the sense of "inspired or appointed by God."

At the other end of the spectrum were the Gnostic Christians. They were far more oriented to Greek philosophy than the Ebionites, with the result that they saw Jesus as a divine redeemer whose humanity was at best incidental, and at worst an illusion. Indeed, on the far right wing of these Gnostics were "docetists," who actually denied the humanity of Jesus, claiming that he was God in disguise and only appeared to be a man. ("Docetism" comes from the Greek word *doket*, "he seems.") They also rankled Ebionites *and* mainstream Christians by contending that there really was no genuine suffering on the cross, since God couldn't possible suffer—that it was all an act or a ruse.

The Jewish-Ebionite Christian view of Christ became dominant in the next two centuries or so in the important Christian center of Antioch in Syria, perhaps because the semitic mindset prevailed there. The Gnostic-Docetic orientation flourished in the Coptic Christian capital of Alexandria, Egypt, where Greek philosophy was treasured and taught. What would gradually emerge as orthodox Christian thinking about Christ was a fusion of these two dramatically opposed views.

A Delicate Doctrinal Balance Beam

After generations of controversy over these two basic positions and all of the shadings in between, a debate fueled by a good measure of regional and party politics, the Council of Chalcedon in 451 CE finally produced a compromise formula that ever after would define who Jesus was. They concluded that he was fully human and totally divine: two complete natures were united (but not commingled) in the one single person. That 2-in-1 formula said, in effect, that Jesus as the Christ is to be regarded as one-hundred percent human *and* one-hundred percent divine—an unprecedented fullness virtually impossible to comprehend and an equilibrium equally impossible to maintain or, for that matter, to explain.

What Chalcedon created, in effect, was a Christological balance beam—or perhaps more accurately, a tight-rope—which required the believer to walk a very narrow and precarious doctrinal line. In retrospect, its subtlety practically made it inevitable that later Christians, theorists and simple believers alike, would lose their doctrinal balance and fall from orthodoxy in one direction or the other—toward an emphasis on either the humanity or the divinity of Christ. Two things above all have resulted from this delicately finessed, compromise affirmation of the dual nature of Jesus as the Christ. The first is the plethora of images of him generated over the subsequent ages. The second is a great deal of vagueness, confusion, and even outright heresy among modern Christians.

Jesus Christ Through the Ages

The claim of the anonymous author of the New Testament Epistle to the Hebrews that "Jesus Christ is the same yesterday and today and forever" (13:8) may be true in some abstract metaphysical sense, but from an historian's perspective it is demonstrably false. For as many modern scholars have shown, every age has conceived and portrayed Jesus Christ differently, more often than not in its own image, so as to reflect its own values and meet its own needs.

A Chameleon Christ?

What is most striking about these images is not only their variety, but the diametric contrasts that they often display, and that commonly recapitulate the ancient human-versus-divine controversy already noted. Some, for example, have emphasized Christ's image as the ideal human and others have regarded him as the perfect image and embodiment of God. Some have seen Jesus the Christ in his own historical context as a Jewish rabbi, albeit one with an extraordinary authority and familiarity with God; while others have seen him as the enfleshment of the eternal Logos—the divine principle responsible for the creation and the ongoing order and process of the cosmos. Monks have seen in him an embodiment of humility and ascetic self-denial, while motivators have imagined him as a great model of worldly success. Mystics have seen in him a lover and bridegroom (often in highly erotic terms), while celibates extolled him as the exemplar of the chaste life. Crusaders and conquistadors have seen him as a militant and triumphal soldier—like the "royal Master" who leads Christian legions against their foes in a popular modern hymn—while pacifists have revered him as the "Prince of Peace." Monarchs and their ecclesiastical supporters have portrayed him as a regal "Pancrator," the almighty, divine ruler of the universe, while their down-trodden and oppressed subjects and parishioners have related to him as a fellow sufferer of imperial injustice and the exigencies of life. Enlightenment rationalists of the eighteenth century downplayed Jesus Christ's divinity and saw in him a simple, if sublime, ethical teacher, while their Romantic successors saw in him a mystical poet of the spirit. Capitalists

127

have seen him as the model of the self-made entrepreneur, as well as a bastion and defender of the *status quo*; Marxists have seen him as an opponent of the profit-motive and proponent of social egalitarianism, justice, liberation, and even revolution.

In light of such contrasting views, it is easy to see Jesus Christ not as "the same yesterday, today, and forever," but rather as "all things to all people." Clearly he has been molded to fit the spirit of each successive age and the predilections of many different people—a sort of symbolic mirror in which each individual or group or society sees a self-reflection or an idealized self-image. (See figure 4.3.) The question remains whether this seemingly "chameleon Christ" still has any value today in the human search for self-identity and meaning.

Jesus Christ in Modern Belief

As we have seen, the definitive ancient Chalcedonian doctrinal formula about the person of Jesus Christ was a compromise between the views of two Christian factions. It declared that this one person had embodied two natures, human and divine, and formulated that conclusion in abstruse terms that few today can begin to understand.

The truth is that most modern Christians have no idea precisely what such official pronouncements about Jesus Christ say, much less what they

A Lost Incident from the Life of Jesus?

(found miraculously preserved on a restroom wall at a very fancy Ivy League college)

And Jesus turned to his disciples and asked of them, "Who do people say I am?"

And they answered and said unto him, "Some say that you are Elijah returned, others say another of the prophets, and still others claim that you are the Christ, the Son of the living God."

"And who do you say that I am?" he asked.

And they replied, "You are the eschatological manifestation of the Ground of Being, the incarnation of the divine Logos in whom we find our ultimate meaning and *raison d'etre* over against the *Angst* and alienation caused by the existential predicaments and uncertainties that plague human life."

And Jesus said, "Huh?"

FIGURE 4.3

mean, but simply harbor the vaguest notion that he was *somehow* both human and divine. A Christological survey of Christians today, however, would probably show that the majority take the divinity of Jesus Christ more seriously than his humanity. In their minds, at least, his divinity supercedes—or overwhelms—his humanity.

My experience in talking to both college students and churchgoers (and sometimes even churchgoing students) suggests that, like Christians in general, they tend to fall off the balance beam of Christological orthodoxy in one of two directions. A minority among the faithful view Jesus as strictly human—a great teacher perhaps, or an example to be followed—with "divinity" watered down to a kind of exceptional saintliness or righteousness. Most who identify themselves as Christians, however, emphasize his divinity to such an extent that his humanity gets severely compromised or swallowed up altogether by piety and sentimentality.

This latter tendency is reflected in a good many Christian hymns, including the popular Christmas carol that has the baby Jesus (already "the little Lord") in the manger, being awakened by some noisy cows, and yet "no crying he makes." What sort of healthy human baby wouldn't cry if startled awake? A better question is: what sort of human religious sentiment cannot abide a crying, much less diaper-dirtying, baby Jesus? (What did we think those "swaddling clothes" were for, anyway?) One old Bible-belt Southern hymn actually says: "They's flies on you, and they's flies on me, but they ain't no flies on my Jesus!" Nothing could more clearly express the popular sense among Christians that Jesus was not human in the same way as everyone else.

Jesus Christ At the Movies

This tendency toward an overly divinized Jesus Christ is visible in artistic renderings of Jesus, especially in paintings. One of the most popular portraits of Jesus in this century has been "Salman's Head of Christ," which makes Jesus appear to be aloof, distracted, other worldly, and even "pretty" in a thoroughly non-human way. The polar opposite impression is given by the various versions of the "Laughing Jesus" portrait that have appeared in the past few decades, all of which depict Jesus in expressions of very-human glee, ranging from mild risibility to utter raucousness. These jolly portrayals have been received by many traditionalists, predictably, with dismay and outrage. The very idea that Jesus could have had a good belly laugh!

The same thing can be seen in cinematic portrayals of Jesus. Most of the popular movies about Jesus—such as *The Greatest Story Ever Told* (1965) and *Jesus of Nazareth* (1976)—have Jesus appearing either wooden or plastic, as though an alien being inhabiting a human body, but not quite comfortably. Jesus appears to float from scene to scene, wide-eyed and rarely blinking, and never seems to be quite "all there." Sometimes the results are utterly spooky, and sometimes downright comical. What makes the actors (or directors) play Jesus that way? It must be the power of popular piety, which tends to make Jesus into "God in a man-suit." These are obviously not movies about the historical Jesus, but portrayals of the Christ of faith—and of an overly divinized, docetic one at that.

Divinity-based popular piety was the reason for the outcry against two modern films that tried to capture the spirit of the ancient creeds: *Jesus Christ, Superstar* (1973) and *The Last Temptation of Christ* (1988). Whatever else you can say about these movies, their depictions did show a very human Jesus—a man with anxieties and anger, fears and fantasies, love and lust. One scene in *The Last Temptation* shows him casting himself to the ground with a debilitating migraine, apparently brought on by the incredible pressures of his calling. Another shows him on the cross, delirious with pain and heat-exhaustion, fantasizing about leading a normal married life, having sexual intercourse with his wife, rearing children, and living into old age.

The public outcry from conservative religious groups over such scenes was loud and long. They were incensed! Why? Because their Jesus couldn't possibly have angst or doubts or terrors or thoughts about sex. He was, after all, God! But the ancient creeds say he was also human—completely human—and how could one be completely human without such emotions and notions? Seen from another angle, how could one possibly imagine divinity and humanity converging in one human being without causing serious psychological turmoil and anguish, and perhaps a headache or two?

The reason that such portrayals of Jesus offend so many so deeply is precisely that popular Christian piety tends to lean in the Gnostic direction. Irrespective of the ancient creeds or the Jesus of the synoptic gospels, both of which clearly attest the reality of his humanity, people gravitate toward a docetic view of Christ that emphasizes his divinity to the virtual exclusion of his humanity. That preference may account for why John's gospel seems to be more often quoted than the others, including on end-zone placards! (As noted in the previous chapter, the Jesus of John's gospel is already somewhat docetic.) Those so inclined are far happier with the more sentimentalized and ethereal portrayals of Jesus found in the movies mentioned earlier. *Superstar* and *Last Temptation* simply tilt uncomfortably in the direction of the humanity of Jesus Christ.

Yet, if truth be known, even such movies as these are not really dealing with the historical Jesus. While emphasizing the humanity of the Christ in painting or film or fiction may be a step toward recapturing the historical Jesus, the latter can be truly encountered only through sound historical-critical research focused primarily upon the ancient gospels, something that movie-makers rarely do.

A Hollow Humanity and Continuing Conundrum

But most Christians probably are not really interested in the historical Jesus, having opted long ago for their preferred semi-human but fully divine Christ. Of course, by ancient and medieval standards, that choice amounts to a *heresy* (the Greek root of which literally means "choice"). And once that particular choice has been made, the theological quicksand deepens perilously. What inevitably happens is that the residual humanity that Christians intuitively know they still must account for is turned into a hollow container for Christ's divinity. Well-meaning Sunday school teachers, most of whom lack formal training in theology or the history of doctrine, reinforce this image when they explain to their equally uninformed students that

Jesus was human in body, but his soul was divine: that he was human on the "outside," but divine on the "inside." In fact, such a view is, historically speaking, a heresy, and one for which these teachers—and any students led astray by them—would have been painfully tortured and executed by an Inquisition not so many centuries ago.

For reasons that should be obvious, orthodox Christianity has never taught that Jesus was human without and divine within. An authentic human being is more than just a physical body; a real human being has an inner dynamic, which religions tend to call the "soul" or "spirit." Without a human soul or spirit, however you conceive these, a person could not be fully human. (Just ask any kid who has seen body-snatchers and zombies in science fiction and horror movies.) If Jesus had been merely a deity "wearing" human flesh, he would not have been a real individual, but a half-man, half-God, "neither fish nor fowl," neither this nor that—what medieval philosophers called a *tertium quid* ("a third something-or-other"). In other words, if one doesn't start with a completely human Jesus and *then* talk about his full divinity, one is already "off the track" as far as the ancient creeds about the person of Jesus Christ are concerned.

Nor should such "deviants" be faulted much on this score. In a sense, the Chalcedonian formula that tried to bring together divinity and humanity was doomed to failure—at least at the popular level, and at least as long as these qualities are conceived (as theists must) as mutually exclusive and discontinuous. A professional theologian or philosopher of religion might be able to employ abstract concepts and arcane terminology to hold divinity and humanity together in perfect balance (though I cannot think of one who has actually managed to). For laypeople, however, it seems inevitable that divinity, when juxtaposed with an equal portion of humanity, will overshadow it in their imaginations—in much the same way that a quarter will always be heavier (not to mention more valuable) than a nickel, despite the fact that they are equal in number. Similarly, even if divinity and humanity are allotted equal portions, given the qualitative superiority of the former, it will inevitably overwhelm the latter.

What is a modern Christian to do? How is one to make sense of this ancient notion of "divinity," and balance it with what we understand today as "humanity"? Is there any way to make Jesus-as-the-Christ not only intelligible, but also inspiring?

In light of the inherent difficulty of the traditional Christological claim that Jesus was of two natures, human and divine, and in the face of all of the many and varied images of Jesus Christ produced throughout the ages, and given the modern confusion about him, some would argue that the best corrective would be to attempt to recover the historical Jesus discussed in the previous chapter, or to pay more attention to the work of those scholars who are striving to do so. For, the argument might run, only in the historical Jesus will modern Christians find the humanity that might restore the Christological balance that the Christian faith seems to demand.

There are major problems with that stance. The first is that the most recent quests for the historical Jesus have produced little more than a sketch of who he might have been, and what he might have said and done.

As we saw in the preceding chapter, the earliest and best sources for the historical Jesus are already testimonies to a Christ of faith, however unformed and ill-defined that image may have been until Chalcedon. The second is that the "humanity" of Jesus Christ in the ancient creeds is not identical with, or to be confused with, the historical Jesus, but is rather an ideal or image of what a human being (or being human) means. Thus, even if the historical Jesus *could* be recovered with great detail and certainty, the relationship of his revealed humanity to the divinity perceived by the early and later Church would still be a problem.

Two New Christs for the Third Millennium

It seems, then, that Christianity is simply "stuck" with the idea of one man with two natures, divine and human, however that is to be formulated. At the same time, it is also quite clear that the conceptual categories used fifteen hundred years ago to reconcile those natures are no longer intelligible, much less compelling, in the modern age. How then should we proceed Christologically? How can we make sense of this man Jesus who became the object of religious belief and devotion precisely because divinity was attributed to him early? As a tentative way of proceeding, let me suggest two "working Christologies" that might begin to do justice to the divinity and humanity of Jesus Christ in a way both plausible and meaningful to modern people. The first we'll call "A Mythical Christ," and the second, "A Mystical Christ."

A Mythical Christ

In the face of how little can be recovered about the historical Jesus, it could be argued that he really has very little or nothing whatsoever to do with the Christ of faith! Some have even maintained, and quite convincingly, that the compelling image of the Christ of faith, and therefore the power of the Christian faith itself, would still remain even if it were proven that the historical Jesus had never existed.

The basis for such a seemingly outlandish claim is this: the enduring and compelling power of the Christ of faith may well reside—as it has throughout the ages—precisely in the fact that he is a mythical figure in the best sense of the word. That is, the details and unfolding of his story, factually accurate or not, simply resonate with people spiritually and affect them deeply in some salutary way. That means that many or even most of the things we saw in the previous chapter as dubious historically and factually—for example, the virginal birth and the bodily resurrection—may in fact be "real" because they point to actual qualities that human beings embody and experience in their deepest selves. Their reality might be seen as strictly psychological (in the Jungian archetypal sense), or as spiritual, or as some combination of these.

According to this interpretation, from incarnation and Bethlehem to Jerusalem and ascension, the Jesus narrative—its characters, settings, and events—represents the origin, progress, stages, and destination of our human spiritual journey. The virginal birth, for example, suggests that we are all pregnant with, and ready to give birth to, divinity; Jesus' journey toward Jerusalem and his crucifixion represent our own spiritual paths toward bliss—that for which we are willing to give our lives; and the resurrection is the affirmation that all life, spiritual and otherwise, comes out of death and that, conversely, death is never simply the end of life. Jesus Christ, then, is something like what Joseph Campbell identified as an archetypal spiritual "hero," whose journey toward realizing the inner convergence of humanity and divinity is really ours. Thus we might identify with this Christ because his quest is ours—in effect, we are he!

Such an interpretation, of course, differs radically from traditional Christian interpretation of Jesus Christ. For this mythical Christology takes individuals and events that were "back there" and "back then," not as definitive or prescriptive for the present, but as exemplars of profound and timeless truth. In any event, it would permit modern New Testament scholarship, which to some looks so very negative and destructive with respect to the historical Jesus, to be seen as an ally of faith rather than an enemy. For it would turn our spiritual attention from the shadowy and foreign first-century figure about whom we can know so precious little, to the Christ-reality that is part and parcel of the innermost human experience—from the external "letter," which scripture itself says is a killer, to the "spirit" that brings life.

A Mystical Christ

A number of writers have come forward in the past few decades to suggest another interesting rereading of Jesus Christ, a thoroughly non-traditional and curious version of the two-natures-one-person doctrine. On the one hand, it presents Jesus Christ as a human teacher; but on the other, it has him proclaiming his own and everyone else's inherent divinity. This portrait is based in large part on ancient Gnostic Christian sources, and especially the Gospel of Thomas. Discovered at Nag Hammadi, Egypt in 1945, Thomas is a collection of sayings attributed to Jesus that often depict him as a teacher of esoteric spiritual wisdom.

In one place, for example, Jesus is quoted as saying "Whoever drinks from my mouth will become like me, I myself shall become that person, and the hidden things will be revealed to him" (Thom 108). Those words sound as though they are affirming not so much Jesus' divine uniqueness as his oneness with his hearers, if only they "drink from his mouth" (that is, heed his teachings) and receive the hidden secrets therein. He is also quoted as saying:

> I am the light that is over all things.
> I am all: from me all came forth,
> and to me all attained.
> Split a piece of wood; I am there.
> Lift up the stone, and you will find me there (Thom 77).

The theology suggested by such claims is one of pantheism, panentheism, or monism—representing the divine as immanent in everyone and every-

4

The Christ of Faith in the History of Christianity

thing, profoundly uniting them—rather than a more traditional Jewish or Christian theism, which teaches that the world is distinct from the transcendent deity "above."

Even the sayings of Jesus in the gospels of the New Testament take on a new meaning when read in a Gnostic light. When Jesus says in Luke 17:21, for example, that the domain of God is within (or "amidst," or "among," or "present," depending on the translation), he could be referring to the inner divine spiritual essence that all people share by virtue of their origins. Likewise, when in John's gospel Jesus prays that his followers "should all be united, just as you, Father, are with me and I with you; may they be [one] in us . . . ," (John 17:21) he may intend for his hearers to conclude, not that he was unique in his oneness with God and his own divinity, but that they also are one with God and thus essentially divine.

Some of the ancient Gnostic Christians, as we have seen, denied the humanity of Jesus. But what is more germane for our purposes here is not what they believed about Jesus, but what they believed he had taught about humanity's relation to God. A new Gnostic Christology, then, might deviate from the old Gnosticism by affirming the complete humanity of Jesus. But it would go on to argue that his basic message about the immediacy of God's presence implied not only his divinity, but that of every person. This mystical image of the Christ would agree with the traditional, orthodox Chalcedonian formula that Jesus was totally human and totally divine, and thus with centuries of orthodox Christian belief that these two natures require reconciling. But it would depart dramatically from orthodoxy in its denial of Jesus Christ's uniqueness in that respect. Instead, he would become the "very human" teacher of the "very divinity" of himself and all humankind.

A Monistic Mutuality?

These two proposed Christologies actually have much in common. For both accomplish a plausible, and perhaps even compelling resolution of the notions of humanity and divinity that have so long been central to the Christian understanding of Jesus as the Christ. Furthermore, they both do so by rejecting the absolute distinction between humanity and divinity demanded by Christianity's traditional theistic framework, which posits God as an "Other" and "above." Both the mythical and mystical Christologies sketched above imply a deity (by whatever name) that is immanent in all people, a divinity that is in continuity rather than discontinuity with humanity. In other words, both Christologies are far more congenial with the monistic, pantheistic, or panentheistic views of God discussed in chapter 2 than with a theistic model.

Thus both the mythical and the mystical Christologies present a picture of Jesus Christ very amenable to an Eastern view of spirituality and religion. As our earlier survey of the theologies indicated, the Eastern religions do not view Ultimate Reality (what Christians would call "God") as a transcendent Other Being affecting the cosmos from above or beyond it, but more as Being Itself, an Inner Presence within all things. They therefore regard divinity not as something distinct from humanity, but as essential to it.

As suggested in chapter 3, many of the reported sayings of Jesus, both canonical and non-canonical, can be imagined as words uttered by a Hindu guru or Zen Master. Indeed, some have claimed that is precisely what Jesus was: an Oriental spiritual master. After all, Jesus is recorded as insisting that his disciples take his "yoke" upon them, and the Sanskrit-Hindu word for "yoke" is *yoga*! He told one man that he had to be "born again," which taken literally connotes reincarnation. He is supposed to have said something about loving God with heart, soul, mind, and strength, at the very least an interesting parallel to the four traditional *yogas* (disciplines) or *margas* (spiritual paths) recognized in Hinduism. Add these to the notion that the domain of God is within and the assertion of his spiritual "oneness" with "the Father," and one has at least a strong circumstantial case for Jesus as an Eastern teacher who was one with the "I AM" (*Jahweh*?) who was the "Way" (*Tao*?), the "Truth" (*Dharma*?), and the "Life" (*Ahimsa*?).

Unfortunately, the argument runs, Jesus' listeners, including his disciples, were so steeped in their own theological tradition that they misheard and misreported his meaning and intent. They therefore turned him into a savior-figure more in keeping with their monotheistic presuppositions than with his (allegedly) monistic perspective. The fact of the matter, however, is that our two compatible alternative Christologies do not depend on whether the historical Jesus really believed, taught, or represented their details or dynamics. They are, for all intents and purposes, self-validating— true if, and only if, they resonate with our human experience and illuminate and facilitate the human spiritual journey.

Whether Christianity as a whole or any particular Christian would be willing or able to "turn East" and to move in the theological direction suggested by our two alternative Christologies is an open question. As chapter 8 will show, however, such a conceptual shift is neither unthinkable nor unprecedented. It has, in fact, been effected again and again by a few radical Christian individuals and movements in virtually every generation of the faithful.

Conclusion

What every believer should know about the Christ of faith in the history of Christianity is that the traditional view of the one proclaimed "Lord and Savior" evolved over the centuries, and is only one among many possible interpretations of that focal figure. Thus, from the standpoint of the modern age, Jesus' person and teachings are by no means clear or unambiguous or open to only one interpretation. The thoughtful and informed Christian believer, then, is left with the responsibility of reading and weighing the sources in order to answer the pivotal traditional Christological questions concerning the person and work of Christ: not who he *was* and what he *did*, but who he *is* and what redeeming work he *does* on humanity's behalf.

Frustrating as it is not to have a definite, once-and-for-all answer to those questions, we are not completely at sea or wits' end in our pursuit of a livable and workable solution. The many images suggested above are a start: they may be researched and reflected upon, and tried and tested for their authenticity and adequacy in light of each individual's own understandings of God, the universe, and human nature and existence; and more than likely some of those images will emerge as more credible and viable than others.

The altogether natural but most grievous error is to turn Jesus the Christ into a mirror of ourselves, in which we see merely who we are on the surface; or a Rohrschach ink blot into which we can read all of our predispositions and prejudices, and so render him simply an idealized version of our superficial selves. There is much to be said for self-discovery and self-knowledge in such a process, I suppose; but I suspect that for any image of Christ to be truly salutary, much less redemptive, it would have to move us beyond simple self-assurance and self-satisfaction, call us into question, direct us toward our spiritual depths, and engender positive transformation and—ultimately—self-realization.

DISCUSSION QUESTIONS & EXERCISES

In order to see clearly the distinction between the historical Jesus and the Christ of faith, Robert W. Funk suggests that most Christian believers can be classified in a spectrum that contains at least four distinct divisions: (1) The JESUS PARTY makes Jesus of Nazareth the primary term in the revelatory process; knowledge of the historical Jesus does or should matter for how we define the Christian faith; faith was and is faith in Jesus himself; the focus is on the teachings of Jesus on God's domain or reign. (2) The APOSTOLIC PARTY insists that knowledge of the historical Jesus does not matter for faith—it has no real significance beyond the satisfaction of historical curiosity—it is faith in the faith of the first eyewitnesses that matters. (3) The BIBLE PARTY takes the New Testament as the final and definitive revelation of God to human beings; it is faith in the faith of those who interpret the New Testament. (4) The CREEDAL PARTY bases its claims on the decisions of the ancient councils, which it takes to be responsible for defining the orthodox faith; it is faith in the faith of those members of the institutions who are responsible for orthodox belief.

A. If you are a Christian, to which party or part of the spectrum would you see yourself as belonging or being closest to in belief? Why?

B. If you are not a Christian, to which party would you be most drawn? Why?

C. In either case (A or B), do you see any problems with (or gaps in) this list of parties or the description of them? What? How would you improve the list (that is, what party or parties might you add, delete, or redefine)?

D. What do you think about the two Christologies (mythical and mystical) suggested toward the end of this chapter, and particularly about the ways in which they deal with the humanity and divinity of Christ? Can you think of a more compelling way to deal with these two attributes of Jesus Christ? If so, describe and explain it.

RECOMMENDED READING

John Dominic Crossan. *The Birth of Christianity: Discovering What Happened in the Years Immediately After the Execution of Jesus.* San Francisco: HarperSanFrancisco, 1998.
  — an interdisciplinary study that reconstructs a picture of a primitive Christianity that was more closely associated with the historical Jesus than with Paul

4

The
Christ of
Faith in the
History of
Christianity

Justo L. Gonzalez, *Church History: An Essential Guide.* Nashville: Abingdon Press, 1996.
— a brief, but excellent historical overview, with an emphasis on institutional development, by the author of the more theologically-focused and exhaustive (3 vols.) *A History of Christian Thought* (Abingdon, 1988)

Gerd Lüdemann, *Heretics: The Other Side of Early Christianity,* transl. John Bowden. Philadelphia: Westminster John Knox Press, 1996.
— a re-examination of the earliest, and perhaps most disharmonious, era of Christianity, with a new appreciation of the suppressed heterodox stream as a more authentic expression of the intentions of Jesus than the orthodox "winners"

Jaroslav Pelikan, *The Illustrated Jesus Through the Centuries: His Place in the History of Culture.* New Haven, CT: Yale University Press, 1997.
— an adaptation of the acclaimed 1985 *Jesus Through the Centuries: His Place in the History of Culture* (Harper and Row), this volume adds artistic illustrations to reflect the changing images of Jesus in Western consciousness

Gregory J. Riley, *One Jesus, Many Christs: How Jesus Inspired Not One True Christianity, but Many.* San Francisco: HarperSanFrancisco, 1997.
— a fresh portrayal of Jesus as a classic Greco-Roman hero-martyr figure to whom the earliest Christians were drawn despite deep doctrinal disagreements about such issues as his person, divinity, ministry, and resurrection

Rodney Stark, *The Rise of Christianity: How the Obscure, Marginal Jesus Movement Became the Dominant Religious Force in the Western World in a Few Centuries.* New York: HarperCollins, 1997.
— a compelling argument, based on modern sociological data and careful historical research, that Christianity grew rapidly simply by offering people (and especially the underprivileged, women, and marginalized Jews) the promise of security and happiness

SIN AND HUMAN NATURE IN THE CHRISTIAN TRADITION

Objectives of this chapter:

- to examine various interpretations of the phrase "image of God" as applied to human nature

- to explore and compare four different theories of evil, including the one that has dominated Christian thought

- to analyze the Garden of Eden story in order to question common assumptions about what is and isn't really there

- to underscore the extraordinary influence that Paul of Tarsus and Augustine of Hippo have had on Christianity in the matter of sin

- to scrutinize in particular the origin, meaning, and significance of the ideas of "The Fall" and "Original Sin"

- to acknowledge dissonant strains of Christian thought that have ignored or downplayed the importance of sin

- to suggest the theological consequences of denying or diminishing the importance of sin

- to examine the concept of hell and its place in Christian belief and thought

- to note some troubling issues that endure in the traditional Christian view of sin and its effects

All religions have as their principal concern and primary focus Ultimate Reality. Christians worship that Reality as "God," while Hindus call it "Brahman," Buddhists refer to it as "Shunyata" or "Tathata," Taoists speak of it as "Tao" or "the Way," Muslims name it "Allah," the Oglala Sioux address it as "Wakan Tanka," and so forth. Whether these names refer, finally, to the same metaphysical entity or principle is a matter of debate, for the concepts attached to these names are diverse and often conflicting. Still, all of the major religions of the world seem to posit a belief in some such Supreme Sacred, even when they also acknowledge multiple divinities or other spiritual beings worthy of devotion.

Every religion also has a keen interest in humanity's relation to its Supreme Reality, and develops a corresponding view of human nature. Nearly all religions see human beings in some sort of unsatisfactory situation or predicament, though they agree as little about exactly what that is as they do about the nature of the Ultimate itself. Whatever the human plight, however, it requires an appropriate kind of resolution or amelioration, which is precisely what each religion claims to afford.

Christianity's distinctive view of human nature and the human predicament evolved out of its biblical theistic view of God (discussed in detail in chapter 2 above), and particularly from the thought of the first-century missionary Paul and the fifth-century theologian Augustine. On the basis of their ideas about the radical nature and effects of sin, Christianity developed what appears to be the most negative view of human nature of any religion of which we are aware. Not coincidentally, as we shall see in chapter 6, it also posited the most radical means of salvation. After all, a religion must offer a healing process commensurate with the pathology that it detects— in this case, humanity's corrupt nature and desperate existential situation.

The Image of God

The starting point for Christian thinking about human nature is the traditional belief, based on Genesis 1:26–27, that human beings were created, male and female, in the "image" and "likeness" of God. Unfortunately, the passage that contains that impressive phrase fails to explain what it means, and thus leaves room for much speculation.

An Image Investigated

The "image of God" has sometimes been naïvely taken to imply a physical resemblance between Creator and creature. Perhaps that interpretation is one reason that God is called such things as "the Man Upstairs." It may also account for much of the pious resistance of Fundamentalists to the scientific theory of evolution: who would want to think of God as a great celestial ape, a kind of supernatural King Kong?

Most mainstream Christian theologians since Augustine of Hippo (d. 430 CE), however, have minimized the physical connotations of "the image of God," no doubt largely because of the impact of Greek philosophy on Christian thought. Accordingly, they have interpreted the phrase as referring to such things as the human soul, or intellect, or spirituality, or creativity, or freedom of will, or capacity for communion with God, or some combination of these. The phrase "image of God" has sometimes been used to designate our seemingly unique gift (at least among earthly creatures) of self-consciousness or self-transcendence, which is to say, our ability to think reflectively and abstractly, to contemplate the future, to inquire about the meaning of life, to have a self-image, and to reach beyond ourselves in search of Ultimate Reality. Apparently the "image of God" can be whatever anyone believes makes us uniquely human and divinely connected.

Whatever they have supposed this "image" to be, however, most traditional theologians have understood it in light of the third chapter of Genesis—the so-called "Fall" story. That they have done so is curious in light of the fact that the "image" in question is part of one creation story and the "Fall" a component of another. The Garden of Eden narrative belongs to the older, alternative creation account of Genesis 2, in which no image of God is granted to humanity at its inception or even mentioned. Yet something very much like an image of God is implied in the story line. Far from being bestowed by God initially, however, as it is in the Genesis 1 story, it is actually *seized* by the primordial pair against the intention and will of the Creator. More about that later.

A Flawed Deity and a Damaging Fall

But just what kind of God does this implied image of Genesis 2 and 3 bespeak? Well, for one thing, the deity of the Eden story is hardly the purely spiritual Being that most Christians today probably would envision and embrace. Pictured here instead is a very anthropomorphic (that is, human-shaped) God, one who can take a casual garden stroll in the cool of the day and make enough noise to be heard in the process. The story also assails the popular notion that God is omniscient, by depicting Jahweh calling out to learn Adam's whereabouts, and finally realizing from the shame-ridden man's responses to a series of questions that an act of disobedience has occurred. And why would an all-knowing God not have foreseen that the new humans would be tempted and disobedient? Would not such a God have planned better? Or—to raise an even more serious theological issue—was the whole thing a set-up, part of a secret divine plan and thus a foregone conclusion? If that was the case, then the couple did God's will and should not have suffered punishment for their disobedience! Such a scenario calls into question not the righteousness of Adam and Eve, but the moral rectitude of God.

The truth is that the garden story portrays a deity that is not an omniscient-omnipotent Divine Spirit, but One who is "all-too-human" and limited in nature, knowledge, and power. The good news here, theologically speaking, is that this God is not a mean-spirited, conniving Supreme Being of questionable morality, but merely a short-sighted, hapless bumbler, struggling in the end for damage-control and wildly punishing everyone and everything in sight and in perpetuity: womankind, mankind, serpenthood, and even the ground. What suffers most as a result of the garden story, however, is not the nature or character of God (much less the well-being of all humankind), but the validity of the theological preconceptions that have commonly been misapplied to this ancient narrative.

Such intriguing issues aside (for the moment at least), it is clear that until recently mainline Christian theologians have regarded the "Fall" story as either literally or substantially true, and have generally concluded that the image of God in humanity is somehow compromised, tarnished, or even lost altogether as a result. Simply put: the Fall severely damaged humanity's likeness to and relationship with God.

To be sure, there have been some technical disagreements between (and among) Catholic and Protestant theologians on this score. Generally speaking, Roman Catholic theologians have tended to identify the *imago dei* with both human reason and certain supernatural gifts originally possessed by the primordial couple, and to hold that only the latter were lost in the Fall. By contrast, Protestant theologians have tended to identify the image of God with the moral function of the human will, and to maintain that it was lost, or at least severely compromised, in the Fall. Despite these relatively minor theological disagreements, however, both the Protestant and Catholic traditions have agreed that some prehistoric event or natural proclivity resulted in humankind's descent from a primordial state of grace (often called "original righteousness" or simply "innocence") and into the throes of evil and sin.

The Question of Evil

Before we examine the specific matter of sin, it makes some sense to look at the larger question of evil, its nature, and its relation to God. We touched on evil in chapter 2 with regard to its implications for the theistic concept of God and the problem of theodicy, but it bears closer scrutiny here. For not all people have viewed evil in the same light or taken it with the same degree of seriousness. In fact, a variety of theories of evil, some religious in origin and nature and some not, have been entertained and embraced over the course of human history. (See figures 5.1 – 5.3)

Evil as a Judgment Call or Deviation

In modern Western cultures a relativistic view of evil seems increasingly to prevail. That view holds that there is really no such thing as evil per se, but that we label this or that as "evil" purely as a value judgment arising from cultural norms, upbringing, education, experiences, feelings, thought processes, and tastes. Thus something that you regard and try to avoid as "evil," your neighbor may see as acceptable or even good.

For example, a strict Southern Baptist Christian may regard alcoholic beverages as inherently evil, while a devout Roman Catholic Christian may consider them perfectly fine if used in moderation; yet both may agree on the absolute evil of abortion. An Episcopalian might well agree with the Catholic position about the acceptability of beer and wine, but part company with both the Catholic and the Baptist on the issue of abortion by declaring it morally acceptable in many cases and strictly a matter of a woman's choice. And each of these persons might well be an absolutist about his or

Evil = a Value Judgement

A Mere Opinion

Evil = a Deprivation of/ Deviation from the Good

A Matter of Degree

Evil = an Attribute/Aspect of the Good

A Mixed Blessing

Evil = a Force Opposed to the Good

A Marked Contrast

FIGURE 5.1

her own views. But because they share not only the same society but indeed the same Christian religion, it is both easy and reasonable to conclude as many do today that nothing is inherently good or evil, and that what is "right" or "true" is just a matter of perspective: "It's up to the individual" or "It all depends." That stance is *relativism*.

Ironically, relativism itself can be more or less absolutist. A thorough-going relativist, for example, might say that all morality and truth are absolutely a matter of individual interpretation because there is no such thing as Absolute Right or Truth. A milder form of relativism, however, might maintain that while there well may be such Absolutes, finite and limited human beings can never hope to know them with any certainty, and there is finally no way to be completely sure which view is closer to the Truth or which action more approximates the Right.

Four Theories of Evil – A Case Study #1

The Issue: Explain terrorism and the terrible harm and suffering it brings to innocent people.

1. Evil as a Value Judgment: One person's "terrorist" is another's "freedom fighter." From one perspective, so-called "terrorism" looks like acts of sheer evil. From the vantage point of the perpetrator, however, it is a measured and justified response to years or decades of imperialist injustices. So-called terrorism is the only effective tactic for a military underdog to combat the awesome power and brutality of its wealthy enemy oppressors, who see themselves as purely "innocent" rather than as the quiet and detached terrorists that they are in their own right.

2. Evil as a Deprivation of / Deviation from the Good: All people are basically good, even terrorists. Their situation has simply driven them to extremes that belie their fundamentally positive human nature. "Desperate times produce desperate people using desperate measures." A terrorist is a basically decent person who has been forced into "deviant" behavior by dire, and often dreadful, circumstances.

3. Evil as an Attribute/Aspect of the Good: Terrorists are agents of a righteous God's inescapable justice, punishing those who deserve it because of their greed and self-interest, which give them riches at the expense of the poor of the world. Terrorists are doing God's will and work.

4. Evil as a Force Opposed to the Good: Terrorists are tools of the Devil and willing or clueless puppets of the cosmic forces of evil and darkness. They are mean, immoral, wicked misanthropists. May the righteous God and we, God's servants, strike them all dead!

FIGURE **5.2**

Plato held a far less relativistic, but still not a thoroughly absolutist, view of evil. He taught a philosophical (or metaphysical) system in which there certainly were such eternal absolutes as Beauty and Truth and Goodness (along with many other values, all of which he called "forms" or "ideas"). But all of his absolutes were positive: that is, there was no such quality (form, ideal) as Ugliness or Falsehood or Evil. Such negatives were merely aspects of existence that represented *deprivations* of or *deviations* from the positive values and their effects. Thus, for him, "evil" was simply a way of talking about the lack of goodness in any person, thing, or deed. In other words, Plato did not believe that "evil" itself had any substantive reality—or what philosophers would call "ontological status." But unlike the afore-mentioned relativists, Plato *did* think that Goodness had such reality. In a sense, then, he was relativist *about evil*, for he defined it only in relation to the Good. About the latter, however, he was definitely an absolutist.

A good analogy for Plato's view of Good and evil might be the sun and a spacecraft. Suppose a cosmonaut pilots her vehicle toward the solar disk. The closer the vessel gets to it, the hotter and hotter it becomes because of the effect of the star's tremendous power. When the pilot steers away from the heat and light and heads toward deep space, however, the space ship gradually gets cooler and cooler, then downright frigid. But this happens, not because it is now moving toward a giant cosmic ice cube generating cold-ness, but simply as a result of having *deviated* from the course toward the sun and having thus been *deprived* of its influence. Like evil in Plato's sys-tem, the coldness of the craft—however real it feels to the shivering pilot—has no real source or substance.

Evil as a Divine Deed

By contrast, the ancient Judaism we find reflected in the Hebrew scrip-tures took evil very seriously and treated it as real. It was not, however, per-ceived as a power or force separate from God, as Christianity has traditionally done. Judaism attributed it to God! In Isaiah 45:7, for example, Jahweh (God) speaks through the prophet saying: "I make weal and create woe." Throughout the Hebrew Bible, in fact, God is either blessing folks or sending curses upon them. Some would say, and with some justification, that this dispensing of help and harm is what occupies most of God's atten-tion and time there.

Some of our own everyday conversation about evils that befall us reflects, however naively or inadvertently, the view that God really is their cause. After all, what do we refer to as "acts of God"? Tornadoes, hurricanes, floods, and other "natural" disasters! And when someone dies unexpectedly, isn't there always someone around talking about its having been "God's will," or even saying things like "God took him"? Such assertions capture precisely the ancient Hebrew (that is, Christian "Old Testament") view of evil as an aspect of God's nature—a divine attribute.

Ancient Judaism's attributing evil to God explains why, as we saw in chapter 2, Satan is such a minor character in Hebrew scriptures, appearing only a handful of times in only four of the thirty-nine books recognized as canonical by the Council of Jamnia (and by Protestant Christians, who mostly accept its decision); and in those few appearances, Satan never takes on the role of an opponent of God. Rather, Satan is depicted there as an agent of God, in God's charge and control. (Regardless of what you've heard, by the way, there is no revolt in heaven or expulsion from God's court anywhere in the scriptures. The "Lucifer" who falls from the heavens in Isaiah 14:12 is the dead Babylonian King Nebuchadnezzar, a former "star" that had "fallen"—or bitten the dust, actually.) Satan's primary function as God's agent in these writings is to accuse or tempt human beings, or to test them by inflicting undeserved suffering on them. The last of these is precisely what is going on in the story of Job, which provides Satan his biggest role

Four Theories of Evil – A Case Study #2

The Issue: Explain earthquakes and the human suffering they cause.

1. Evil as a Value Judgment: Earthquakes are purely a natural phenomenon, a necessary self-adjustment of the earth's crust. From the standpoint of human beings who happen to be in their way, they seem evil. In the longer view of geologic time, however, they are not only good, but even essential for maintaining the tectonic equilibrium of the earth's surface.

2. Evil as a Deprivation of / Deviation from the Good: A perfect world in which the earth's surface was always dependable and human suffering did not exist would be wonderful. But we live in an imperfect world in which the forces of nature are unstable and often unpredictable, and in which humans have not quite learned to live in harmony with them, to keep out of their way, or otherwise minimize their effects. Hence we sometimes see or feel the awful and unsettling effects of natural phenomena, including human suffering. We then call them "disasters" and "evil," simply because they do not conform to our utopian ideals, they do not serve our selfish interests, and they bump us out of our illusions of comfort and security.

3. Evil as an Attribute/Aspect of the Good: Earthquakes, as well as other so-called "natural disasters," are really caused by God as a way of meting out divine retribution against the unrighteous. We don't call such events "acts of God" for nothing!

4. Evil as a Force Opposed to the Good: Earthquakes and other death-and-destruction-dealing natural phenomena are part of Satan's great arsenal, which has tormented and afflicted humanity ever since the Evil One's fall from God's good graces. Only righteous living, prayer, and the hope for God's eventual victory can fend off such things.

FIGURE 5.3

in the entire Old Testament (a grand total of seven verses of one chapter!). All of the evils that befall Job—the loss of his children, his fortune, his health, his peace of mind, and the respect of his wife and friends—are sent by Satan with God's blessing to test that good man's righteousness.

Another way to put the ancient Jewish view is this: they didn't regard Satan as a Devil, that is, as a counter-force in opposition to God. As we also saw in chapter 2, the main reason that it didn't occur to them to make Satan a Devil is that they were strict monotheists. They knew that to posit an evil counterpart to God was, in effect, to conceive a second God, and—like the equally strict Muslims on this score—they were far more willing to attribute evil to God's doing than to compromise their basic creed and conviction that there is one and only one God.

It could be said that the ancient Jews simply had the good sense to understand that if God was the sole Creator and providential overseer of everything, then any evil that occurred had to be either God's doing or to happen in accordance with God's will, or perhaps even with God's blessing. They knew that when it comes to ultimate responsibility in a monotheistic system, the buck stops wherever God is conceived to be.

Evil as the Devil's Doing

Christians traditionally have not seen a problem here. They have claimed to be monotheists while insisting that evil is a negative force that stands over against God's good power. From the New Testament writers on, Christians have identified that negative force as Satan, and have treated Satan (in a very un-Jewish way) as the Devil, a definite power and agent of evil who opposes God's will, resists God's power, and threatens God's people. In so doing, Christians have maintained a fourth view of evil (besides that of relativism, Platonism, and Judaism). They have taught that evil is a separate, countervailing power or force over against the good; and they generally have ignored the threat of this view to their claim that there is only one God.

Why the earliest Christians—who, after all, were mostly Jews—departed so decisively from their traditional view of God is a matter of some speculation. The simplest adequate explanation is that a lot had happened to Jews in the previous five or six centuries, subsequent to the composition of the early books that defined the Old Testament worldview. Not the least important factor was increasing contact—through commerce, invasion, and exile—with other peoples with different ideas, some of which challenged their own strict monotheism.

One of those alternative views was provided by Zoroastrianism, a religion born in ancient Persia (modern Iran), probably in the seventh century BCE. Against the prevailing polytheism of that time and place, the prophet Zoroaster (or "Zarathustra") taught either that there were two gods, one good and one evil, or one god with two opposing spirits, one good and one evil (depending on which modern interpreter you read). It just so happens that Zoroastrianism sometimes referred to the evil god or spirit as "Satan."

In the following few centuries, Jews had plenty of contact with the Zoroastrians, especially after being defeated and carried into exile by peoples from that area. Consequently, by the time the New Testament was written, Jewish thought had had sufficient opportunity to absorb beliefs about an evil power or force, though in deference to their heritage of strong monotheism they still hesitated to call it a god. But that is exactly how Satan is portrayed in the New Testament and traditional Christian thought: as the Devil, an ungodly force in his own right, though not called a "god"; and evil is his doing, not God's. That is the main reason that God generally appears so much kinder and gentler in the New Testament than in the Hebrew scriptures.

Genesis 3 and "The Fall"

Nowhere is the difference between the Christian and Jewish views of evil more obvious than in the history of the interpretation of the Garden of Eden story. In the Jewish narrative, Satan plays no role whatsoever, not even as God's agent. In the Christian interpretation, however, Satan-as-the-Devil looms large, and most Christians assume (quite wrongly) that Satan is a character—perhaps even the main character—in that ancient tale. But as we shall see, Satan is only one of many such "assumed" components completely missing from the text.

What is Missing and What Myth Is

Whenever Christian folks today think and talk about sin, they almost inevitably have in mind images of Adam and Eve, Satan and an apple, a deceptive serpent, humanity's loss of immortality, and a divine expulsion from Paradise. Their point of reference, of course, is chapter 3 of Genesis, which tells the familiar story of the so-called "Fall" of humanity. Unfortunately, the tale is so familiar that most Christians haven't read the text carefully, much less analyzed it, but have simply assumed that they knew what it was all about.

Most Christians would therefore be surprised to find out that Satan never makes an appearance, there is no apple, the serpent (much less the Devil) deceives no one, humanity doesn't fall, Adam and Eve do not lose their God-given immortality, and by any standards of justice or simple fairness, the punished pair cannot even be held responsible for having sinned! Most Christians would also be astonished to learn that the God who appears in that story is human-shaped, limited in knowledge, deceptive, and egregiously unfair in the punishment of a largely innocent couple, not to mention their multitudinous, hapless heirs.

Before addressing the contents of the story of Adam and Eve, however, it is important to identify its literary genre as religious myth. That is not to say, of course, that it is a lie or that it is not to be taken seriously. It is to say that the story neither is nor purports to be historical fact. As a myth, it does endeavor to tell spiritual or theological truth, just as the parables of Jesus conveyed to their hearers important truths by means of obviously fictitious narratives. With myth, then, it is not simply a question of "Is it truth or is it fiction?" A myth routinely couches truth *in* fiction. The very function of myth, in fact, is to employ fiction to convey spiritual truths that are more profound than factual truth or truthful facts.

It is also important to recognize that the creation myths found in Genesis are by no means the earliest extant creation stories. The story found in Genesis 1 was written around 400 BCE , and Genesis 2–3 before that, around 850 BCE. Noticeably older are (1) the Babylonian *Enuma Elish* from around 1100 BCE, (2) the Canaanite myth of Baal and Anat written around 1200 BCE and (3) the Babylonian *Epic of Gilgamesh*, dating to around 1750 BCE. Creation myths are a part of nearly all religions, though most have composed their own. Christianity and Islam, by contrast, appropriated and co-opted the Hebrew stories found in Genesis to suit their own needs, as we shall see.

When we turn to the actual contents of any creation myth like the Garden of Eden story, the best approach is to "bracket out" or suspend, as much as possible, all of our presuppositions and recollections about the characters that appear there; and to read it, insofar as possible, from its author's perspective. When we do this with Genesis 3, we may be astounded to discover what really is—and especially is not—there. (See figure 5.4.)

A Savvy Serpent and Divine Deception

The first thing that appears in this story is the serpent, which is never identified by the author as Satan. Satan plays no part whatsoever in the garden, or in Genesis, or in the Pentateuch. What we have in the garden is simply a serpent, though one notable for his ability to think and talk. (Talking animals are quite common in religious mythology.) Depending on the English translation, this serpent is "subtle," or "cunning," or "crafty." Most Christians assume that that means "sneaky" or "devious," but the original Hebrew word suggests something much closer to "mentally acute" or "sharp-witted."

Indeed, the details of this story suggest that the serpent is not devious, but "perceptive": he "knows what's what" and "tells it like it is." He informs Eve that she will not drop dead by sundown if she eats the fruit of the tree in question, as God has told her (thus misleading her to believe that it was quite poisonous). On the contrary, he tells her that she will gain moral knowledge from the eating; and, sure enough, she eats, and survives—and "wises up"! That was one smart—*and* truthful—serpent!

So the canny serpent understood the situation clearly and accurately predicted the outcome. Even God's own assessment of the situation at the end of the story is testimony to the serpent's veracity, echoing as it does the creature's words earlier in the chapter: "Behold, they have become like us, knowing good from evil . . . . " That is exactly what the serpent had said would happen! In fact, if there is any deception going on in this story, it is on the part of God, who had said that the humans would die the very day that they ate of the fruit. It appears that God had misled them.

Some try to save God's reputation in this regard by saying that what God really meant was that they would lose their immortality; but this explanation adds layers of interpretation and bestows a gift on humanity (immortality) that nowhere is even implied by the Jahwist author, either here or in the preceding chapter. Immortality, it seems, like knowledge of good and evil, is a divine prerogative in this story. And so, having lost the struggle to

Down and Out in the Garden of Eden

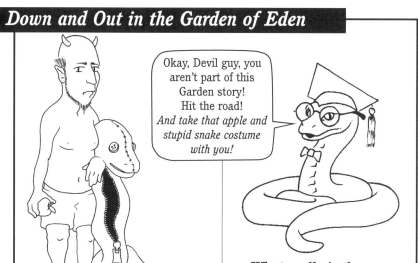

Okay, Devil guy, you aren't part of this Garden story! Hit the road! *And take that apple and stupid snake costume with you!*

What is not there.

1. A sneaky Satan in disguise.
2. Deception by the serpent about the consequences of eating.
3. An apple.
4. A sin committed by morally responsible adults.
5. An omniscient God who could have foreseen such disobedience, and taken steps to prevent it.
6. The primordial couple causing evil to come into the world.
7. A righteous God meting out justice befitting the crime.

What really is there.

1. A Savvy Serpent.
2. Deception by God about the consequences of eating.
3. An unnamed fruit.
4. An act of disobedience by two innocents who don't yet know good from evil.
5. A God who "puts two and two together" and then struggles for damage control.
6. Evil already there, only knowledge of it at issue.
7. A jealous God, harshly punishing the naïve couple— and everything else.

FIGURE 5.4

retain the exclusive rights to the knowledge of good and evil, God is especially concerned to protect this last bastion of divinity from human participation: "Now, lest they put forth their hand, and eat of [the tree of life] and live forever . . . . " God does not want them to do that; and nowhere does the story imply that God had intended immortality to be their destiny.

In this regard, the divine declaration "you are dust and to dust you shall return" (Gen 3:19) is not further punishment for the man, but a reminder of human mortality. It is probably there to give one reason that the ground (Hebrew *ha-adhamah*) should be cursed: it is a close relative of the man (*ha-adham*), who was made from it. To read into that story "otherwise you would have lived forever" is to play fast and loose with the text and the author's apparent intention.

Omniscience, Omnipotence, and Other Omissions

It must be noted that in this whole narrative, God is hardly the omniscient, omnipotent deity of our modern-day conceptualizations. The ancient writer depicts God as a somewhat inept male human who first appears in the story taking a stroll. The three questions that God then asks are hardly rhetorical: "Where are you?" and "What is this you've done?" are not intended by the author as a testing of Adam. They are real, matter-of-fact questions. Likewise, God's "Have you eaten . . . ?" sounds like the product of a sudden insight—a putting together of "two plus two" or a cartoon light-bulb being illuminated above God's head. None of these sounds like the utterance of one who is all-knowing. Indeed, by the end of the story (as we have seen) God appears to be scrambling to protect the last remaining divine prerogative, immortality. Shouldn't we expect a deity with normal foresight to have posted a guard or constructed a high wall around both trees in the first place? This is a God of afterthought, not foreknowledge.

As for the rest of the story, there are other details besides Satan, a serpent's deception, and divine omniscience that most people think are there, but that really aren't. There is no apple in the story, only "fruit." We can't be sure what that fruit may have been in the author's mind. (For the sake of evolutionists, it may have been a banana!) But the best candidate—suggested by the narrative itself—is the fig, since fig leaves appear readily at hand for makeshift clothing once the couple realizes its nakedness. Why then have European countries remembered this fruit as an apple? Perhaps because apples have been more familiar there than any fruit of the Eastern Mediterranean region. Apples may also have had an additional appeal for artists painting scenes of the ancient garden and the so-called "Temptation": apples are prettier, more colorful and visually appealing, and easier to paint than figs!

The story's most astonishing omission is sin. Not only is the word "sin" not used; the concept cannot fairly be applied to the actions of Eve and Adam. For, having not yet partaken of the tree of the knowledge of good and evil, they clearly had no knowledge of good and evil, which is to say that they had no moral sense at the moment of their decision to disobey God. How, then, can they reasonably be blamed for this or any act of disobedience? To punish them (and especially so severely) is the equivalent of thrashing a toddler for taking a pretty toy from the seductive display in a supermarket checkout line, or incarcerating a mentally-challenged adult for helping himself to candy at a convenience store. Without knowledge of good and evil, the primordial couple could not possibly have understood that to disobey would be wrong. After the fact, of course, they had the knowledge of good and evil, and presumably could have seen in retrospect (and in the story they apparently do see) that to disobey was wrong. But that was too late.

Their situation prior to the eating is perhaps best compared to that of people of normal maturity and intelligence who have committed heinous crimes but who, under our legal system, cannot be found guilty if it can be demonstrated that their moral judgment was impaired at the time, that is, if it can be shown that they could not distinguish good from evil. They are deemed "unfit to stand trial." Wouldn't one expect a moral God to have been at least that understanding toward those who did not yet have a knowledge of good and evil? Not in Genesis 3!

Righteous Indignation or Child Abuse?

What is more, this God—having failed to take appropriate and timely precautions—tries to remedy the situation by punishing everything in sight, and some things not yet even in the picture. God punishes not only the serpent, who had told Eve the truth, but all serpenthood forever. (This, by the way is proof positive that this was not, in the mind of the story's author, Satan posing as a serpent. Nobody would blame and punish all soldiers because a robber disguised himself as one for a bank-heist.) God also punishes not just Eve, but all of future womanhood, with excruciating pain in childbirth and (Catch-22!) lust for their husbands. God then condemns, not only Adam, but all males in perpetuity to endless hard labor in order to eat.

But the final blow here is this: God punishes the ground, which, as we have seen, amounts to "guilt by association" of the worst sort: Adam, you see, having been shaped from the ground, had dust as his only ancestor and, aside from Eve, his closest relative! So the ground has to be punished, which further adds to the punishment of the males who ever after will have to toil in tilling before it will feed them. (Can this be the origin of the adage that "There's no free lunch"?) With this last punishment, one gets the impression that, albeit in righteous indignation, this God has simply "lost it"—in a fit of *ungodly* rage.

I like to compare this story to a more modern scenario. Let us suppose that a mother had made her three-year-old son some of his favorite chocolate-chip cookies, and placed a plate of them on a table well within the toddler's reach and grasp. (Silly woman!) And imagine that she had said to him, "Son, if you eat these before dinner, Mommie will kill you." His friend, an all-too-sharp (that is, "subtle") five-year-old from across the street, observing the scene and hearing the threat, says to the toddler: "Of course, she's not going to kill you. Parents are always saying things like that. She knows the cookies are delicious and is just trying to keep you from eating them and spoiling your dinner." The younger child then does exactly what anyone with any sense (not to mention omniscience) could have predicted: he eats a cookie or two.

What would you think of his mother if you found out later that she had returned, had seen chocolate stains on her child's guilty little face, and, having put two and two together, punished him severely for disobeying her? What would you think if you found out that, because of that rather predictable deed on the child's part, the mother also had written into her will that any children her son might have (and that they might produce in turn, etc.) should be punished as well? You'd call her, quite properly, an abusive—maybe even insane—mother; and you'd wonder why she hadn't done the sensible thing and put the plate of cookies out of the child's reach in the first place! Yet, for some strange reason, in this story we give the character God the benefit of the doubt in a similar situation. We call this God "just" and "righteous" for putting temptation close at hand and punishing people who, in their naïve and childlike innocence, couldn't have known any better than to do a deed that any deity (or human) with common sense could have foreseen and prevented.

A Nearly Forgotten Story of Newly-Found Status

It is no wonder—but may come as a surprise for most Christians—that the rest of the Hebrew Bible almost completely ignores this story. There is plenty of sinning in the books that follow Genesis, of course, but no one there thinks to blame it on the primordial couple. Rather, people are accounted culpable for their own deeds, and punished accordingly. No one thinks to develop a general theory of human sin on this seemingly heinous gastronomic *faux pax* until we get to much later Jewish and Christian interpreters. That happened first among commentators in the so-called "Intertestamental Period." But the garden story gained its most intensive and influential interpretation in the mid-first century CE from the Jew-turned-Christian, Paul.

Before turning to Paul, however, it is necessary to elaborate on an earlier comment about "the image of God." Again, the Jahwist author of the Garden of Eden story does not use the phrase, but the words he (or she) places on God's lips at the end of the story can be fairly taken to imply that something very much like an "image of God" has been seized by the human couple. "Behold," says God, "they've become like one of us, knowing good from evil." That sounds like an elevation of status in the eyes of the deity, not a "Fall" as Christian theologians have interpreted it. Eve and Adam have arrogated unto themselves—if one can talk about moral innocents "arrogating" at all—a divine prerogative: likeness to God, which is to say, an *image* of God.

Another theory of the garden myth suggests that the tree of knowledge of good and evil found in Genesis (2:9, 17; 3:5, 22) has nothing to do with sin or morality at all, but that the metaphor "good and evil" is actually a biblical code phrase for sexual experience. If that's the case, then when God says, "Behold, they have become like one of us, knowing good and evil," it is really an expression of the anger of the heavenly host, who heretofore have been the only ones capable of creation; now humankind can in fact live forever because they can also create. The net result of this alternative explanation is the same as that noted in the moral interpretation. A divine prerogative has been seized and the human status has been elevated, rather than diminished.

In any event, the Garden of Eden story is very reminiscent of the ancient Greek myth of Prometheus, the Titan creator of humanity, who stole fire from Zeus and the Olympian gods in Greek mythology in order to warm his poorly-designed (furless) creatures. The punishment that he had to endure was as excessive as the Edenic couple's: he was to be chained to a rock for eternity and have his liver eaten out by a large bird every day, only to have it regenerate every night for the next day's feeding. Both stories depict deities as extremely petty and excessively punitive. How grave a loss would it have been for the Olympic gods to share fire with humanity, and what harm would it have done to Jahweh for the primordial couple to be either moral or sexual? From a modern perspective, at least, these appear to be very "small" gods!

Paul and Augustine on Sin

It might surprise most Christians to know that for many of the world's religions the basic human predicament is not defined in terms of "sin" at all. The monistic religions born in India and China define the basic spiritual problem of humanity as ignorance—specifically, ignorance of its oneness with Ultimate Reality. And although the three great religions born in the Middle East define the human predicament in terms of sin, they put two very different spins on that term. Judaism and Islam both define sin in terms of deeds that break covenant or otherwise offend the will of God (Jahweh or Allah), but that can be atoned for by people's repentance and reform or by rituals performed on their behalf. Christianity, thanks largely to Paul and Augustine, goes its own way, and in the process produces the most negative view of human nature found in any religion.

"Missing the Mark" (a Misdemeanor)

There are various Hebrew and Greek words in the Christian Bible that are translated into English as "sin." They have different shadings of meaning, but most have a root sense of missing the mark, going astray, erring, or failing. That fact would lead one to conclude that in the Bible and Christianity as a whole, sins are understood (as in Judaism and Islam) basically as bad deeds or impious acts.

That is probably also the common popular definition among Christian lay people. When most people think about the word "sin" today, or use it in conversation, they probably are referring to some behavior that they deem, or believe that God deems, immoral. And if they wish to decide whether or not a person is sinful they probably add up her or his deeds, weighing the negative ones in terms of their numbers and gravity and perhaps balancing them against any possible mitigating circumstances or offsetting positive traits or actions. Should there be a clear preponderance of bad or good deeds in this individual's history or patterns of behavior, then one might feel justified in pronouncing that person (more or less) sinful or (more or less) righteous.

Now this view of sin is a perfectly valid one, and may even be the best possible definition of the word. But it was not Paul's fundamental understanding; and because of his enormous impact in shaping the faith and its doctrines, it has not been that of Western Christianity either. His extraordinary influence, later reinforced by Augustine, led both Roman Catholicism and Protestantism to view sin not as an improper or immoral act—a kind of misdemeanor—but as something far more fundamental, profound, and devastating.

A Congenital Condition

Christianity derives its distinctive view of sin, and thus its basic understanding of human nature, ultimately from Paul's definition of sin as a *universal condition*. This, and its subsequent reinforcement by an almost equally influential fourth century North African theologian-made-Saint named

Augustine, impressed itself indelibly upon Christianity. Not coincidentally, it was also Paul and Augustine who made the Genesis 3 story so pivotal for Christian thinking.

Paul did not have to add up a person's bad deeds in order to calculate whether she or he was sinful. To him, all people were sinners from birth, for all were children of Adam and heirs of his sinfulness: " . . . sin came into the world through one man, and death came through sin, and so death spread to all because all have sinned"; and thus "one man's trespass led to condemnation for all," for "by one man's trespass the many were made sinners" (Rom 5:12, 18, 19). The "one man," of course, is Adam; and his sin was not just a bad act or "trespass" but something that came into the world and made everyone ever thereafter sinners. Thus, sin for Paul was not so much that one deed as the resulting *universal condition* that leads to acts or deeds that may properly, but only derivatively, be called "sins." People weren't sinners because they sinned, but sinned because they were sinners. The inherited condition preceded (and caused) the act.

Paul didn't quite put it this way, but he would not have objected much to the assertion that in their natural condition, all human beings are innately "rotten to the core"—including newly-born babies! Indeed, the only difference that these seeming "innocents" might have over a seasoned adult sinner is the lack of the hand-eye coordination required to accomplish actual acts of sin. But the condition is there, ready and waiting for the skills to develop enough to produce sinful acts. And to Paul, the condition is damnable whether it has triggered any actual bad deed or not.

Of course, the notion that all people are basically bad and the belief that a baby is sinful even at birth probably are neither emotionally appealing nor rationally convincing to most people. In fact, such pessimistic ideas are downright dismaying. But there is at least some empirical evidence for Paul's viewpoint. For one thing, all you have to do is listen to the evening news or read the morning newspaper to get the impression that things are bad all over: murder, kidnapping, terrorism, rape, robbery, embezzlement, war, repression, treason—the list of evil human deeds is endless and the examples countless. Just listen to police activity on a radio scanner some evening, or ask a seasoned police officer after a long shift what he or she thinks of human nature. And any parent who has endured the well-known "terrible twos" may find Paul's viewpoint plausible, and perhaps even comforting: the parents have done nothing wrong to make this mean-spirited, self-centered, miniature human being what it is; it is simply a congenitally sinful human nature bursting forth into expression.

It might be added here that one of the original reasons for the infant baptism practiced by the Roman Catholic church and many Protestant denominations was to offset the damning effects of this inherent, inherited sin. Unfortunately children baptized as infants still seem to go through the terrible twos.

Deceptive Deeds and a Durable Doctrine

Be that as it may, the chief effect of this sinful condition is that it debilitates humanity as a whole and every individual, making it impossible for them to do anything truly good. From Paul's perspective, we may do things that look like good deeds, just as a tree may produce beautiful, but poisonous fruit. But upon examination, our apparently "good deeds" are exposed for what they are: sinful acts.

Thus a Boy Scout who goes out of his way to help an elderly person across a busy street is revealed to have done so because he needed to do his "one good deed" for the day. That is, he did it out of selfishness, which makes it a sin (though presumably not as heinous a sin as if he had beaten her up and stolen her purse). Or the person who gives a large donation to feed the hungry or house the homeless—both apparently "good deeds"—actually does so in order to feel better about his or her selfish, luxurious, and wasteful lifestyle, or to appear charitable, or to gain admiration, or (worst of all) as an advertising gimmick to improve business and increase personal wealth (and thus further open the gap between the rich and the poor). Again we have an apparently good deed that is really a sin. Humans simply cannot do really good deeds "under their own steam," according to Paul. Even of himself he said: "I do not understand my own actions. For I do not do what I want, but I do the very thing I hate" (Rom 7:15).

This Pauline understanding of sin has had tremendous consequences for the mainstream Christian concept of salvation. For no matter how much we want it, how hard we strive to achieve it, or how seemingly righteous we become as a result of our own efforts, all our desires and deeds are for naught. Paul labeled as "works righteousness" all human endeavors to do good, to gain God's favor, or, in modern parlance, to "get saved"; and his unshakable conviction is that "works righteousness" doesn't work. Why? Precisely because of our sinful condition, which, as we have seen, prevents us from doing anything but sin. (See figure 5.5.)

Although this viewpoint became the foundation for Western Christian theology, it is at odds with much of what passes for Christian belief in modern thinking and much that is taught in Christian homes, churches, and Sunday schools. I remember being told by well-meaning Sunday School teachers as a child—or at least being left with the clear impression as a result of their instruction—that "good little boys and girls go to heaven, but bad little boys and girls go to hell." Now that saying may well be true; but from Paul's perspective all little boys and girls go to hell, at least if they die in their congenital condition.

Here again, sad to say, there is at least some empirical evidence to support this seemingly absurd and certainly disarming notion: just recall the selfishness, meanness, and downright cruelty of children to one another at school or play, and their uncanny ability to wreak nearly total destruction upon adult activities and possessions. My old grandmother used to call such normal infantile behavior "devilishness." Paul would have agreed. (Come to think of it, my grandmother had read Paul a lot!)

Original Sin—an Ongoing Stigma

Paul's view on sin did not gain immediate acceptance in Western Christianity as the definitive doctrine about the human condition; and among Eastern Orthodox Christians, it never did quite catch on. Sometime after the

FIGURE 5.5

fourth century, however, and largely as a result of the enormously influential North African theologian, Augustine of Hippo, the Roman Catholic Church adopted Paul's view. Building upon his ideas, Augustine had fashioned a systematic theology that used the Apostle's radical view of sin as its very cornerstone, and that made a deep and enduring impression upon the Church's view of human nature, sin, and salvation.

Augustine's understanding of sin revolved around what he called *peccatum originale*, or "Original Sin," a term and concept that he invented to enunciate in clear doctrinal form what Paul had taught three and a half centuries before. By sinning, it seems, Adam had somehow tainted his soul and passed that imperfection on to the whole human race, and with it the proclivity, the compulsion, even the necessity to sin. In other words, "Original Sin" is what Augustine called the natural human condition that Paul had described; and on the basis of that idea he referred to the entire human race as a *massa perditionis*, or "mass of damnation," destined for hell.

In order to explain how Original Sin got passed on from generation to generation, Augustine suggested a theory called "traducianism," which holds that a child's soul is somehow acquired from the parent. Thus any spiritual defect that Adam had incurred would be transmitted to future generations genetically, as it were. What kept Augustine from embracing traducianism completely was that a part of him wanted to keep the creation of each individual soul in God's hands, an idea called in his day "creationism." The downside of this alternative view for him, of course, was that it left inherited sin with no mechanism to account for it.

From a Divine Desire to an Ill Will

What was less ambiguous to Augustine than the origin of the soul was the origin of sin itself. The trick was to show how sin had emerged, but without attributing its inception to God; or, in other words, to figure out how to blame sin on humanity without implying a design flaw that made the Creator culpable.

Augustine solved this problem with the idea of concupiscence, which means something like "burning passion" or "ardent desire." It had been created by God, he theorized, to assure the propagation of living things. (Concupiscence is what causes two bunnies of different sexes to produce hundreds more.) And as a part of God's plan for creation, it was a good thing. The problem was (said Augustine) that human beings, beginning with Adam, failed to control it properly. When they did that, one of two things happened: either their spiritual side took over and they committed sins of pride—which in effect meant that they forgot their fleshly aspect and tried to play God; or they lost track of their spiritual side and wallowed in the "muck" of their physical natures and the material world. For Augustine, then, all sins could be classified as either spiritual or fleshly (corporeal). The result of both types was the same: the ideal balance between the two human aspects was lost—and all because of the innate condition of Original Sin.

According to Augustine, the principal impact of Original Sin was upon the human will. Only Adam had (and only prior to his disobedience) a completely free will, that is, the ability to exercise moral choice between good or evil.

(Free will for Augustine is not a matter of selecting such things as what to wear, eat, or do for a living—unless, of course, such decisions have moral implications.) But once Adam made the ill-advised choice of evil in the garden, said Augustine, he passed that tendency on to his progeny. The result was that human beings do have a limited freedom of the will, but only to do one kind of evil or another: our imaginary Boy Scout, for example, must choose between helping the old lady out of selfishness or mugging her out of greed. The option to do good is, after Adam, simply not open to people in their natural state. (Eve somehow gets lost in Augustine's shuffle here, despite that fact that fellow North African theologian Tertullian in the third century had faulted her alone for the Fall, and thus had placed the blame for Jesus' death upon all womanhood.)

Alternative Views and Augustine's Victory

As dominant as the Pauline-Augustinian view of sin and its implicitly negative view of human nature and moral freedom have been, they have not held total sway in Christianity. As chapter 8 will show, a number of individuals and movements have arisen over the centuries to claim that humanity is not all that "damned bad." But even in ancient times there was no Christian unanimity on the matter.

An Optimistic Opponent

Augustine did not go unchallenged in his assertion of Original Sin. His most famous critic was the contemporary British monk, Pelagius. Pelagius argued, in effect, that Augustine's limited free will made God an ogre. What kind of deity, for example, would require obedience to laws and commandments, knowing all the while that the descendants of Adam could not possibly choose to act righteously because of their congenital condition? In Pelagius' view (to use a modern example), such a god would be like a father who discovered his seven-year-old son tied hand-and-foot by his playmates and left in his room, all in good fun. What if that man, without releasing the child, ordered him to clean up his room under threat of extreme punishment extending to all of his descendants? To Pelagius, that all-too Augustinian scenario did not yield a very positive picture of God.

Pelagius summed up his anti-Augustinian view in the phrase "If I ought, I can!" If God's expectation and demand and commandments were that humans be good, then they must have it in their power to do so. Otherwise, God would be unreasonable and unjust—to recall our "cookie caper" example, an abusive parent. Pelagius acknowledged that after Adam, human obedience to God and God's commandments was more difficult, perhaps even exceedingly so. But he was also deeply convinced that though it might take a tremendous effort and exertion of will, people could be righteous. (See figure 5.6.)

Growing Into God?

Long before either Augustine or Pelagius was born, some important Christian authors had presented views of evil and sin quite contrary to Augustine's "Fall" explanation. Not coincidentally, the most prominent of

Do We Have Freedom of the Will?

What is at issue in most theological and philosophical discussions of freedom of the will is not mundane choices (like what to eat, what to wear, what to do for a living, or whom to marry) but morality: the ability to choose between doing good and doing evil. The classic debate on the matter in Christianity — replayed in succeeding generations — was between Augustine and Pelagius in the fifth century. Augustine said that because of Adam we had limited freedom, namely, to choose between one kind of sin or another. Pelagius believed that we could choose righteousness, but that thanks to Adam, it wasn't at all easy. Their positions boiled down to this:

FIGURE 5.6

these writers were from the Eastern part of the Roman Empire, and their location may have been one reason that their ideas didn't catch on in the Western Church.

Clement and Origen, for example, lived in Alexandria, Egypt during the second and third centuries. Like many Christians in their part of the world, they embraced a mystical form of spirituality. That meant that they believed their own spiritual essence to be the inner presence of God. As a result, their theologies tended to downplay or ignore altogether such doctrines as the Fall of Adam and the determinative power of sin, which (thanks largely to Paul) were already staples in Western Christian thought. Much less pragmatic and legalistic, the Alexandrians taught that humanity was meant for perfection, which could be achieved through the exercise of free will because of the *deification of humanity* effected by the incarnation of Jesus. Indeed, Origen had once declared that the Word of God had become human so that humans might learn from that humanity how they might become God. Human nature was not only *perfectible*, it seems, but positively *deifiable*!

At about the same time, Irenaeus, a native of Asia minor (think "East") who had become a bishop in France, was arguing in a similar vein that humanity had not been created perfect in the image of God and fallen from that lofty status, but had been made perfectible, with the potential to grow into the image of God. Hence, evil and sin were, in effect, merely inevitable "growing pains" in the process of humanity's spiritual development.

A Win for Wickedness?

Although such "Oriental" Christian views of human nature were largely ignored by the Western Church, the contributions of Clement and Irenaeus in other respects were so significant that the ecclesiastical powers-that-were made them saints anyway. Whether Origen might also have been thus honored despite his radical theology is uncertain, since he rendered himself ineligible by castrating himself after taking Matthew 19:12 literally. (Yet another reason to reject Fundamentalism?) Pelagius, by contrast, was a clear loser in the Church's eyes, and the Church never canonizes its losers— or names churches, schools, or cities after them. (The oldest city in the United States, by the way, is St. Augustine, Florida. Don't bother to search your atlas for St. Pelagius.)

Unfortunately for the Church and its official doctrines, however, most modern readers will probably find Pelagius' argument for human freedom of the will more convincing and satisfying than Augustine's; and Irenaeus' view may seem more in keeping with everything we now know and hope about human growth and development, psychological and otherwise. Nevertheless, Augustine's views remain the basis for Catholic and Protestant Christianity's teaching, not only about the natural human condition but also concerning the sort of divine action that is required to remedy that condition. (More about that in the chapter that follows.)

The reasons that Augustine's view won in the long run are many and complex. One likely explanation is that convincing people that they were "damned sinful" put them in a more vulnerable position and direly in need of the Church, its ministrations, and its ministers, than did Clement's and

Origen's deification motif, Irenaeus' developmental model, or Pelagius' free will doctrine. In other words, Augustine's view of the depth and seriousness of human sinfulness may well have prevailed for largely political reasons: it made the rites and rituals of the Church seem indispensable and those who administered them powerful. To put it bluntly: it kept the clergy employed. Thus the Church's suppression of these and other so-called "heresies"—not only in the various unjust and cruel Inquisitions of the Middle Ages, but in the equally shameful witch trials of later times—may be explained in terms of the fear in high places that such "deviant" views could render the Church dispensable in the eyes of the laity. Another explanation, of course, is that the Church was itself exhibiting in such ungodly proceedings the very condition of Original Sin that it was claiming for all humankind!

The widespread acceptance of the Pauline-Augustinian view of sin by Roman Catholicism (and later, Protestantism) had two important effects. First, it gave mainstream Christianity an extremely pessimistic view of human nature and potential. Second, following naturally from the first, Paul's radical view of sin necessitated a soteriology—that is, a doctrine of salvation—sufficiently radical and dramatic to overcome completely "from above" this seemingly hopeless condition of sin. Some would argue, and with some justification, that it was really the other way around: that the radical view of human nature was devised in order to explain the necessity of the atoning death of the Son of God. There is no winning this chicken-and-egg conundrum, and no need to do so. The real point is that the Pauline-Augustinian views of sin and salvation are compatible, even if not finally compelling.

The Continuing Controversy

As we have already noted, many religions in the world have no doctrine of sin at all, preferring instead to talk about ignorance as the key to human existential shortcomings, the cause of misdeeds, and the main hindrance to whatever "salvation" is conceived to be. But the ones that do define the human predicament in terms of sin (most notably Judaism and Islam) define "sin" basically as bad deeds, acts either not in accordance with or absolutely at odds with God's divine will or law. Judaism in particular teaches that humanity is born not in a state of sinfulness or moral bondage, but naturally empowered to choose between good and evil, especially with God's help, which is provided in an ongoing way as a matter of heavenly routine.

Only Christianity portrays us as so radically sinful that we are unable to effect our own salvation, and thus leaves us, as it were, "painted into a theological corner." God will have to act decisively, perhaps even dramatically, to help. But how? A divinely dispatched lawgiver bringing more commandments won't work. A priest to do more sacrifices won't be enough. Nor will a prophet with more stern chastisements and frightful warnings in the name of God. Not even a great teacher will suffice. No, humanity is far too sinful to respond positively to any of these traditional bearers of salvation or their gestures. Hence, someone very special and heaven-sent will have to come and do something quite powerful and unprecedented. (Can you see where this logic is headed?)

In the history of Christianity, however, the debates over the interrelated issues of human depravity and freedom of the will have never been completely settled. From the sixteenth century to the present especially, the argument seems to have been revived with renewed vigor in every generation. For example, when liberal sixteenth-century Dutch humanistic Christian philosopher Erasmus wrote a treatise entitled *On the Freedom of the Will*, Martin Luther quickly responded with *On the Bondage of the Will*, the titles nicely capturing the authors' opposing positions on the subject. A century later, it was the followers of a man named Arminius arguing against the successors of Swiss reformer John Calvin and their doctrine of total human depravity, which along with their doctrine of Predestination all but eliminated freedom of the will. The debate even resurfaced in eighteenth-century America, with the ultra-Calvinist Jonathan Edwards arguing against such liberals as Charles Chauncy on the matter—and emerging victorious in the eyes of the Puritan ecclesiastical establishment.

One who appears to have bucked the trend in that century was Englishman John Wesley, the founder of Methodism. He had to admit to the "charge" issued by Lutheran and Reformed (Calvinist) Protestants that he was an "Arminian" (that is, a believer in free will—a dreaded, latter-day Pelagian). He even confessed to a belief in human perfectibility. Wesley's more positive regard for human nature ultimately prevailed to the degree that the Methodist tradition grew out of his belief and example. Wesley is a notable exception, however, for in nearly every case in which the conservative Augustinian position has been challenged by a liberal Pelagian stance, the former has "won" the debate, at least in the eyes of "mainstream" Christianity (Catholic and Protestant), and at least until the twentieth century.

Today, however, even in churches originally built on Augustinian, Lutheran, and Calvinist-Reformed theologies, popular piety (not to mention common sense) seems to accept and affirm the fundamental goodness of humanity and to take freedom of will for granted. To that extent, Pelagius, Erasmus, Arminius, and Wesley seem to have been harbingers of things to come: they may have lost their individual battles on the subject of human nature, but their liberal faith is winning the war.

A Pair of Persistent Problems

As important as the radical notion of sin as a universal condition has been in the history of Christian thought and practice, it does raise at least two nagging problems. The first is the curious if not downright troubling fact that, for better or for worse, this premise of ineradicable sin originated with Paul rather than with Jesus himself. Indeed, it is very difficult to find *any* sayings of Jesus that suggest that humanity is so utterly debilitated by sin as to be rendered powerless to do good. Had he believed that, why would he have been remembered as telling an accused adulterous woman to stop sinning (John 8:7–11); and as commending to another the love of God—with heart, soul, mind, and strength, all apparently uncorrupted enough to be exercised—and love of neighbor (Mark 12:29–31 and Matt 22:37–39)? For that matter, why would he have even invited people to follow his teachings, if he thought that they were powerless to do so?

The other troubling aspect of the Pauline-Augustinian doctrine of sin is its possible long-term effects on those taught to believe such a thing. Although no expert on child-rearing, I am convinced that if children are constantly told that they are evil and worthless, there is a good chance that they will become adults who are precisely that. Conversely, if children are reared with a positive sense of their basic goodness and worth, they will become reasonably healthy adults with wholesome self-images and strong self-esteem. In this regard, there is cause to worry about a religion whose basic view of humanity is that in its natural state it is a "mass of damnation" corrupted by sin, powerless to do good "under its own steam," and bound for hell. Especially in contrast with Eastern faiths, which not only have no strong doctrine of sin but actually begin with a premise of everyone's essential divinity, Original Sin seems a formidably debilitating doctrine.

One of the marks of Christian Liberalism is an optimism about human nature and its inherent possibilities only slightly less grand than that Oriental view. Contrary to Paul and Augustine and their "orthodox" advocates, Liberals tend to believe that humans are basically good, innately capable of improvement, and worth the effort. That view, I suspect, corresponds pretty well with the opinions of the majority of modern people on the subject, including most Christians. For most people probably think that they and most of their fellow human beings are either basically good or at the very least a mixture of goodness and evil. They do not really harbor the idea that folks are as damned and wretched as the official formulators of Christian orthodoxy claimed. Of course, people who think in such a Liberal way may be right or wrong. They may even be bound for the very hell they have disparaged and disavowed! But this is for certain: they are running counter to the historic foundational teachings of mainstream Christianity.

The Concept of Hell

No treatment of sin and human nature would be complete without some attention to the concept of hell. For as far as most Christians through the centuries and many Christians today are concerned, the principal detrimental effect of sin is being dispatched there at death for an eternity of damnation. Indeed, some seem to think that were it not for the threat of everlasting torment and suffering in the nether regions, sin would not be such a big deal at all.

A Place of Perpetual Punishment

Like the concept of heaven, which will be discussed in the next chapter, the idea of hell has a rich and varied history. For ancient Jews, there was not a place of punishment at all, but *Sheol*, which meant either simply the grave or burial pit or, somewhat later, the abode of the dead, where phantasmic remnants of the formerly-living maintained a shadowy state of suspended "inanimation"—a kind of limbo, though no one called it that. This latter belief was a stretch for Jews, for as we saw in chapter 3, Hebrew thought had never conceived of a separable soul that could outlive the body. Thus it is difficult to know whether ancient Jews took this shadowy post-mortem existence as a metaphor or an actual reality. In any event, it is clear that Jews regarded this "hell" as the destiny of all: good and bad, righteous and unrighteous, godly and godless.

By Jesus' day, perhaps due to the influence of the Persian Zoroastrian religion, which had a clear concept of hell and of a demonic god or spirit to oversee it, some Jews probably had come to believe in a literal hell as a place of punishment and suffering. To what extent Jesus himself did is unclear. For the very few times he is reported in the canonical gospels to have alluded to such a place, his intent appears to have been more rhetorical than theological. To be sure, Matthew does have Jesus speaking of a last judgment and quoting God's anticipated pronouncement upon the accursed: "You, condemned to the everlasting fire prepared for the devil and his messengers, get away from me!" And he has Jesus add that "the second group will then head for everlasting punishment" (25:41, 46). But such sayings are rare in the recorded teachings of Jesus, and many scholars consider them to be creations of the later Church, where the idea of hell may have been more developed.

But even if Jesus did say such a thing, just how far one can push the meaning of the words of a teacher noted for his use of metaphor and parable is not clear. Indeed, most of the gospel references to "hell" on the lips of Jesus are translations of the Greek word *Gehenna*, which was the site of the smoldering garbage dump near Jerusalem, a place where the abominable practice of child sacrifice had often been carried out.

It was Paul and his successors who developed the idea of a literal hell as the destiny of the unrighteous (for example, 1 Cor 6:9–11; Eph 5:5; Gal 5:19–21; 2 Thes 1:8–9). And Christian thinkers, Protestant and Catholic, not to mention poets and painters, have followed his lead and elaborated on the horrors of hell as a place of fiery and unrelenting punishment.

Getting the Hell Out?

In modern times, theologians—mostly Liberal Protestants—have questioned the idea of hell on two grounds. First, the very notion of a nether world of punishment and suffering beneath the earth is posited on the antiquated concept of a three-storied-universe (Heaven-Earth-Hell) that is incompatible with our modern scientific worldview. Second, the idea that an infinitely, or even relatively, merciful and compassionate God could create a realm of cruel, vindictive, torturous, and (above all) eternal punishment seems totally incongruous and incredible.

Thus, some Christians have reinterpreted hell to refer either to a temporary, purgative, penitential state after death or to the sorry and sad condition of a human soul deprived of communion with God. Other contemporary Christians have simply eliminated hell from their consciousness and concern, and often along with it the idea of Satan. They find it more meaningful to focus attention on positive things: God, mercy, compassion, grace, love, and so forth. It is perfectly possible, after all, to acknowledge human sinfulness in its most profound sense and as having negative consequences without having to posit a place of excruciating and unending—and therefore purely retributive—punishment.

Conclusion

What every Christian should know about sin, and probably doesn't, is that it derives doctrinally from the thought of Paul and Augustine; that it originally referred to a universal condition inherited somehow from Adam; that it has been central to the mainstream teachings of Western Christianity, both Catholic and Protestant; and that it implies the most negative view of human nature to be found in any of the world's major religions. But Christians should also know that this view of sin did not derive from the teachings of Jesus, nor has it been the only view held by Christians over the centuries.

As we shall see, however, that orthodox view of sin is the premise upon which most of the other important teachings of the faith stand, particularly those regarding Jesus Christ and salvation. For only if we human beings are too profoundly sinful to save ourselves do we require a divine redeemer to have been sent to die for our sins. The theological problem here is that to deny orthodoxy's premise of our utter inability to save ourselves is to lessen the necessity for someone else—a redeemer-figure like a Jesus Christ, for example—to come and effect our salvation. Specifically, it all but eliminates the need for the atoning death of Christ. If, as Liberal Christians like to believe, people are not all that "damned bad," but only somewhat and curably so, then a moral teacher or example would suffice. Moreover, if folks were basically or essentially good (or even divine), then they would really need only a spiritual guide or master like Buddha to make them aware of their own inner potential (or divinity) and help them realize and release it.

While Liberal Christian interpretation has often portrayed Jesus in much that way, traditional Christianity has continued to insist that the cross is the central symbol of the faith precisely because it represents Jesus' atoning death. To the degree that the Liberals' assessment of human nature is valid, however, a major portion of Christian doctrine will need to be overhauled from the ground up. Such a reassessment will necessarily include the person of Jesus and his alleged role as the Christ, and especially the nature and purpose of his redemptive work. To that matter we turn next.

DISCUSSION QUESTIONS & EXERCISES

A. As background for the Garden of Eden story, read Genesis 1:1–2:4a and
    Genesis 2:4b–25 and list the two orders of events. Compare the lists and
    explain the differences. Find the *Enuma Elish* in a good library or on the
    Internet. Read it and note the parallels between that creation myth and
    the myths in Genesis 1–3.

B. It can be argued that the first person created in Genesis 2:7 *(ha-adham)*
    is sexually undifferentiated—an androgyne or hermaphrodite, perhaps.
    What evidence can you find for that argument, either here or in the Gen-
    esis 1 creation story (or both)? How does what you found affect the read-
    ing of the story?

C. The Garden of Eden story in Genesis 3 is an extension of the second cre-
    ation story. If Paul had focused instead on the first creation story as a
    basis for his view of humanity, how might Christian theology have been
    different? Explain.

D. Elizabeth Cady Stanton, in the late nineteenth century, said in her anger
    toward the male establishment of the church: "Take the snake, the fruit-
    tree and the woman from the tableau, and we have no fall, no frowning
    Judge, no Inferno, no everlasting punishment—hence no need of a
    Savior. Thus the bottom falls out of the whole Christian theology. Here
    is the reason why in all the Biblical researches and higher criticisms, the
    scholars never touch the position of women." To what degree do you
    think she was right? Why?

E. Read Matthew 25:31–46. How does one receive salvation according to
    that text? How does that text fit in with your church's definition of
    salvation?

F. Do you think people are born sinful? Do you think that people are
    naturally good, bad, both, or neither? Why? Given your belief in this
    regard, what kind of redeemer or savior figure (if any) might humanity
    need to "save" it or help it improve? If you belong to a Christian denom-
    ination, how closely do your ideas agree with its official doctrines or
    teachings about the human condition and salvation?

RECOMMENDED READING

Martin Buber, *Good and Evil: Two Interpretations.* Translated by Robert Gregor Smith and
    Michael Bullock. New York: Charles Scribner's Sons, 1953
    —a classic on the subject by one of the greatest Jewish philosopher-theologians and
    mystics of the twentieth century

William Ceckner, ed., *Evil and the Response of World Religion.* St. Paul, MN: Paragon House Publishers, 1997.
  — a very readable survey of the variety of perspectives on evil found in the world's great religious traditions by a wide range of experts in each
Desiderius Erasmus and Martin Luther, *Discourse on Free Will.* Scranton, PA: Frederick Ungar Publishing Co., 1985.
  — the classic (and lively) exchange in the ongoing debate in Christian history on the subject of freedom of the will, with the contrasting views of the premier Catholic humanist (pro) and the great Protestant Reformer (con)
John Hick, *Evil and the God of Love.* New York: Harper and Row, 1966.
  — another classic treatment by arguably the most outstanding philosopher of religion of modern times
Robert A. Johnson, *Owning Your Own Shadow: Understanding the Dark Side of the Psyche.* San Francisco: HarperSanFrancisco, 1991.
  — an extremely brief, readable, and reassuring treatment of the human experience of evil in a Christian context from a Jungian perspective by a psychoanalyst who also happens to be a mystic
Kristen E. Kvam, Linda S. Schearing and Valarie H. Ziegler, eds., *Eve and Adam: Jewish, Christian, and Muslim Readings on Genesis and Gender.* Indianapolis: Indiana University Press, 1999.
  — a comprehensive anthology that surveys more than 2,000 years of Jewish, Christian, and Muslim commentary on the creation stories found in Genesis and their negative and positive effects on society (for example, in the discrimination against and the support of the equality of women)
Elaine Pagels, *The Origin of Satan.* New York: Random House, 1995.
  — a ground-breaking study of the evolution of the idea of Satan in the Christian tradition from its Jewish roots, suggesting that it was really a social construct that sprang primarily from the need to demonize one's enemies
Huston Smith, *The World's Religions.* San Francisco: HarperSanFrancisco, 1991.
  — an updated version of the highly readable, eye-opening, and best-selling *Religions of Man*; a presentation of the essentials of the world's major religions by the ranking scholar in the field
William Willimon, *Sighing for Eden: Sin, Evil and the Christian Faith.* Nashville: Abingdon, 1985.
  — a modern reading of the garden myth by a university chaplain who believes that it is a metaphor for the human condition as everyone experiences it existentially

GRACE AND SALVATION iN THE CHRISTIAN TRADITION

Objectives of this chapter:

- to recognize the central place that grace occupies in Christian thought and teachings about salvation

- to define the atonement for sin accomplished in the death of Jesus as the definitive gracious act of God

- to delineate the roles of faith and good works in Christian doctrine and their proper relationship to grace

- to explain the idea of predestination and its prominent yet problematic place in the history of Christian thought

- to survey the effects attributed to salvation by grace, particularly sanctification, and other gifts of the Holy Spirit

- to examine various interpretations of the place of morality in the Christian life, as well as contrasting approaches to Christian ethics

- to explore conflicting Christian ideas about eternal life and heaven, specifically immortality of the soul and resurrection of the body

- to raise and address the question of whether Jesus Christ and the Christian faith are the only valid and effective spiritual paths

W e have heard all of our lives that "Jesus died for our sins" and that "Jesus saves." Behind those catch phrases is a great deal of Christian theology that boils down to this: Jesus had to die to save humanity because the descendants of Eve and Adam are too sinful to save themselves. People might die *because* of their sins, but they cannot die *for* their sins; for nothing they can do through living or dying will help them out of their predicament. Help must come from without and from above.

As the previous chapter has shown, traditional Christianity paints human beings into a theological corner. It takes its basic view of human nature from Paul's radical understanding of sin as a universal condition and from Augustine's more systematic elaboration of his predecessor's ideas as the doctrine of Original Sin. In this view, human beings lead lives of quiet or not-so-quiet desperation because their corrupted nature inevitably leads them to commit despicable acts of sin. Thus humanity, a "mass of damnation," is in a badly broken relationship with God. At the same time, Christian doctrine asserts that by Adam's sin we lost the ability to do anything about this terrible situation. Our sinful condition permits us to do nothing but acts of sin, despite worthy intentions and efforts, or even how much good we seem to do in the process. Every attempt to achieve righteousness in God's eyes, however sincere and concerted, is doomed to failure from the start. Even if we long only for harmony with God or eternal life, our very desire is grounded in a selfish yearning and hence impure. Theologically speaking, we are helpless and hopeless. (See figure 6.1.)

No religion could leave humanity in that untenable situation, of course, and traditional Christianity does not. It offers a way out of this predicament, a means of salvation as radical and unique as its view of sin. In other words, after delivering the bad news, it offers its *good news*, which, after all, is the literal meaning of "gospel." It should not be surprising that the solution provided by the normative Christian view of salvation, grace, is consistent with the premise, sin; nor should it come as a shock that most of the terms and images associated with salvation come from the same Paul who declared us so utterly and hopelessly sinful.

Salvation by Grace Through Faith

In his letters, Paul employed a rich mixture of terminology and imagery that have given the Christian faith many synonyms for salvation: "reconciliation," "redemption," "justification," "expiation," and "atonement." All of these derived metaphorically from different cultural contexts and thus carry different connotations and shades of meaning; but for Paul and the subsequent Christian mainstream that he helped to define they all meant essentially the same thing: getting *right with God* or simply *righteous*. Likewise as a result of Paul's influence, orthodox Christianity has maintained that because our innate depravity prevents us from achieving this goal ourselves either individually or corporately, God has mercifully done so for us through the instrument of grace.

Grace as a Gift

"Grace" is one of those words that is tossed around a great deal in Christian circles, but seldom explained and little understood. It appears in hymns, sermons, devotional literature, and conversation without ever being defined, as though everyone surely knows what the term means. My own experience in talking to life-long Christians of all ages, however, is that although most are very familiar with the beloved hymn "Amazing Grace" and may even know it by heart, they have at best a foggy notion of what grace entails. And, despite the fact that time and again they have referred to themselves as "wretches" in the second line of that song, they have never made the crucial connection between that word and the abject human sinfulness that, according to mainstream Christianity, grace is supposed to rectify.

For traditional Christianity, God's grace is the *only* means of salvation. Over the centuries, there has been a good deal of controversy about the details of grace and its workings; but there has also been general agreement that "grace" connotes an *undeserved* gift on God's part, which overcomes our

I am not worthy! I am not worthy!

Paul's sin-redemption theology permeates the language of Christian worship. Notice the stark declarations of human unworthiness and the emphasis on God's righteousness, mercy, and forgiveness as the only hope in the following traditional prayers from the eloquent Eucharistic liturgy of the Anglican-Episcopal *Book of Common Prayer*. (Italicized words and phrases are for emphasis.)

We acknowledge and bewail our manifold sins and wickedness, which we from time to time most grievously have committed, by thought, word and deed, against Thy divine Majesty, provoking most justly Thy wrath and indignation. *We do earnestly repent*, and are heartily sorry for these our misdoings; the remembrance of them is grievous to us; the burden of them is intolerable. *Have mercy* upon us, have mercy upon us, most merciful Father; for Thy Son our Lord Jesus Christ's sake *forgive us* all that is past; and grant that we may ever hereafter serve and please Thee in newness of life, to the honor and glory of Thy name; through Jesus Christ our Lord.

And although *we are unworthy*, through our manifold sins, to offer unto Thee any sacrifice, yet we beseech thee to accept this our bounden duty and service, *not weighing our merits but pardoning our offenses*, through Jesus Christ our Lord.

We do not presume to come to this Thy table, most *merciful* Lord, trusting in our own righteousness, but in thy manifold and great mercies. *We are not worthy* so much as to gather up the crumbs under Thy table. But Thou art the same Lord whose property is always to *have mercy*. Grant us, therefore, *gracious* Lord, so to eat of the flesh of Thy dear Son Jesus Christ and to drink of his blood, that we may evermore dwell in him, and he in us.

FIGURE 6.1

estrangement and restores us to a status of acceptability and even favor in God's sight. The root idea in the concept of grace is that it is *free*. (In fact, the old Church Latin word for it was *gratia*, whose adverbial form is *gratis*, a word that we have taken over into English to mean "free of charge.") In a nutshell, grace is a *present*, not a reward.

The term "grace" appears throughout Paul's writings, but one of the clearest of his statements about it is this:

> For there is no distinction since all have sinned and fall short of the glory of God; they are now justified by his grace as a gift, through the redemption that is in Christ Jesus, whom God put forward as a sacrifice of atonement by his blood, effective through faith. He did this to show his righteousness, because in his divine forbearance he had passed over the sins previously committed; it was to prove at the present time that he himself is righteous and that he justifies the one who has faith in Jesus (Rom 3:22b–26).

This rich passage is packed with the major Pauline concepts that would become the basis of Christian orthodoxy: justification, grace, redemption, sacrifice, atonement, blood, faith, righteousness. The best place to begin to understand this constellation of ideas, however, is with Paul's understanding of the role of the Law in the divine plan of salvation.

The Law That Fails and the Love That Frees

According to Paul, prior to the supreme act of grace in Christ, God had always been reaching out in love and mercy to provide humanity with measures for their salvation. The greatest example of God's intention and effort in this regard was the Law (Torah), graciously given to the Israelites as a part of what Paul called "The Old Covenant" in the expectation that they would obey it. But the Law had proven an insufficient measure, precisely because humanity was so incapacitated by sin that it could not live up to its demands. The Law, then, had not only demonstrated the utterly hopeless plight of humanity in its "fallen" state, it had actually left God's chosen people more damned and desperate than before (Rom 5:13, 20). For the Law required good works; but humanity had proven again and again incapable of meeting that expectation, and thus had fallen into deeper and deeper despair. So God had had to devise another means of salvation, because, in Paul's own words, " . . . a person is justified not by works of the law," and "no one will be justified by the works of the law" (Gal 2:15–16). The new instrument of justification was, of course, grace.

As indicated in the previous chapter, there is a logical—or, more accurately, a theological—problem with this scenario. One wonders why a God of common sense, much less omniscience, would not have foreseen the Israelites' inability to obey the Law and jumped directly to a more profound and effective form of grace. Here again God appears to be fumbling, just as in the case of Adam and Eve in the Garden: trying one thing, then scrambling to Plan B when the first attempt proves ineffective. Again, why God did not foresee the inadequacy of the Law or the inability of the Israelites and humanity and thus save everyone a lot of time, effort, frustration, and grief Paul never addresses or even seems to wonder. He simply never faces the seeming ineptitude of this God, perhaps because he was working out his theology while on the go and therefore piecemeal—making it up as he went along, as it were. In any case, the inefficiency of God in the salvation of humanity remains a major if not fatal flaw in Paul's system.

Perhaps an image will help to explain Paul's view of sin and grace: let us think of sin as a huge wall that separates humanity from God, one that we can neither tear down nor scale. In giving humanity the Law, God had made an opening in the "wall of sin," had posted the Law next to it, and had said, in effect, "Obey my commandments and come on through," only to find that humanity was too incapacitated by sin to do so. So God, in an act of unprecedented compassion and undeserved mercy, took a dramatically different approach and created a substantial breach in the wall. God then reached through the opening and all the way across the intervening distance in order to bestow upon humanity unmerited love and forgiveness, to empower us with the Holy Spirit, and above all to restore us, through the person and work of Jesus Christ, to a loving relationship with God. (See figure 6.2.)

The gratuitous nature of this divine action cannot be emphasized too strongly. It is—and indeed has to be—unconditional ("no strings attached"; "no ifs, ands, or buts"), unearned, and undeserved. Otherwise, it is not really a gift. Throughout the centuries, Catholic and Protestant theologians have interpreted grace differently and have varied their emphasis on or enthusiasm for the doctrine, but they have substantially agreed that salvation is free, and ultimately attributable not to human effort, but to God's gracious activity in Jesus Christ. And their reasoning has always come back to this presupposition: that humans are just "too damned sinful" for salvation to depend on them. It simply *has* to be a gift.

Clearly, the idea of grace flies in the face of much of what many Christian children are taught by their parents and church school teachers, and what many adults are led to believe by clergy. Such "authorities," often only marginally educated in their own theological heritage, leave the impression (if not declare outright) that salvation is something that one should desire and make a decision to seek and obtain. The message of Paul and the Christian mainstream, however, has always been that redemption does not come as a result of one's own yearnings, searchings, or efforts, but only as the free gift of God's love.

Atonement in Christ and the Cross as the Crux

As the pivotal passage from Romans 3 quoted above indicates, Paul depicted Jesus Christ as the locus of God's ultimate gracious action toward humanity; and Paul's ideas in this regard became the basis of Christian thought about salvation, which revolves around two key, related concepts: *incarnation* and *atonement*. "Incarnation" ("enfleshment") means the embodiment of God in the person of Jesus, and we covered that doctrine in chapter 4. "Atonement"—a synonym for "reconciliation," referring to the bringing together of the once-estranged duo, God and humanity, into a situation of "at-one-ment" with one another—is effected by Jesus' saving

Paul & Gracie, Part II: A Loser Gets Lucky

FIGURE 6.2

"work": not his life and ministry so much as his self-sacrificing death for humanity.

Perhaps the best-known and most succinct expression of Paul's view on atonement comes in the first half of the fifth chapter of his letter to the Romans, some of which we noted in our preceding chapter:

> For while we were still weak, at the right time Christ died for the ungodly. Indeed, rarely will anyone die for a righteous person— though perhaps for a good person someone might actually dare to die. But God proves his [sic] love for us in that while we still were sinners Christ died for us. Much more surely, then, now that we have been justified by his blood, will we be saved through him from the wrath of God. For if while we were enemies, we were reconciled to God through the death of his [sic] Son, much more surely, having been reconciled, will we be saved by his life. But more than that, we even boast in God through our Lord Jesus Christ, through whom we have now received reconciliation (Rom 5:6–11).

Paul's reference to "life" in the next to the last sentence of this passage does not mean the earthly life of the historical Jesus, but the "life" of the risen and ascended Christ. For in the view of Paul, it was not the miraculous conception of Christ (about which he said nothing) nor the life and teachings of the historical Jesus (about which he appears to have known or cared little), but only the death of Jesus on the cross that is the key to human salvation.

It is prudent at this point to recall that Paul, by his own admission, had not known the earthly Jesus, the teacher and prophet of God's unmediated and present domain. It is even doubtful whether Paul had ever attempted to familiarize himself with whatever sayings and deeds of Jesus might have been available through oral tradition. (Remember, there would be no gospels until after Paul's death.) What is certain is that the teachings and actions that constituted the ministry of the man of Nazareth played no appreciable role in Paul's writings or his theology. For Paul, only two things were important about Jesus: his alleged divinity and his atoning death. Together these and these alone made human salvation possible.

In all of this, Paul saw a clear parallel between Adam and Christ: as Adam had been disobedient, and thus had brought sin and death and condemnation into the world, so had Christ been obedient, and consequently had brought righteousness and life and acquittal. As Paul himself put it:

> Therefore just as sin came into the world through one man, and death came through sin, and so death spread to all because all have sinned—sin was indeed in the world before the law, but sin is not reckoned when there is no law. . . . But the free gift is not like the trespass. For if the many died through the one man's trespass, much more surely have the grace of God and the free gift in the grace of the one man Jesus Christ abounded for the many. . . . If, because of the one man's trespass, death exercised dominion through that one, much more surely will those who receive the abundance of grace and the free gift of righteousness exercise dominion in life through the

one man, Jesus Christ. Therefore, just as one man's trespass led to condemnation for all, so one man's act of righteousness leads to justification and life for all. For just as by one man's disobedience the many were made sinners, so by the one man's obedience the many will be made righteous (Rom 5:12–19).

Paul's language here is from the law courts, as is one of the important terms he uses often for salvation: "justification" (literally, "acquittal" or "pronouncement of innocence"). As we have seen, he used other imagery drawn from other contexts as well. But the message was always the same: Jesus undid the human tragedy that Adam had wrought.

Thus Paul was certain and clear that the death of Jesus was the gracious act of God that brought atonement. But when it came to the sticky question of just *how* one person's execution—however unjust or agonizing—could possibly be effectual and salutary for successive generations of people, Paul was at best sketchy and suggestive. Instead of presenting a clear and unambiguous explanation of cause (cross) and effect (atonement), he offered several terms to suggest to his contemporary readers some provocative images that would be meaningful to them: *expiation* (through sacrifice), *ransom* (from captivity), *redemption* (from slavery), and *victory* (in warfare). Through such colorful similes or metaphors, Paul hoped to convey a sense of the purpose of Jesus' atoning death.

Analyzing and Arguing Atonement

One important result of Paul's ambiguity about the mechanics of Christ's redemption—that is, *how* it accomplished humanity's salvation—is a succession of theories of atonement, which were produced, promulgated, and debated throughout the Middle Ages and later eras, and which, for the most part, coexist in Christian thought in modern times despite their logical incompatibility with one another. There were actually five such historic theories that elicited a fair amount of support among theologians. One, the *satisfaction theory*, was derived from ancient Jewish ritual practices and thus regarded Christ as a sacrifice to God that appeased the deity, who had been so offended by human sin. Another, the *substitution theory*, held that the death of Jesus was not so much a sacrifice as a payment to God for the debt owed by humanity by virtue of sin. Yet another, the *ransom theory*, reasoned that sinfulness had put humanity on the Devil's "turf," and that God had made the payment to Satan necessary to free us. A fourth, the *victory theory*, suggested that far from being a payment to the Devil, Christ through his "obedience unto death" effected a defeat-in-principle of the power of evil. Still another, the *moral theory*, held that the real point of Jesus' obedience and death was to provide an example for humanity to follow.

What is most intriguing, and perhaps frustrating, about these theories is not so much the imaginativeness or ingenuity that they reflect, but the vastly different dynamics that they embody. The first two are directed toward God, either by appeasing or compensating the deity for humanity's trespasses. The third and fourth are aimed at Satan and spell the end of his demonic control over humanity, though in dramatically different, even diametrically opposed ways. (Did God pay off or punch out the Devil?) The fifth suggests a change in the disposition, not of God or of Satan, but of humanity itself. This serious lack of unanimity on such an important issue bespeaks yet another gap in Paul's theology: the absence of an *explanation* of the efficacy of the cross.

Of all of these, the satisfaction theory has tended to be the most popular and influential in Christian history, not only in Roman Catholicism's view of the Mass as a sacrifice of the Lamb of God on an altar, but in the "bloody" hymns and sermons of American Evangelical Protestantism. (See figure 6.3.) Conversely, the moral theory has received the least support among orthodox theologians, primarily because it suggests that if humanity needed only an example to follow, it must not have been so thoroughly sinful after all.

Factoring in Faith (While Guarding Grace)

In the history of Christian thought, the word "faith" has had two very different meanings, one *propositional* and the other *relational*. On the one hand, it has denoted "belief in" or "assent to" particular truths, teachings, ideas, or doctrines—in other words, the acceptance of certain propositions. To have faith in this sense is simply to affirm something as true that cannot be empirically or rationally verified. On the other hand, "faith" has had the meaning of "trust," as when we talk about friends or spouses being "faithful" to one another, meaning simply that they maintain a *relationship* based on mutual confidence. For a Christian to have religious faith in the first, propositional sense is to believe *that* there is a God and probably *that* this God has done and can do certain things. To have faith in the relational sense, by contrast, is to place one's trust in God, God's grace, or the ultimate triumph of God's righteousness.

Of these two meanings, the relational is the more biblical, for in both of the Christian biblical Testaments, "faith" generally connotes reliability, steadfastness, confidence, and trust. The object is usually a person (or personal God) rather than a proposition, and nearly always implies a personal relationship. The object or content of religious faith in this sense is not a truth presented rationally, but the providence, purposes, promises, and performance of a caring and dependable God in history. Paul certainly used "faith" in the sense of trust. He sometimes made the object of faith God's grace itself, and at other times Jesus Christ. But that variation is understandable in light of the key role that Jesus Christ (and particularly his atoning death) played in Paul's views of God's gracious plans. To Paul, God's grace and the saving work of Jesus Christ were virtually synonymous.

Preachers sometimes suggest, if not outright declare, that in order to obtain God's forgiveness and mercy one has simply to get, and perhaps give verbal or visible testimony to, faith. From the standpoint of traditional Christianity, however, this understanding is backwards. For it makes grace not unconditional, but conditional; that is, dependent upon the faith that a person generates. But if we are too "damned sinful" to do any good thing, and "works righteousness" (the attempt to earn heaven by doing good) doesn't work, then we have to deny this interpretation of faith. For in effect it turns faith into just one more work, performed by the exertion of the will. Or stated in another way, if you have to do *anything* to earn grace, including generating or having or professing faith, it isn't grace at all, but a prize or reward.

If we are to maintain a strict Pauline line, therefore, faith itself (like good works) is best regarded as both secondary and subsequent to grace. Grace is what saves, for that is God's act, and God must be in charge of the process, since only God is inherently righteous. Faith, being a human activity, is a *response* to grace. As Paul himself puts it: "For this reason it depends on faith, in order that the promise may rest on grace . . . " (Rom 4:16). In

---

Washed in What?!

" . . . our paschal lamb, Christ, has been sacrificed." (1 Cor 5:7b)

The image of Jesus Christ as a sacrificial lamb has been a pivotal part of Christian thought ever since St. Paul introduced that metaphor. The traditional Eucharist — itself a rehearsal of Christ's sacrifice, performed on an altar — includes references to the image, as in the ancient hymn, *Agnus dei:* "O Lamb of God, who takest away the sins of the world, have mercy upon us . . . grant us Thy peace."

In Evangelical Protestant Christian circles, however, special attention has been given to the blood of Jesus and its cleansing effect, leading to some rather macabre "washing" imagery that is not, in itself, biblical. Take a look at some lyric fragments from a few old favorite hymns:

> **There is a fountain filled with blood**
> **Drawn from Immanuel's [Christ's] veins;**
> **And sinners, plunged beneath that flood,**
> **Lose all their guilty stains.**
> *—William Cowper*

> **What can wash away my sins?**
> **Nothing but the blood of Jesus; . . .**
> **Oh! precious is the flow / That makes me white as snow;**
> **No other fount I know / Nothing but the blood of Jesus.**
> *—Robert Lowry*

> **Have you been to Jesus for the cleansing power?**
> **Are you washed in the blood of the Lamb? . . .**
> **Are your garments spotless? Are they white as snow?**
> **Are you washed in the blood of the Lamb?**
> *—Elisha A. Hoffman*

> **Would you be free from your burden of sin?**
> **There's pow'r in the blood, pow'r in the blood . . .**
> **There is pow'r, pow'r, wonder-working pow'r**
> **In the precious blood of the Lamb.**
> *—L. E. Jones*

What is perhaps most strange about these hymns is that their tunes are invariably upbeat and lilting, and usually sung with great toe-tapping gusto and glee.

FIGURE **6.3**

6

Grace and
Salvation in
the Christian
Tradition

other words, you don't get grace because you have faith; you get grace and then have faith (that is, trust) in it and its Giver. To be sure, Paul sometimes invites misinterpretation when he makes statements like this: " . . . since we are justified by faith, we have peace with God through our Lord Jesus Christ" (Rom 5:1), and " . . . a person is justified, not by the works of the law but through faith in Jesus Christ" (Gal 2:16). Such wording makes faith sound like the cause, and justification the effect. But when such statements are read in the larger context of Paul's rhetoric, his intention becomes clear. Indeed, immediately following the passage just cited from Romans, Paul refers to "Jesus Christ, our . . . Lord through whom we have obtained access to this grace in which we stand . . . " (Rom 5:2a). Again and again Paul's point is that when it comes to salvation, God is the agent and benefactor, and humanity is but the recipient and beneficiary.

The most precise statement of the case is that *we are saved by grace through faith*: "For by grace you have been saved through faith; and this is not your own doing; it is the gift of God—not the result of works, so that no one may boast" (Eph 2:8). Ironically, this clear explication of Paul almost certainly was not written by Paul, but by a follower using his name. Had Paul himself consistently used his terms so carefully, there might be less confusion about the relationship of grace and faith today.

From time to time, some Christian theologians have wrestled with the question of what it is that could empower such thoroughly sinful human beings to respond to God's grace. For would not their radical sinfulness rule out the slightest ability to accept an offered gift of salvation? Some have therefore argued for what they called a "prevenient grace" that precedes saving grace—perhaps as a natural trait or innate capacity—and that sufficiently empowers the individual to respond to the full measure of redemptive grace. Some object that such attention to humanity's ability or inability to respond to grace may well be theological overkill, and that the concept of prevenient grace is a needless inflation of Christian doctrine. But at least those responsible for this seemingly dispensable notion have gotten Paul's point: when it comes to salvation, God is—indeed *must* be—completely in charge.

Given his radical view of sin, Paul himself might well have said (as some Protestant theologians later did) that it must be saving grace itself that affords a person the ability to respond, since *any* faith generated by the person on his or her own could arise only from a corrupted nature. Like some later theologians, he might also have been concerned that even such a seemingly innocuous notion as prevenient grace somehow mitigated the utter sinfulness on which the dramatic atonement was predicated, and thus threatened to reduce the necessity of Jesus' saving work. And Paul certainly didn't want to do that!

No Other Name?

Another important consideration is whether, as many Christians have been taught and firmly believe, the salvation offered by God in Jesus Christ is offered *only* in him and *exclusively* to those who have heard and embraced the Christian gospel. That seems to be the point of Jesus' oft-quoted assertion in John 14:6: "I am the way, and I am truth, and I am life. . . . No one gets to the Father unless it is through me." That apparent exclusivism is reinforced by the claim made by Luke in Acts 4:12 that "There is salvation in no one else, for there is no other name under heaven given among mortals by which we must be saved." Has God, then, left some people without a witness or means of salvation? Is Jesus the only Way, Truth, and Life? Is he the only redeemer? Does no one come to God except through him? Is there really no other name by which people may be saved or redeemed?

Traditional Christian claims of the unique efficacy of Jesus Christ are much more troublesome today than they once were. Prior to the twentieth century, given the limitations on travel and communications, most Christians (and especially those in the Western hemisphere) had little or no contact with people of other cultures or their religious traditions. It was thus far easier to consign to eternal damnation those distant nameless and faceless persons who were devoted to the great religious traditions inspired by such exalted spiritual figures as Muhammad, Krishna, Lao Tse, and the Buddha, and who were edified by venerable scriptures like the *Qur'an*, *Bhagavad Gita*, *Tao Te Ching*, and *Dhammapada*. All of these were simply unknown in the Western world.

But Christians today are much more likely to meet, know, and form friendships with people who adhere to such non-Christian traditions, and who thus may profess very different yet plausible beliefs, even on such fundamental issues as the human predicament and salvation. Christians are also more likely to be exposed and drawn to other of the world's religious traditions, not only in high school and college classrooms, but through public libraries and popular bookstores, movies, and television programs. All of this should lead Christians at least to consider the possibility that a truly gracious and loving God might have provided various paths and means of salvation for people of various cultures. They might wonder, more specifically, whether the same God that Christians worship might be the source of inspiration behind other religious and spiritual traditions and the scriptures and doctrines they have produced. Such considerations might further prompt Christians to examine a number of religious issues—God, the life of the spirit, human nature, and perhaps even their own religious tradition—from the vantage points of these alternative altars.

Christians wanting to explore or embrace such inclusive ideas may take comfort in the fact that in his own relations, as well as in his sayings and parables about the present reign of God, Jesus himself was anything but exclusivist. Also, the very same New Testament books that contain the highly exclusivist assertions cited above provide ammunition for the counter-argument as well. For in John 10:16, Jesus is quoted as saying: "Yet I have sheep from another fold, and I must lead them, too." And in Acts 10:34, Peter is reported as sharing this new realization: "I truly understand that God shows no partiality, but in every nation anyone who fears him and does what is right is acceptable to him." Such statements hardly square with the "One Way" Christians who claim that only Jesus Christ and Christianity are valid paths to God, and that all who follow other spiritual masters and religious traditions are, to put it bluntly, going to hell.

Predestination: Its Purpose and Its Problems

One of the most troublesome and misunderstood doctrines in the history of Christian thought is predestination. What makes it problematic, especially in modern times, is that it tends even by its terminology to run counter to widely held notions of individual freedom and self-determination. Oddly enough, however, all of the great pre-modern theologians who formulated Christian orthodoxy, Protestant and Catholic, affirmed the doctrine of predestination. In its simplest form, this doctrine holds that God determined before creation who would be saved, not on the basis of divine foreknowledge of their character or actions—that would reduce grace to a pre-planned reward—but on the basis of arbitrary divine choice. Thus, though Christ died *in theory* for *all* humanity, in fact the positive effects of his death would accrue only to those pre-determined by God to be its beneficiaries.

As if that scenario were not hard enough for the modern mind to accept, one sixteenth-century Reformation theologian, John Calvin, argued for "double predestination," which meant that God had specified—again, prior to creation—both who would be saved and who would be damned. In the long run, the results are about the same: for those unchosen in "single" predestination are consigned to damnation by default. But Calvin's view does seem to suggest an almost sadistic image of God, which may simply be the unintended result of still more theological overkill.

The Biblical Witness—A Blow to the Will?

As distasteful and perhaps downright silly as the notion of predestination may seem to modern consciousness, the arguments for it are surprisingly strong. For one thing, there is considerable biblical evidence that the God of the Judaeo-Christian tradition is one who picks and chooses. In the Hebrew scriptures, for example, Jahweh designates the children of Israel as a chosen people, apparently not on the basis of their merit, but simply because God wanted to do so. That means that God did not choose (elect, or predestine) any of a number of other people in Israel's immediate vicinity. Psalm 65 also suggests that God chooses only some individuals to receive divine hospitality (v. 4). Indeed, such precedents in what Christian theologians regarded as their Old Testament provided them more than enough justification for the formulation of a doctrine of predestination.

But they had much more ammunition than that! For in the New Testament, many passages written by or attributed to Paul suggest predestination. One of them, for example, says:

> We know that all things work together for good for those who love God, who are called according to his [sic] purpose. For those whom he [sic] foreknew, he also predestined to be conformed to the image of his Son, in order that he might be the first-born within a large family. And those whom he predestined he also called; and those whom he called he also justified; and those whom he justified he also glorified (Rom 8:28–30).

Another passage, probably written by someone influenced by Paul rather than the apostle himself, is even more explicit:

Blessed be the God and Father of our Lord Jesus Christ, who has blessed us in Christ with every spiritual blessing in the heavenly places, just as he chose us in Christ before the foundation of the world to be holy and blameless before him in love. He destined us for adoption as his children through Jesus Christ, according to the good pleasure of his will, to the praise of his glorious grace that he freely bestowed on us in the Beloved. In him we have redemption through his blood, the forgiveness of our trespasses, according to the riches of his grace that he lavished upon us (Eph 1:3–8).

Though any scripture is subject to various interpretations, these and other similar statements in the New Testament suggested to the formulators of orthodox Christian doctrine that God has a master plan, conceived prior to creation, and specifying who would receive redemption. Also noteworthy in this passage is the phrase "according to the good pleasure of his will," which clearly means "because God wanted to." The implication of arbitrary or unconditional choice is evident.

Exactly what Paul and others had in mind in composing such seemingly predestinarian statements is not entirely clear. For one thing, it is difficult to determine to what extent they may have been using hyperbole with such language as "before the foundation." But the very notion of predestination seems to coincide with the tendency of the New Testament to refer to the Church as "The New Israel," which is to say "the recently chosen people of God." That image both confirms and reinforces the pattern of divine election that the premier theologians of Christianity over the centuries have discerned in their Old Testament.

But the motivation of Paul and all subsequent proponents of predestination was not purely scriptural. They also had a theological reason for affirming such a seemingly exclusive and irrational doctrine: it reinforced the idea that God alone is in charge of salvation. It was a way of saying, "Not only is salvation beyond human control, the decision concerning your salvation was made before the world was created. The matter is thus completely and utterly out of your hands."

A Comforting and Gracious Doctrine?

Strange as it may seem, some predestinarian theologians, like John Calvin in sixteenth-century Switzerland, found this a comforting doctrine. Two centuries later in colonial America, Jonathan Edwards even described predestination as "exceedingly bright, and sweet"! Some people in their respective congregations apparently had been spending a great deal of time wringing their hands over whether they were or were not saved. The doctrine of predestination, then, was a useful pastoral tool, a way of saying to worried parishioners: "Stop worrying! The whole thing is settled! There is nothing you can do: it's up to God. Relax!"

Both Calvin and Edwards also concluded that one could not finally know where they stood in God's plan. But, lest folks take the fact of predestination as an invitation to live wild and immoral lives (secure in the knowledge that their behavior could not affect God's primordial decision about their fate one way or the other), both suggested that all Christians should live as though they were among "God's elect." If they happened not to be, they could go to hell comforted by the fact that they were still playing a small part in God's overall plan.

Though predestination may seem to be at odds with our twentieth-century love of freedom and self-determination *and* to imply an arbitrary and dispassionate deity, the theologians who affirmed and promulgated it thought that it bespoke a gracious God. Their reasoning was this: it is not God's fault that humanity is sinful; all deserve damnation as a result of Adam's disobedience; so if God chooses to save even a few out of divine charity, to God be thanks and praise! After all, we didn't criticize Mother Teresa of Calcutta because she didn't provide care for all the world's poor, did we? An absolutely just God would have let humanity as a whole perish, and rightly so. But God is merciful, and goes out of the way graciously to save a portion of humanity. It is God's mercy that should be emphasized, not the limits thereof—or so goes the argument.

Perhaps here again an illustration will help clarify. Suppose a great ocean liner, piloted by Captain God, comes upon the wreckage of another ship, steered to its destruction by one Captain Adam. (We shall picture this captain as a male here, because that is the way Paul, Augustine, and the orthodox theologians who hatched and maintained the doctrine imagined God.) Amid the flotsam are visible the bobbing heads of a thousand people crying out to be saved. Captain God quite graciously (since the wreck wasn't his doing and isn't his responsibility) interrupts his own course to engage in a rescue, and manages to save five hundred souls (as they say) before proceeding toward the original port of destination. (Calvin's "double predestination" of course, would have God ordering the heads of the remaining victims pushed under the water until they drowned—but let's not dwell on that scenario!) Upon arrival, Captain God is not faulted for his failure to save half the potential drowning victims, but given a medal of honor for managing to save the rest who surely would have been fatalities without his selfless efforts. (Still, it could be argued that a modern female skipper—and a more feminine God—would have made sure that all were saved.)

Of course, this illustration points to a number of serious theological questions that the idea of predestination raises. For one thing, if God decides to be gracious, why to just a portion of humanity, and why so arbitrarily? Why doesn't God elect to save everyone, or at least offer salvation to everyone in accordance with some strict guidelines? (In terms of our illustration, wouldn't God's vessel—a Love Boat, naturally!—be unlimited in capacity? Why, then, save only five hundred? Why not rescue all?) Is it reasonable to maintain that a truly merciful God, a loving Parent to boot, would exclude any from divine grace, and allow even one child to suffer eternally or perish utterly?

Those who have taken the position that God (or the Ultimate, however conceived) in fact eventually would save everyone are called "universalists" (not to be confused with the Universalist denomination that was in fact founded on this idea, and that later merged with the Unitarians). Universalism is found in nearly all of the world's religions, sometimes as the mainstream view. (Pure Land Buddhism is a good example, for it teaches that the warm compassion of the Amida Buddha extends to and guarantees a celestial salvation for all eventually, even non-Buddhists.) In Christianity, however, universalism is almost invariably a minority report. Still, there have been universalists in all brands of Christianity over the centuries—people who have held that however salvation is to be conceived, everyone gets it sooner or later. For, they have reasoned, a God of infinite mercy and compassion—a God that truly *is* Love—could have it no other way. Traditional Christians are not convinced, and have devised a multitude of explanations (none of them convincing) for how a God who *is* Love can write anyone off forever.

Predestination's Limited Scope . . . and Appeal

Whatever difficulties the modern mind may have with the idea of predestination formulated by the great Christian theologians, we should at least note that it is quite restricted in its implications, especially in comparison with some current, non-Christian beliefs. For one thing, it is strictly theological, and confined to the issue of one's ultimate spiritual destiny. Thus, contrary to some popular misconceptions, the Christian doctrine of predestination has nothing whatsoever to do with what one will have for lunch, where one will vacation next summer, whom (or whether) one will marry, to what vocation one will dedicate one's life, or even how long one will live. (The biblical dictum that our days are "numbered" simply means that we have a finite time to live, not a definite or predetermined length to our lives.) In short, the doctrine of predestination has only to do with whether or not one will be saved.

In this regard, Christianity's strictly theological doctrine of predestination is much less comprehensive and confining than many modern forms of determinism. Proponents of astrology, for example, assert that our basic personality types, directions of our lives, and even specific events are predetermined by the configuration of stars and planets at the moment of our birth. Recent studies by both geneticists and sociologists further suggest that we are far more the product of our innate genetic structure—and far less by either environment or free will—than we ever imagined. Added to these examples are the common truisms with which we are all familiar: "When your number's up, your number's up"; "God has a plan for my life, a destiny for me to fulfill"; "It just wasn't meant to be." Whether any of these fatalistic assertions is true is beside the point; they reflect a deterministic attitude that is far more sweeping than the narrowly focused theological doctrine of predestination, which applies solely to the question of one's salvation.

Nevertheless, of all the doctrines connected with the notion of grace, predestination has been the most difficult for the Church to embrace, despite the fact that many of its greatest spokespersons—Paul, Augustine, Thomas Aquinas, Martin Luther, John Calvin, and even twentieth-century Neo-Orthodox Protestant theologian Karl Barth (a list notable for its absence of women)—all affirmed it. In Roman Catholicism, the idea has been, at best, peripheral; most Protestant denominations have downplayed or rejected it; and even those who have not (such as the Calvinistic Reformed and Presbyterian bodies) have planted it more firmly in their official creeds and historic confessions than in the hearts and minds of their members. Its limited appeal does not prove the doctrine of predestination wrong, of course, since rarely has truth been obtained by referendum. What is certain is that the idea runs counter to the sensibilities of most who live today in the "free world," and perhaps especially offends the citizens of "the land of the free," for whom the concepts of individual liberty and freedom of choice are staples of consciousness.

The Effects of Salvation

What does God's free bestowal of grace accomplish? For the believer, according to Paul, it is nothing less than a "new creation":

> So if anyone is in Christ, there is a new creation; everything old has passed away; see, everything has become new! All this is from God, who reconciled us to himself [sic] through Christ and gave us the ministry of reconciliation; that is, in Christ God was reconciling the world to himself, not counting their trespasses against them, and entrusting the message of reconciliation to us. . . . For our sake he [sic] made him to be sin who knew no sin, so that in him we might become the righteousness of God (2 Cor 5:17–19, 21).

According to this passage, God treats us as a judge would, but with incredible leniency. It is as though we were objectively guilty criminals led before a judge who knows that we are guilty, but who nevertheless chooses to disregard our offenses and to pronounce us "not guilty." It is again worth noting that "righteous" and "justified" both had legal connotations in Paul's day.

Real Righteousness

Far-fetched though this courtroom illustration may sound, our own judicial system quite frequently pronounces objectively guilty parties "not guilty" in the eyes of the law because of technicalities, extenuating circumstances, or easy juries; and sometimes it convicts innocent people by mistake, making them legally guilty, despite their objective innocence. Paul's idea that objectively guilty sinners might be declared innocent suddenly makes more sense than it appeared to initially.

It is noteworthy that Paul typically embeds the term "righteousness" in the phrase "righteousness of God," thereby underscoring his belief that humanity has no legitimate claim to it. As he affirms in the passage quoted earlier (Rom 3:21–26), only God is inherently righteous; humans have to be *made* righteous, presumably out of the vast storehouse of God's own righteousness. The term sometimes used for this process is "imputation"—as in "God imputes righteousness to us"—which suggests that God ascribes or attributes to us the "not-guiltiness" that we could not attain ourselves.

The major effect of this "imputation" of righteousness, this "not guilty" verdict despite our obvious sinfulness, is that humans are left in an ambiguous situation: objectively sinful, but righteous in God's gracious eyes. Martin Luther used the Latin phrase *simul iustus et peccator*, which means "at one and the same time righteous and a sinner," to describe the paradoxical situation of the recipient of God's grace. For the gift of grace does not automatically render the recipient morally upright, much less faultless. Indeed, Paul was quite open about his own persistent tendency to continue sinning: "For I do not do the good I want, but the evil I do not want is what I do" (Rom 7:19). The reason for this behavior, he says, is that sin still dwells and works in him, despite his having received God's grace, forgiveness, and righteousness.

Spirit-Possession and Other Salutary Side-Effects

Counteracting this sin in the believer is the spirit of Christ (or the Spirit of God, or the Holy Spirit—Paul uses the terms practically interchangeably), which is also at work in him or her, presumably as part of God's gift:

> But you are not in the flesh, you are in the Spirit, since the Spirit of God dwells in you. Anyone who does not have the Spirit of Christ does not belong to him. But if Christ is in you, though the body is dead because of sin, the Spirit is life because of righteousness. If the Spirit of him[sic] who raised Jesus from the dead dwells in you, he [sic] who raised Christ from the dead will give life to your mortal bodies also through his [sic] Spirit that dwells in you (Rom 8:9–11).

Two things should be noted at this point. First, Paul here and elsewhere makes a sharp differentiation between "flesh" and "spirit" that was foreign to the holistic view of humanity in both his own Jewish tradition and the teachings of Jesus. Second, the term "Holy Spirit," which theologians later employed in a very specific way to distinguish the third Person of the Holy Trinity, Paul uses here and elsewhere in a more general sense; for him it merely signifies the presence of Christ within the believer.

Paul's language about this inner presence occasionally borders on the spooky, suggesting a kind of possession: ". . . it is no longer I who live, but it is Christ who lives in me . . . " (Gal 2:20). What Paul seems to be getting at here is the same point that he has been making all along, namely, that human beings cannot accomplish anything truly good "under their own steam." Only after they have received not only grace, but also the Holy Spirit are they capable of doing good. Of course, even then they don't deserve any credit, for God is the true author of the good they do as well as of the grace they have: "For we are what he has made us, created in Christ Jesus for good works, which God prepared beforehand to be our way of life" (Eph 2:10).

Coming as important side-effects of the receiving of grace and the Spirit are other appealing gifts (Greek, *charismata*):

> Now there are varieties of gifts, but the same Spirit; and there are varieties of services, but the same Lord; and there are varieties of activities, but it is the same God who activates them in everyone. To each is given the manifestation of the Spirit for the common good. To one is given through the Spirit the utterance of wisdom, and to another the utterance of knowledge according to the same Spirit,

to another faith by the same Spirit, to another gifts of healing by the one Spirit, to another the working of miracles, to another prophecy, to another the discernment of spirits, to another various kinds of tongues, to another the interpretation of tongues. All these are activated by one and the same Spirit, who allots to each one individually just as the Spirit chooses (1 Cor 12:4–11).

It appears that the blessings brought by the Holy Spirit are many and varied!

The two last-mentioned of these gifts, involving "tongues," have proven to be the most controversial. The Greek word is *glossolalia* (literally, "a speaking"), which connotes spontaneous utterances in a language that is unknown to speaker. This was a gift that Paul himself downplayed, suggesting that though he himself had experienced this phenomenon, it should be restrained in worship and allowed only under strict guidelines (1 Cor 14). Most Christian denominations have therefore been either cautious or downright disparaging with regard to such charismatic expressions. Within the last century or so, however, a number of "Pentecostal" and "Holiness" denominations and sects have emerged within evangelical Protestantism, as well as charismatic movements and groups in mainline Protestant and Catholic churches, all of which have—Paul's reservations notwithstanding—placed a great deal of emphasis on tongues, as well as prophecy and healing.

Making Sense of Sanctification

Some of these groups also stress the idea of "sanctification." The term is used in the New Testament, though rather ambiguously: at times it appears synonymous with "justification," while at others it suggests a process at work within those justified, a sort of growth in grace under the influence of the Spirit. Even in this latter sense, however, Paul makes it clear that one's salvation is not dependent on this growth process, but is guaranteed by the justification itself. Thus, in a sense, sanctification (literally "holy-making") may be the icing for the believer, but it is certainly not the cake.

But Paul lists other gifts of the Spirit that are at once more ordinary and, in his eyes, more important: ". . . the fruit of the Spirit is love, joy, peace, patience, kindness, generosity, faithfulness, gentleness, and self-control" (Gal 5:22). At the top of this list is love, which in New Testament terminology is a special type. The Greek word is *agape* (usually pronounced "ah-GAH-pay"), which means "selfless love" or even "self-sacrificing love" and refers both to God's love for humanity as exhibited in the death of Christ, and to the sort of love that is expected of those who "walk in the Spirit."

Paul does not believe that the Spirit, or sanctification, or the gifts are delivered to individuals in isolation from other people; all of his thought assumes community. When one receives grace, that person is "in Christ," an odd use of language that makes sense only when one realizes that by "Christ" here Paul is thinking not of the earthly Jesus, but of a cosmic spiritual reality—presumably the risen, exalted, and glorified One that he had reportedly experienced on the Damascus road. He also appears to believe that once "in Christ," the believer is automatically in company with others so "graced." Indeed, he speaks of such people as "members of the body of Christ" (1 Cor 12:12). But with that notion we have encountered the concept of the Church, to which we shall turn attention in the next chapter.

Christian Ethics

The fact that Christian orthodoxy's commitment to the idea that salvation comes by grace alone has clearly determined the role of ethics in the faith. After all, if God grants salvation not on the basis of the merits earned by one's deeds, but purely as a divine act of mercy, then living a virtuous life would seem to be beside the point.

A Law Unto Oneself?

In fact, throughout the history of the faith some have concluded that Christians are perfectly free to do whatever they wish, unrestricted by moral law. They have generally been labeled "antinomians" (opponents of the law), and summarily denounced as such. In ancient times, antinomianism was prevalent among Gnostics because of their radical body-soul dichotomy, which left the flesh to do pretty much what it wanted while the soul sought an eternal home. The first Christian antinomian is generally acknowledged to have been Marcion (c. 140 CE), himself a Gnostic at heart, who created an idiosyncratic canon that excluded the Hebrew Scriptures precisely because of what he perceived to be their preoccupation with the Law. The Middle Ages produced antinomian sects that expressed their sense of Christian freedom through sexual excess. In the Reformation, antinomianism was advocated by certain Anabaptists and one Johann Agricola, who claimed that for those under gospel dispensation the biblical moral law was null and void. Anne Hutchinson, who lived in the seventeenth century, is probably the most famous American "antinomian," though she probably was really only anti-clerical, challenging the Puritan establishment of the religiously repressive Massachusetts Bay Colony, and being banished and excommunicated for her efforts.

Antinomianism would seem to be the least of orthodox Christianity's problems today. In fact, just the opposite appears true For if the messages of most TV preachers about obeying God's Law, the efforts of some parents to get the Ten Commandments posted in public school classrooms, and the various appeals to Old Testament precedents on issues from abortion to capital punishment and from child-rearing to homosexuality are any indication, the spirit of moralism and legalism is rampant. And, left unchecked, it undermines the whole system of grace established by Paul, since it reverts to the kind of commandment-keeping of which he declared us incapable because of sin. Even if he was wrong about that, it is not clear that moralism and legalism would be preferable to his sin-premised doctrine of salvation. Given obvious human foibles, faults, and frailties, one could do worse than to hold out for *some* kind of divine grace.

Consequential or Cooperating Goodness?

By far the majority of Christian moral theorists have insisted that, the decisive nature of divine grace notwithstanding, ethics and morality—or simply "good works"—have an important place in Christian theology and life, but as the consequence of salvation rather than its cause. That is, Christian ethicists since Paul have generally held that good works are the result of one's having received the grace of God, rather than the reason for it. In other words, Christians are not made righteous because they do good things; they do good things because they have been made righteous; they are not "saved" because of the good that they have done; they do good by virtue of their having been saved.

Yet Christian theologians and shapers of doctrine have not totally agreed on the place of good works in the Christian life. The Roman Catholic tradition, in particular, has given them an important role in the achievement of salvation, a kind of "cooperating" relationship with grace. Protestant thinkers influenced by Martin Luther, however, have continued to insist that good works are purely consequences of the divine grace that imputes God's righteousness, and that they are finally attributable to the empowering effects of God's Holy Spirit. But other Protestants—most notably those in the Calvinist tradition—have placed a greater emphasis on the importance not only of good works, but of the Law itself, even for those Christians predestined to salvation. (It is from the Calvinists, by the way, that we Americans allegedly get our so-called "Protestant work ethic.")

The vast majority of Christian lay people, however, Catholic and Protestant alike, have been largely unaware of and unconcerned with such theological subtleties, gravitating instead to a more clear-cut, rule-based ethics. Popular Christian piety, therefore, often focuses on the Ten Commandments, or the love of God and neighbor, or the Golden Rule, sometimes to the point of making these definitive of the faith itself. What bothers traditional theologians about such reductionism, of course, is that it seems to detract from the importance of grace, the atonement, the cross, and Jesus himself; and that it further leads people to imagine their salvation to be based on their own moral efforts and good deeds rather than on the graciousness and righteousness of God.

Obligations or Outcomes or Opportunities?

Given the basic Pauline understanding of good works as a consequence of God's grace and the fundamental lack of agreement in subsequent generations about just what that means, it is perhaps not surprising that Christian moral theorists have produced many different ethical systems and have come to a great variety of conclusions about a wide range of specific issues. What is especially curious, however, is that so many of their ethical approaches appear to be based strictly on human volition and obedience to rules—in clear violation of Paul's misgivings about so-called "good works."

Broadly speaking, the principal options that have been explored by Christian ethicists have been three: (1) a legalistic, rule-based ("deontological" or "non-consequentialist") ethics, which assesses moral behavior against definite norms, usually seen as God-given; (2) an "ends-justify-the-means" ("teleological" or "consequentialist") ethics, which determines right action in light of probable outcomes; and (3) a contextual ("situational") ethics based on broad general principles applied to particular circumstances. Deontological ethicists, for example, have insisted that there are certain unequivocal commandments, rules, and laws—"thou shalts" and "thou shalt nots"—that are obligatory irrespective of consequences. For them, the question is "What does God demand?" Consequentialists, by contrast, focus on outcomes, and employ "the greatest good for all concerned" as the criterion for appropriate action. They ask, "What will be most beneficial in the long run?" Situationalists have gone another way altogether by insisting that such Christian principles as the ideal of love should be applied on a case-by-case basis to specific circumstances. They simply wonder, "What is the loving thing to do?"

The first of these three, the most prescriptive style of Christian ethics, dominated the thinking and writings of both Catholic moral theologians and Protestant ethicists through the first half of the twentieth century, even though it appears to be a reversion to commandment-based understanding of humanity's relationship to God. Situational ethics, which has gained more advocates in recent decades, is more relativistic, in that it leaves it up to the individual to determine what principles are compelling or appropriate *and* what acts or actions these principles suggest. Most relativistic of all, however, is the consequentialist approach, for it leaves morality seemingly unattached to either a given moral code or chosen ethical ideals. Predictably, perhaps, both situationalist and consequentialist ethics have drawn much criticism from traditionalists on the grounds that, rather than deferring to the wisdom and will of a demanding and righteous God, they place too much responsibility for decisions about right and wrong on flawed and fallible individuals and whatever principles and goals might strike their fancies.

Issues—Nagging and New

Besides determining the kind of ethics they would embrace, Christian ethicists—as well as Christians simply trying to act ethically—have had to decide which areas of human life should be the focus of their moral concern. Throughout the centuries, Christian ethics has dealt with such very important issues as gender roles and sexual behavior, war and peace, human rights, civic responsibility, abortion, and euthanasia.

Predictably, sincere Christians have held widely varied opinions, in most cases because of the divergent ethical systems they have adopted. Some, for example, have declared pacifism as the only stance appropriate to followers of the Prince of Peace, while others have supported the concept of a "just war" and even promoted one or another holy war. Some Christians have pronounced sex outside of marriage as categorically wrong, while others have allowed love and circumstances to set more flexible rules. Some Christians have used the Bible and its teachings to support slavery, apartheid, racial supremacy, and segregation; others have used scripture as a basis for abolition, integration, egalitarianism, and civil rights. Some have found in scripture and theology a justification for the subordination of women, while others have found the roots of feminism. Some have used scripture to support vengeance and capital punishment; others have found in God's mercy a precedent and demand for Christians to oppose the death penalty, even for the most heinous crimes.

Perhaps the most controversial ethical issues in the next few decades will be biomedical. Genetic engineering, for example, finds Christians on both sides of the fence, with some arguing against "playing God" on biblical grounds, while others counsel the moral obligation to proceed with responsible experimentation. Some Christians regard any form of suicide, assisted or otherwise, as unconscionable, as well as euthanasia and "pulling the plug" on those being kept alive by artificial medical means; others see the prolongation of life by extraordinary means as contradictory to God's loving nature and will. Some Christians find the use of donor organs and fetal tissue repugnant, especially if they are bought and sold, while others consider it the ultimate expression of Christian charity. And, in what is almost certainly the most heated and persistent debate in the last few decades, some Christians have used scripture to support the right of women to choose abortion, while others have adduced biblical testimony against it. Indeed, this last example suggests an illustration of how complicated the matter of ethics can be among Christians. For some odd reason, anti-abortion "Pro-lifers" generally have been *for* capital punishment; and, yet more ironic, at least one Christian Pro-lifer has been sentenced to death for murdering a physician (himself a Christian layman) who, among his many other medical duties, performed legal abortions.

Christian ethics, then, has been racked with confusion and controversy, and promises to be equally or more so in the foreseeable future. The only finally "safe" Christian stance about ethical decisions and moral action upon which most if not all Christians would agree, then, is that it is better to be intentional and consistent in one's approach to behavior than to act impulsively or fail to act by default.

Eternal Life and Heaven

No doubt the principal effect of salvation in the minds of most Christians—the "big payoff," as it were—is eternal life. Unfortunately, however, Christianity inherited two conflicting views of human nature, one Jewish and the other Greek. For that reason, the Christian faith has always been of at least two minds about human beings' ultimate destiny, and that fact has left Christians for almost twenty centuries in a confused state about the nature of eternal life.

Resurrection: A Jewish Concept of Afterlife

As we saw earlier, the Jewish tradition had no concept of an eternal soul or spirit that might survive after death. The human "spirit" (Hebrew, *nephesh*) was something like vitality, personhood, or simply the self, and perished with the body. As a result, when in Jesus' day the reformist Pharisees were entertaining the possibility of eternal life, they did it in terms of "resurrection of the dead" or "resurrection of the body." For with a basically holistic view of human nature and without a survivable inner spiritual or psychical essence in their conceptual arsenal, the only possibility for life was in terms of a whole person, which had to include a body. The only hope for eternal life, therefore, was for God to work a great future miracle and raise and restore the dead body to the status of a complete and living person.

This late notion of eternal life did not catch on in Judaism. But it did find a home in Christianity, having arrived there through two primary sources: the reported experience of Jesus after death and the teachings of Paul. In the former case, it is noteworthy that Jesus' experience of life after death, as recorded in the four canonical gospels, was one of bodily resurrection and an empty tomb, and not just a disembodied spirit. Indeed, none of the scriptural resurrection accounts suggests that any part of Jesus endured the crucifixion except the dead body. These gospel accounts impressed themselves on the later historic confessions of the Church: in the words of the Apostles' Creed, for example, Jesus was "crucified, dead, and buried," and the Nicene that "he suffered and was buried." Period. There is no mention of any spiritual survival. (To be sure, one ancient version of the Apostles' creed adds that "he descended into hell," a phrase clearly added to provide salvation to the holy and righteous saints of yore who would otherwise have been denied their just reward. But read in Hebrew terms as a reference to *Sheol* or "the grave," even that "hell" addendum would simply mean that he was truly dead and buried.) Both creeds tell us in the very next breath that he arose from the dead, not that his ghost appeared (although some gospel accounts suggest that his body seemed capable of appearing and disappearing somehow). With such powerful affirmations of a bodily afterlife for Jesus, it is no wonder that the idea of the resurrection of the dead as the destiny of all people became fixed in the Christian tradition.

Add to that the writings of Paul, which often set forth the idea of resurrection. Especially telling in this regard is his lengthy discussion in 1 Corinthians 15, written to Greek Christians who were having trouble swallowing the idea of bodily resurrection. To them, the whole idea was preposterous and what many people today would call "gross." Paul is hard-pressed to convince them of the truth of the idea; and though in his argument he makes use of a puzzling distinction between physical bodies and "spiritual bodies," it is clear that he is not talking about eternal, separable souls. After all, he was writing to Greeks with a long history of belief in immortal souls. If Paul had been envisioning eternal life in terms of disembodied spirits, he wouldn't have wasted the ink on that Greek congregation. No, Paul believed in some kind of resurrection: that those who are dead "in Christ" would rise from the dead. (See also 1 Thes 4:13–18.)

It is because of the weight of such scriptural testimony that the conclusion of the Nicene Creed declares, "I look for the resurrection of the dead," and the Apostles' Creed asserts, "I believe...in the resurrection of the body, and the life of the world to come." Such ancient statements of faith are clear reflections of late Jewish thought, which entertained the idea of eternal life but, lacking a concept of an immortal soul, had to do so in physical and this-worldly terms.

Competing Concepts and Christian Confusion

But because of the Greek-philosophical orientation of its early theologians, Christianity has also taught that humans have immortal souls that are released at death. So by the second century the Church and its Greek-influenced theologians had, in effect, inverted the message of Jesus: instead of God's reign coming from Heaven to Earth, immortal souls of the righteous would be separated from their bodies at death, and ascend to heaven to live forever.

The idea that the souls of the saved have an eternal heavenly home as their final destination and reward, however, did not come from the Greeks, but derived from the Persian Zoroastrians. They had envisioned a heavenly "House of Song" as the realm of the God of Light, Ahura Mazda, to which the souls of the righteous would retire sometime after death. Jews, of course, had had a concept of heaven, but as a place where God and the angels resided. Angels, by the way, were never understood by the Jews as promoted human beings; rather, they were a species unto themselves, agents or messengers created to do God's bidding in heaven and sometimes on earth. The Zoroastrian-Christian idea of heaven as a human goal or eternal residence would have been utterly foreign and bewildering to the Jewish mind, and therefore to Jesus.

In any case, the convergence of the two very different understandings of human nature, Hebrew and Greek, has left modern Christians engaging unwittingly in double-think or double-talk about eternal life. On the one hand, they will stand up in a Sunday morning worship service and recite an ancient creed that ends with an affirmation of belief in "the resurrection of the dead" or "the resurrection of the body," which clearly envisions eternal life as future and physical. But when asked directly, these same people will freely declare their conviction that when a person dies, he or she goes to "a better place." And they don't mean a peaceful grave, but heaven, the immediate enjoyment of which presupposes the survival of a separable, survivable, and immortal soul of the Greek-philosophical sort.

This clash of Christian rhetoric about eternal life is particularly evident in conversation among Christians after the death of one of their own: some comfort one another with the assurance that the deceased is "at rest" and that all will rise when Jesus comes, while others allow as how the dear departed is already with God, Jesus, and a host of loved ones in heaven. And they nod and say "Amen" to each other and never notice that they are talking from opposite sides of their religious and theological tradition. Rarely does anyone notice, much less wonder about, the contradiction.

Which of these two views is correct or true, or whether there is eternal life at all, neither the scientist nor the theologian can state definitively. What can be said, however, is that it is well-nigh impossible, at least on rational grounds, to affirm both Greek immediate immortality and Hebrew future resurrection. It is also clear that the Greek idea of an immediately immortal soul is attractive because it is more comforting in the face of death, one's own or a loved one's. The Hebrew idea of a resurrection, however, is more clearly scriptural as well as more miraculous; for it bespeaks not a natural phenomenon, but a decisive and awesome future act of divine re-creation and restoration.

Two things complicate the issue for the modern Western mind. The first is the scientific worldview that all of us share as a result of having been born in the twentieth century, and that renders both the idea of a non-material, non-empirical "soul" and the prospect of an unprecedented future resurrection almost equally incredible. That fact alone leads some Christians to take the whole idea of eternal life in a loose, metaphorical sense, and to hold no real hope for a literal, personal survival, either spiritual or physical. But further complicating the matter is the belief in reincarnation or transmigration of souls that is a staple of Eastern religions like Hinduism, Buddhism, and Taoism. These three ancient traditions all teach that the human spiritual essence is at once uncreated, eternal, and capable of incarnating in future life forms, either human or non-human. More and more people in the Western world (and in Christian churches) are being exposed to such ideas and are entertaining them as distinct possibilities. For mainstream Christians that presents a problem, since for most of the history of their faith, its scripture, and its theology there has been little or no place for reincarnation.

How, then, does the notion of eternal life fit in modern Christian thought? The best general answer is that most Christians have a less than specific belief in it as one element of God's redeeming activity in Christ and through the Holy Spirit. Exactly what part it plays in that activity depends (as is the case with every other religious issue) on each Christian's theological and philosophical presuppositions and convictions.

Conclusion

What every believer should know about the Christian faith with respect to salvation is that, thanks again largely to Paul and Augustine, just as it holds the most radical view of sin of any religion, it also promotes the most radically grace-based view of salvation. For other religions either regard sin hardly at all or treat it as a relatively ancillary problem—a matter of bad behavior or lack of obedience—and see its cure as a matter of following commandments, moral teachings, or examples. Traditional Christianity, by contrast, presents sin as a congenital condition that requires the gracious forgiveness of a merciful God and the atoning death of its savior-founder, and that sees righteousness and morality as the consequence rather than the cause of salvation.

Not all Christians in all eras have found this orthodox view acceptable, however. Theorists and laypeople alike, for example, have often found themselves (sometimes consciously and sometimes unconsciously) rejecting the radical view of sin on which the idea of atonement is based. Indeed, as we shall see in detail in chapter 8 below, one of the marks of both traditional Eastern Orthodox and modern Liberal Christian traditions, as well as a number of distaff Christian movements and individuals, is a more positive view of the natural human condition than orthodoxy has maintained since the days of Augustine. That change of viewpoint has led Liberal thinkers in particular to shift their attention from Jesus' death to his life and teachings, from the assertion that "Christ died for our sins" to the view that "Jesus lived and taught so as to guide us to a godly life." Ironically, many Christians who would be scandalized to be identified as Liberals would not, if pressed, want to defend the claim that people are utterly sinful from birth. Yet they find themselves repeating the inherited rhetoric and rituals of orthodoxy that defend and dramatize the absolute necessity of Christ's atoning death, despite the fact that they don't really think folks are all that "damned bad."

Once again, then, we have discovered within the Christian faith and among the Christian faithful a great deal of diversity on virtually every topic and issue. That diversity expresses itself in many ways and in many places, but particularly in the veritable maze of denominations and sects to be found in the Church today. To the idea of the Church and the multiplicity of churches we turn our attention in the next chapter.

DISCUSSION QUESTIONS & EXERCISES

A. Put into your own words Paul's view of salvation, and especially how atonement, grace, faith, and works fit in. Construct your strongest possible argument for it. Then do the same thing against it. Which do you find the more persuasive? Why?

B. What view, if any, do you have of "salvation"? How or where did you come to that view? Why do you believe it is valid? What does it imply about humanity in general? Do you really believe that implication? Is it, for example, psychologically sound?

C. Do you believe that you have a soul or spirit? If so, which or both? How would you define it or them, and what evidence can you give for their existence? Do you believe that the soul or spirit is uncreated and eternal, created and immortal, or simply finite and mortal? Do you believe in reincarnation? Why or why not? Whether you believe in reincarnation or not, what evidence can you give to support the idea? If human cloning is ever accomplished, where will the clone's spirit or soul (as you understand it) come from and when and how will it be joined with the body?

D. Of the three basic types of ethics mentioned in this chapter, which one comes closest to explaining how you determine (or believe you should determine) right or wrong behavior for yourself or others? What difference would it make in your life if you switched to another ethical system? Why?

E. If you are a Christian, do you think that devout Hindus, Buddhists, Muslims and others who do not put their faith in Jesus Christ have a chance at salvation? Why or why not? How about atheists and agnostics? What does your view imply about the nature of God? Are you comfortable with that implication?

RECOMMENDED READING

Gustav Aulen, *Christus Victor: An Historical Study of the Three Main Types of the Idea of the Atonement.* New York: Macmillan/Collier, 1986.
— the classic treatment of the main theories of atonement, with a strong case for the "victory" rationale

Denise Lardner Carmody and John Tully Carmody, *Christian Ethics: An Introduction Through History and Current Issues.* Englewood Cliffs, New Jersey: Prentice-Hall, 1992.
— a very readable and quite thorough survey of the kinds of ethical systems that have emerged in Christianity and the sorts of issues that have attracted the greatest attention

James D. G. Dunn, *The Theology of Paul the Apostle*. Grand Rapids, MI: Eerdmans, 1997.
   — based on the Letter to the Romans, this is an exhaustive thematic exposition of Paul's theology in light of recent scholarship, covering the key topics (God, humankind, sin, Christology, salvation, the Church, and Christian life)

John Hick, *A Christian Theology of Religions: The Rainbow of Faiths*. Philadelphia: Westminster John Knox Press, 1995.
   — a highly accessible, even entertaining presentation of a religious pluralism that sees Christianity as "one true religion among others," by the foremost philosopher of religion of recent decades

Hyam Maccoby, *The Mythmaker: Paul and the Invention of Christianity*. San Francisco: Harper and Row, 1986.
   — "an entirely different and unfamiliar view" of Paul as the real founder of Christianity, with special attention to the Ebionites as a vital source of information about him

Donald W. Musser and Joseph L. Price, eds., *A New Handbook of Christian Theology*. Nashville: Abingdon, 1992.
   — an excellent resource for topics in Christian theology, with especially good articles on "Atonement," "Ethics—Christian," "Grace," and "Soteriology" (but none, strangely enough, on "Sin")

Wilfred Cantwell Smith, *Faith and Belief: The Difference Between Them*. Oxford: Oneworld Publications (Penguin), 1998.
   — a marvelous study of the relationship between faith and belief in Hinduism, Buddhism, Islam, and Christianity by one of the great comparative religionists of our time

A. N. Wilson, *Paul: The Mind of the Apostle*. New York: W. W. Norton & Co., 1997.
   — a very thorough examination of Paul of Tarsus that sets him in his proper Roman and Jewish contexts and makes the case that this "richly imaginative, but confused, religious genius" was also a "prophet of liberty" and "poet of the inner life" who in fact founded the religious movement that became Christianity

THE CHURCH AND THE CHURCHES FROM PENTECOST TO THE PAROUSIA

Objectives of this chapter:

- to understand the basic meaning and various nuances of the New Testament term "church"

- to explore in particular the Pauline images of the Church as "The Body of Christ" and the faithful as being "in Christ"

- to examine the growth of the Church as an institution, with special regard for its traditional aspects and functions

- to view the ambiguous and controversial role and status of women, and the problematic teachings of Paul about them

- to define and distinguish between the terms "denomination," "sect," and "cult," especially as these apply to Christianity

- to provide a guide to Christian denominations by sorting them into four major groups

- to describe the American pattern of separation of church and state, as well as its major alternative

- to examine critically the persistent Christian belief in the Second Coming of Christ and alternative ways of interpreting the book of Revelation

7

The Church
and the
Churches
from
Pentecost to
the Parousia

Suppose a stranger should approach a typical American Christian layperson and ask, "To what church do you belong?" What would his or her first response be? Chances are, it would be one of two kinds of answers: either a denominational affiliation ("I'm a Presbyterian."), or the designation of a particular building in a specific location ("I belong to the Church of the Sacred Heart on Main Street."). Either of those would be a perfectly sensible answer. Strictly speaking, however, neither would be a biblical response.

The word "church," as used in the New Testament, means neither an institution nor a physical structure. Both of those meanings are late and derivative at best. "Church" in its original scriptural sense refers to a specific category of people, namely, those who have received God's grace in Jesus, who therefore are "in Christ," and who congregate in fellowship in his name to celebrate their oneness in him.

The Church in the New Testament

In the Greek vocabulary of the New Testament, "church" is *ekklesia*, from which we get the term "ecclesiastical." The literal meaning of *ekklesia* is "those called out," "assembly," or "congregation." The term is used in these early Christian writings to refer to the community of those who have heard the gospel, have accepted Jesus as Messiah in the distinctively Christian sense of that title (*Christos* in Greek), have been baptized, have received forgiveness and perhaps one or another of the gifts of the Holy Spirit, and who meet together to worship and to share the Eucharist, or meal of thanksgiving. The Church—the capital "C" denoting both the ideal and the institution, as opposed to the basic idea or an individual congregation—is the community of the New Covenant that has supplanted that of the Old Covenant, which is to say, Israel. For that reason, some of the writings of the New Testament refer to the Church as "The New Israel."

"The Church" as an Afterthought

Surprisingly, perhaps, the idea of "church" apparently played little or no role in the teachings of Jesus. Indeed, only one of the four gospels (Matthew) has him even mention the word, and he uses it there a grand total of three times. One of these is in a famous passage on which a great deal of subsequent Church history and doctrine are based: it is Jesus' alleged declaration to Peter, "And I tell you, you are Peter, and on this rock I will build my church, and the gates of Hades will not prevail against it" (Matt 16:18). Despite the fact that the Roman Catholic Church has used this verse throughout its history as the cornerstone of its argument for the primacy of Peter and the authority of the papacy, the appearance of the word here (as well as twice more in chapter 18) looks very suspicious to modern biblical scholars simply because it is not reported anywhere else as a part of Jesus' vocabulary.

Indeed, if the Church had been an important part of the original mission of Jesus, one would expect to find mention of it often in his recorded sayings in all of the gospels. The fact that it does not appear at all in three of them and only a few times in the fourth leads many New Testament scholars to

7

The Church
and the
Churches
from
Pentecost to
the Parousia

conclude that its several appearances in Matthew may be the result of the term's having been remembered back onto the lips of Jesus by Matthew or his sources, by whose time (sometime around 85 CE) "church" was a well-established concept and reality.

The term "church" does occur in the book of Acts, at first referring to the Christian community that gathered in Jerusalem after Jesus' death. Later it appears in reference to other local congregations (for example, in Antioch, Caesarea, and Ephesus), as well as in a more universal sense. But it is in the epistles of Paul that the final concept of "Church" begins to take shape. His many uses of the word in several senses, from local to universal, laid the foundations for *ecclesiology* (thoughts about the nature of the Church).

A Body without By-Laws or Buildings

Paul's most vivid image for the Church is "the Body of Christ." That metaphor appears briefly in Romans 12, and in considerably expanded form in 1 Corinthians 12. There, after going on at length about how God has arranged the human body so that despite the diversity of its parts it functions as a whole, he declares:

> Now you are the body of Christ and individually members of it. And God has appointed in the church first apostles, second prophets, third teachers; then deeds of power, then gifts of healing, forms of assistance, forms of leadership, various kinds of tongues. Are all apostles? Are all prophets? Are all teachers? Do all work miracles? Do all possess gifts of healing? Do all speak in tongues? Do all interpret? (vss 27–30)

From Paul's description here and elsewhere, we can see that the earliest church was not an institution as we would think of it, with humanly elected or appointed officers in clearly defined chains of authority and command, but a loosely organized association of people divinely ordained and gifted.

Indeed, because of his emphasis on the various divinely-bestowed "gifts," the earliest church is sometimes called a "charismatic community." That is not to say that everyone spoke in tongues or healed or prophesied, but that the community, although lacking such formal organizational structures as offices and rules, was informally but nonetheless strongly united by their common experiences, viewpoints, and mutually supportive talents or "gifts"—and by the Holy Spirit.

Nothing even resembling a building or organization was ever implied in Paul's use of the word "church." Perhaps because they met in numbers too small to require them, the earliest Christians did not have special buildings for religious purposes. Also, for the first three centuries or so, Christianity was an illegal and largely underground religion, the equivalent of a "cult" in the very worst modern sense of that word; and the threat of arrest and persecution forced them to meet in secret in places like homes and even tombs. Distinctive architectural forms or religious symbols would have posed an unacceptable risk. Besides, early Christians may have been too preoccupied with things of the spirit or their expectation of the imminent return of Christ to see any need for buildings.

So, returning to the stranger's question about what church one belongs to, we can say that the answer most in keeping with the attitude of both the New Testament and the earliest Christians would be along these lines: "I belong to the one and only Body of Christ. Now if you ask me the where-abouts of this universal Church, I'll have to tell you that some are at home, some are at work, some are at school, some are shopping, and some are undoubtedly asleep. Most will meet together next Sunday in church-build-ings that bear particular denominational names. Now if you're asking about what building I attend or what my denominational affiliation is, those are different matters. Now as always, the real Church is flesh and blood and spirit, not brick and stone and mortar, much less organizations or rules or bylaws." On second thought, perhaps it would be more merciful to the ques-tioner just to look puzzled and shrug.

The Growth of the Institution

The initial growth of the Church as an institution was spurred by two factors. First, the second coming of Christ, which most early Christians expected, didn't occur. As long as Jesus' return was anticipated, there was no reason to get organized, since he would surely establish a new order that would render all human institutions obsolete. Second, when Constan-tine became both the emperor and a Christian in 313 CE, Christianity was legalized.

No longer burdened by the day-to-day struggle for existence, Christians now had the psychological "space," as it were, to get organized—hammer-ing out beliefs, defining ministerial offices, formalizing ritual practices, and determining their canon of scriptures. Only then did there appear ecumeni-cal councils, elaborate creeds, the first dedicated church buildings, and the makings of a hierarchical clergy. Still, it would be at least a century before the Church would have sufficient organization and power to begin to look at all episcopal ("bishop-ruled") or papal in any modern sense.

Traits and Tasks of the Church

In the years immediately following Constantine's conversion, the Church hammered out its identity and established its authority, usually in reaction to heresies (beliefs deemed erroneous). Gradually the Rome-based, Latin-speaking, western-European branch of Christianity that would eventually become the Roman Catholic Church defined itself in terms of four "marks" (Latin: *notae*), which had been suggested in a phrase at the end of the late-fourth-century Nicene Creed: " . . . the one, holy, catholic and apostolic Church."

These "marks" are generally listed in a slightly different order from that in the creed. The first, *unity*, derived not only from the idea of the Church's oneness in Christ, but increasingly with the perception of the Papacy as the sole heir of Peter, Christ's chosen leader of the Church. The second mark, *catholicity*, originally signified the Church seen as a whole as opposed to spe-cific local congregations, though from the fourth century on the word "catholic" more and more took on the function of a proper name (as in Roman Catholic Church). The third mark, *holiness*, was attributed to the

7

The Church
and the
Churches
from
Pentecost to
the Parousia

presence of the Holy Spirit and the resulting righteousness of the members, and was associated with the specific rituals called "sacraments" that gradually emerged as special conduits of God's grace. The fourth mark, *apostolicity*, derived from the reputedly unbroken chain of "apostolic succession" by which Church leaders traced their authority back to the first disciples of Jesus, and to Peter in particular.

After the Reformation in the sixteenth century the various Protestant bodies that had broken with Rome naturally downplayed, redefined, or rejected unity and apostolic succession as necessary marks. They also increasingly avoided the "tainted" word "catholic," though some did retain it, ostensibly in its original sense, in their recitation of ancient creeds. Protestants tended to replace these three traditional attributes with a single distinguishing feature: the "right" preaching of the Word of God, which they believed to be the true source of real unity, catholicity, and apostolicity anyway. As for the remaining Roman Catholic mark, holiness, most of the mainline reformers retained "duly administered" sacraments as the second mark of a true (Protestant) church, although they generally reduced the number of those rites from seven to two—holy communion and baptism— by eliminating confirmation, penance, holy orders, matrimony, and anointing of the sick.

More radical Protestant reformers and groups and their successors, such as the continental Anabaptists and the Baptists and Quakers of Old and New England, did away with the concept of "sacrament" altogether and increasingly defined "holiness" in terms of personal piety, visible saintliness, and disciplined living. That change marked an almost total reversal in the criteria by which the Church identified itself: these so-called "Left-Wing" or "Free Church" Protestants replaced external, institutional authority based on historic and hierarchical validation with *internal, individual authority based on the unmediated and sanctifying presence of God's Spirit*. This was not necessarily a better or worse definition of the Church, but it certainly was a different one, and it continues today to pose a barrier to ecumenical dialogue between the Roman Catholic Church and many Protestant denominations.

What makes a group of Christians a church (or the Church) today, therefore, depends on which Christians you ask and what specific historical branch of Christianity they represent. Some would say it is the authority of the papacy, the episcopacy, or the clergy passed on from ancient times. Others might contend that it is the proper preaching of the Word of God, administering of the sacraments, or both. Still others would claim that it is the ongoing presence and activity of the Holy Spirit within and among the faithful. You might even find Christians somewhere who would maintain that it is some or all of the above, and then would argue over the correct proportions. But most Christians, I suspect, would have little or no idea about what constitutes them or any other group as a church, much less as *the* Church.

And yet, all branches of Christianity have tended to agree, at least tacitly, upon the true functions of the Church. The four traditionally listed and their corresponding New Testament Greek terms are these: (1) the *proclamation* of the gospel to those who are not followers (*kerygma*), which includes what is commonly called "evangelism" as well as missions aimed at conversion; (2) the *teaching* of the doctrines of the faith to those who are within the fold (*didache*), which includes most Sunday sermons, Christian education, and the like; (3) the *community* of believers in a fellowship of love (*koinonia*), which includes all community-building and mutual-support activities within the membership; and (4) the loving *service* on behalf of people in need beyond the congregation (*diakonia*), including acts of charity, missions of mercy, and so forth.

Obviously not all congregations or denominations have given equal emphasis to these functions; nor, for that matter, has any body of Christians done complete justice to any one of them. But they do remain noble ideals and goals for any group that would aspire to be *a* church, and provide standards by which Christians in any age can measure their right to identify with *the* Church.

The Role and Status of Women

One of the most liberally inclusive statements made in the entire Bible is found in Galatians 3:27–28. There Paul declares: "As many of you as were baptized into Christ have clothed yourselves with Christ. There is no longer Jew or Greek, there is no longer slave or free, there is no longer male and female; for all of you are one in Christ Jesus." For a first-century Jewish Palestinian male, that is an extraordinary statement; for in his cultural context, women, slaves, and Gentiles were generally held in low esteem indeed, not only socially, politically, and economically, but religiously as well. Paul's words make it sound as though in this New Israel all traditional barriers have been eliminated.

The problem is that other statements that he makes (or, in some cases, that others writing in his name make) suggest something very different— especially with regard to women. In 1 Corinthians 11, for example, he argues that "any woman who prays or prophesies with her head unveiled disgraces her head—it is one and the same as having her head shaved." Men, however, should not cover their heads, he says. Why? Because men, not women, are "the image and reflection of God." There is very little logic or theology here, but there certainly is an attitude, and one that Paul regards as non-negotiable: "We have no such custom, nor do the churches of God" (vss 2–16). And that's that!

Paul's successors, writing in his name and probably in his spirit, asserted that women are to be submissive to their husbands in the same way that children are obedient to their parents and slaves to their masters (Col 3:18–4:11); and that they are to be listeners and learners, not speakers, in worship (1 Tim 2:11–12). In fact, according to the writer of 1 Timothy, a woman's only hope for salvation is through childbirth (2:15). While childbirth was not the matter of choice then that it is today, no doubt some women were physically incapable of bearing children. According to the author of 1 Timothy, there was no hope for them.

One famous text in the authentic letter of Paul to the Corinthians insists that women should not be heard in church: " . . . women should be silent in the churches. For they are not permitted to speak, but should be subordinate, as the law also says. If there is anything they desire to know, let them

7

The Church
and the
Churches
from
Pentecost to
the Parousia

ask their husbands at home. For it is shameful for a woman to speak in church." I Cor 14:34–35. One fairly recent interpretation suggests that Paul was actually quoting somebody else's position here, and then arguing against it. (Imagine how the Pope and those conservative Protestant ministers who have opposed the ordination of women partly on the basis of this passage would feel if they got to heaven and found out that they had been supporting Paul's opponents all this time!) But most recent translations of this passage, including the one just cited, clearly attribute the desire to "keep women in their place"—at least in ecclesiastical matters—to Paul himself.

None of what Paul and his successors say about women in these and similar passages sounds particularly egalitarian, or seems to comport with Galatians 3:28. Yet such statements have long been used to exclude women from positions of leadership and authority in various Christian denominations. Ecclesiastical bodies as diverse as the Roman Catholic Church and Fundamentalist Protestant churches, for example, still refuse to ordain women as clergy, and justify their positions at least partly on the basis of Paul's more exclusive passages. Such mainline Protestant denominations as the Episcopalian, United Methodist, and Presbyterian ordain female ministers and sometimes even elect female bishops, but in such relatively small numbers that few would claim gender parity in ecclesiastical power. Paul's idealized concept of the Church as "neither male and female," therefore, remains at best unrealized.

In recent years, however, women have increasingly asserted their right to an equality of role and status despite scriptural restrictions. Their principal appeal has been to the example of Jesus, who seems to have freely associated with women in public, stood up for their rights, and included them among his closest disciples. Recent scholarship has found that women played extraordinary roles in the Christianity of Paul's day, exercising leadership at every level and in every aspect of the young Church's life, including missions. Whether or not these examples can outweigh the less-than-liberated attitudes of Paul and his successors toward women remains to be seen.

The Broken "Body of Christ"

The number of institutional Christian bodies in America with a significant profile—those with ten-thousand members or more and having a national headquarters of some kind—is around two hundred. If you add the small, local "non-denominational" Christian expressions, from huge independent "mega-Churches" to tiny store-fronts, the number is in the tens of thousands. Thus Christianity today is characterized by a confusing diversity of institutional forms. A useful first step in sorting out the pieces of this puzzle is to clarify three terms often carelessly used: denomination, sect, and cult.

Denomination, Sect, and Cult

One often hears people speaking about or espousing "the Catholic religion" or "the Methodist religion." Technically speaking, however, these are not religions at all, but "denominations" of the same religion, namely, Christianity. I find it helpful to think of denominations as analogous to brandnames, even though they sometimes seem to be offering different products entirely.

The term "denomination" usually applies to older, larger, well-established Christian groups that can trace a European lineage directly or indirectly to the Reformation Period of the sixteenth century or earlier. By this definition, Roman Catholics, Lutherans, Reformed Protestants, Presbyterians, Anglicans, Episcopalians, and Baptists and Methodists of many varieties—to name only the most prominent—would be said to belong to denominations. One rarely sees the term used outside of Christianity; subdivisions within Islam or Buddhism are commonly called "schools" or "sects" or both. As a religious term, "denomination" appears to be almost exclusively Christian.

The word "sect" is also used to denote a subdivision of Christianity, but one that comprises organizations that are younger and probably smaller than most denominations, and that promote at least one belief or practice that is idiosyncratic and markedly out of the Christian mainstream as well. In America, the "home-grown" Christian-based groups that emerged in the nineteenth century—the Mormons, Adventists, and Christian Scientists, for example—more than likely would still be considered sects, though by now all of these have been around long enough and are so well established and accepted that they probably have achieved the status of "denomination." Unlike "denomination," the term "sect" is also used with reference to other religions to denote branches, as in "the Shi'ite sect of Islam" or "the Nichiren sect of Buddhism."

The term "cult" has acquired a very negative connotation in recent decades, probably for the wrong reasons. For one thing, it derives from the Latin word for "growth" (as in "cultivate" and "culture"), and thus suggests a place where spirituality is nurtured; for another, it has nothing to do with the word "occult" (from the Latin word for "hidden"), with which it has been incorrectly and unfortunately associated. Indeed, for most of its history the Roman Catholic Church has used the word "cult" positively to describe smaller, accepted groups with a special devotional focus, such as The Cult of the Sacred Heart. In recent decades, however, with the proliferation of small, non-Christian, and sometimes strange and scary religious and quasireligious groups springing up seemingly everywhere, the term "cult" has come to have a very different meaning. Especially in casual conversation and media news reports, it almost invariably implies a small, fanatical, weird, and probably dangerous religious group, led by some charismatic and mesmerizing crack-pot.

Much more useful, however, is a neutral, purely descriptive sense of the term. Accordingly, a "cult" is a small, fairly new group with beliefs and practices that are out of the religious mainstream of its surrounding society or culture. In this sense, no self-consciously Christian group would properly be called a "cult," however strange its ideas and ways. But we would rightly speak of the Society of Krishna Consciousness (or Hare Krishnas), Baha'i, and New Age Religions as "cults" in that they are fairly recent additions to the American religious milieu and certainly not in tune with the prevailing

7

The Church
and the
Churches
from
Pentecost to
the Parousia

Judaeo-Christian tradition. We would not, however, automatically be casting aspersions on them with that designation. Such a neutral, descriptive use of the word "cult" would free us to distinguish between good cults (those that encourage or "cultivate" religious beliefs and values that have a positive spiritual effect on their members) and bad cults (those that are harmful or dangerous in some demonstrable way, rather than being merely "different" or "strange").

What often happens today, however, is that small, new and different religious groups—including some Christian ones—are simply assumed to be deviant and deleterious, and are dismissed out of hand merely by labeling them "cults." This often means no more than: "It's different and I don't understand or like it." (It's like the definition of "cult" in Wiley's Dictionary in an old "B.C." cartoon strip: "The church down the street from mine.") Dismissing a religious group in this way protects us from the disarming possibility that its teaching might have merit, or that it might be as worthy as or even more compelling than our own, or that it may siphon off members and revenues from our own churches. Labeling an "odd" religious group a "cult" may also allow us to deprive its adherents of their constitutional rights, which include the free exercise of religion. After all, if it isn't a religion but a cult, then we don't have to recognize its members' rights, do we?

Unfortunately, certain sects or denominations of Christianity—Mormons, Jehovah's Witnesses, and Adventists, for example—are often denounced and dismissed from pulpits and in print as cults. And on the basis of such dubious distinctions we sometimes allow parents of "acceptable" denominations to kidnap and deprogram (that is, brainwash) their teen-age or even adult children who have joined one of the non-normative religious groups, such as the Unification Church ("Moonies") or Hare Krishnas. Our self-serving justification for this blatant abrogation of religious and civil rights is that we are rescuing people, not from a religion or a sect, but from a cult.

Roman Catholic and Eastern Churches

Another way of making sense of the baffling religious landscape is to recognize certain patterns in what appears to be a denominational crazy quilt. Most of the "standard-brand" Christian denominations, for example, can be divided into four historical families or groups: Catholic, Ethnic Non-Western, European Protestant, and American Sectarian. (See figure 7.1.) They can be further distinguished on the basis of their various understandings of scripture, worship, authority, theology, and even style.

The Roman Catholic Church is arguably, but not unquestionably, the oldest expression of Christianity in the world, for it traces itself back—through an historical process that it calls "apostolic succession"—to none other than Peter the Apostle, whom it regards as the first Bishop of Rome or Pope. In addition to claiming him as the leader of the Church Universal, the Catholic Church distinguishes itself by its seven sacraments, its belief in and attention to saints (especially the Virgin Mary as the "Mother of God"), its exclusively male and celibate clergy, and its devotional use of statues (which is *not* to say that Catholics worship statues). The term "Catholic" also extends to churches like the Anglo-Catholic and Byzantine Catholic that, while

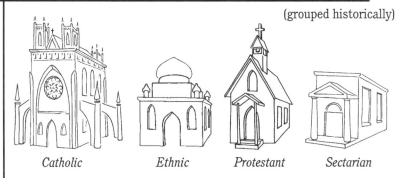

Christian Denominations and Sects

(grouped historically)

Catholic   Ethnic   Protestant   Sectarian

All of these churches claim roots in the Ancient Period (29–500 CE). The Great Schism between West and East occurred in 1054 CE.		Reformation and its aftermath, 1500–1800CE	American proliferation, 1830s–1890s and beyond
Roman Catholic Church Byzantine Catholic Churches Anglo-Catholic Churches	Eastern Orthodox Churches (Russian, Greek, Serbian, Romanian, Bulgarian, et al.) Coptic (Egypt) Mar Thoma (India) Syrian (Jacobite)	Lutheran Reformed/ Presbyterian Anglican (Episcopal) Methodist (United, et al.) Mennonite, Amish Baptist (Southern, et al.) Society of Friends (Quakers) Congregationalists (United Church of Christ)	Latter Day Saints (Mormon) Restoration Churches (Churches of Christ, Disciples of Christ) New Thought Groups (Divine Science, Religious Science, Science of Mind, Unity, et al.) Christian Science Pentecostal & Holiness (Assemblies of God Churches of God Nazarenes, et al.) Adventists (Seventh Day et al.)

Note: *Churches included above explicitly identify themselves as Christian. Some (like the Mormons, Jehovah's Witnesses, and Unity) are frequently accused by outsiders as being either non-Christian or "cults" in the most pejorative sense, and usually because these bodies don't subscribe to one or another doctrine that the accusers deem essential to the faith. Some well-known churches are excluded (such as Unitarian-Universalists) because they do not see themselves explicitly as Christian, though some of their members may self-identify as such.*

FIGURE **7.1**

7

The Church
and the
Churches
from
Pentecost to
the Parousia

remaining national or regional, observing distinctive rites, and sporting distinctive architecture, yet recognize papal authority and maintain strong ecclesiastical ties with Rome.

Chief among the Ethnic Non-Western Churches is the Eastern Orthodox family, which includes Greek Orthodox, Russian Orthodox, and a dozen or so others. The rift between Rome and the Eastern bodies began in the ancient period of the church, and was rooted in both practical and doctrinal issues. But the official split (or "Great Schism") finally occurred in 1054 CE and produced two related but largely independent communions: the Roman Catholic Church and Eastern Orthodoxy.

Of the two, the Eastern Churches are less organizationally unified, with each acknowledging its own spiritual leader or Patriarch. The Roman Church, by contrast, finds its basic unity in the Pope. Eastern Orthodox Churches distinguish themselves by requiring bishops to be celibate but allowing priests to be married; by forbidding the use of statues in worship and devotion; and, as we shall see in chapter 8, by exhibiting a much more mystical spirituality and theology than is generally found in Western Christianity, either Catholic or Protestant. Despite these profound differences, however, both the Roman Catholic and the Eastern Orthodox Churches have clear hierarchical structures of power and authority, a strong connectional relationship between local churches (much like those within a multinational corporation), and an appreciation for order and ornateness—some would add "sensuality"—in worship. In the United Sates, both groups have also shared the experience of having to struggle for acceptance and rights at various times, largely because of their ethnic ties with immigrant groups and the suspicion of "foreignness" that those ties unfortunately raised among other ex-foreigners who had been here longer.

Also in the "Ethnic" group are the ancient Coptic Church of Egypt, the Ethiopic Church of (where else?) Ethiopia, and the Mar Thoma Church of India, all of which claim Apostolic founding and thus an antiquity at least rivaling Roman Catholicism's. These three remain rather bound to their countries of origin, and thus have relatively few followers either in the United States or the Western world in general.

Protestants and Sectarians

The third major group of Christian denominations in America are those deriving directly or indirectly from the Protestant Reformation in sixteenth-century Europe. These include the Lutheran, Reformed, and Anglican (Episcopal) Churches. In addition are those like the Mennonites and Amish, who are descendants of the continental Anabaptist groups; and the far more numerous Baptists, Congregationalists, Presbyterians, and Quakers, all of whom came from English or Scottish Puritanism. Still other denominations, such as the United Methodist Church and the United Church of Christ, represent various patterns of schisms and mergers of two or more older European bodies.

These denominations cover the style spectrum from the very structured, hierarchical, connectional, liturgically ordered and ornate (such as the Episcopalians), to the plainer, more spontaneous, and congregationally-governed groups (such as the Baptists), with various "mixed" churches (like the Methodists) in the middle. The more formal denominations in worship and organizational structure are considered "sacramental" because, as we have seen, they—like Roman Catholics—recognize certain rituals (sacraments) as especially ordained and empowered by God. Others are called "non-sacramental," either because they don't think of rituals (and especially communion and baptism) in this way, or because they eliminate them altogether. As a rule of thumb, churches that baptize only people old enough to profess their faith and that ordain and appoint their ministers locally (that is, in the congregation) are of this latter, "non-sacramental" type. Conversely, churches that baptize infants and that have clergy that are certified, ordained, and appointed by authorities beyond the local congregation are generally "sacramental."

The fourth group of denominations—called "American Sectarian" because of their origins in this country as small, independent groups—comprises "home-grown" churches, most of which were born in the religious ferment of the 1800's. These include various so-called "Restoration" Churches (for example, Churches of Christ and Disciples of Christ), The Church of Jesus Christ of Latter Day Saints (Mormons), Adventists (Seventh Day and otherwise), Jehovah's Witnesses, Christian Scientists, Assemblies of God, Churches of God, and Nazarenes, to name but the most prominent.

Many of these bodies have experienced a long, hard struggle, not only for acceptance, but indeed (like Catholic and Orthodox Christians in the nineteenth century) for basic religious rights supposedly guaranteed to everyone under the First Amendment. As already indicated, some are still denounced by conservative Christians as "cults" for the sole reason that their doctrines deviate significantly from the Christian mainstream. In fact, these groups have been around long enough, grown large enough, and achieved enough respectability among the general public to qualify them for the classification "denominations." At minimum, they have established themselves as safe sects.

Transdenominational Types

Other designations largely ignore or cut across the above denominational lines and groups. The term "Mainline," for example, is sometimes used to identify those denominations that have roots going back to the Reformation and a more or less liberal approach to both the interpretation of the Bible and social issues. Churches at the other extreme, insisting on a literal interpretation of scripture, a firm belief in certain basic doctrines (usually including the imminent return of Christ) as essential, and a strict observance of absolutist moral codes, are called "Fundamentalist," a term that first came into use early in the twentieth century. Yet another designation is "Evangelical," which applies to those denominations that take the Bible very seriously, though not necessarily completely literally, and who focus on the need for personal conversion and thus equate evangelism with soul-saving. A fourth group consists of the "Pentecostal" or "Holiness" churches, which place special emphasis upon the so-called "gifts of the Spirit," particularly *glossolalia* (speaking in tongues), healing, and prophecy, as evidence of sanctification (also called the "second blessing" or "fire baptism") that some are believed to receive in addition to the simple "justification" that ensures salvation.

Some denominations can rather easily be identified with one or another of these labels. United Methodists, for example, are generally regarded as Mainline, Southern Baptists as Evangelical, and Assemblies of God as Pen-

7

The Church
and the
Churches
from
Pentecost to
the Parousia

tecostal. Yet—in defiance of our best attempts to classify—specific congregations, groups, and individuals within these denominations may bear a different label. Some United Methodists for example, proudly claim to be Evangelical, and even a few are Pentecostal, while some Southern Baptists whom you would expect to be Evangelical (but rarely Pentecostal) may rightly be called Liberal in outlook and agenda. Most Evangelical Lutherans are not really "Evangelical" in the generic sense, but Mainline or Liberal. In fact, they would be considered downright radical by typically ultra-conservative Missouri Synod Lutherans, who are by most standards Fundamentalists. And, to add to the confusion, at least two of the distinctions are compatible, so that it is common to find Christian believers who are both Pentecostal *and* Fundamentalist.

Yet another way of categorizing churches is according to their appreciation of structure in worship and polity (governance). (See figure 7.2.) For some reason, churches that have a more set pattern of ritual (or "liturgy") also typically have a predilection for a hierarchical and connectional organizational structure that places authority outside the congregation (for example, in a bishop), as well as for ornateness in art and architecture; while those more prone to spontaneity in their worship seem to prefer a more local (congregational) authority and independent self-determination, as well as for simpler and plainer buildings and sanctuaries. The former are sometimes called "high church" or "sacramental," and may generally be said to evince an appreciation for rationality and objectivity in matters of faith. The latter, by contrast, are labeled "low church" or "non-sacramental," and tend to appeal subjectively to religious experience and affections. It is fair to say that neither style is correct or even better, except insofar as its distinctive style might more closely comport with the dispositions, tastes, sensibilities, and preferences of particular individuals.

None of these designations and distinctions, of course, should be seen as hard or fast; nor can any of them begin to do justice to the hundreds of denominations and thousands of splinter groups that have formed from all the major groupings, or the countless independent little religious bodies—some of them claiming to be "non-denominational" in one sense or another—that have grown up over the years. Nor should any of the categories presented above be used to pigeonhole, prejudge, dismiss, or even criticize any Christian denomination or sect without a clear understanding of what it teaches and does. The most that such labels can do is to help the puzzled observer see some sort of pattern in what otherwise may look like a muddled mosaic of contemporary Christianity.

From time to time, there have been efforts to simplify the denominational multiplicity. One such effort, most notable for its failed good intentions, was the Restoration movement in early nineteenth-century America. The stated purpose of one of its founders was to eliminate the denominational labels by calling all Christians what they were: "Disciples of Christ." What he wound up accomplishing, of course, was the creation of yet one more denomination, which would quickly suffer a series of schisms that yielded even more denominations (for example, Churches of Christ). On a more positive note, the twentieth century has seen some successful denominational mergers as

A Spectrum of Church Types

For some reason, Christian denominations that prefer structured worship, also tend to like ornateness, hierarchy, and an "objective" piety; while those that lean toward spontaneity in worship appreciate simplicity, local control, and a "heart-felt" piety.

Denominational Spectrum

HIGH	Catholic & Orthodox
	Anglican/Episcopal
	Lutheran
	Presbyterian/ Reformed
Mixed	United Methodist
	United Church of Christ
	Baptist
LOW	Pentecostal/ Holiness

Note: The placement of the denominations is approximate. Churches within a denomination will form a spectrum of their own, with some more formal than others.

High Church Characteristics

Sacramental (rituals like baptism and communion as conduits of God's grace: hence baptism of passive infants; Eucharist as miraculous divine intervention—Christ's Real Presence in the bread and wine)

Structured Worship (fixed order/liturgy; set prayers, creeds; scripture prescribed by lectionary; sermons composed)

Audio-Visual Richness (ornate sanctuaries and buildings; bright colors; clergy in fancy vestments; complex hymnody and choral pieces; statues, stained glass, candles, incense, banners)

Hierarchical Polity (interconnected churches; clergy ordained and appointed by Bishop or equivalent; local churches "owned" by the denomination; tight connections with other churches of same brand)

Objective Piety (hymns, songs, sermons, prayers focused without: on the majesty and mercy of God)

Low Church Characteristics

Non-Sacramental (rituals like baptism and communion as signs and seals of believers' faith: hence, believers'—not infant—baptism; Lord's Supper as memorial and sharing—Jesus "present" in participants' hearts and minds)

Spontaneous Worship (flexible order; prayers, testimony, and sermons at Spirit's bidding)

Audio-Visual Simplicity (plain auditoriums and buildings, neutral colors, clergy in street clothes; simple, singable songs; little or no visual art)

Congregational Polity (independent congregations ordain and choose clergy locally; own their own church facilities, property; loose associations with other churches)

Subjective Piety (hymns, songs, sermons, prayers, rituals, etc. directed within: at feelings of the believer)

FIGURE **7.2**

a result of a movement of conversation and cooperation called "ecumenism" (from the Greek word for "the whole inhabited world"), including the two already mentioned (the United Methodist Church and United Church of Christ). It is safe to say, however, that schisms continue to outnumber mergers by a wide margin, which means that the Body of Christ is more "broken" today than ever before.

The Problem of Christian Missions

Of the functions of the Church listed earlier in this chapter, perhaps the most controversial and problematic in recent times has been proclamation, especially as manifested in foreign missionary activity. Two things in particular have been the occasion of misgivings: the apparently questionable motives for past missionary activity and a growing modern sensitivity to other peoples and cultures.

Methods and Motives: "One Way" or "Many Paths"?

Only relatively recently has it begun to trouble Christian sensibilities and consciences that historically the Christian faith was often spread as a part of imperialistic ventures and conquests—a fact that adds new meaning to the hymn title "Onward, Christian Soldiers." Undoubtedly, the two best examples are the Holy Roman conquest of Europe in the fourth and fifth centuries and the Spanish, French, and English confiscation of the so-called "New World" in the late fifteenth through the seventeenth centuries. Portuguese, Dutch, and English Christian colonialism had a major, and not altogether salutary, impact on various parts of Africa and Asia as well.

If only by looking at the case of our own Native Americans, we know that enormous cultural and psychological violence was often done as a result of this sort of wedding of Christian mission and shameless imperialism. Indeed, it may not be too cynical to say that much of the historical spread of Christianity has been the result of a holy lust for political power and a baptized greed for other people's land and riches.

Another, and not unrelated, problem is that the typical Christian missionary mentality throughout most of the past two millennia has been exclusivist, which is to say that in embracing Christianity, one had to renounce all other religious and spiritual beliefs and practices, however deeply-ingrained or dear. This attitude, grounded in the widespread Christian conviction that there is only one valid route to salvation, is not unique to Christianity. Islam, for example, takes a similar approach.

But it is also important for Christians to know that such culture-specific religions as Hinduism and Shinto have had little or no sense of having a universal appeal and thus no missionary impulse for most of their history; and other more self-consciously universal faiths, like Buddhism, that have had such an impulse have propagated their message only through peaceful means and with a goal of finding points of commonality and compatibility with whatever indigenous religions they encountered. Furthermore, the people of most of South and East Asia have historically maintained that, if one religion is good, two must be better, and three better still. For, they believe, all religions address the various aspects and passages of life to different degrees of effectiveness. They simply cannot understand how or why Christians could see their own faith as the one and only true religion. It is largely for this reason that, despite many centuries of missionary efforts, Christianity has had comparatively little success in the Orient.

The Christian missionary impulse itself is being deflated today by two basic facts of life. First, the ever-increasing ease of communication and travel has made us more and more aware of and—one would hope—sensitive to the many cultures in the world, including their religious and spiritual traditions. At the same time, we are seeing a dizzying proliferation of subcultures in our own country, largely as a result of immigration. More frequent contact with people of other cultures who treasure their own time-tested and deeply-held beliefs and practices has made many Christians much less prone to present their own faith as *the* one Way.

Missions of Mercy and Mutuality

In the face of such a pluralistic world and diverse society, mainline churches have tended to direct more and more missionary effort toward such charitable activities as building and staffing schools and hospitals in the world's poorer regions. Evangelical denominations, by contrast, have continued to insist that, whatever other good things missionaries ought to be doing for the unfortunate of the world, they should certainly be paying attention to converting people of other faiths, on the premise that those faiths are erroneous and paths to hell.

But the promotion of Christian missions has had some unintended and often undesired results. For even when the faithful were successful in compelling or convincing peoples to convert, the prior beliefs of these new Christians inevitably affected their newly adopted faith and practice and modified the Christian religion itself. As a result, Roman Catholicism among Native American converts is very different from the way it is held and practiced among African tribal initiates; and both of those vary widely from the style of Catholicism taught and experienced in the Vatican and much of Europe and North America. Indeed, it is not an exaggeration to say that, as Christianity spread to other cultures, it was almost always as much affected by them as they were by it.

The Relationship Between Church and State

In the United States, we are so used to the idea of the separation of church and state that we need to remind ourselves that there are other patterns whereby church and state may be related. Indeed, for most of the history of Christianity and in most places that it has flourished, church and state have not been separate at all, but organically and officially intertwined.

Church-State Co-mingling and Establishments

That pattern began, not surprisingly, with Constantine in the early fourth century. As a Christian convert and a consummate politician, the Emperor thought it his duty to intervene in such affairs of the church as doctrinal disputes. The first Ecumenical Council (Nicea, 325 CE) met at his direction, and

7

The Church
and the
Churches
from
Pentecost to
the Parousia

his purpose was clearly political: he wanted to keep peace and stability in the empire, and religious disputes that rocked the ship of state needed to be resolved for the sake of social and imperial security.

This pattern of mixing the affairs of state and church continued throughout the Middle Ages. Not long after Constantine, Christianity became not just the preferred, but the official religion of the Empire. From about the ninth century on, Europe was officially The Holy Roman Empire, and both the Pope and the monarchs wielded sacred and secular power on a common turf, often stepping on one another's political toes in the process.

That medieval pattern is called "establishment of religion," or "established religion," which means that a particular religion is officially set in place by law and supported by the political authorities and public funds. To be a citizen, then, is to be a church member, and vice versa. Most of the nations of Europe have had an established "State Church" at some point in their history, and some, like England, still do. In modern times, however, State Churches generally recognize and permit alternative Christian denominations and sects as well as other religions to exist and function, and allow their citizens freedom of religious affiliation and practice.

Established religion was the norm for most of our original American colonies. One of our great national myths says that the Pilgrims came to America in order to establish religious freedom. To be sure, the Pilgrims had suffered religious repression, and were indeed seeking religious freedom for themselves. But the strict and theocratic Calvinism that these Puritans solidly established in New England, and especially in the Massachusetts Bay Colony, was as repressive to others as the Church of England had been to them.

The majority of the original thirteen colonies had by law (or charter) an established religion. The Southern Colonies (Virginia, the Carolinas, and Georgia), for example, were officially Anglican; and the New England colonies (Massachusetts, Connecticut, and New Hampshire) were "established" Puritan or Congregational. That meant, especially in New England, that one not only needed to be a church member in order to vote, but a person of any other religious persuasion was subject to fine, imprisonment, banishment, or death. In fact, late in the seventeenth-century, Massachusetts executed four Quaker Christians for advocating religious liberty and freedom of conscience. Despite such grievous excesses, however, most of the inhabitants of the thirteen colonies when the Constitution was written probably favored the idea of an established religion, and thus no separation of church and state. But given the diversity of denominational preferences from colony to colony, they probably could never have agreed upon which one to establish.

Even where there was toleration, as in Catholic Maryland after 1649, it was usually limited to Christians who believed in the Trinity (as opposed to Unitarians, Jews, and +*Muslims, among others). Notable exceptions to these patterns were Rhode Island, founded by a free-thinking religious "Seeker" named Roger Williams, and Pennsylvania, founded by a Quaker, William Penn, both of which colonies provided much needed havens of religious freedom and models of tolerance.

Separation of Church and State

Credit for the principle of separation of church and state rightfully belongs to the framers of our Constitution, most of whom were deists (see chapter 2 above), not traditional Christians. In fact, one of the motives of the deists was to protect their minority religious views *from* the traditional Christians, who had been in the majority at least since the Puritan Pilgrims. The clear leader in this defensive strategy and the chief architect of church-state separation was none other than Thomas Jefferson, who advocated the idea against other options being proposed and considered.

Some colonists, for example, favored a "national establishment" resembling the Anglican Church in England. Their main argument was that it would provide the new nation with an additional sense of unity. More strongly and widely supported was a system called "multiple establishment" favored by Patrick Henry, which would have provided government aid to all Christian groups. The principal objection to this idea seems to have been practical: that benefits would be unequal, and administration would be a bureaucratic nightmare.

Jefferson had a stronger objection to Henry's idea, however: that in a democracy, the best way to support and encourage religion in general is to be completely neutral and impartial concerning religions in particular; and the best way to give religious freedom to all is to deny religious freedom to none, even those whose faith appears strange, suspicious, or just plain silly. In his "Virginia Statute for Religious Freedom," he had already penned these words: "No man shall be compelled to frequent or support any religious worship place, or ministry whatsoever."

Largely because of Jefferson's prestige and persuasive power, the system that America's founders finally adopted and incorporated into the Bill of Rights in 1791 was the complete disestablishment of religion. The first one-third of Amendment 1 reads: "Congress shall make no law respecting an establishment of religion, or prohibiting the free exercise thereof." With these sixteen words, Congress effectively tied its own hands with respect to showing religious favoritism.

Constitutional Concerns and Conflicts

In recent years there has been much debate and a considerable amount of legal wrangling, all the way to the Supreme Court, over the implications of the separation of church and state. The disagreements have mainly been of two types. The first type has been called "borderline" cases, in which public institutions, and therefore funds, seem to be supporting one or another faith and its practice (for example, when a public school recognizes certain holy days as holidays, or a municipality decides to use tax money or public space for a Christmas nativity scene). The second type involves the so-called "free exercise" cases, in which individuals, families, or small groups representing minority religions—sects or cults as defined above—have had to sue for their constitutional rights (for example, when a Rastafarian wants to smoke marijuana as a spiritual rite, or a Native American Church wants to use hallucinogenic cactus as a sacrament).

7

The Church
and the
Churches
from
Pentecost to
the Parousia

Uneven honoring of the religious freedom implied in separation of church and state has been a fact of American religious life, and has caused problems for a great many people over the years, including those on the Supreme Court. For a long time, for example, American Roman Catholics endured bigotry, discrimination, and repression in the face of what amounted to a Protestant-heavy religious nationalism; and Christian sects founded after the Constitution (especially Jehovah's Witnesses, Christian Scientists, Seventh-Day Adventists, and Mormons) have had it even worse: they have had to fight tooth and nail through the courts to have their beliefs and rights recognized, much less respected. But non-Christians (for example, the Society for Krishna Consciousness, Eckankar, Moonies, atheists, etc.) have had it worst of all, often being forced to go to extraordinary lengths to practice their constitutional right to belief or unbelief.

It is thus true only in theory that all Americans have had and do have freedom of religion under the Constitution, and that church and state are separate. The sad reality is that American religious history teaches us that a person in the "land of the free and the home of the brave" has unquestioned religious freedom only if he or she happens to be a member of a Christian denomination that existed when the Constitution was ratified, or subscribes to the Evangelical-Protestant, nationalistic-American-consensus-religion of the culture. Otherwise, separation of church and state is liable to compromise and violation in subtle and not-so-subtle ways and at every turn.

Compounding the problem are religious groups that seek to breach the "high wall of separation" of church and state by imposing their beliefs on others. Is it, for example, appropriate for Catholic and Evangelical Protestant "Right to Life" groups to interfere physically with women seeking legal abortions, or, for that matter, to seek tax revenues to support their own parochial schools? Is it legal for TV evangelists and such organizations as the Moral Majority (and its later incarnations) to campaign for and fund specific conservative causes and candidates? Is it appropriate for clergy to run for public office or, for that matter, to serve as chaplains with officer rank in the military—and thus be paid by the government *and* be subject to the orders of secular superior officers? Is it even proper for church properties to go untaxed, thus increasing the tax burden for all other owners of real estate, including agnostics and atheists?

Despite such sticky questions, the separation of church and state was and is still a great idea, and works to the benefit of all religions. For if government has the right to support a religion, it also has the right to control it and perhaps corrupt it. That certainly happened to the Lutheran Church in Hitler's Germany, with the result that conscientious Christians had to form an underground "Confessing Church" in order to restore some semblance of religious freedom and integrity.

Americans would do well, therefore, to be on guard against any incursion of religion into our public institutions, even if it sounds as well-intentioned and seemingly harmless as morning prayer in public schools or nativity scenes on public property. For whatever might be gained by Christian groups in the short-run, the long-term effect could well be to reduce or remove the precious protection that all people, religious and non-religious alike, should enjoy under the system of separation of church and state.

Expectation of the Second Coming

Some Christians claim that there is no great need for concern about such things as separation of church and state, since there is not much of a future for either. For they firmly believe that we are living in "the last days," that is, on the threshold of the imminent *parousia*, or Second Coming of Christ. As pointed out in an earlier chapter, it is not at all clear to modern biblical scholars that Jesus expected to return, since his reported words to that effect are ambiguous or of doubtful authenticity. Ardent believers in an imminent Second Coming, however, are the least likely to have any interest in the findings of modern biblical scholarship, and thus yearn fondly for the end-time that they are convinced is upon us.

Much ink has been spilled, therefore, and much money spent (and earned) in the last several decades in the production of books whose thesis is that the end is near, and which purport to read and interpret recent and current events as signs of the imminent *parousia*. Many TV evangelists in particular have developed this theme—along with related ideas of Antichrist, Armageddon, Tribulation, and Rapture—and have convinced a good many people that "it won't be long now." Study groups on the book of Revelation, almost always led and taught by amateurs rather than professional or credentialed scholars, have cropped up all over the country. Frightening movies have been based on apocalyptic themes, and even bumper stickers have trumpeted such assertions as "In case of Rapture, this vehicle will be driverless!"

A Weak Case and a Poor Track Record

What those who proclaim and teach the imminent Second Coming of Christ fail to point out (or perhaps even to realize) is that much of their case is naïvely based on a particular type of biblical interpretation that has few defenders among real biblical scholars. For one thing, it is Fundamentalist, and therefore literalistic, which we saw in chapter 1 to be problematic in and of itself. On top of that, it is futuristic, in that it assumes that such scriptures as the book of Revelation are unfulfilled prophecy originally intended for a future age (ostensibly ours). While that could be true, it surely is not obviously so; for there are other, quite plausible, perhaps even compelling ways to interpret those scriptures that some see as boding an impending cosmic cataclysm.

One thing that should make us suspicious of the futuristic method of interpretation is the fact that Christian history has had many futurists who have interpreted the signs of their times as obvious indications of an imminent end, and they have invariably been wrong. Joachim of Fiore, an Italian monk of the late twelfth century, for example, predicted on the basis of calculations of symbolic numbers contained in the book of Revelation that the

7

The Church
and the
Churches
from
Pentecost to
the Parousia

end would most certainly occur in the year 1260. Fortunately for him, he died in 1206, and so was not around to be disappointed; but many of his Franciscan-monk followers fervently preached the end-time all over thirteenth-century Europe. Many Protestants at the time of the Reformation, including Martin Luther, also believed that they were living in "the last days." They, too, appear to have been mistaken.

In American religious history there have been many notable and influential individuals who have predicted the end with great conviction. William Miller, the grandfather of Adventism, for example, predicted 1843 as the crucial year; and Charles Taze Russell, founder of Jehovah's Witnesses, later expressed a similar certainty about the year 1914. Both men and their movements experienced respective "Great Disappointments"; and in both cases their end-time convictions generated denominations with organizational structures and policies clearly intended to guarantee long-term institutional survival and success. Best-selling author Hal Lindsay rose to popularity in the 1960s by predicting 1988 as *the* year, only to have to revise that number upward in his many subsequent books—profits from which he almost certainly invested!

The No-Gain Numbers Game

Many futurists have been fascinated with the Beast described in Revelation, and have often associated or even equated it with the Antichrist mentioned in the first two letters of John (but not in Revelation). In those letters, however, the term "antichrist" appears to refer not to a particular being, but simply to anyone who opposes Christ. Yet, even the non-religious popular imagination has been captured by the image of an individual Antichrist, and even more, it seems, by the number of the Beast mentioned in chapter 13 of Revelation: 666. (Just watch late-night TV reruns of the 1976 Gregory Peck movie, *The Omen*!)

Martin Luther thought that that number referred to the Pope, whose official Latin title, *vicarius filii dei* ("vicar of the Son of God") has the Roman-numerical value of 666. Some English and American Christians in the 1940s concluded that, since Hitler was obviously the most demonic man of modern times, his name *must* have the numerical value of 666; and, surely enough, they devised a scheme that made it so. (It let A=100, B=101, C=102, etc., so that H-I-T-L-E-R = 107+108+119+111+104+117 = 666. One of my industrious but injudicious students once figured out and informed me that "Dr. Paul" produced 666 using the same system!) Some liberal American Democrats of the 1980s even pointed out (jokingly, in most cases) that each of the names of Ronald Wilson Reagan had six letters, hence 6-6-6. Most recently, the number has been pinned—probably in jest—on Bill Gates of Microsoft, and even on a cuddly purple dinosaur who is a favorite of small children. (See figure 7.3.)

What such creative arithmetic tells us, of course, is nothing about the end-time or the alleged Beast, but a great deal about the likes and dislikes of the enumerator. But it should also make us at least a tad skeptical of the futurist method of interpreting the supposed prophecies.

Revelation Relativized

The many past failures of the futurists should not, however, lead us to the conclusion that the book of Revelation is worthless and useless. There are three other perfectly good ways to interpret the vivid and often perplexing imagery of that difficult scripture.

There is, for example, the *historicist* method, which says that that book (as well as all scriptures) is best understood in its own historical context. Viewed in this light, Revelation is a Christian literary work of the late first century (c. 96 CE) written for Christian readers who were experiencing persecution under the particularly severe Emperor Domitian. It is thus an encoded treatise that affirmed belief in Christ and the eventual victory of the faith and the faithful against staggering odds. The Beast, then, obviously becomes the Roman Empire that was threatening to devour the young and vulnerable Church. The seven heads of the dragon in Revelation 12 refer to the famous seven hills of the capital city, and the ten crowned horns in Revelation 13 to the ten emperors that had ruled her since the death of Jesus. As for 666: the name of Nero Caesar, when converted to Hebrew letters (which were also Hebrew numerals) adds up to that very number; and he had been one of the most vicious of all Roman emperors in his persecution of Christians.

A second alternative to the futurist way of interpreting Revelation is the *praeterist* method (from the Latin word *praeter*, meaning "already"), which says that Revelation contains prophecy that has already been fulfilled. This viewpoint was espoused by none other than Augustine, who believed that the birth of the Church—which Paul had called the Body of Christ—had constituted the Second Coming. Thus for Augustine the *parousia* had occurred four hundred years before his own fifth century, at the Pentecost event recorded in Acts 2. According to this view, instead of staring at the eastern

7

The Church
and the
Churches
from
Pentecost to
the Parousia

A Biblical Code Deciphered!

1. Given: CUTE PURPLE DINOSAUR
2. Change all "U"s to "V"s, as in Latin:
    CVTE PVRPLE DINOSAVR
3. Extract the Roman numerals:
    C, V, V, L, D, I, V
4. Convert to Arabic values:
    100, 5, 5, 50, 500, 1, 5
5. Add the numbers up: 666.
6. Conclusion:

    The Beast of Revelation 13:18 is Barney!

— *Circulated on the Internet, Source Unknown*

FIGURE **7.3**

skies for signs and a savior, therefore, Christians should be busy *being* Christ in the world and thus fulfilling their roles *as* the Second Coming.

Yet another way of interpreting Revelation is the *symbolist* method, which says that the real value of the book is its treasure-trove of Christian imagery, and its clear and impassioned affirmation of the Lordship of Christ. The symbolist approach treats Revelation as a great extended metaphor with vivid images to be savored and enjoyed, rather than dissected, deciphered, or decoded. Rather than looking forward, as the futurist method does, or to the past, as the historicist and praeterist approaches do in different ways, symbolist interpretation finds the meaning of Revelation in the present—in the confessional life of the Church and in the hearts and minds of the faithful.

Whether or When?

No one can finally say, of course, whether or not Jesus will come again, and if so, how soon; though it must be admitted that the whole idea seems utterly implausible if not preposterous from the standpoint of our modern Western worldview. One can also say that even the scriptural evidence is shaky, and that the track-record of previous end-time predictors is exceedingly poor.

It may also be added that, should the Second Coming actually occur, we have no reason to think that Jesus would come in some form that would be recognizable or acceptable to Christians today, any more than he was to the religious people of his own day. In fact, if the previous pattern were followed—a Christian Messiah born in the most humble circumstances in the least likely of places—the Christ might well appear in the person of a poor woman, and probably a member of a minority, underprivileged, and oppressed race or ethnic background. She might even be physically challenged in some way . . . a welfare recipient, perhaps, and probably homeless.

We might also speculate that She would not recognize much of what passes for standard Christianity today as having much at all to do with the teachings of the reign of God that had dominated the teachings of the adored Incarnate One of the First Coming. Would this Returned One, for example, recognize all of the expensive and elaborate church buildings, when the First One was remembered to have uttered not a single instruction to His followers about constructing the reign of God in brick and stone? Would She understand how Christians today can justify their luxurious and comfortable lives and healthy bank accounts and retirement portfolios in a world of widespread and abject inequality and starvation and deprivation and suffering? Remember, He reportedly cautioned His followers not to lay up treasures on earth but to show mercy and charity to the poor, oppressed, and imprisoned. Would Her values and priorities be different?

Perhaps those who claim that they long for the great return and the judgment that they expect to follow it should be careful what they wish for. Should their fondest hopes be realized, unlikely as that may be, they might be surprised to find themselves flocked with the goats rather than numbered among the sheep.

Conclusion

What most Christians should know about the Church and the churches, but probably don't, is the complicated historical forces and processes that formed them. They should also be aware of the rich variety of beliefs and practices and institutions that can be found in twentieth-century Christianity under the banner "church."

Just imagine a recently-landed alien from some far-off planet who is trying to figure out this religion called "Christianity." She visits and experiences first a high Catholic Mass celebrated by the Pope in St. Peter's Basilica on Christmas Eve. "What do you call this?" she asks a bystander. "Christianity" is the response. The alien then transports herself to a small, rural Appalachian Pentecostal clapboard church where people are singing, dancing, speaking in tongues, and passing live, venomous rattlesnakes back and forth. "And what is this?" she asks. "Why, Christianity, of course!"

Most American Christians find themselves in liturgical traditions somewhere between these extremes of ornate, sacramental formality and plain, chaotic spontaneity, and they naively take their brand of Christianity to be rather generic and normative. But there is no generic Christianity. Every permutation of the faith and its embodiment in a church of whatever name—even if it claims to be "non-denominational"—is the result of a long tradition of belief, interpretation, disagreement, schism, and in rare cases merger. The result is a potpourri or smorgasbord or crazy-quilt, with every constituent part equally deserving and undeserving of the names "Christian" and "church."

The positive side of this situation is that it gives a wide range of options to those of us who live in a country in which the choice of any religion or none at all is constitutionally guaranteed and thus a matter of individual decision. Theoretically, then, we have a host of options; the fact is that statistically most people die in the same Christian group into which they are born, having made no apparent decision for one and against others. Statistics also show that most of the relatively few people who do convert to another faith or denomination do so not for religious or spiritual reasons, but because of marriage or convenience: "I was a Methodist until I got married, when I joined her Baptist church. But after we moved, the Presbyterian church was *so* close to our new house. . . ."

It is too bad that most Christians know little or nothing of the history of the church as a whole or of their own particular denomination or sect. Nor, for that matter, do they know which teachings and practices distinguish them from Christians of other varieties, much less from people of other religions. That situation does not bespeak a healthy Christianity and cannot bode well for the future of the faith in an increasingly pluralistic world. Nor will it change unless and until all churches begin to take Christian education—real education, administered by trained professionals—as a matter of great urgency and high priority.

7

The Church
and the
Churches
from
Pentecost to
the Parousia

DISCUSSION QUESTIONS & EXERCISES

A. If the possibility that Jesus did not intend to found the Christian religion or the Church could be proven beyond a shadow of a doubt, would it really matter or not? How and why? (Now argue the other side!)

B. What, if anything, do the phrases "Body of Christ" and "in Christ" mean to you? Would what we know today about the operations of the human body (that Paul didn't when he coined the first of those phrases) affect the idea of the Church as Christ's Body or not? How and why?

C. Do you think that women ought to be ordained priests and ministers? Why? What do you think the historical Jesus would say about that issue? Why?

D. Into which of the four historical groups does your church fit? How about that of your closest church-going relative or friend? Is it sacramental or non-sacramental? If you don't know, what sources of information might you seek and what questions would you ask in order to find out?

E. Do you think that Rastafarians and Native Americans should be able to use mind-altering drugs as sacraments in their religions, even if these are illegal substances in the larger society? Do you think Catholics and Episcopalians should be able to use wine at Sunday Holy Communion if restaurants in the area cannot legally serve it to their guests until noon (or at all) on that day? Explain your answer in both cases, and any connection you might see between them.

F. Is Christian pluralism good or bad? What should be the purpose of an Ecumenical Council or consultation today, whether between Christian denominations or with Judaism, Buddhism, etc.? What "bottom lines" are there that keep all Christians from worshipping together? How valid are they?

RECOMMENDED READING

Catherine L. Albanese, *America: Religion and Religions, 3rd edition.* Belmont, CA: Wadsworth Publishing Co., 1998.
   — an outstanding and engaging history of religion (which is to say, of religious proliferation) in America along the themes of "oneness" and "manyness," a great way to get a sense of religious diversity in America
Milton V. Backman, Jr., *Christian Churches of America: Origins and Beliefs.* Revised edition. New York: Charles Scribner's Sons, 1996.
   — an excellent (and time-honored) resource for discerning denominations and sorting sects in the veritable maze of Christian diversity

Kenneth B. Bedell, ed., *Yearbook of American and Canadian Churches 1997.* Nashville: Abingdon Press, 1997.
— another long-time favorite source book of denominational information, prepared and edited for the Communications Commission of the National Council of Churches of Christ

Frank S. Mead, *Handbook of Denominations in the United States, 10th ed.,* revised by Samuel S. Hill. Nashville: Abingdon Press, 1996.
— yet another resource for demystifying denominational diversity in the U.S., in its tenth edition (with an eleventh almost certainly planned) because of its continuing value

Donald W. Musser and Joseph L. Price, eds., *A New Handbook of Christian Theology.* Nashville: Abingdon Press, 1992.
— see especially John H. Leith's excellent article on "Ecclesiology"

Letty Russell, *Church in the Round: Feminist Interpretation of the Church.* Louisville, KY: Westminster John Knox Press, 1993.
— one of the premier feminist theologians sketches her image of the Church of the future around the themes of partnership, sharing, hospitality, and working for the liberation of all people

Charles H. Talbert, *The Apocalypse: A Reading of the Revelation to John.* Louisville, KY: Westminster John Knox Press, 1994.
— a brief and readable, but surprisingly thorough, scholarly look at the book of Revelation, and a great introduction to the modern historical-critical approach to the study of scripture in general

Damian Thompson, *The End of Time: Faith and Fear in the Shadow of the Millennium.* Boston: University Press of New England, 1997.
— a tracing of the Zoroastrian, Jewish, and Christian roots of millenarian or apocalyptic (that is, "end-time") fervor through its many historic manifestations, including Nazism and Marxism as well as movements in the Orient and contemporary America

Daniel Wojcik, *The End of the World As We Know It: Faith, Fatalism, and Apocalypse in America.* New York: New York University Press, 1997.
— a surprisingly comprehensive and comprehensible overview of, and explanation for, the amazing number and variety of apocalyptic leaders and movements that America has produced, including such recent phenomena as the Waco Branch Davidians and the Heaven's Gate suicide society

7

The Church
and the
Churches
from
Pentecost to
the Parousia

ALTERNATIVE CHRISTIAN VIEWS, THE WORLD'S RELIGIONS, AND THE FUTURE OF THE FAITH

Objectives of this chapter:

- to recognize the stance of Christian Liberalism as an alternative to Western Christian orthodoxy's view of human nature

- to show Christian Liberalism's relationship to the modern scientific worldview, to enumerate its basic principles, and to suggest its historic place and future promise

- to survey some of the minority mystical movements that have appeared throughout the history of Christianity

- to distinguish between two basic kinds of spirituality, noting how they relate to traditional and alternative Christianity

- to examine the lessons that Christianity might learn from the Eastern religious and philosophical traditions of the world

- to indicate how attention to its own mystical tradition, dialogue with Eastern religions, and a spirit of Liberalism can help Christianity survive and prosper in its third millennium

8

Alternative
Christian
Views,
the World's
Religions,
and the
Future of
the Faith

*T*he preceding chapters have concentrated on what has been the dominant theological view of Western Christianity, the so-called "fall-sin-redemption model." As we have seen, that model was derived from Paul and Augustine, whose doctrines of universal human sinfulness required Jesus to be the savior-figure whose atoning death alleviated that condition—at least for those predestined to benefit from his sacrifice. So prevalent has been that understanding of what constitutes the heart of the Christian faith that—despite some disagreement about the attendant notions of the image of God, predestination, and freedom of the will—for most Catholics and Protestants alike the fall-sin-redemption nexus provides the basic conceptual framework for their belief and doctrine, and thus defines orthodoxy.

But along the way we have also encountered three other important threads. First, I have mentioned Liberalism as a form of the Christian faith different from that of orthodoxy, and particularly divergent from Fundamentalism in its rejection of a literalist approach to scripture, its openness to the findings of modern science, and its far more optimistic view of the human condition. Second, I have at least hinted that there is a long tradition of an alternative Christian spirituality, one grounded in mysticism and therefore yielding an interpretation of the faith quite distinct from the traditional. Third, I have made comparisons between traditional Christianity and other world religions, and particularly those of the East that are rooted in a monistic view of reality. Although these three threads—Christian Liberalism, mystical Christianity, and Eastern religions—seem a bit like unrelated loose ends, I shall now attempt to tie them together, so that by the end of the chapter both their relationship to one another and their importance to the future of Christianity will be evident. But first, let us examine each of these threads in more detail.

Christian Liberalism and the Modern Worldview

In a religious context, Liberalism is a bit difficult to define because it has different shades of meaning. In its most general sense, it reflects the tendency for any long-enduring religion to produce a sub-tradition characterized by free-thinking and flexibility in interpretation, belief, and practice. Such liberalism is grounded in the conviction that, for any religion to survive and remain relevant, it has to move beyond the specific views and practices of its founder and to question, adapt, absorb, and change as it moves from time to time and place to place, applying the original principles of the faith to each new historical era and cultural context. A synonym of "liberal" in this broad sense might be "progressive."

Christian liberalism in this rather loose (and hence, uncapitalized "l") sense, would characterize any person or movement in the history of the faith that has felt free to disagree with, or deviate from, official, orthodox doctrines and practices. Since that norm has been rooted in the interconnected notions of fall, sin, and redemption, then any Christians who have rejected or minimized any or all of these three fundamental tenets might be termed, however anachronistically, "liberal." We might characterize as "liberal," then, such important figures as Pelagius, Arminius, Erasmus, and Wesley,

8

Alternative
Christian
Views,
the World's
Religions,
and the
Future of
the Faith

all described in Chapter 5 as having granted humanity a greater measure of untarnished image of God and human freedom and potential than did their bastion-of-orthodoxy contemporaries—Augustine, Calvin, Luther, and Jonathan Edwards, respectively.

So Christian liberalism, even in this general sense, both presents and pre-supposes a more positive, optimistic assessment of human nature than Christian orthodoxy. Also inherent in liberalism in this broad sense is a willingness to deviate from external authorities (like popes, councils, creeds, and even scripture) on the basis of such internal norms as reason and experience, as well as an openness to a wider range of information and viewpoints.

The Enlightenment, Its Cosmos, and Its Critics

But modern Christian Liberalism is different from—and much more focused and radical than—this more generic type (thus, its capitalized "L" when used as a noun). For it defines itself in light of the modern scientific worldview, which we described briefly in chapter 6. This worldview, you may recall, while rooted in the European Renaissance of the thirteenth and fourteenth centuries, is largely the product of the Enlightenment of the seventeenth and eighteenth centuries, a movement forged by such thinkers as Francis Bacon, John Locke, and Isaac Newton.

The two linchpins of this worldview are *rationalism*, which values human reason, and *empiricism*, which trusts sensory data. Together, they define the only path to scientific knowledge: the pursuit of truth by making rational sense of empirical data. But these two principles, which seem so obvious and innocuous today, constituted an implicit rejection of revelation, which long had been a staple not only of Christianity, but of nearly all religions. As if that were not enough, they produced a worldview that was and is the greatest challenge to the Christian faith in its entire history, and indeed to spirituality and religion as a whole.

Enlightenment rationalism and empiricism combined to produce a particular image of the constitution and operation of the world—as well as of the universe and nature—hence, "worldview." This worldview says that the universe is basically a physical entity that works in accordance with inviolable natural laws (for example, gravity, motion, and thermodynamics) and in a predictable and experimentally demonstrable way. The only real "mystery" to be encountered in this cosmos is that for which we have insufficient data or for which we have not yet empirically observed or rationally discerned the underlying causes, all of which are presumed to be natural.

Predictably, the reaction of most religious authorities to this worldview was negative on a number of grounds. For one thing, it seemed to give God less and less to do, since it replaced Providence with natural law. It also seemed to eliminate completely the possibility of miracles. More than that, it called into question the very existence of God, and of such things as souls and heaven, precisely because these lacked empirical reality—that is, they could not be seen, heard, touched, smelled, or tasted. The emerging worldview simply seemed far more comfortable with and affirmative of material reality than it did with the spiritual realm that Christianity valued so.

It was only a matter of time until this new empiricist, materialistic world-view produced a "natural selection" explanation for human origins and evolution, and a "Big Bang" theory of creation—both of which seemed to entail an implicit contradiction of biblical accounts of a divine Creation. A sharply negative response to this new worldview and its implications from Christian circles was a foregone conclusion, and the fiercest and most vocal was Fundamentalism, whose reactive stance on biblical interpretation was outlined in chapter 1.

Christian Liberalism and Its Fundamentals

But not all reaction to the modern scientific worldview was negative. Modern Christian Liberalism—sometimes called "Modernism" and "Modernity"—accepted and embraced modern science, its methods, its findings, and even the challenges to religion that it seemed to pose. This modern Liberalism thus added to the optimism and openness of the general liberalism of the past a new spirit of *objectivity*, derived from the modern scientific worldview's twin pillars, rationalism and empiricism.

Modern Liberalism has even been willing to apply the scientific worldview to biblical and theological studies, employing the methods and findings of such academic disciplines as history, psychology, and sociology, which share that worldview. In biblical studies, that has meant the use of the *historical-critical method*, which analyzes scriptural texts carefully, contextually, comparatively—and always from a post-Enlightenment perspective on how the world and human beings function—an approach that has been especially hard on miracles. In a similar vein, the liberal theologians of the nineteenth and twentieth centuries have been inclined to examine doctrine more with reference to the believers and their subjective experiences than to the purported object of Christian devotion and faith, God, since the former can be treated as empirical data, while the latter is non-empirical and therefore rationally inaccessible.

Despite the impact of modern Christian Liberalism in the field of religious studies, to call it a "movement" or even a "methodology" would be to give it a coherence that it has never had, probably because its emphasis on individual reason and experience naturally tends to produce diverse viewpoints and approaches rather than a unified agenda. Despite the impressive label "Liberal Theology," Liberalism can claim no specific theology or particular spirituality. A liberal Christian is free to be a theist, pantheist, panentheist, or monist. (Christian agnosticism and even Christian atheism, though a stretch, are not inconceivable.) A Liberal may also be a devotional pietist, a mystic, or a social activist. In sum, Liberalism is more an attitude, an orientation, and an approach than a theological or spiritual model.

Adding up what we have said above, however, we can identify several broad characteristics that define Christian Liberalism. We have already noted that it bears the traits of optimism, openness, and objectivity. Let us now expand upon those a bit, in order to produce what we might paradoxically term the "fundamentals" of Christian Liberalism.

First of all, Christian Liberalism values internal authority, particularly reason and experience, over against any external authority, whether it be

8

Alternative
Christian
Views,
the World's
Religions,
and the
Future of
the Faith

clerical, papal, traditional, creedal, or even scriptural. In a nutshell, Liberalism insists that religious claims must make sense and comport with common human experience, and refuses to believe them unless they do, regardless of who asserts them. Liberals may elect to follow external authorities, but would find acceptable those grounded in reason and education rather than those claiming the validation of revelation and ordination.

Second, Liberalism tends to maintain that human nature is basically good rather than sinful or corrupted. While not ignoring human shortcomings and social problems, liberal Christians nevertheless tend to be optimistic about human nature and confident about human potential. Accordingly, they are deemed naïve, and are often accused, and usually correctly, of being "humanists." Of course, as Christians, they must be *religious* humanists rather than secular humanists—a distinction often lost on their critics.

Third, because of the legacy of the Enlightenment, Liberalism tends to assume that the world and humanity work in accordance with natural law and that they always have. In the sciences, this important presupposition has sometimes been called "the principle of uniformity of process." When applied to the scriptural accounts of various miracles—walking on water or curing a lunatic by casting out demons, for example—that principle makes the need for rejection, reinterpretation, or recontextualization a foregone conclusion.

Other characteristics of Christian Liberalism are more self-evident and can be treated briefly. Perhaps as a result of its strong rationalistic strain, Liberalism has been open to examining and weighing the truth claims of other religious faiths and philosophies, as well as those of the sciences, on the same grounds as the teachings of Christianity. And, sensitive to individual and cultural differences, liberal Christians tend to be tolerant of people with other views. Thus, while they may disagree strongly and often with one another and others about a variety of things, they would never consign any proponent of an opposing view to hell—even if they were inclined to believe in such a place.

Doubts about Divinity and Other Doctrinal Difficulties

Naturally, these characteristics of the liberal Christian mindset have raised questions about some of the basics of the Christian faith. First and foremost in this regard is the very idea of God, a concept generally accepted as referring to a non-empirical, supernatural reality. In traditional Christianity, God is a spiritual reality whose existence and activity (and claims about such matters) must be taken on faith. This God of the traditionalists is transcendent, but from time to time intervenes in human affairs or interrupts the natural processes in order to effect a miracle. But liberal Christians, with their modern worldview, tend to find no acceptable evidence of such occurrences, and thus cannot take seriously—or at least literally—such miracles or the scriptural reports of them.

Liberals also have typically had intellectual difficulties with a number of doctrines, some of them quite central to the faith. One of the most important has been the Divinity of Jesus Christ, for the very idea of "divinity" seems so far removed from both everyday experience and the natural order as to be problematic. To declare further that this particular man (and only he) had two complete *and* completely disparate natures, one human and one divine, but remained a single, integral person, stretches their credulity too far. Liberals have thus found doubly difficult the incarnational claim of orthodox Christianity about the person of Jesus Christ.

Because they view the world from the human perspective and their own experience, liberal Christians have, as a rule, emphasized the full humanity of Jesus and his role as a teacher and example rather than his alleged divinity and atoning blood-sacrifice on the cross. In fact, it was liberal German scholars in the nineteenth century who first made the distinction between the human Jesus of history who lived and walked the earth, and the Christ of faith whose image as the dying redeemer was the focus (and product) of the early and later Church. Liberals have always found the former more hospitable, attractive, and compelling and the latter commensurably alien, suspect, and problematic.

Other doctrines have posed serious problems for liberal Christians on rational grounds. The doctrine of the Trinity, for example, appears illogical in its assertion that God is one entity with three eternal, separate, and distinct persons (not personalities, modes, or roles), who yet somehow constitute a single undifferentiated deity. The idea of a literal, eternal hell involves another contradiction: a loving, merciful God who is so vengeful as to let millions of souls suffer divinely-devised and eternal torment. Likewise, liberal Christians find it difficult to assent to the doctrine of the Virgin Birth, not only because they believe that nature doesn't now and never did work that way, but also because the scriptural evidence for this particular virginal conception is at best thin and contradictory. Even the seemingly essential belief in the physical resurrection of Jesus is suspect on the same grounds. Liberals generally find some way to reinterpret these doctrines symbolically or metaphorically; otherwise, they ignore or reject them altogether.

The "Heresy" of Liberalism

All of that sounds very negative; and in truth there is a side of Christian Liberalism that can reasonably be seen as deconstructionist or downright destructive, for it questions and undermines some beliefs that many regard as essential to the faith. But there is a very positive side of Liberalism as well. For one thing, Christian Liberalism flies in the face of orthodoxy's presupposition about humanity and its dire plight: while acknowledging the existence of sin (though they are often uncomfortable with that history-laden and tradition-loaded word), Liberals take it as incidental rather than essential to our nature. Some liberal theorists have even concluded that human salvation is really a growth process in which men and women gradually achieve their inherent, but undeveloped potential. Indeed, for many Liberals that is the real meaning and message of the Christian faith.

Another positive aspect of Christian Liberalism is that it does not force believers to choose between two conflicting worldviews or to exist in the uncomfortable "twilight zone" between them. It does not compel them to choose between science and scripture, or to convince themselves that the latter is really the former (as in the case of so-called "creation science").

8

Alternative
Christian
Views,
the World's
Religions,
and the
Future of
the Faith

Christian Liberalism does not equate faith with naïve, literal belief in ancient events reported by people with very different worldviews and story traditions, not to mention their individual agendas and biases. Liberalism not only allows but encourages people to approach recorded tradition with intellects intact and engaged. In other words, it does not force believers to check their minds along with their coats and hats at the sanctuary door.

That Christian orthodoxy would have problems with Liberalism is understandable. For starters, the latter's radical appeal to reason is an implicit rejection of revelation and an open invitation to question the validity of the decrees and proclamations of religious authorities. What is more, orthodoxy's entire salvation system depends on the need for an extraordinary act of grace and mercy, such as that found in the cross of Jesus Christ. If, as Liberals contend, we are not that damnably sinful by nature, then perhaps Jesus could have been—or actually was—a simple teacher or moral example rather than a sacrificial "Lamb of God." To Liberals, that makes much more sense than the blood sacrifice model of the atonement.

From an orthodox perspective, then, modern Liberalism is *heresy*, a charge that contains a large measure of truth. For "heresy" comes from the Greek word for "choosing," and that is exactly what Liberals do: they choose what to believe and how to believe it. From their perspective, that task is both a wonderful gift of freedom and an awesome burden of responsibility. To defenders of Christian orthodoxy, of course, it is the slippery slope to hell.

Levels of Liberalism

Liberalism as an attitude or mindset is not an absolutist position, but a matter of degree at both the individual and the institutional level. A person or church may be more or less liberal, depending on how rigorously she, he, or it applies logic and empiricism to matters of faith and belief. In fact, Liberalism appears in varying degrees within virtually every denomination of Christianity, including those that are officially conservative.

American Roman Catholicism, for example, has been widely regarded as liberal among the world's Catholics, precisely because its members—and especially its laypeople—have shown a willingness to think for themselves and to disagree with papal teachings on such issues as birth control, priestly celibacy, and the ordination of women. (Nevertheless, Dutch Catholics have had the reputation of being the most liberal of all the "children of Rome" for at least the past four hundred years.) Among America's Protestant groups, some are more liberal than others. Episcopalians, the United Church of Christ, and the Disciples of Christ (but *not* Churches of Christ!) are generally regarded as liberal, both theologically and socially (for example, on issues like drinking and dancing). So are most Lutherans and Presbyterians today, despite the fact that their origins go back to Luther and Calvin, respectively, both bastions of Protestant orthodoxy. United Methodism, by contrast, has always had a liberal streak, attributable in large part to its founder, John Wesley, who insisted on the validity of reason and experience, and who was optimistic about the ability of every believer to "go on to perfection."

But such patterns collapse in a number of intriguing ways. On the one hand, in many denominations, including the most conservative, the educated clergy are often more liberal theologically and socially than their lay constituents. Southern Baptist colleges and seminaries, for example, tend to be far more liberal than congregations of that same denomination. On the other hand, even in liberal denominations there are individuals and congregations and even geographical regions that don't fit the expected mold. Some United Methodist individuals and groups (to cite but one instance) are downright conservative, choosing to focus on such aspects of their founder and his teachings as his high regard for scripture and tradition.

The most liberal religionists of all, no doubt, are the Unitarian-Universalists, who are virtually without official creed, insisting that each member work out a reasonable faith for himself or herself. The denomination (or religion in its own right) is a fusion of two earlier groups, the first so named because it rejected the Trinitarian concept of God, and the second for their belief that whatever salvation is, everyone eventually gets it. In fact, whether or not Unitarian-Universalists are Christians depends on which particular church you are talking about or which individual member you are talking to. Some of them would insist that they are humanists, pure and simple.

Lessons from Liberalism

While the thoroughgoing skepticism of many Unitarian-Universalists may be too radical for most Christians, it is quite clear that Christianity has taken a turn in that direction and will have to embrace the attitude of Liberalism in a major and deliberate way in order to survive, prosper, and maintain its relevancy in the Third Millennium. The modern scientific worldview is simply too pervasive, productive, and compelling to ignore; and all of us reared in the West are so acculturated into it that we simply accept it as the way the world operates. Any faith—Christian or otherwise—that demands of its followers that they deny their senses and minds in order to believe, or that tries to shield them from the prevailing worldview, is doomed to anachronism, retrogression, and eventual oblivion.

Also, any faith that asks its followers to take human nature as profoundly or even fundamentally corrupt is bound for failure in an era in which optimism and self-improvement are cultivated, and the findings of psychology and sociology valued. Liberalism honors and embraces such attitudes and activities, and sees Christianity and its teachings as reinforcements for them. Liberalism also embraces the popular modern spirit of freedom and self-determination, and maintains an openness to a variety of beliefs, perspectives, and ideas—religious, philosophical, and scientific. Surely that is a useful stance in an age of diversity of belief and pluralism of ideas.

In short, what Christian Liberalism values most is precisely what modern people most treasure: reason, evidence, freedom, and optimism. Ironically, it might also be seen as demanding a greater degree of faith than forms of Christianity that claim to have scriptural or historical proofs for their tightly held tenets, *and* that further reinforce their teachings with threats of

8

Alternative
Christian
Views,
the World's
Religions,
and the
Future of
the Faith

eternal damnation that feed on *fear* rather than foster *faith*. Liberal Christians, unconvinced by such assurances and intimidation, boldly walk the tightrope of faith, as it were, without a safety net.

Christianity's Other Alternative Expressions

As we have seen in the course of this book, every era of the history of Christianity has produced spiritualities and theologies that, being mystically-inclined, were dissonant alternatives to the prevailing Christian orthodoxy. What follows is a brief (and by no means exhaustive) overview of some of these heterodox perspectives, all of which have laid their own claim to the label "Christian." Many of them were formally recognized and rejected by ecclesial powers, labeled heresies, and actively suppressed. Others maintained a low profile, or emerged in times and places where the domination and control of the Church was minimal, and so escaped official condemnation. From the standpoint of official Western Christian orthodoxy, however, all were and are out of the acceptable mainstream.

The Knowledgeable Gnostics

Between the first and third centuries CE, there was a formidable group of Christians whose interpretation of the faith did not follow the orthodox fall-sin-redemption framework. These were the Gnostic Christians, so called because they understood Jesus as a teacher of esoteric, sacred knowledge or wisdom (*gnosis* in Greek).

Gnosticism itself was older than Christianity. Pre-Christian Gnosticism had taught that the world was not created by a personal transcendent God, but *emanated* from an impersonal God, like light from a flame. Indeed, Gnostics often used light imagery for this God-source, and understood souls or spirits as divine "sparks" given off by It. Humans housed, or rather, imprisoned this Light-deity in their material bodies, which meant that the emanating God was immanent in them. Gnostics believed that it was humanity's general ignorance of their radiant inner divinity that kept their spirits entrapped. Salvation was thus seen as the liberation of these spirits for their journey back to their Source. This process of reunion was facilitated through knowledge—not facts so much as an esoteric wisdom that had to be invoked—or more precisely, *evoked*—by some divine teacher-figure.

Some early Christians, influenced by these ideas, interpreted the person and significance of Jesus accordingly. These Gnostic Christians taught that Jesus was just such a divine purveyor of saving knowledge, a teacher who had pointed to his own inner divinity in order to enlighten people about theirs. They therefore did not adopt the cross as their central symbol, because their focus was not the death of Jesus, but his teaching.

Gnostic Christians produced their own scriptures, including gospels. But Gnosticism did not prosper or endure institutionally, because the "cross Christians" achieved dominance and suppressed them, their ideas, and their scriptures. Some Gnostic writings (such as the Gospel of Thomas) have survived, in whole or in part, as so-called "pseudepigrapha," and may be found today in most good libraries and bookstores. Many people familiar with these scriptures have argued quite convincingly that the Christian Bible should now be expanded to include them.

The "Other" Orthodoxy

Faring much better than Gnosticism institutionally was Eastern Orthodoxy, which today comprises over a dozen ethnic Christian communions, the largest and best known in America being the Greek and the Russian Orthodox Churches. As we saw in the previous chapter, Eastern Orthodoxy officially broke with Roman Catholicism in 1054 CE, after long and deep disagreements on a number of matters, not the least of which was the primacy, power, and authority of the papacy. But deeper than differences over matters of polity or practice was what might be called Eastern Orthodoxy's "incarnational" spirituality and theology, an orientation that looks . . . well, Eastern.

Eastern Christianity has never reflected the theological views of Paul and Augustine to the same degree as Roman Catholicism and Protestantism. Eastern Orthodox theology is much more closely akin to such ancient Egyptian (Coptic) Christian theologians as Clement and Origen of Alexandria (discussed in chapter 5), both of whom were mystical in their spirituality. As a result, their theologies tended to downplay or ignore altogether such staples in Western Christian thought as the Fall of Adam and Original Sin. Instead, they taught that humanity was meant for perfection, which could be achieved through the exercise of free will because of the divinization of humanity effected by the incarnation of Jesus.

Following such thinking, Eastern Orthodox Christianity has always taught that God's nature (much like that of Brahman and the Tao from yet farther East) is inaccessible, but permeates the universe with its energies. Thus the aim of worship and prayer, and indeed of the spiritual life as a whole, is nothing less than the *deification* (Greek, *theosis*) of the individual and total *union* (not just communion) with God, an achievement they see as a realization of the new humanity revealed in Jesus' incarnation. For Eastern Orthodoxy, God became human so that humans might become divine. It would be difficult indeed to find a more positive view of human nature than this one, or one more diametrically opposed to that of the Catholic and Protestant mainstream.

The Mystical Minority

Yet, a similar view to Eastern Orthodoxy's can be found within the Roman Catholic mystical tradition. Mysticism is the human activity that seeks a direct, unitive, and blissful spiritual experience of the Ultimate or Supreme Reality (which is to say in Christianity, with God) by turning inward. As a spiritual activity, it is much more common in Non-Western religious traditions, whose teachings are based on the very idea of the presence of divinity within. Predictably, it is quite rare in the theistic traditions of Judaism, Christianity, and Islam, precisely because its goal, oneness with God, is inherently subversive of the sharp distinction between humanity and God—that is, the idea of ontological transcendence—that Western theism

8

Alternative
Christian
Views,
the World's
Religions,
and the
Future of
the Faith

maintains. Yet, mystics traditionally have at least courted (and sometimes reported) the experience of utter absorption into, and complete oneness with, the Infinite One.

In the Middle Ages (500–1400 CE), Catholic mysticism was especially prevalent—as much as a minority movement can be—finding eloquent expression in a number of remarkable but largely forgotten women (for example, Julian of Norwich, Mechthild of Magdeburg, Hildegard of Bingen, and Theresa of Avila) as well as a few good men (for example, Bernard of Clairvaux, Francis of Assisi, and John of the Cross). The most radical exponent of the medieval Western Christian mystic tradition was Meister Eckhart (1260–1327), a German Dominican Catholic priest, who claimed that nothing is so near to human beings as their very being, which is none other than God. In fact, his Latin definition for God was this: *esse est deus*, which literally means "to be is God"! Having insisted that his own essence and God's essence were one and the same, he asserted that people must learn to penetrate everything in order to find God within them and themselves. On one occasion, he even compared God to a great "underground river," an impersonal image of depth that is a far cry from a heavenly Father. It should come as no surprise that Eckhart was accused of pantheism and declared a heretic by papal decree. He might have been better received and treated had he been Greek Orthodox . . . or Hindu.

Usually the Catholic Church looked askance at these people, primarily because the direct experience of God that they sought and claimed threatened the role and function of the Church, its sacraments, and especially its leaders as mediators of God's grace and revelation. Still, the Church managed to include most of these mystics in spite of their radical spirituality, but kept them in safe isolation in religious orders and monasteries. Some of them were even named saints, perhaps because posthumously they seemed more holy—and less threatening—to the established order.

The Quiet Quaker

Quakerism was founded in the mid-seventeenth century in England by a man named George Fox. It was essentially a late and left-wing expression of Puritanism, the Protestant movement that had begun in that country early in the previous century for the purpose of removing the last vestiges of Roman Catholicism from the newly formed Anglican (that is, English) Church. In other words, the Puritans wanted the established state Protestant Church of England "purified," and hence their name.

Fox's brand of Puritanism was very radical, if only because its teaching entailed a dramatic move away from the traditional theism of Christianity and in the direction of monism. The heart of his doctrine was that each individual contained an "Inner Light," or spark of divinity. Quaker spirituality was focused on the believer's getting in touch with that sacred personal center through quiet meditation. That goal made early Quaker worship distinctive: the people met and sat in silence (what the Japanese Zen Buddhists might call *zazen*), unless and until a participant felt moved by God's Spirit to speak. There was no order of worship, no sacrament, no scripture reading, no audible prayer, no sermon, no music, and no clergy. All of these were regarded as intrusive distractions from the believer's immediate (that is, unmediated) access to the Inner Light, which was none other than God.

This declaration of divinity within was, of course, a far cry from the Pauline-Augustinian emphasis on human sinfulness and innate depravity maintained by most Christians and emphasized by other Puritans. And church officials in all of the mainline groups—Protestant as well as Catholic by then—perceived the threat that this Quaker teaching posed to the need for a divine savior-figure to die for a sinful humanity. Quakers saw humanity as possessing an unfallen, inward "image of God," and they longed and sought for a pure experience of it—with no "third party" help, human or super-human.

American Metaphysical Religions and Not-So-New Thought

The inner-focus of the Quakers, as well as the mystics and Gnostics before them, has found many and various American expressions in what are sometimes called "metaphysical religions." The elder-statespersons of the American metaphysical movement are generally acknowledged to have been the Transcendentalists, whom we saw in chapter 2 to have been, in fact, "Immanentalists," theologically. But the metaphysical movement, which drew on a number of sources, including spiritualism, mesmerism (hypnosis), and Eastern religions, found its purest expression in the deliberately Eastern-laced Theosophy produced by Madame Helena P. Blavatsky late in the nineteenth century. But Theosophists, like most of the Transcendentalists before them (and the similarly "metaphysical" Scientologists who would appear in America much later), self-consciously and deliberately placed themselves outside the Christian fold.

The same metaphysical "spirit of the age," however, also produced a number of explicitly Christian expressions. Chief among these in durability and size is Christian Science, which was founded in the late nineteenth-century by Mary Baker Eddy. In her pivotal book *Science and Health with Key to the Scriptures* and other writings, she taught that (1) God is both a Principle and a Person (Father-Mother); (2) matter is not self-existent (that is, "really real"), but a shadow of the truth of God; therefore (3) sin and sickness are not realities, but mistaken thoughts to be cured by the Truth (Christian Science); and (4) human beings are essentially divine and immortal, not to mention naturally whole and well. (It should be noted that whenever the word "Science" appears in the name of a religious denomination, it almost invariably means "esoteric, spiritual Wisdom.") It is on the basis of such teachings that Christian Scientists even today reject traditional (that is, truly scientific) medical procedures and remedies.

Another American-born Christian metaphysical expression, closely related to Christian Science, is New Thought. In most ways less radical in its teachings than Christian Science, it did not utterly deny the reality of matter or renounce modern medicine; still, New Thought was and today remains quite far removed from Christian orthodoxy. New Thought was, in effect, a nineteenth-century revisionist version of Christianity, pioneered by Emma Curtis Hopkins, Charles and Myrtle Fillmore and others. It taught the immanence of God as the "Christ presence" in everyone and everything, and

8

Alternative
Christian
Views,
the World's
Religions,
and the
Future of
the Faith

as the source of truth, health, prosperity, and peace. New Thought managed to produce quasi-denominations with names like "Religious Science," "Divine Science," and "Science of Mind," but it found perhaps its most visible institutional expression in the Unity School of Practical Christianity, a small alternative Christian denomination, usually called simply "Unity." It is best known for its Silent Unity telephone-mail prayer ministry and *The Daily Word*, a daily-devotional booklet published monthly.

Unity (not to be confused with Unitarianism) teaches, in typical New Thought fashion, that God is Good and "the One Presence and Power in the Universe and in our lives," and thus explicitly denies the reality of Satan or any such power of evil. Unity asserts that Jesus was "the Christ" in the sense that he was in perfect touch with his own inner divinity, his Christ-nature. His mission, therefore, was to put all others in touch with their own innate Christ-natures. In this regard, he was a kind of spiritual "Elder Brother" or "Wayshower," performing a role resembling that of a Gnostic teacher . . . or Buddhist sage.

Unity spirituality, therefore, is not sin-focused; nor does it place much emphasis on the death of Jesus or make use of the cross as a symbol. The Bible is interpreted spiritually or "metaphysically" (which is to say, "metaphorically"), and personal devotions and corporate worship emphasize positive affirmations (for example, "I am an expression of God, and I am well and whole"). Many of the old (mostly Protestant) sin-fall-redemption hymns are revised to present more positive messages, free from references to human wretchedness, bloody-death atonement, and heaven as a celestial place. So different is the version of Christianity presented by Unity, that it is often attacked as a "cult" by Fundamentalist and Evangelical Christians, much as Gnostic Christians of an earlier era were pronounced heretics. After all, New Thought in general and Unity in particular are in many respects really revivals of *old* Gnostic Christianity.

Contemporary Christian Theology and Creation Spirituality

Twentieth-century Catholic and Protestant theologians have explored and endorsed some theological models that, despite their differences from one another, resemble each other by looking less like traditional Western theism and more like Eastern monism. What they have in common, and what ties them to the East, is an appreciation for divine immanence.

In the early mid-century, for example, Roman Catholic priest and paleontologist Pierre Teilhard de Chardin (d. 1955) produced a "process theology" that viewed God not only as an immanent force within the natural universe, but one evolving *along with it* toward full maturity—what Teilhard called "The Omega Point." At about the same time, Protestant theologian Paul Tillich (d. 1965) likewise rejected or at least greatly compromised the notion of divine transcendence, maintaining instead that God was "The Ground of Being" or even "Being Itself," and as such was immanent as the "depth dimension" of all existing beings.

In the 1960s came the radical work of Thomas J. J. Altizer, whose "Death of God" theology was based on the idea that at the heart of the Christian message was a God who had voluntarily renounced transcendence in favor of immanence. That transformation occurred first as the divine Incarnation in the person of Jesus, and then universally as the Holy Spirit that Jesus released to infuse the world, which for Altizer meant primarily human culture. Still later (mostly in the 1980s and 90s) proponents of "Eco-theology" or "Eco-Feminist Theology" have explored similar themes relating to an immanent divinity, but one inherent in nature—or *as* Mother Nature—rather than in human culture.

Of the "new theologies of immanence" to come to prominence in recent years, one warrants special attention here if only because of its deliberate rejection of traditional Christian theology. It is the Creation Spirituality of Matthew Fox, a former Roman Catholic priest and now an Anglican priest, whose ground-breaking book, *Original Blessing: A Primer in Creation Spirituality* (1983), proved him to be yet another fox in the hen house of Christian orthodoxy.

In that work Fox presents a self-consciously Creation-centered understanding of the Christian faith as an alternative to the "fall-sin-redemption" model. Augustine's doctrine of Original Sin is a major stumbling block, Fox argues, for it both engenders guilt and self-doubt in believers *and* places ecclesiastical authorities in unhealthy positions of power as mediators of the needed divine remedies. Over against this traditional pattern, Fox offers a positive and empowering view of human nature.

Fox's Creation Spirituality departs from orthodoxy at four major points. First, he denies that the theistic, dualistic, patriarchal pattern is the best way to conceive of God. Instead, he prefers panentheism: the view that God and the cosmos interpenetrate one another in such a way that God is both profoundly immanent and somehow transcendent as well. Fox also professes a predilection for language about God that is holistic and feminist, since these are more congenial for the expressing of God's intimacy with and presence in the world. Second, Fox denies that Original Sin is the proper starting point for understanding the human situation or salvation. Instead, he begins with "Original Blessing" through God's immanent creative energy, which he calls *dabhar Jahweh* (Hebrew for "the Word of God" that was the creative force active in Genesis 1). This divine power is present within all of creation, he says, making it inherently good. Point three follows logically: Fox refuses to accept the idea that human nature is basically fallen and sinful. Rather, since they embody God's creative word in an especially profound way, humans are essentially divine. Fourth and finally, he asserts that the importance of Jesus lies not in his atoning death, but in his role as a "prophet-artist" who calls others to their own divinity and helps them "birth" it.

Fox sees his Creation Spirituality as rooted in the Wisdom literature of the Hebrew Bible, in the New Testament Gospel of John, and ironically, perhaps, in the "cosmic Christ" imagery in the same Pauline epistles whose sin-emphasis he so flatly rejects. To further support his theology, Fox cites an impressive array of witnesses, most of whom are unorthodox or downright heretical. Fox likes Irenaeus of Lyons, the medieval mystics (and especially Meister Eckhart), and Teilhard. Looking beyond the Christian tradition he finds complementary themes in Native American tribal religions, Eastern religious and philosophical traditions (especially Buddhism and Taoism),

8

Alternative
Christian
Views,
the World's
Religions,
and the
Future of
the Faith

secular poetry and the other arts, and even the post-Einsteinian "New Physics," to which we shall later refer.

The Most Common Denominator

Despite obvious variations in expression and terminology, a common denominator connects Matthew Fox's Creation Spirituality to the other modern theologies, as well as to most of the "alternative" Christian movements previously mentioned in this section. Simply stated, it is their shared dynamic of *interiority*. For all of these "alternative Christianities" have a mystical character that posits God as an immanent Reality.

To describe these alternative expressions as "interior" is to recognize that there are basically only two types of spirituality to be found in the world's religions: *relational* and *unitive*. Relational spirituality dominates the Western religions, which are based on a theistic framework that posits the Ultimate Reality as an "Other," a personal God who is an object of worship and devotion. Spirituality in such a theological context seeks both *communication* and *communion* with this God who dwells apart. Unitive spirituality, by contrast, is found mostly in Eastern religions and their monistic philosophies, which present the Ultimate as a non-personal "Inner"—a Presence or Force infusing nature and human nature. This kind of spirituality posits God's presence not only at the core of the individual's being, but *as* that person's very essence, and seeks *union* with it; hence, its *mystical* character and *interior* dynamic.

In fact, both kinds of spirituality are found in all of the world's religions. In both Hinduism and Buddhism, for example, despite their generally monistic orientation, there are numerous sects devoted to this or that divinity or quasi-divinity, with whom they feel a special relationship. The reverse pattern appears in monotheistic Judaism and Islam, where one finds mystical strains in such movements as Kabbalah and Sufism, which locate God within as the very essence of every human being. Likewise, as noted earlier, mystical spirituality has issued at least a "minority report" in Christianity in virtually every era—from ancient Gnosticism to contemporary Creation Spirituality. It is less a coherent tradition than a recurring dynamic that seemingly "won't go away," despite the efforts of traditionalists to suppress its heterodoxy.

Aldous Huxley called this dynamic of mystical interiority "the perennial philosophy," and touted it, not just as the common denominator of all of the world's religions from prehistoric times to the present, but as the very root from which they sprang. That view stands in sharp contrast to the more traditionalist, theistic Christian understanding, which considers mysticism as at best problematic, and at worst deviant. Nonetheless, this enduring expression of human spirituality is commanding such increasing attention in the Western world that Christianity will no longer be able to ignore or suppress it.

Alternative Christianity and the New Age

In the face of the challenges of a new millennium, Christianity would do well to search out and re-explore the largely hidden expressions of unitive spirituality and theology in its own tradition. One clear sign of the need to do so is the burgeoning of the so-called "New Age Religion"—or what is sometimes called "New Alternative Spirituality"—in the last few decades. This phenomenon is very diffuse and difficult to define, having no institutional coherence and drawing from many disparate traditions. Its many sources include mysticism, nature worship, spiritualism, occultism, Wicca, and Native American and Oriental spiritualities. Yet there is a common theme that apparently makes the whole movement so attractive: an emphasis on interiority in the life of the spirit. Whatever else it is, New Age Religion is inherently mystical.

Why that makes it so appealing to contemporary people is uncertain. No doubt one reason is the impact of the field of psychology, in particular the many forms of depth psychology, with its focus on internal motives and impulses rather than external behaviors. It may also result in part from the increasing influence of Eastern religions. The enormous popularity of actors and other artists in our society may also be a factor; for all artistic disciplines demand both the search for and the analysis of internal sources of inspiration that are best described as spiritual. That in turn may help explain the number of well-known actors who have embraced such non-Christian religions of interiority as Tibetan Buddhism and Scientology, and who have freely shared with the public their new-found faiths through the various media.

For these and other reasons, no doubt, more and more Christians are becoming interested in Christian Gnosticism. Increasing numbers are also studying mystics like Hildegard of Bingen and Meister Eckhart, both of whom are more widely known than at any time in history, including their own. With the rise in visibility and popularity of such long-neglected voices as these, the face of Christianity may be changing before our eyes.

None of these trends seems to endorse traditional, orthodox Christianity's relational spirituality or its transcendent "Other" celestial God who occasionally intervenes from on high. They instead suggest something close to the mysticism of the alternative Christians discussed earlier, and resonate with the theological *immanence* implied there and taught explicitly in the religions of the East.

Christianity and the Religions of the East

The last of our three loose threads, then, is Christianity's relationship to the other great religious traditions of the world, and especially those of the East. Though Christianity has always been more or less aware of other religions, it has only been in serious dialogue with them for little more than a century. Prior to that, non-Christian religions were regarded *a priori* as misguided and error-ridden at best, and works of the Devil at worst. For most of the past two millennia, Christians have remained both suspicious and blissfully ignorant of the spiritualities and teachings of other religions.

Imported Immanence and Its Implications

Eastern teachers and spiritual masters began to appear in the United States after the first World Parliament of Religions, held in Chicago in 1893; and with the waves of immigrants from the Orient and Middle East produced

8

Alternative
Christian
Views,
the World's
Religions,
and the
Future of
the Faith

by the relaxed policies of the Immigration Act of 1965, Eastern religions have reached a critical mass of visibility. One result of these two important events is that it has become clear to more and more people that these exotic traditions have much to offer that traditional Christianity does not. That "something" is, above all, a conceptual framework rooted in the idea of *divine immanence*; and that means *monism* or something very close to it.

As we have seen, monism has not been so much absent from Christianity as underrepresented and unrecognized. The implicit theology of Meister Eckhart and many of his fellow mystics was monistic; and in fact he was accused and condemned as a pantheist, which he was—for a pantheist is really just a monist who uses the name "God" for the Ultimate One within all things. (See figure 2.4 in chapter 2.) Eckhart had found it necessary to leave the dominant theology of his tradition in order to conceptualize and articulate his own unitive experience of God; yet surprisingly, neither he nor any of his fellow mystics ever developed a systematic theological framework within which to articulate their unitive experiences.

Thus, even if Christianity should move in the direction of some of its own minority expressions, it might still benefit greatly from the mystical spirituality and monist philosophies of Eastern religions. In this vein, let me suggest here several things that I believe Christianity would do well to learn from the Eastern religions. These lessons will help the faith not only to appreciate its own alternative traditions, but to become more responsive to the challenges of the Third Millennium.

The Monistic Model Revisited

In Hinduism, the Ultimate is *Brahman*, and the individual's spiritual essence is *atman*; and *atman* is *Brahman*. In Buddhism, one's own essential Buddha-nature (*Dharmakaya*) is one with the spiritual essence of all of nature and of all beings within it. In Taoism, the Way (*Tao*) is in and flows through all things as their very being (*tzu-jan*). For these three great systems, the individual, spiritually speaking, *is* the Ultimate—essentially one with the One, and therefore with all others.

That theological framework or model, which we described in detail under the banner of "monism" in chapter 2, is far more compatible with a unitive spiritual quest than is a theistic one; and, as we have suggested, more and more Americans seem to be drawn to precisely such a quest. This is not to say that the monistic model or its cognates, pantheism and panentheism, should become *the* definitive theology of Christianity; for certainly many Christians experience God as a transcendent Other, and there is no good reason to pronounce the experience invalid or the theological image wrong. Rather, a new Christian monism would provide an alternative conceptual framework for articulating the experience of those Christians who encounter God more as an Inner Presence than as an Other Power. A dialogue with Hinduism and other Eastern faiths would help Christianity to develop alternative ways of capturing and conveying the mystic's distinctive sense of God, and of God's indistinct nature with respect to the universe and humanity.

Eastern Elucidation for Difficult Doctrines

The study of Eastern religions might also shed new light on many historic Christian doctrines, especially those that have always been the most difficult to fathom. The difficult notion of the Trinity, for example, might be complemented and clarified by the Hindu concept *Trimurti* (literally, "Three Forms"), which refers to the widespread belief in India that the non-personal Ultimate, Brahman, self-expresses in three primary, personal forms: Brahma, Vishnu, and Shiva. Analysis of this concept could help Christians to sort out the dynamics of their own Trinitarian belief, which also posits an impersonal-sounding Godhead that is unitary yet comprises three separate Persons.

Another point at which Eastern monism might make a contribution is in the area of Christology. As we saw in chapter 4, Christianity from ancient times has taught that Jesus Christ was the unique convergence of perfect humanity and perfect divinity, or God Incarnate ("in the flesh"). Catholic sacramental theology has extended that idea by maintaining the "real presence of Christ" in the *natural* elements of bread (grain) and wine (grape) in the Holy Communion. Eastern monistic-pantheistic-panentheistic theologies, however, expand the idea of incarnation infinitely, by conceiving it as *universal*. For when the Ultimate is the inner essence of all sentient beings, then all sentient beings are essentially divine. It might be interesting, therefore, to shine this Eastern light into some obscure Christological corners.

In this regard, the teachings attributed to Jesus in the canonical and non-canonical gospels might take on new meaning for Christians if viewed through the lens of the broader, Eastern understanding of incarnation. Wouldn't Jesus' claim in the Fourth Gospel of oneness with "the Father," along with the "I am" sayings, be more inspiring if seen as statements about human spirituality in general rather than as the particular self-referential boast of a uniquely divine individual? And wouldn't such a generalization comport nicely with his reported saying that the domain of God is "within"? Even his much-touted advice to Nicodemus about the need to be born again would make new sense in light of a system that has always taught human incarnation as a quite natural, ongoing, and cyclical process of rebirth.

Another example of a doctrine that might find greater clarity in an Eastern light is the Virgin Birth. It might prompt a good deal of useful reflection, for example, if Christians knew that the Buddha and Lao Tse are believed by their followers to have been miraculously conceived, *but* that they are not therefore presumed to have been uniquely divine. In light of such information, Christians might be stimulated to explore the idea of virginal birth as a metaphor for the birthing or actualization of everyone's true Buddha-Christ nature, that is, the incarnate or enfleshed divinity that all humans innately possess. This process of self-realization is precisely what "Enlightenment" means in Eastern religions—in contrast to its empiricist-rationalist connotation in the Western world.

Furthermore, the power of the image of the Virgin Mary and the widespread devotion to her in Roman Catholic Christianity might be newly envisioned in the context of some Hindus' devotion to the *Mahadevi* ("Great

8

Alternative
Christian
Views,
the World's
Religions,
and the
Future of
the Faith

Goddess") and most Buddhists' reverence for the feminine-featured *bodhisattva* (compassionate being) variously called *Kwan Yin* (China), *Kannon* (Japan), and *Tara* (Tibet). Even the artistic renderings of these Eastern female figures are often so strikingly similar to those of the Blessed Virgin of Catholicism that one begins to wonder whether they are either Jungian archetypes that have emerged from the collective human unconscious or various expressions of the feminine face of Deity Itself.

Unitive Mysticism

Christianity could also gain from Eastern religions a better understanding of what mysticism is. As already noted, the search for God within is always difficult in a theistically-based doctrinal setting that treats God as an absolute Other. It is not surprising, then, that most of the mysticism that has emerged in Christianity has been of a compromised variety, what has sometimes been called "devotional mysticism" in order to distinguish it from the purer "unitive mysticism" found in the monistic Eastern religions. Devotional mysticism focuses attention on or even visualizes an object of devotion: usually it is a manifestation of God or some such expression of divinity as Jesus or his Sacred Heart or a saint. The sought-after effect is a heightened sense of *love*.

Unitive mysticism, by contrast, aims at clearing the mind of all images in order to experience a dissolution of individuality and the absorption of the believer into the *bliss* of oneness with the Absolute One. Unitive mysticism is much more typical of Eastern religions, precisely because their most profound philosophies are *monistic* rather than theistic, and thus based on the premise of divine *immanence*. Still, devotional mysticism can be found in some Eastern expressions, just as unitive mysticism has occasionally appeared in the West, for example, in Christianity's Meister Eckhart and Islam's Sufi tradition.

Ways to the Way

Christianity might also gain from Eastern religions an appreciation for variety and inclusiveness in the spiritual quest. Like their fellow Western monotheists (Jews and Muslims), traditional Christians have always tended to make exclusivist claims that their God is the only God and that their faith is the only path to that God. By contrast, the people of Southern and Eastern Asia have generally accepted the idea that diverse religious traditions can be both right and valuable in their own ways. The image of "many paths to the mountaintop" is often used, though given the spiritual interiority of the Eastern religions, "many paths into the depths of the cave" might be more appropriate.

Perhaps because they have been around longer than Christianity, Eastern religions are also more inclined to recognize a variety of spiritual orientations and styles *and* to affirm each as valid. Hinduism has been the most systematic in this regard in its distinguishing of four primary *yogas* (disciplines) or *margas* (paths): (1) the *deeds* (*karma*) approach, which embraces both ritual and ethical behavior; (2) the *insight* (*jnana*) path, comprising doctrinal study and intellectual inquiry; (3) the *love* (*bhakti*) path, which expresses devotion and adoration for a particular god or goddess; and (4) the *mystical* (*raja*, literally "royal") discipline aims at the kind of unitive experience described above. For convenience, these can be called "religion of the hands," "religion of the head," "religion of the heart," and "religion of holiness," respectively.

As suggested in chapter 4, once these four religious types are recognized, it is not difficult to see them reflected in Jesus' reported saying about loving God with *heart*, *soul*, *mind*, and *strength*. Hinduism's four paths might also help Christians make better sense of the variety of practices and doctrines, not to mention the denominational diversity (or "chaos of cults"), that their own faith has produced. The observance of the Roman Catholic sacraments, then, might reflect *karma marga* because of their "hands-on" quality; the metaphysical teachings of Christian Science could be seen as having a *jnana marga* orientation because of its "heady" approach; the evangelistic revivalism common among Southern Baptists might be an example of *bhakti marga* because of its emphasis on "heart-felt" experience; and the silent, introspective worship of the early Quakers might seem a kind of Christian *raja marga* because of its quiet cultivation of a profound inner "holiness." Perhaps recognizing the variety of valid paths would lead to tolerance not only for fellow Christians and their different beliefs and practices, but for the adherents of other religions as well.

Toward Tolerance?

Despite a certain prestige accorded to the mystical path, the Hindu *yoga-marga* system is predicated on the belief that there is a path for everyone, and that all are effective. Exposure to such an open and accepting—not to mention loving and generous—attitude might prompt even conservative Christians to consider the possibility that a truly gracious and merciful God may well have provided in the many religions and their divergent sects a variety of viable and righteous routes, if only as a way of accommodating the inevitable individual and cultural differences within the human family. Wouldn't a loving parent do as much for all of his or her children?

I grew up in northern Kentucky, right across the Ohio River from Cincinnati. When I was a child, there were no fewer than five bridges connecting "my" side of the river with the Queen City, and all of them got me and my fellow "hillbillies" there in fine fashion. Some of the bridges were faster routes than others, and different ones led to different parts of the big city. One bridge even sang a rather soothing *OM* under moving tires because of its surface of metal grating. But all of them worked. Could not the world's religions simply be seen as alternative bridges to God?

Savoring Silence

Christianity might have yet one more practical lesson to learn from Eastern religions. Hinduism and Buddhism in particular have spent centuries in perfecting such meditative techniques as *yoga* and *zazen*, and in employing short, monotonal *mantras* (chants) as spiritual practice exercises. But perhaps the greatest gift that the monistic East can offer Christianity is a profound misgiving about words and a genuine appreciation of silence with

8

Alternative
Christian
Views,
the World's
Religions,
and the
Future of
the Faith

respect to Ultimate Reality. For, while it is true that "the Silence" has been practiced in Christianity among such widely different groups as Catholic Trappist monks and sectarian Unity laypersons, the most prominent and influential figures in Christian history have been people of many rather than few words. The East, by contrast, has always questioned the efficacy of words in the realm of spirituality, and has maintained a healthy skepticism towards verbosity.

Hinduism, for example, counsels silence as the best way to approach the infinite depths of Brahman. Next best is the use of the simple monosyllable *OM*, and the last resort is the negative ascription *neti neti* ("not this, not that" or "neither/nor"), which indicates only what the Ultimate is not. Many forms of Buddhism sum up their entire piety in a single short chant ("*namu amida butsu,*" or "*namu myoho renge kyo,*" or "*om mani padme hum*"), while Zen Buddhism counsels sitting in complete silence, pausing to utter only a few puzzling words sure to confound the intellect. The Chinese scripture, *Tao Te Ching,* begins by telling us that the Tao (Ultimate Reality) really cannot be discussed, and later declares that even the name "Tao" is wrong!

Again and again Eastern religions remind us that *the best religious language is always closer to poetry than to prose; but in the realm of the spirit, silence is golden.* Christians probably already know the first part of that intuitively, as evidenced by the general esteem in which the poetic Psalms and metaphorical parables of Jesus are held. Psalms 46:10 quite specifically counsels, "Be still, and know that I am God!" Perhaps more attention to the East could improve the West's knowledge of how this sort of sacred stillness could be better accomplished, as well as provide some hints about what experiences and benefits might result.

Tying the Threads

In reviewing Christian Liberalism, Christianity's alternative mystically-oriented traditions, and the monistic religions and philosophies of the East, I have argued that Christianity really needs some of the important dynamics of each. Specifically, I have contended that if the Christian faith is to survive and prosper in its third thousand years, it will have to open itself as never before to: (1) Liberalism's attitude of *objectivity*, its *optimism* about human nature, and its *openness* to the presence of truth not only in other religions and philosophies, but in modern science as well; (2) Christian mysticism's largely ignored and suppressed *spirituality of interiority*; and (3) Eastern religions' *philosophy-theology of divine immanence*.

Much That is Mutual

The three already have significant points of contact. Liberalism, for example, shares with Eastern religions an appreciation for and tolerance of religious diversity. But two of the threads are much more fundamentally related, even cognate: Christian mysticism as a spirituality and Eastern monism as a immanentalist philosophy or theology are simply two sides of the same unitive coin. That connection leads to yet another: with their shared notion of innate divinity, Christian mysticism and Eastern monism also reinforce Liberalism's optimism about human nature.

In its openness to a variety of sources of truth, Liberalism reflects an attitude that is more typically Eastern, yet it is firmly rooted in the Christian tradition. This salutary combination makes it vital for the future of Christianity. For it gives Christians permission to seek and discover meaningful and useful beliefs and practices outside their own confessional circles of faith. It enables them to find, for example, inspiration in the *Upanishads* or the *Tao Te Ching*, edification in *yoga* or *zazen*, comfort in the idea of *karma*, or hope in the possibility of *moksha* (release from the cycles of reincarnation).

An Enhanced Liberalism for the Liberally Enlightened

But beyond such affinities, Liberalism very much needs Christian mysticism and Eastern monism. For while it represents an attitude or orientation that can be an important catalyst in the forging of a new Christian outlook, which is exactly what the faith needs, Liberalism has no spiritual or theological substance. It must look elsewhere for that. In this regard, it may very much require mysticism and monism for its own survival. As we have seen, modern Liberalism is defined in large part by its positive response to the post-Enlightenment worldview that prevails today in the Western world. The problem for Liberalism here is that there are clear signs that that modern worldview may already be *passe*.

The neat, mechanical Newtonian picture of the universe is now being challenged, and even referred to in scientific circles as "conventional" or "the old" physics, in contrast to the "New Physics" of Albert Einstein, Max Planck, Niels Bohr, Werner Heisenberg, and their successors. Relativity theory and quantum mechanics especially require us to confront the vagaries of infinity, randomness, and the relativity and instability of both time and space. The New Physics has thus reintroduced mystery into the cosmic picture in a very profound way. As English biologist J. B. S. Haldane observed, "The universe is not only stranger than we imagine, it is stranger than we *can* imagine." The comparatively flat, materialistic, and mechanistic Newtonian universe that Liberalism so boldly embraced and came to find so congenial simply no longer exists.

Strange as it may seem, a number of physicists have observed that the image of the universe that is now emerging is highly compatible with ancient Hindu, Buddhist, and Taoist cosmologies. Some theoretical scientists have even said that they are rediscovering "God" in their researches and theories, but their musings clearly bespeak Something (not Someone) much closer to *Brahman*, *Shunyata*, or *Tao* than to the deity of traditional Judaism, Christianity, and Islam. If Christian Liberalism is to keep pace with modern science, it may need to reexamine the Wisdom of the East and its distinctive style of thought about Ultimacy. In other words, this movement born of one Enlightenment may find its maturity—as well as its soul—in an Enlightenment of a very different sort.

Conclusion

The modern era has often been identified, quite correctly, as an age of pluralism of belief. That means that more than at any other time in history,

8

Alternative
Christian
Views,
the World's
Religions,
and the
Future of
the Faith

a wide variety of viewpoints and interpretations—some religious and some not—exist today side by side, providing conflicting interpretations of the universe and the human situation. What makes these especially challenging to the modern mind is the fact that they are often equally plausible and therefore quite difficult to choose among.

Modern pluralism has affected Christianity deeply in this regard. Perhaps the most serious challenge thus far has been the post-Enlightenment world-view itself, because its empirical and inductive approach to truth seems to call into question or rule out altogether many of the things traditional religions have held dear: spiritual realms, revealed truth, supernatural or transcendent realities, faith, and so on, up to and including God or an Ultimate Reality by whatever name. On top of that, the increasingly visible historic world religions, and particularly those of the East, have made their presence felt in dramatic new ways that can no longer be ignored; and they have been joined by a host of new religions and quasi-religions that have appeared in this country in recent years, some imported and some home-grown. And, as if that weren't enough, leading exponents of such modern Western secular philosophies as Existentialism have tended to ignore or deny the existence of God or gods altogether. All of these together have challenged the truth claims of religion in general as well as the credibility of particular tenets of the Christian faith.

Perhaps more troubling than these external systems of belief to traditional Christianity today, however, have been the various Christian spiritualities and theologies, both old and new, that have emerged and reemerged in recent decades to question Christian orthodoxy at its very roots, and from within the circle of faith. Much attention is now being paid to the alternative Christian movements and groups treated in this chapter, all of which have challenged or rejected outright the traditional Christian view of (1) a remote, transcendent God who intervenes into the natural order from time to time, and (2) humanity as an inherently sinful species in need of redemption through the atoning death of a divine emissary. They have preferred instead an Ultimate One more profoundly immanent in nature and human nature. To that extent, at least, and whether wittingly or not, they have "turned East"; and such a turning seems likely to become even more widespread and relevant as people from all walks of life become more familiar and increasingly enamored with Oriental spirituality.

If there has been a trend in Christian theology in the past several decades, it has been precisely that kind of movement away from the traditional theistic view of God that undergirded Christian scripture and theology for two millennia. Many of the more acclaimed recent theologies have stressed the immanence of God within the natural world and thus moved deliberately in the direction of monism, pantheism, or panentheism. If I were to make a prediction about the future of the Christian faith from a strictly theological standpoint, it would be that at the professional level at least, it will continue to move toward an emphasis on divine immanence. And where theologians have gone, Church doctrine has generally followed, with popular belief and practice ultimately affected. Sometimes, however, it is the other way around: popular spirituality moves in a particular new direction, and the ecclesiastical authorities and theoreticians then struggle to play catch-up. Whichever may be the present case, a further evolution of Christian theology toward a greater appreciation of God's profound immanence—and of Christian piety toward a deeper experience of God's presence—seems inevitable.

Such an evolution is hardly unthinkable. After all, Jesus stood the traditional view of his own faith on its head and afforded a fresh, sensitive-to-the-oppressed approach to God; and early Christian works unknown until recently are promising to change the composition and character of the canon, further expanding its theological imagery. A reconsideration of God's image today, then, would be no more than an episode in the ongoing process of fine-tuning our necessarily provisional thinking about God.

The only alternative would seem to be to revert, either wholesale or piecemeal, to a worldview held by people two millennia ago and half a world away, one that is ever more irrelevant to who we are and who we need to become. The inevitable consequence of such a stubborn devotion to an antiquated mindset would almost surely be the decline—and perhaps even the death—of what should be a living faith.

8

Alternative
Christian
Views,
the World's
Religions,
and the
Future of
the Faith

DISCUSSION QUESTIONS & EXERCISES

A. In light of the listed characteristics of Christian Liberalism, how liberal are you as a Christian (or would you be, if you were a Christian)? Why? What are the "upside" and "downside" of Liberalism for you? Why?

B. Of the "heterodox" mystical Christian movements and viewpoints listed in this chapter, which one is most intriguing, attractive, or compelling to you? Why? What do you think Christianity would look like today had these types of Christianity dominated and prevailed over the fall-sin-redemption "orthodoxy"?

C. Given the two kinds of spirituality described in this chapter—relational/devotional and unitive/mystical—which one comes closest to yours, or to one that you might embrace? What explanation (psychology, environment, personality, education, or what?) would you give for why this one seems more right for you?

D. Some say that artists (painters, poets, actors, musicians, etc.) are more prone to a unitive/mystical spirituality. Why do you think they make this claim? What in your experience would tend to support or undermine such an assertion?

RECOMMENDED READING

Ian G. Barbour, *Religion and Science: Historical and Contemporary Issues* (revised and expanded edition). San Francisco: HarperSanFrancisco, 1997.
— previously published under the title *Religion in an Age of Science*, this impressive book represents the fruits of decades of work by the leading contemporary authority on the interface between religion and science

Fritjof Capra, *The Tao of Physics: An Exploration of the Parallels Between Modern Physics and Eastern Mysticism,* revised edition. Boston/London: Shambala, 1991.
— an updated version of the 1984 bestseller that reconciles Eastern philosophy and Western science in a brilliant vision of the universe, excellent despite its somewhat dated scholarship in both areas

Jacques Dupuis, *Toward a Christian Theology of Religious Pluralism.* Maryknoll, NY: Orbis Books, 1999.
— a Jesuit Catholic priest and scholar explores the possibility that world's religions other than Christianity may be a part of God's divine plan and vehicles for the redemptive operation of the Holy Spirit

Diana L. Eck, *Encountering God: A Spiritual Journey From Bozeman to Banares.* Boston: Beacon Press, 1994.
— an account, by a renowned scholar of comparative religion and devout Christian, of how personal experiences in India led to the conviction that dialogue with other faith traditions (and their practitioners) is crucial for Christians in today's world of religious diversity

Meister Eckhart, *The Best of Meister Eckhart,* ed. Halcyon Backhouse. New York: Crossroad Publishing Co., 1993.
— a selection of the wonderfully outrageous writings of the most radical Christian mystic of the medieval period, and perhaps of all time

Matthew Fox, *Original Blessing: A Primer in Creation Spirituality.* Sante Fe: Bear and Co., 1983.
— the cornerstone book of the Creation Spirituality theological model, treated at some length in this chapter: readable, engaging, and thought-provoking

Richard Elliott Friedman, *The Hidden Face of God.* San Francisco: HarperSanFrancisco, 1995.
— a work that encompasses religion, science, history, cosmology, and mysticism, in which the author explores the changing image and role of God, and the implications for human behavior, as humankind comes of age

Aldous Huxley, *The Perennial Philosophy.* New York: Harper & Row, 1970.
— the classic comparative work alleging that a core of mystical spirituality lies at the heart of all religions

George A. Maloney, *Gold, Frankincense, and Myrrh: An Introduction to Eastern Christian Spirituality.* New York: Crossroad Publishing Co., 1997.
— a wonderful introduction to the distinctive aspects of Eastern Orthodox Christianity, especially valuable for Catholics and Protestants

Ed. L. Miller and Stanley J. Grenz, *Fortress Introduction to Contemporary Theologies.* Philadelphia: Fortress Press, 1998.
— a very readable and brief introduction to current Christian thought, intended for lay readers, informative despite its clear bias in favor of orthodoxy

Geoffrey Parrinder, *Mysticism in the World's Religions.* Oxford: Oneworld Publications, 1995.
— a reprint of the 1976 Oxford University Press classic, which defines mysticism and distinguishes between mystical monism and mystical theism, with clear and helpful illustrations from different religious traditions

John Shelby Spong, *Why Christianity Must Change or Die: A Bishop Speaks to Believers in Exile.* San Francisco: HarperSanFrancisco, 1998.
— an Episcopal Bishop's search for a scientifically credible image of God, leading to the idea of an inner deity as the source of life, love, and being, with implications for ethical inclusiveness

Leslie D. Weatherhead, *The Christian Agnostic.* Nashville: Abingdon Press, 1990.
— a reprint of the mid-century liberal Christian classic by a retired British cleric who extols the place of reason and doubt in the Christian life and gives many intriguing interpretations of major Christian doctrines along the way

Gary Zukav, *The Dancing Wu Li Masters: An Overview of the New Physics.* New York/Toronto/et al.: Bantam Books, 1979.
— the first, widely acclaimed, award-winning, and in many ways the best of what would become a succession of compelling attempts by various authors (like Capra, mentioned above) to reconcile Western science and Eastern consciousness

8

Alternative
Christian
Views,
the World's
Religions,
and the
Future of
the Faith

CONCLUSION

T his book has covered a very large territory and presented a great deal of detailed information about the Christian faith under the banner "What Every Believer Should Know about the Faith, but Probably Doesn't." Now it is time for a parting disclaimer: every Christian does not really need to know all of this stuff! I can almost hear the diligent reader of the preceding pages breathing a sigh of relief over not having retained all the facts, and details contained therein. Then I can imagine an aftershock of outrage: "If I really didn't need to know all of this, why did you make me wade through it?"

The answer is simple: although I cannot imagine anyone but a professional scholar in the field of religious studies keeping the bulk of this material in the mind's long-term memory banks, I do think that it is important for every Christian to be exposed, at least, to the kind of information about the Christian faith contained in this book. The feedback I get from my college courses and church seminars on the Christian faith assures me that such exposure is, in a word, liberating: it frees people to admit doubts, ask questions, seek information, and above all *think* about their belief systems—all of which are essential to constructing and maintaining a vital faith.

What every believer should know about the faith is not a host of historical facts or doctrinal details, but this: that nothing about the Christian religion dropped out of heaven fully formed, intact, and perfect—not its scripture, not its beliefs, not its doctrines, not its practices, and certainly not its many institutional expressions. Every aspect of the faith is the product of a long and ongoing tradition of the sincere struggles of imperfect people to grasp the meaning of God, God's nature, and God's connection to the cosmos, nature, history, and their own lives—and then to figure out ways to act upon their tentative and sometimes tenuous perceptions.

That basic truth about the Christian religion has two major consequences. First, the Christian faith is by no means a monolith. As this book has shown, the long process of human religious grappling has produced a wide variety of interpretations and understandings of Christianity, all with confident, contradictory, and often competing claims to authenticity and authority. Indeed, it may even be misleading to use the common phrases "the Christian tradition" or "the Christian faith," so variegated is the faith's terrain. In truth, the *only* honest and accurate way to end the phrase "If you are a Christian you believe. . ." is with the statement ". . .that Jesus is somehow important to humanity's relationship to God." But in the articulation of that "somehow" Christians of various persuasions will diverge in dozens of directions.

A second consequence of the human role in the shaping of Christianity is this: that it is not only all right, but a good thing for believers to think about the faith. It is also perfectly normal and permissible to have doubts, big ones and small ones, about its major and minor doctrines, including the very existence and nature of God and the identity and purpose of Jesus Christ. For doubt is a natural by-product of thought, and a stimulus to further inquiry and the intellectual and spiritual growth that it brings. Questioning and doubting and trying out new facts and theories never have been, and are not now, inimical to faith. Neither are differences of opinion, disagreements, and disputes. These have been part and parcel of the Christian faith from the outset; indeed, they are the very tools that have forged and shaped it into all of its many permutations.

But I know from experience that relatively few Christians have been encouraged in the spirit of inquiry, or taught to regard doubt as an ally of faith; and that sometimes they have actually been discouraged from paying any intellectual attention to their beliefs; and when they have found themselves thinking (or, in the case of college students, being required to think) about such things in a critical way, they have felt threatened and frightened and guilty. A few have even reported a temporary loss of faith when they began to analyze their beliefs closely—an occurrence that suggests that their faith was not all that firmly grounded or deeply rooted in the first place. By far the majority, however, have found that in the long run such critical inquiry both increases their understanding of the Christian religion and strengthens their personal faith.

Humankind's most distinguishing feature and valuable gift is the mind, which is indeed "a terrible thing to waste" in any area of life, including religion. It is therefore quite ridiculous to think that even a transcendent Creator God would have bestowed upon the human species both an inquisitive, curious nature and the mental faculty to exercise and satisfy it, and then expected people to disown these in matters of spirit and faith—much less punish them for using those gifts. It is equally absurd to imagine that a gracious God would hold mere mortals—who occupy but a tiny speck of matter in an unimaginatively huge and ancient universe for what amounts to the briefest eye-blink of cosmic time—eternally accountable for not figuring out every issue and grasping every shred of Ultimate Truth.

It is much more reasonable to believe that such a God would be disappointed if we failed to appreciate and utilize our great gift of intellect with all our might and for whatever time is available to us. If this volume has succeeded at all in arousing in the reader the spirit of inquiry and encouraging the use of the mind with respect to her or his faith, it has served its purpose.

GLOSSARY

Acts—the fifth book of the Christian* New Testament canon*; a theological* account of the first years of the Church* and Christian* mission almost certainly written by the author of the Gospel according to Luke some fifty years after the death of Jesus

A.D. (abbreviation for *Anno Domini,* "Year of [Our] Lord")—the traditional way of denoting the years from the birth of Jesus (or thereabouts) to the present; now increasingly being replaced with "CE"*

Adventism, Adventists—a family of American Christian* sects*—the largest of which is the Seventh-Day variety—that evolved from the Millerites, a loosely organized group of people who accepted the (erroneous) predictions of an imminent end-time made by William Miller in the 1830s and early 1840s

agape (pronounced *ah-GAH-pay*)—the New Testament* Greek word for distinctively Christian* love, that is, selfless, self-sacrificing; it was for Paul* the chief of the gifts of the Spirit for those touched and saved by God's grace*

agnosticism (adj. *agnostic,* from a Greek word meaning "unknown")—the state or condition of not knowing what to believe about Ultimate Reality*, its existence, nature, etc.; though in the Western world the term is usually applied to those who are non-committal about belief in God's existence, it is sometimes extended to include uncertainty about other religious doctrines as well

Allah (literally, "The God")—the name for Ultimate Reality* in Islam*

American Protestant Revivalism—a trans-denominational* style of Christianity* originated in England and quickly imported to colonial America (particularly New England) in the early-to-mid-eighteenth century; it is characterized by an emphasis on heart-felt faith, a "born-again" conversion experience, and the excitement of a fiery preacher orating dramatically to "win souls," preferably in a non-religious and informal setting (e.g., a field, tent, or stadium)

Ancient Period—a term used by historians to designate the era of human history prior to about 500 CE*; when used specifically in the history of Christianity*, it denotes roughly the time between the crucifixion of Jesus (c. 29 CE) and the death of Pope Leo I (461 CE)

Anglican—a reference to the Church of England, a Protestant* denomination* founded in the early sixteenth-century by King Henry VIII for largely political reasons (he couldn't get the Pope to annul his marriage to a Queen who seemed to be able to bear only daughters, whom he considered unfit to inherit the throne); its ecclesiastical* head is the Archbishop of Canterbury

apocalyptic, apocalypticism—(1) at its root, a designation for a type of literature that employs colorful (some would say "strange") imagery (especially animals and numbers) and other mythopoetic language in order to draw a sharp contrast between the evil present age and the new age that is expected to replace it in some dramatic and cataclysmic way; the best example in the New Testament* is the book of

G

Note: Cross-references to other items in the glossary are indicated with asterisks (*), and are extensive enough that the links in one or two terms could conceivably lead the reader to more terms and their flagged words, and eventually to all of the other entries. Thus used, the glossary can serve as a compendium of the entire book. On the other hand, these links can be ignored or used selectively, especially by the reader who has some knowledge of the terms referenced. In any case, all foreign words and non-biblical titles have been italicized.

Revelation*, from whose Greek title (*Apocalypsis*) the genre takes its name; (2) a type of religion or spirituality* that reflects an urgent hope for the quick arrival of the age that the literature anticipates

Apocrypha (adj. *apocryphal*)—the books contained in the Roman Catholic* Old Testament* whose authority is questioned by Protestants*, who exclude them from their canon*, but sometimes include them in their preferred translations of the Bible* as "Intertestamental"

apostle (adj. *apostolic*)—literally, "one sent out," as on a mission; the term is generally confined to a disciple commissioned by Jesus (especially one of the Twelve), or to Paul of Tarsus*, who (despite having never been a disciple of Jesus) claimed to have been given the status by the risen Christ* in a vision

Apostolic Succession—the notion, officially held by the Roman Catholic* Church* (and by a few Protestant* denominations* as well), that the power and authority conferred upon clergy at ordination have been passed on in an unbroken line from the apostles* themselves, and from Peter in particular; most Protestant* groups, by contrast, claim that the necessary power and authority come more directly to their clergy from God

Arminius, Jacobus (1560–1609)—a Dutch theologian* active a generation or so after the death of John Calvin*, and an opponent of the major themes of that Swiss theologian's Reformed* theology*—especially the notions of the total depravity of humanity, humanity's lack of free will, and Predestination*—in favor of a more positive view of human nature

Arminianism—the anti-Calvinist, pro-human-nature theological* movement and orientation derived from Jacobus Arminius*; in official Reformed* Protestant* circles, it amounts to heresy*

atheism (adj. *atheistic*; a proponent is an *atheist*)—disbelief in any Ultimate Reality*, which in the Western world generally means a rejection of a specifically theistic* God; broadly speaking, there are two types of atheism: *casual* ("Now that I think about it, I guess I don't believe in God.") and *doctrinaire* ("I absolutely do not believe in God, for the following reasons . . . .")

atman—in Hinduism*, one's inner spiritual energy-essence, roughly equivalent to the Christian* "soul" or "spirit," but non-personal, uncreated, eternal, recyclable, and totally one with the Ultimate Reality*, *Brahman**

atonement/Atonement (adj. atoning)—(1) in general, a technical term for reconciliation* (literally "at-one-ment"); (2) in Christianity*, one of many synonyms for "salvation"* derived from Paul*, around which many theories about the mechanics of redemption* were constructed in the Medieval Period* and later, including satisfaction, substitution, ransom, victory, and moral

Augustine of Hippo, St. (adj. *Augustinian*) (354–430 CE)—a Tunisian (North African) Bishop and theologian*, and arguably the most influential thinker in all of Christian* history; author of the phrase "Original Sin"

autograph—the original manuscript of any biblical* book, written either by the author or a scribe under the author's immediate supervision; all are lost

B.C.—abbreviation for "Before Christ*"; the traditional way of denoting the years before the birth of Jesus (or thereabouts); now increasingly being replaced with "BCE"*

BCE or B.C.E.—a fairly recent abbreviation of "Before the Common Era," a replacement for "B.C.*" increasingly used in deference to the sensitivities of non-Christian people

Bhagavad Gita—a Hindu* scripture, a small portion of an incredibly long epic; it tells of a conversation between an Indian Prince and the incarnation (Krishna) of a god (Vishnu); popular in devotional (faith-based) Hinduism

Bible (adj. *biblical*, from the Greek *ta biblia*, "the books")—a collection of writings by various authors, reflecting much variety in genre, style, viewpoint, historical context, factual content, etc.; for Jews it is the Hebrew *Tanakh**, while for Christians*, it comprises the Old Testament* and the New Testament*

Body of Christ—one of the favorite images for the Church* used by Paul*

Brahman—in Hinduism*, the Ultimate Reality* or Supreme Spirit; not a god or goddess, but a Power or Principle immanent* in the universe, nature, and human nature as *atman**

Buddha (Sanskrit, *"Enlightened One"*)—the title given to Siddhartha Gautama, the founder of Buddhism*, as a result of the pure consciousness or awareness that his followers believed that he had achieved through meditation at around the age of thirty-five

Buddhism (adj. Buddhist, which is also the designation of a follower)—the religion that originated in India in the sixth-century BCE* with the life and teachings of Siddhartha Gautama, the Buddha*; today it consists of a variety of sects in three major schools: Theravada (southern and southeastern Asia), Mahayana (eastern and northeastern Asia), and Vajrayana (Tibet and surrounding countries)

Calvin, John (1509–1564)—French-Swiss Protestant* reformer, originator of the Reformed* Protestant* tradition; notable for his emphasis on the depravity of humanity, the importance of the Law* in the Christian* life, and his belief in (double) Predestination*

Calvinism—practically synonymous with the Reformed* Protestant* tradition that began with Calvin*; its doctrinal* linchpins have been five: (1) total human depravity; (2) predestination*; (3) the atonement* of Christ as limited in its redemptive effects to those elected* to receive God's grace; (4) divine grace* that cannot be refused; and (5) divine grace that cannot be forfeited or lost once received

canon (adj. *canonical*, the opposite being *non-canonical*)—the scripture taken by any religious tradition to be authoritative and focal (for example, the Bible* and the *Qur'an**)

Catholic, Catholicism—usually shorthand for the Roman Catholic Church or Roman Catholicism*, the term also includes other denominations* in communion with Rome and recognizing the primacy of the Pope (for example, Byzantine- and Anglo-Catholic Churches)

CE or C.E.—a fairly recent abbreviation for "Common Era," a less Christocentric way of designating the years of the era earlier known as A.D.*

Chalcedon—the ecumenical* council that, in 451 CE*, finally established the compromise formula that Jesus was one person with two complete natures (human and divine)

charismatic (from the Greek, *charismata,* "gifts")—(1) in a general Christian* sense, descriptive of the unofficial basis on which the leaders of the earliest Church* served, namely, by applying their natural (or perhaps supernatural) talents; (2) in a more specific Christian sense, being possessed of and exhibiting such gifts of the Spirit as glossolalia*, prophecy, interpretation, and healing—all of which are especially valued and promoted in modern Pentecostal-Holiness* denominations*

Christ (from the Greek *Christos,* "Annointed" or "Messiah*")—a title applied to Jesus by Christians*, irrespective of its original connotations in Judaism; also, a term representative of all of the heightened images of Jesus generated and venerated by the faithful over the centuries

Christian Science—the religious movement and later sect* started by Mary Baker Eddy in the late nineteenth-century and best known for its reliance upon faith rather than modern medicine in the treatment of illness or injury

Christianity (adj. *Christian*)—the religion *about* Jesus (rather than that *of* Jesus), based not so much on what Jesus taught, but on what was said about him and his mission after the fact; its theological and institutional origins are traceable more to Paul than to Jesus himself

Christology—(1) loosely, any view of Jesus as the Christ*; (2) more formally, the branch of Christian* theology* that deals with "the person and work of Christ," that is, who he was (divine? human? both? how?) and what he accomplished for human salvation (taught? exemplified? died?)

church, Church—(1) in its original New Testament* connotation, the "assembly" or "congregation" (*ecclesia*) of those who have received God's grace*; (2) a denomination* of Christianity*; (3) any local congregation; (4) a building used for Christian worship; and (5) [usually capitalized] the universal, cosmic, metaphysical* reality envisioned by Paul* and encompassing all other meanings

Church of England—see "Anglican"

congregational, Congregational (noun *Congregationalism*)—(1) a particular type of church* polity* in which authority and decision-making, ordination, and facility ownership resides in the local congregation; (2) [capitalized] a distinctive Protestant* denomination* in the Reformed* tradition and prominent in colonial New England

consequentialist ethics—the form of ethics that looks to the likely outcomes of behavior rather than either set rules or broad principles in determining appropriate actions in any given circumstance

Constantine—the early fourth-century Roman Emperor who (in 313 CE*) became a Christian* and made Christianity not only legal, but (by virtue of his own status) credible; he was also instrumental in creating the earliest Christian councils and therefore the earliest official Christian creeds*

Creation Spirituality—a theology* developed in the late twentieth century by Roman Catholic* (later Episcopal*) priest Matthew Fox; a conscious departure from the "fall-sin-redemption" model of mainstream Christianity* in that it emphasizes the inherent divinity in all people

creeds—official statements of belief, the most ancient and best known of which (the Apostles' and the Nicene) were produced as a result of the decisions made by the earliest ecumenical* Church* councils in the fourth and fifth centuries CE*

cult—originally, any group that "cultivates" a distinctive spirituality*; in recent years, a pejorative term for any small, new religious group sufficiently out of the mainstream to be perceived as dangerously heretical or fanatical (often misconnected to the word "occult," which has an entirely different Latin root)

deism—the theology* that holds that the transcendent* creator God made the universe self-sufficient, so that divine intervention is not only inessential, but unthinkable; the religion of most of America's most prominent Revolutionary founders

denomination (adj. *denominational*, noun *denominationalism*)— a subdivision of Christianity*, best reserved for those groups (Catholic*, Protestant*, and Eastern Orthodox*) that are traceable to the Reformation* or earlier, though often applied to more established sects* as well

deontological ethics—(also called "non-consequentialist ethics") the way of determining appropriate behaviors and acts in accordance with set rules, laws, commandments, or other guidelines (which are generally regarded as a "given," divinely or otherwise)

Docetism (from the Greek *doket*, "he seems")—an ancient view, associated with Gnosticism* and popular among some early Christians*, that Jesus was not really a human being, but merely God disguised in human flesh; and that he therefore did not really suffer on the cross

doctrine (adj. *doctrinal*)—a teaching, tenet, or belief derived from certain principles, whether religious or otherwise

dogma (adj. *dogmatic*)—a teaching, tenet, or belief promulgated by some authority as true and therefore non-negotiable (that is, a doctrine* "carved in stone")

Eastern Orthodox (Church), Eastern Orthodoxy—the branch of Christianity* (comprising some fifteen national, regional, or ethnic communions, mostly in eastern Europe—for example, Greek Orthodox and Russian Orthodox) that formally broke with Roman Catholicism* in 1054 CE* over a number of issues of doctrine and practice, the most important being the primacy of the Pope over Christianity (each Orthodox body has its own Patriarch as its head)

Ebionism (from the Hebrew for "the poor")—an early group (and later sect) of Jewish Christians who had a very pragmatic view of Jesus, emphasized his humanity and his role as teacher and example, valued the Torah* and either the Gospel* of Matthew or the non-canonical* Gospel of the Hebrews, and rejected both the Virgin Birth and the teachings of Paul*

ecclesiastical (from the Greek, *ekklesia,* "assembly," "congregation," *and later* "church")—a reference to anything having to do with the Church*

ecclesiology—any view or doctrine* concerning the Church*, its nature, or its function

Eckhart, Meister Johannes (c.1260–c.1327)—a German Dominican monk and theologian*, and arguably the most radical of all Christian* mystics* in his claim of absolute essential identity with God

ecumenical (from the Greek *oikoumenikos,* "of the whole world")—(1) with reference to early Church* councils, the term implies representation from all parts of the Catholic* world; (2) in the Modern Period*, it has taken on the additional meaning of conversations and consultations between various denominational* bodies, including the Roman Catholic Church, with an eye toward greater cooperation and perhaps even merger

Edwards, Jonathan (1703–1758)—a New England Puritan*, cleric, theologian*, and educator best remembered for his staunch Calvinism* and his contribution to an emergent American Protestant Revivalism*

Election (applies to people called the "elect" or "elected")—a common synonym for Predestination*

Elohim—one of the names for God used in the Torah*; a plural noun, curiously enough, it is rather less personal than "Jahweh*," with which it is often paired; it is usually rendered as "Lord"

empiricism (adj. *empirical,* when referring to data or evidence; *empiricist,* when referring to a viewpoint or person)—(1) broadly, reliance on sensory-input-based experience or observation; (2) narrowly, a philosophical theory (specifically, an epistemology) that all knowledge originates in experience (as opposed to being inborn or intuition-based); its chief proponent was John Locke (1632–1704)

Enlightenment—(1) in the Western world, a philosophical movement of the seventeenth and eighteenth-centuries that emphasized empiricism* and rationalism*; (2) in Eastern religions, the goal of the spiritual life: the overcoming of ignorance of one's true, essential nature

episcopal, Episcopal (from the Greek *episcopos,* "overseer")—(1) in the more general sense, a hierarchical Church* polity* that employs bishops in key positions of power and authority; (2) in the more specific (and capitalized) sense, what the Church of England (Anglican* Church) came to be called in America after the Revolution, which made anything that sounded English quite unpopular

epistle, Epistle—(1) any letter of correspondence; (2) [capitalized] the letters composed by Paul of Tarsus* and others that were included in the New Testament*

Evangelical Christianity, Evangelicalism—a type of Protestantism* closely associated with (and in fact an outgrowth of) American Protestant Revivalism*; it emphasizes the sovereignty of God, the infallibility of the Bible* on matters of faith and practice (though not necessarily the verbal inerrancy and literal interpretation that Fundamentalists* insist upon), the reality of sin, and the necessity of conversion and a morally upright life; the term "Evangelical" sometimes appears in the name of a denomination that is not, strictly speaking, in the Evangelical Christian* tradition (for example, the Evangelical Lutheran* Church)

evangelist—(1) a gospel* writer, usually capitalized if the reference is to one of the four canonical* gospel authors; (2) a preacher, usually but not necessarily representing Evangelical Christianity*, whose main purpose is the conversion of non-Christians (or casual, lax, and nominal Christians) to a dedicated life of faith, more often than not by means of a profound emotional appeal (versus preaching for edification via a more rational approach)

evil—in Christian* thought, a real power, almost invariably associated with Satan*, and the root source of sin*, against which Christians must struggle and because of which Jesus had to die an atoning* death; other religions and philosophies make evil much less important and formidable, treating it as merely an occasional divine retribution or test, or a human deviation from or deprivation of goodness, or a relativistic*, subjective value judgment

faith—(1) a synonym for "religion," as in "the Christian faith"; (2) assent to certain religious or theological propositions, as in "you just have to accept that on faith"; and (3) the most scriptural and theological* meaning: *trust*, especially in God and God's forgiveness and mercy, and thus a response to (rather than a prerequisite for) divine grace*

Fall—Paul's* interpretation of the spiritual effect of the disobedience of Adam and Eve upon them and all humanity in the Genesis 3 Garden of Eden story, in spite of the clear implication of the story itself that there has actually been an elevation of humanity's status (vs 22); in any case, the alleged "Fall" became the basis of Paul's view of sin as a universal human condition, which in turn was rendered later by Augustine* as "Original Sin"*

Fundamentalism, *fundamentalist*—an expression of Protestant* Christianity* dating back to the early twentieth-century, and holding that there are certain "fundamental" beliefs that are absolutely essential to the faith; the number of these basics varies, but almost always includes a literal interpretation of the Bible* as the verbally inspired Word of God*

futurist interpretation—a type of scriptural interpretation that takes the book of Revelation* as a coded message for the present day—an urgent warning about the imminent return of Christ and end of history as we know it

glossolalia (Greek, "tongues")—the kind of Spirit-inspired, spontaneous utterance depicted in the Pentecost* narrative of Acts 2, mentioned by Paul* in some of his epistles*, and given a special place in modern Pentecostal-Holiness* Christian* denominations*; the resulting language is regarded sometimes as an established language unknown to the speaker and sometimes as a distinctive, otherworldly language of the Spirit

Gnosticism (adj. *Gnostic*)—an ancient Greek system of religious belief predating Christianity*, it taught that human spirits were divine "sparks" trapped in human bodies and required a savior to bring the spiritual knowledge (Greek, *gnosis*) that would release the spirits for a re-union with God (usually portrayed as light); very much an influence on early Christian* thought, though eventually declared a heresy*

Gospel of Thomas—the only complete non-canonical* gospel* extant, consisting strictly of sayings, and reflecting in many cases a different—and some say Gnostic*—Jesus

gospel, Gospel—(1) broadly, the "good news" of the Christian proclamation; (2) any ancient Christian* account of significant events and/or teachings from the life of Jesus, in some cases including resurrection appearances, though some were purely infancy narratives; dozens, including the Gospel of Thomas*, were excluded from the New Testament* canon*; (3) more specifically [and often capitalized], any one of the four such accounts that made it into the New Testament canon: the three synoptics* and John*

grace—in Pauline*-Augustinian* Christian* orthodoxy*, the divine gift that effects the salvation* of humans too incapacitated by sin* to attain their own

Hebrew Bible, Hebrew scriptures—the Tanakh*

henotheism—the worship of one god without denying the existence of other deities—a kind of blend of practical monotheism* and theoretical polytheism*

heresy (adj. *heretical;* a person who embraces a heresy is a *heretic*, all from the Greek *hairesis,* "choice")—any belief or doctrine deemed unacceptable by those in authority in any religion; practically synonymous with "heterodoxy"*

heterodoxy (adj. *heterodox*)—the opposite of "orthodoxy"*, and therefore "wrong belief" or "erroneous teaching" (see "heresy")

hierarchy (adj. *hierarchical*)—a form of church* polity* that organizes its clergy into descending ranks or orders of decreasing power and authority (very much like "chain of command" in the military)

Hinduism (adj. *Hindu,* which is also a noun that refers to a person)—the ancient cultural religion of India, dating back at least three thousand five hundred years (but with roots much earlier) and combining a vast array of practices and beliefs, including polytheism*, monism*, and henotheism*

historical-critical method—the kind of overall methodological approach to the study of scripture that has characterized modern biblical* scholarship for the last century and a half; briefly stated, it means studying the Bible* carefully, contextually, and comparatively; it includes such specific methodologies as textual criticism, source criticism, form criticism, and redaction criticism

historicist interpretation—a type of interpretation that reads the book of Revelation* in its own historical context, as a coded message for late first century (c. 96 CE*) Christians*, who were under threat of persecution at the hands of a quite "Beastly" Roman Empire

humanism (adj. *humanistic* or *humanist,* the latter of which is also a noun that refers to a person)—an attitude or philosophy generally associated with the Renaissance*, it stresses the dignity, worth, and potential of the human species and individual, often, but not necessarily, to the exclusion of supernaturalism; accordingly, a distinction is often made between *secular* humanism (which tends to raise humanity to some sort of position of ultimacy) and *religious* or *Christian* humanism (which retains belief in a sacred Ultimate Reality* or God)

image of God (Latin, *imago dei*)—the unspecified similarity to God granted to humanity (along with an equally vague "likeness") in Genesis 1:26–27; it has been interpreted as mind, soul, spirit, free will, self-transcendence, creativity, and a number of other aspects; there has been general agreement among mainstream Christian* theologians*, at least, that whatever the image is, it was damaged or lost completely in the Fall*

immanence (adj. *immanent,* when applied to God; *immanental* or *immanentalist,* when talking about an idea, theology, or philosophy, all from the Latin *immanere,* meaning "to dwell within")—the theological* quality whereby the Ultimate Reality* can be said to abide within the universe; in the strongest, ontological* sense, it means that the essence of the Ultimate and the essence of the universe and its components are the same—as in pantheism* and panentheism*; in a weaker sense, an ontologically transcendent* Ultimate can be said to be immanent as *active* in the universe, while still remaining distinct (or "Other") in being or essence—as in theism*

incarnation, Incarnation (adj. *incarnational*)—in its most general sense, an embodiment or enfleshment of a god or goddess—what in Hinduism* is called an *avatar*; in traditional Christianity* [capitalized] it refers to the belief and doctrine* that Jesus (and he alone) was God, or the Second Person (Son) of the Trinity*, or the eternal, divine Logos* of God "in the flesh"

Islam (adj. *Islamic* or *Muslim,* which is also a noun referring to a person)—the Western-type, strictly monotheistic* religion founded in Arabia by Muhammad* (d. 632 CE) and dominant in the Middle East, North Africa, and many parts of Asia; its Five Pillars are the creed, prayer, fasting during the month of Ramadan, almsgiving, and pilgrimage to Mecca, the faith's holiest city

"J," Jahwist—one of the four (or five) authors of the Pentateuch* identified by modern biblical* scholarship, distinctive for using the personal name for God, "Jahweh*"; credited with the "Adam's rib" creation account of Genesis 2 and the Garden of Eden story of the following chapter (probably ninth century BCE*)

Jahweh (always pronounced and sometimes spelled "Yahweh")—the proper name for God in the Torah, reportedly revealed to Moses in Exodus 3:14; in the vowel-less Hebrew original, it is "JHWH" and its meaning is some variation on "I AM"; non-Jewish people sometimes inject enough vowels into the four original consonants to produce "Jehowah" or "Jehovah"; especially among orthodox Jews, this name is unspoken (even in worship) in deference to its holiness, often being replaced by the euphemism *Adonai* ("Lord")

John (adj. *Johannine*)—a name ascribed to the author of the Gospel* of John, the canonical* epistles* of John, and, to a lesser extent, the book of Revelation*, despite the fact that these were more than likely different individuals; the adjective is often (1) employed to denote any commonality of viewpoint (or, some would say, "the school of thought") that might be perceived in some or all of these writings; and (2) used in contrast with the word "Synoptic"*, because of the similarities of the first three Gospels and the utterly idiosyncratic character of the fourth

justification—one of Paul's* many synonyms for "salvation,*" in this case a metaphor drawn from the law courts

karma (English adj. *karmic*)—in both Hinduism* and Buddhism*, (1) deeds, (2) the consequences that they bring upon the doer, and (3) the universal law that "you reap what you sow" and "what goes around, comes around"—for example, that all get their just deserts eventually

kingdom (domain, reign, rule) of God—clearly the central theme of the teachings of Jesus, as reported in the Synoptics*; the main idea is that a divine domain will replace earthly reigns, and that it is immediate (that is, unmediated) and both present and yet not fully realized

L—all of the source materials, oral and written, other than Mark and Q* that Luke (only) used in the writing of his gospel*

Lao Tse—(a Chinese honorific title meaning "Old Man") the perhaps-legendary sixth-century BCE* Chinese author of the *Tao Te Ching*' and founder of Taoism*

Law, The—(1) the Torah* or Pentateuch* ; (2) the body of commandments given by God to the Israelites through Moses as part of the divine covenant with Israel; according to Paul's* Christian* interpretation, its effect was to damn the recipients even further, their persistent disobedience proving how incapacitated they were by sin

Left-Wing Protestantism (adj. *Protestant*)—the most radical of the sixteenth century Reformers (for example, the Anabaptists), who rejected more of Roman Catholic* belief and practice (including sacraments in general and infant baptism in particular) than Luther*, Calvin*, or their followers

liberalism, Liberalism (adj. *liberal* or *Liberal,* which may also refer to an advocate or adherent)—(1) in general, the tendency of any religion to develop a religious tradition of interpretation that applies the principles of its founder with some degree of flexibility, as opposed to following that person's example and teachings to the letter; (2) more specifically, the recurring Christian* sub-tradition of opposition to the dominant Pauline*-Augustinian* emphasis on human sin*, depravity, and lack of free will (among other issues); and (3) most specifically [capitalized], the largely transdenominational* wing of Christianity* that has accepted the principles of the Enlightenment* and the resulting modern scientific worldview*, and adjusted its perspectives on faith, God, scripture, etc. accordingly

Logos (from the Greek, *logos,* "word" or "reason")—a Greek philosophical term and concept used often since ancient times in Christian* theology* to denote the eternal principle of divinity that constituted the second Person of the Trinity* (the Son) and that was incarnate* in Jesus of Nazareth, making him the Christ*; the strongest scriptural basis for the notion is the Gospel of John* (especially the first fourteen verses of the first chapter)

Luther, Martin (1483–1547)—the German monk who started the Protestant* Reformation* by publicly posting his *95 Theses* against certain practices of the Roman Catholic Church*, and by widening his critique to include many of the most dearly held beliefs and institutions of Rome, including the Papacy itself

Lutheran—an adjective referring to (1) the Protestant* theological tradition stemming from Luther's thought, as distinct from the Reformed* or Calvinist* tradition; and (2) the name of the Christian* denomination* (and eventually a family of denominations*) founded upon his thought by his followers after his death

M— all of the source materials, oral and written, besides Mark and Q* that Matthew (only) used in the writing of his Gospel*

mass of damnation —Augustine's* phrase describing humanity in its natural condition—at least after the Fall*—as a totally depraved species

Medieval Period—the era of Western and Christian* history, running roughly from five hundred to fourteen hundred CE*, described in this book as a time of "Development and Domination" during which the Roman Catholic Church* achieved a remarkable, if not absolute, measure of unity and power

Messiah (adj. *Messianic,* from the Hebrew, *Mashiach*)—in its original Jewish meaning, a longed-for successor to King David who, like his renowned ancestor, would be a great political and military leader and would restore Israel to its past glory, prosperity, and security; Christianity* obviously changed that "job description" by spiritualizing it in a way that made Jesus the clear fulfillment of prophecy

metaphysical—(1) in its most precise sense, descriptive of the branch of philosophy (metaphysics) that addresses the nature of reality, whether that be seen as material, spiritual, or something else; (2) in a more popular, modern sense, a reference either to a spiritual realm believed to be beyond the everyday, physical one, or to the belief in such a realm

Metaphysical Christianity—a type of Christianity* that arose in America in the mid-to-late-nineteenth century and that "spiritualized" the faith and its scriptures, with a special emphasis on its healing effects; included in this category are Christian Science*, Theosophy*, and the various sects* under the New Thought* umbrella

Middle Ages—the Medieval Period*

Modern Period—the era of Western and Christian* history running roughly from 1650 to the present, and characterized in this book as a period of "Diversity and Doubt"

because of the combined effects of the Reformation* and the Enlightenment* in the undermining of traditional faith claims

modern scientific worldview—the prevailing worldview* in the Western world ever since (and as a result of) the Enlightenment*

Modernism, Modernity—another name for Liberalism*, most frequently used in Roman Catholic* circles

moksha (Sanskrit)—in Hinduism*, the longed-for "liberation" or "release" from the nearly endless cycles of rebirth (*samsara**) achieved by one or another spiritual discipline (*yoga**)

monism (adj. *monistic*)—(1) the philosophical belief that all reality is essentially of one kind of substance, whether matter (materialistic), mind or spirit (idealistic), or something else (neutral); (2) in Eastern religions especially, the belief in an Ultimate Reality* that is a non-personal Something—for example Brahman* or Tao*—and definitely *not* a god

monotheism (adj. *monotheistic;* a proponent is call a *monotheist*)—a belief in only one God of the theistic* type, or a theology* based on such a belief

Mormons (adj. *Mormon*)—the nickname for both The Church of Jesus Christ of Latter Day Saints and the Reorganized Church of Jesus Christ of Latter Day Saints; a Christian* religious sect* founded in America by Joseph Smith in the 1830s on the basis of certain claimed visions, which supposedly led him to discover the *Book of Mormon*, an allegedly inspired scripture on a par with the Bible*

Muhammad or **Mohammed** (570–632 CE)—the Arabic messenger of Allah* and founder of Islam*, who wrote (or spoke) the *Qur'an**

Muslim or **Moslem**—a follower of Islam*; a worshipper of Allah* in the tradition of Muhammad*

mysticism (adj. *mystical* or *mystic,* which is also a noun that refers to a person)—the introspective spiritual* orientation that seeks an experience of one's essential identity with the Ultimate Reality* or God; though found in Western religions as a kind of sub-tradition, it is much more common in Eastern religions precisely because it is far more compatible with a monistic* theology* than with a theistic* one

myth—a story that couches a deep religious or spiritual* truth, but—as with a parable—at a level well below the superficial facts, and therefore requiring interpretation

Nag Hammadi—an Egyptian town near which many Gnostic* texts were discovered in 1945, including several lost gospels*

New Testament—the twenty-seven specifically Christian* books—Gospels*, Acts*, Epistles*, and Revelation*—that were first listed as definitive in the late fourth-century CE* and gradually accepted as canonical* over the next millennium or so

New Thought—a movement in late nineteenth-century American Christianity* that took a self-consciously metaphysical* approach to scripture and doctrine, viewing God as immanent* in humanity, and Christ as one who realized his own inner divinity ("the Kingdom of God* within") and who set out to put others in touch with theirs; it produced such sects* as Divine Science, Religious Science, Science of Mind, and Unity

Nicaea—the first great Christian* Council, which was convened by Constantine* in 325 CE* and established the theoretical basis not only for the doctrine of the Trinity*, but for the full divinity of Christ*

Old Testament—the Hebrew Bible* or Tanakh*, which is accepted as canonical* by most Christians*, though there is some disagreement (mainly between Roman Catholics* and Protestants*) about how many books are to be included

ontological—(from the Greek, *ontos*, "being") a term used by philosophers to refer to the very being or true essence of anything (for example, to declare that something has "no ontological status" means that it has no basis in reality)

oral tradition—the kind of word-of-mouth transmission that lies behind some of the most important parts of the Christian* Bible* (for example, the Genesis and Gospel* stories)

Original Sin—a Christian* doctrine* formulated by Augustine* (d. 430) on the basis of his reading of Paul* on sin*; it says that, because of Adam's sin, we are born with a condition (also called "Original Sin") that makes us innately depraved and incapable of exercising the will in a positive, much less saving, moral direction; though the doctrine was clearly based on a reading of the Garden story of Genesis, it is certainly not a part of Jewish thought

orthodoxy (adj. *orthodox*)—(from the Greek for "right opinion") officially correct belief, as determined by any religious authority

"P," Priestly author—one of the four (or five) authors of the Pentateuch* identified by modern biblical* scholarship, distinctive for using ritual-related terminology; credited with the six-day Creation account of Genesis 1 (probably sixth century BCE*)

panentheism (adj. *panentheistic;* a proponent is called a *panentheist*)—the notion (from the Greek *pan,* "all" or "every," *en,* "in," and *theos,* "god") that everything is in God in such a way that God is immanent* in it, while God yet retains a large measure of ontological* transcendence* as an aspect or dimension

pantheism (adj. *pantheistic;* a proponent is called a *pantheist*)—(from the Greek *pan,* "all" or "every," and *theos,* "god") the notion that everything is God or is *essentially* God

Paul of Tarsus (adj. *Pauline*) (d. 64 CE)—the first (and most) important Christian* missionary and theologian*, whose ideas are so central to Christianity* that he may arguably be the real founder of the faith*; the adjective is most often applied to (1) the New Testament* epistles* determined by modern biblical* scholarship to have been authentically his; and (2) theological ideas and traditions that originated with him

parousia (Greek for "presence")—the technical term for Jesus' long-anticipated Second Coming

Pelagius (adj. *Pelagian*)—British Roman Catholic* monk c. 400 CE* who opposed Augustine's* view that Original Sin* is so profound that it renders human beings incapable of exercising free will so as to choose to act morally; Pelagius believed that though disabled by Adam's disobedience, people are not utterly helpless and can do good if they exert enough will power and effort

Pentateuch (from the Greek for "Five Books")—another name for the Torah*, the first five books of the Hebrew Bible* (and therefore of the Christian* Bible as well)

Pentecost (from the Greek for "fiftieth")—(1) originally a Jewish festival (*Shavot*) on the fiftieth day after Passover, celebrating the giving of the Law*; and (2) later a Christian* festival following Easter; the term is important in Christianity* because of (3) the event reported in Acts 2 in which the Holy Spirit came upon the Apostles* in a profound way, in effect birthing the Church*

Pentecostal-Holiness—a type of Protestant* Christianity* that originated around the turn of the twentieth century, that emphasizes such charismatic* gifts as glossolalia*, prophecy, and healing, and that is remarkable for its ecstatic worship; sects* belonging to this category include Assemblies of God, Nazarenes, and many Churches of God

polity—a particular way in which a denomination* or individual church* organizes itself; the extremes are congregationalism* and hierarchy*, though in practice these two types are often mixed in a variety of ways

polytheism (adj. *polytheistic*)—belief in many gods and goddesses, characteristic of ancient cultural religions worldwide—for example, Indian (Hinduism*), Japanese (Shinto), Mesopotamian, Chinese, Egyptian, Greek, and Roman

praeterist interpretation (from the Latin *praeter*, "already")—a type of biblical* interpretation, exemplified by Augustine*, that maintains that the book of Revelation's prophecy of a Second Coming was fulfilled with the coming of the Church* (the "Body of Christ*") at Pentecost*

Predestination (adj. *Predestinarian*)—the doctrine*, promoted by all of the most influential theologians* of Western Christian* orthodoxy*, that whether or not one will receive the benefits of God's grace* and Christ's atoning* death is predetermined by a primordial decision on God's part

process theology—a twentieth century theology*, mostly rooted in the thought of English mathematician and philosopher Alfred North Whitehead (1861–1947) and promoted by theologians Charles Hartshorne and John Cobb, that treated God not only as immanent* in the universe but as evolving with it; most process theologians embrace some form of panentheism*

prophets, Prophets—(1) in general, important characters in the ancient history of Israel, and especially around the time of the Exile (sixth century BCE*), variously described as inspired social critics or poetic denouncers of injustice, they stood at odds and in tension with the more ritual-oriented priests; (2) [capitalized] one of the three divisions of the *Tanakh**, which contains some of the writings by (or attributed to) the most outstanding and memorable of these charismatic* figures (for example, Isaiah, Jeremiah, Ezekiel, Hosea, and Amos)

Protestant Christianity, Protestantism—the sixteenth-century religious and theological* movement that began in Germany with Martin Luther* and spread quickly to Switzerland, England, and Scandinavia; it started as a critique (that is, "protest") of specific practices of the Roman Catholic Church*, soon questioned its fundamental claim to authority, and wound up causing a succession of schisms (splits) that produced the denominational* diversity that is so obvious in Christianity* today

Providence (adj. *Providential*)—the technical theological* term for the kind of ongoing divine activity that one expects in a theistic* religion

Pseudepigrapha (literally, in Greek, "false inscriptions")—(1) Jewish book written between 200 BCE* and 200 CE* that never made it into the Jewish canon* or the Apocrypha*; (2) canonical* and non-canonical* Christian* writings falsely claiming apostolic* authorship (for example, the six pseudo-Pauline* New Testament* letters)

Puritanism (adj. Puritan)—a type of radical Protestantism* that surfaced in sixteenth-century England as an effort to "purify" the Anglican* Church—which had separated from Rome for largely political rather than religious or spiritual* reasons—of its remaining Roman Catholic* ties and trappings; both in its homeland and later in the New England colonies, it was largely Calvinist* in its theology*

Q—(from the German *Quelle*, "source")—a hypothetical, yet well-attested, source (either oral or written) of Jesus' sayings posited to account for material common to Matthew and Luke in the writing of their gospels*, but not found in their (other) common source, Mark

Quakerism (adj. *Quaker*)—a Left-Wing Protestant* Christian* movement (later denomination*) also known as the Society of Friends, founded in England by a radical Puritan* named George Fox (1624–1691); a fundamentally mystical* expression, whose original focus was on the "inner light" of divinity within each person, its most distinctive features were its rejection of clergy, scripture, music, sacraments*, creeds*, and confessions, and its practice of silent worship

Qur'an or **Koran**—the holy canon* of Islam*, consisting of 114 *Surahs* (chapters) and based on the central theme of the mercy and compassion of *Allah**

rationalism (adj. *rationalistic*)—the recognition of reason, usually in conjunction with empirical* data, as the only source of true knowledge (an implicit rejection of revelation)

reconciliation—one of Paul's* many synonyms for "salvation,"* a metaphor that builds on the idea that sinful humanity is alienated or estranged from God

redemption—another of Paul's* many synonyms for "salvation,"* a metaphor drawn from slavery, from which one could be purchased and freed by a person with the disposition and resources to do so

Reformation (Period)—the era of Western and Christian* history that covers the sixteenth century CE* and perhaps a few years on either side (but ending no later than 1650), during which the Roman Catholic Church* undertook to reform itself from within at the same time that some—like Luther* and Calvin*—sought and effected such radical changes in theology and practice as to create Protestantism* and its many denominational* expressions

Reformed Protestantism—the type and tradition of Protestantism*—distinct from the Lutheran*—that originated in Switzerland, especially under sixteenth-century reformer John Calvin*, and produced a variety of churches* that used the name (for example, the Dutch Reformed Church); it is closely related historically to Scottish-English Presbyterianism, and is practically synonymous with "Calvinism"*

relativism (adj. *relativistic*)—the belief that there are no absolutes; that truth depends on one's viewpoint, background, upbringing, education, experience, reason, natural disposition, and so forth; with respect to good and evil*, it is the belief that there is no power behind or reality to either, and that they are basically (and merely) subjective value judgments

Renaissance (noun and adjective)—the era of Western history covering the better part of the fourteenth and fifteenth centuries CE*, noted for the rise of humanism*, a renewed appreciation for classical (especially Roman and Greek) sources and styles, and a burgeoning of the arts, literature, philosophy, music, and the early stirrings of what would become modern science and the modern scientific worldview*

Restoration Churches, Restoration Movement—first a movement—and, ironically, later a constellation of denominations*—that arose as a result of an urge on the part of several Protestant* church leaders in early nineteenth-century America to end denominationalism and restore Christianity* to its (alleged) primordial unity; the resulting denominations include Disciples of Christ and Churches of Christ (but not the United Church of Christ)

Revelation—the last book of the New Testament*, and the only example in the entire Christian* Bible* of a whole book in the apocalyptic* genre

Roman Catholicism (adj. *Catholic*)—arguably the oldest branch of Christianity*, tracing its origins back to the first Bishop of Rome, the Apostle* (and Saint) Peter; its most definitive feature (besides the Papacy itself) is its system of seven sacraments*

sacrament (adj., *sacramental*)—a Christian* ritual believed to convey the grace and blessing of God to the participant-recipient in an especially effective and objective way; the Roman Catholic Church* recognizes seven (communion, baptism, confirmation, penance, marriage, ordination, and anointing of the sick), while the Protestant* denominations* that retained the concept and practice generally acknowledge only the first two of these

salvation—the umbrella Christian* term for the amelioration of the human predicament of sin*, with a host of virtual synonyms, the most important being "atonement*," "justification*," "reconciliation*," and "redemption*"

samsara (Sanskrit)—in Hinduism*, (1) the nearly endless cycles of rebirth that an *atman** goes through on its way to *moksha**; and (2) the everyday world in which these cycles are lived out

sanctification (from the Latin *sanctus*, "holy" or "saint"; literally, "saint-making")—the ongoing process of spiritual growth that Christians are to experience after they have received God's grace*; it leads to the production of truly (as opposed to only seemingly) good works under the power of the Holy Spirit

Satan—(1) in early Hebrew thought, as reflected in the Hebrew Bible*, a very minor figure: a member of God's heavenly court whose job it is to test the faith or be an accuser of humans; (2) in later Jewish thought to some extent, and in Christianity* to a great extent—in both cases, probably as a result of the influence of Zoroastrianism*—a Power or Force of evil* and enemy of God, God's plans, and God's people (aka "the Devil")

sect (adj. *sectarian*)—(1) in Eastern religions, a smaller division of a larger branch (often called a "school") of a dominant religion (for example, Hinduism*, Buddhism*), regardless of the antiquity or size of the group in question; (2) in Christianity*, a smaller, newer, and somehow idiosyncratic branch, at least in comparison with the more established, sizable, and mainstream denominations*

Sectarian Christianity—the eclectic branch of Christianity* that comprises smaller, newer, and mostly home-grown American sects* and denominations*, ranging from Mormons* and Adventists* to Restoration*, Metaphysical*, and Pentecostal-Holiness* bodies

Septuagint (from the Latin for "the seventy," and often written LXX)—a third-century BCE* Greek translation of the *Tanakh**, so-called because it was completed by 70 (or 72) rabbis in 70 (or so) days; probably the Bible* used by at least some of the New Testament* writers

Shahadah—the basic creed and first of the Five Pillars of Islam*; it declares that "There is no god but Allah*, and Muhammad* is God's messenger"—a statement of radical monotheism*

Shema—the basic creed* of Judaism found in Deuteronomy 6:4 (and quoted by Jesus in Mark 12:29), which says "Hear, O Israel, the Lord your God, the Lord is one"— another clear statement of strict monotheism*

Shunyata (or ***Sunyata***, Sanskrit for "Emptiness" or "Nothingness")—Ultimate Reality* in Buddhist* philosophy, conceived in seemingly negative terms in order to (1) capture a sense of its utter mysteriousness; (2) underscore its total dissimilarity to existent beings and things; and (3) convey its role as the Infinitely Potential Source of all actualities (existing entities), which Itself (as Such) does not exist

sin—the root problem and human predicament for which Christianity* provides salvation* as a solution and cure; as a result of the influence of Paul* and Augustine*, traditional Christian* theology* has regarded sin as primarily an inherited *condition* that inevitably causes evil* acts, and only secondarily as the acts themselves (which are also called "sins")

situation ethics—a type of ethics popularized in the 1960s by Joseph Fletcher; it commends the application of broad principles (for example, Love) in specific circumstances rather than either obedience to set rules or concern about outcomes

soteriology (from the Greek *soter*, "to save")—(1) loosely, any view of salvation*; (2) more strictly, the area in formal Christian* theology* that addresses issues relating to salvation (for example, what it is, how it is or was accomplished, etc.)

spirituality (adj. *spiritual*)— the way in which one orients oneself toward Ultimate Reality*; broadly speaking, the two patterns of spirituality seen in the world's religions are (1) *relational*, which aims at a *communication* or *communion* with a transcendent* Other; and (2) *unitive*, which has as its goal total *absorption* into or *union* with an immanent* One

Stanton, Elizabeth Cady (1815–1902)—author of *The Women's Bible* (1895) and precursor of modern feminist biblical* studies and theology*

symbolist (or **symbolic**) **interpretation**—a type of interpretation that reads the book of Revelation* strictly as an early Christian* testimony that is rich in imagery about Christ*, and that can be used freely (but not literally) in modern worship and devotion

Synoptic Gospels, Synoptics—the canonical* gospels* of Matthew, Mark, and Luke, so-called because the profound, parallel similarities (due to Matthew's and Luke's use of Mark as a source) make them "look-alikes" when "viewed together"

Tanakh—the Hebrew Bible* (and Christian* "Old Testament"*), consisting of Law* or *Torah**, Prophets* or *Nevi'im*, and Writings* or *Khetubim*

Tao (Chinese, "Way," "Word," or "Idea")—an ancient Chinese concept, later adopted and adapted in very different ways by Confucianism and Taoism*; it refers to the Absolute and Undifferentiated Non-Personal One that is both the Source of the cosmos and the inner (immanent*) Force that motivates it, but in a most gentle, unobtrusive, and flowing way

Tao Te Ching—an ancient Chinese book of esoteric wisdom attributed to Lao Tse*; a cautious, poetic, and self-effacing description of the Ultimate Reality* as the Mysterious One that is immanent* in nature and human nature, it is the key scripture of Taoism*

Taoism—the ancient Chinese religion said to have been founded in the sixth century BCE* by Lao Tse* and based on the *Tao Te Ching* *; its basic principles are naturalness, non-assertiveness, simplicity—all expressing a fluent harmony with the *Tao**

theism (adj. *theistic*)—the theological* model that holds that God is transcendent* in the strong, ontological* sense (that is, that God's essence is fundamentally different from that of the universe and its contents) and immanent* in the weaker sense of being its Creator and *active* in its history in an ongoing way (see "Providence*"); theists—such as traditional Jews, Christians*, and Muslims*—are usually *monotheists**, claiming that only one such deity exists

theodicy—any effort to offer an explanation for evil* and suffering, especially among the apparently helpless and innocent, within the context of belief in an omniscient (all-knowing, including prescience or foreknowledge), omnipotent (all powerful), *and* omnibenevolent (thoroughly loving) God

theology (adj. *theological*; a person who does theology formally is a *theologian*, all from the Greek *theos*, "god," and *logos*, "word," "thought," or "reason")—(1) informally, any idea or statement concerning God or Ultimate Reality*; (2) more strictly, a formal intellectual discipline that engages such matters as the existence of God, the nature of God, and God's relevance to humanity in some kind of deep, intentional, and perhaps even systematic, philosophically-grounded way (though not *all* formal theologies are systematic or philosophical)

Theosophy—an eclectic American metaphysical* religion founded in the late nineteenth century by Madame Helena P. Blavatsky (1831–1891), blending elements of Christian* theology* with ideas drawn from Eastern philosophy—hence, "Theosophy"

Torah—the first five books of the Hebrew canon*, *Tanakh**, or "Old Testament*"; the most sacred of the three parts of the Jewish scriptures, its authorship had traditionally been attributed to Moses, though modern historical-critical* scholarship has identified at least four writers

traducianism—a theory of the origin of human souls entertained by Augustine* as a way of explaining congenital Original Sin*; it asserted that the human soul (and therefore any flaw in it) is somehow inherited from the parents

transcendence (adj., *transcendent*, when applied to God; *transcendental* or *transcendentalist*, when applied to an idea, theology*, or philosophy, all from a Latin verb meaning "to go beyond")—a word important in theology in two distinct senses, one strong and one weak: (1) *ontological* transcendence*, which is the divine quality of being prior to, above, beyond, and other than (or any combination of these) in such a way that the being or essence of the deity (or Ultimate) in question is clearly different from that of the universe and its constituents, so that "God is not the cosmos, world, or humanity and they certainly are not God."; and (2) *perceptual* or *conceptual transcendence*, which speaks more to human limitations than to the nature of God, holding that whatever God's own nature is (truly immanent* *or* transcendent), it is *beyond* the powers of human perception, conceptualization, and verbalization

Transcendentalism (adj. *Transcendentalist*, which is also used as the designation for a follower of this view)—an American spiritual and literary movement of the early nineteenth-century (most associated with New Englanders Henry David Thoreau and Ralph Waldo Emerson) that was closely related to Romanticism in the appreciation of intuition over reason, and—despite their name—their vision of a divinity of essential or ontological* *immanence** rather than transcendence*

Trinity—the term first coined by a third-century North African Christian* theologian* named Tertullian in order to account for the Father, Son, and Spirit all identified in the New Testament* with (or *as*) God; the concept eventually evolved into the official doctrine* that says that God is in three coeternal and coequal Persons, all joined in a single Godhead

Ultimate Reality—a generic term used in religious studies for the Supreme Spirit or Being in any system of monotheism* or monism*; within the religions, it will be known as "God," "Jahweh*," "Allah*," "Brahman*," and the like

unitarianism—the belief that God is one, and thus generally a rejection of the orthodox Christian* doctrine of the Trinity*

Unitarian-Universalism—a religious denomination* resulting from a 1961 merger of two older groups, both with roots in Christianity*; perhaps the most liberal* and free-thinking of all modern religious groups, its members represent a wide spectrum of religious belief (and disbelief) from atheistic* humanism* to Liberal Christian* theism; but that very diversity, along with the studied lack of doctrinal* precision and certitude that it reflects, often alienates its members from traditional Christianity and mainline churches*

universalism—the idea, found in some religions as the majority position and others as a minority view, that whatever salvation* is conceived to be, everyone gets it sooner or later; the notion is invariably grounded in the thoroughgoing love, mercy, and grace* of God, which simply could not permit any to perish or be otherwise punished or lost forever

Upanishads—a collection of ancient Hindu* philosophical writings antedated only by the venerable *Vedas*, to which they are sometimes considered appendices and called "*Vedanta*" (the *Vedas*' end); the main theme is the proper relation between—indeed, the unity of—*atman** and *Brahman**

verbal inspiration—the idea, promoted with varying degrees of rigor and vigor among Christian* Fundamentalists* and Evangelicals*, that God authored every word of the Bible*, employing the named and unnamed authors as scribes or channels

Wisdom—(1) in ancient Jewish thought, the divine power or principle, depicted as feminine in Proverbs, by which God effected Creation; (2) the body of literature within the Writings* of the Hebrew Bible* that addresses or expresses this idea, especially, Proverbs, Ecclesiastes, and Job

Word of God—(1) the Logos* featured in John 1:1–4 and prominent in many ancient Greek philosophies; (2) Jesus Christ as the Incarnation* of the Logos; (3) any divine revelation; (4) the Christian Bible as a whole or the specific divine revelation couched therein; and (5) the Christian gospel* or the proclamation of it

works righteousness—the attempt to be or become good by doing good things; Paul* declared it ineffective because the condition of sin* rendered humans in their "fallen" state incapable of doing good

worldview—the way people of any society or culture of any era implicitly agree on what reality is and how it works; the overall perspective from which individuals or cultures understand the universe and its life

Writings (Hebrew, *Khetubim*)—the third traditional division of the Hebrew Bible* or *Tanakh**, including Job, Psalms, Proverbs, Ecclesiastes, Song of Solomon and other important writings (See figure 1.3 in chapter 1)

yoga (Sanskrit, "to yoke")—(1) any one of a number (usually three or four) of spiritual disciplines recognized in Hinduism* as effective in making the crucial (and inevitable) connection between one's *atman** and *Brahman**—also sometimes called a *marga* (path); or (2) a specifically physical practice or technique associated with *hatha* (that is, bodily exertion) *yoga*

Zoroastrianism (adj. *Zoroastrian*, which is also the designation for a follower)—the ancient religion founded in Persia, probably around the seventh century BCE* by the prophet Zoroaster (or Zarathustra), who introduced into the polytheistic* cultural milieu of that time and place a monotheism* that focused on the good God, Ahura Mazda, but that nonetheless posited a formidable power of evil* called Ahriman or Satan*, which the good God would eventually have to defeat in a great endtime battle just before a resurrection and last judgment of the dead

INDEX

Acts (of the Apostles) 21,
23–24, 118, 223
Adam 149–155, 156,
159–160, 173, 178, 239
Adventists 209, 211, 213,
220, 222
agape (love) 190
agnosticism 41, 48
Amendment, First 219–220
Amish 211–212
Anabaptist(s) 111, 206
Ancient Period 110–112,
117–120
Anglican/Anglicanism 111,
211, 215, 218, 219
apocalyptic 19, 24, 96, 101
Apocrypha 18
Apologists 119
apostle 20–21
Apostles' Creed 98–99, 124,
195
Apostolic Succession 111,
119
Aquinas, St. Thomas 187
Arminius, Jacobus 164, 231
Assemblies of God 211, 213
atonement/Atonement 45,
118, 173, 176–180, 242
atheism 41, 49
Augustine of Hippo, St. 111,
141, 155–156, 158–167,
186, 197, 223, 231–232
autographs 27–28
Bacon, Francis 115–116, 232
Baptists 206, 211, 212, 213,
215, 225, 237, 249
Barth, Karl 111, 187
Bethlehem 81–82
Bhagavad Gita 68, 183
Bible 11–36, 114, 116, 155,
193, 242
  - feminist interpretation of
  65–68, 243
  - higher criticism of 15–16
  - history of 25–32
  - inspiration & authority of
  14–15, 32–36
  - nature of 11–16
  - structure of 16–25
Body of Christ 204–205, 216,
223
Borg, Marcus 56
Buddha, Buddhism,
Buddhist(s) 70, 79, 84, 141,
153, 187, 197, 209, 216,
240, 245, 247, 249–250
Calvin, John 111, 184, 185,
232, 236

Calvinism/Calvinist 192, 218
canon/canonization 17,
30–32
Chalcedon, Council of 120,
126
Charismatic 189–190, 204
Chauncy, Charles 164
Christ/christos/Christ of faith
95–96, 109–110, 112,
117–136, 177–179, 188,
189, 198, 203, 242, 247
Christian Science/Scientist
209, 211, 213, 220, 241
Christianity, history of
110–120
Christology/Christological
109, 111, 117, 121–122,
125–127, 130–131, 133,
135, 247
church/Church 68, 93, 101,
109–117, 120, 121, 125,
162–163, 195, 198,
201–225, 240
  - functions of 206–207
  - marks of 207–208
  - role and status of women
  in 207–208
Church of England (see
Anglican/Anglicanism)
church-state relations
217–221
Church of Jesus Christ of
Latter Day Saints (Mormons)
209, 211, 213, 220
Churches of Christ 213–214
Churches of God 213
Clement of Alexandria 239
concupiscence 159
congregational/Congregation-
alists 211, 212, 218
consequentialist ethics 193
Constantine 111, 112,
119–120, 205, 218
Coptic 126
Creation/Creator 12, 45, 51,
148, 150
Creation Spirituality
242–244
cross 176, 178, 236, 242
crucifixion 25, 96–98, 133
Crusades 111
cult 117, 204, 209–210, 213,
242
Darwin, Charles 116
Death of God Theology
242–243

deism 44, 49–52, 56–57
denomination 109, 111, 125,
209–210, 213–215, 237
Devil 48, 148, 149
Disciples of Christ 213, 214,
236
Divine Science 242
Docetism/Docetists 126
domain (reign, rule, kingdom) of God 85, 86, 91–93,
96, 124
Eastern Orthodoxy 17–18,
111, 157, 210–212, 239
Eastern religions 52, 53–54,
85, 134–135, 197, 231,
243–244, 245–250, 250–252
Ebionites 126
Eckhart, Meister 52, 240,
245, 246, 248
Eddy, Mary Baker 241
Eden, Garden of 149–155,
175
Edict of Milan/Toleration
119, 120
Edwards, Jonathan 164, 185,
232
ekklesia 203
Elohim 46
Emerson, Ralph Waldo 43
Empiricism 50, 232
Enlightenment (The) 50,
111, 115, 232–234, 251,
232–234, 251
Episcopal/Episcopalians 208,
211, 215, 236
epistles 21, 24, 118, 243
Erasmus 111, 164, 231
Essenes 78
Establishment/established
religion 218
eternal life 194–197
ethics 171, 191–194
Ethnic Christianity 117,
210–211
Evangelical/Evangelicalism
180, 181, 220, 242
Eve 48, 149–155, 173
evil 57, 60–65, 159
  - theories of 143–149
expiation 173, 179–180
faith 180–182, 238
Fall 142–143, 149–155, 160,
239
Fox, George 240
Fox, Matthew 56, 243–244

I

Francis of Assisi (St.) 240
free will (see will, freedom of)
Fundamentalism/Fundamentalist(noun)/fundamentalist (adj.) 29, 32, 33–34, 90, 111, 116–117, 101, 116, 141, 162, 208, 221, 233, 242
futurist interpretation 221–222
Galilee/Galilean(s) 77–78, 87
Garden of Eden (see Eden, Garden of)
gender 65–68
gifts (of the Spirit) 189–190
glossolalia 190, 213
Gnostic(s)/Gnosticism 111, 126, 133–134, 191, 238–239, 242, 244
God 41–70 (et passim)
 - feminine images for 66–67
 - omnibenevolence omnipotence, omniscience of 61–65
 - the Father 125–126, 247
 - the Holy Spirit 42, 125, 171, 176, 189–192, 197, 203, 206
 - the Son 125–126
gospel 119, 125, 173
gospels
 - canonical 12–14, 20–23, 76–77, 119, 121, 134
 - Gospel of John 12, 13, 22, 28, 76, 79, 81, 87, 88, 97, 102, 121–122, 130, 134, 183, 247
 - Gospel of Thomas 133, 238
 - Infancy Gospel of Thomas 83
 - Synoptic Gospels (Mark, Matthew, and Luke) 12–14, 22, 76, 79, 80–83, 86–94, 97, 99, 100, 101, 121–122
grace 143, 171, 173–189
Great Schism 211
Ground of Being 242
heaven 194
Hebrew Bible/Hebrew Scriptures/Tanakh/Old Testament 12, 15, 16, 17–20, 30–31, 48, 61, 66, 95, 146, 148, 154, 185, 191
hell 139, 165–166, 195
henotheism/henotheistic 43, 46

heresy 111, 235–236
Hildegard of Bingen 240, 245
Hindu/Hinduism 52, 53, 61, 70, 79, 84, 85, 135, 141, 197, 216, 240, 246, 247, 248–250
Historical Jesus (see Jesus)
historical-critical method 15–16, 233
Holiness (see Pentecostal-Holiness)
Holy Roman Empire 218
humanism 111
Hume, Thomas 116
Huxley, Aldous 244
image of God (imago dei) 141–142, 154, 241
immanence and transcendence 41–48, 51, 58–59, 134–135, 239, 245–246, 247, 250
imputation 188
Incarnation 45–46, 47, 176, 247
Inquisition 111
Irenaeus (St.) 162, 243
Islam (Muslim faith) 41, 43, 45, 46–48, 53, 66, 79, 112, 155, 209, 239, 244, 251
Jahweh (Jehovah) 85, 146, 154
Jahwist author 154
Jefferson, Thomas 50, 52, 219
Jehovah's Witnesses 210, 213, 220, 222
Jesus/Jeshua (Yeshua) 11, 75–103, 117, 129–131, 171, 176, 180–183, 198, 231, 236, 238, 242, 247
 - birth of 25
 - last days of 96–98
 - lost years of 83–84, 86, 112
 - ministry and message of 86–93
 - of history/the historical Jesus 75–103, 121, 130
 - resurrection of 98–100
 - sayings of 85
 - self-image/titles of 93–96
Job 147–148
John the Baptizer 86–89
Judea/Judeans 87
Judaism/Jews/Jewish 41, 43, 45, 46–48, 53, 64, 66, 146, 148, 155, 194–195, 239, 244, 248, 251

justification/justify/justified 173, 175, 179, 188, 190, 213
King James Version (KJV) 26, 29–30, 85, 90
Lao Tse 183, 247
Law (The)/Torah 18, 175, 192
Liberalism/liberal or Liberal (noun)/liberal (adj.) 34–36, 111, 116, 165, 167, 198, 231–238, 250–251
Locke, John 116, 232
Logos 127
Lord 96, 109, 121, 182
Luther, Martin 111, 114, 164, 222, 232, 236
Lutheran 211, 215, 236
Marcion 31, 191
Mary (Miriam)/Virgin Mary 77, 80, 81, 82, 83, 124, 210
Mary Magdalene 80, 84, 99
Mechtild of Magdeburg 240
Medieval Period/Middle Ages 110–111, 112–113, 191, 240
Mennonites 211
Messiah 78, 83, 95, 121, 203, 224
metaphorical interpretation 68–69
metaphysical religion 241–242
Methodists (see United Methodist Church)
Middle Ages (see Medieval Period)
missions 216–217
Missouri Synod Lutherans 214
Modern Period 110–111, 115–117
modern science/scientific worldview 115–116
monism/monistic 49, 52–54, 56, 133–135, 231, 242, 246, 248, 252
monotheism/monotheistic 46–49, 57, 60
moral theory 179
Mormons (see Church of Jesus Christ of Latter Day Saints)
Moses 50
Muhammad 79, 183
Muslim(s) 141, 148, 218, 248
mysticism/mystics/mystical 69, 111, 231, 239–240, 244, 245, 248, 250

myth/mythical 132, 149–150, 154
Nazarenes 213
Nazareth 81–82
nephesh 194
New Age Religion/New Alternative Spirituality 245
New Testament 14, 20–22, 25, 26, 28, 31–32, 45, 48, 75, 76–77, 79, 80, 83, 91, 92, 94, 101, 102, 127, 183, 185, 203
New Thought 211, 241–242
Newton, Sir Isaac 232
Nicea, Council of 120, 127
Nicene Creed 98, 99, 124, 195, 205
Old Testament (see Hebrew Bible)
oral tradition 26–27
Origen 162, 163, 239
Original Sin 45, 139, 158–160, 239
orthodox/orthodoxy (Western) 23
pantheism/pantheist 44, 49, 52–54, 55, 58–59, 133, 243, 246, 252
panentheism/panentheist 54–56, 59, 252
Papacy, The 112, 205
parables, Parables (The) 88
parousia 119, 221 (see also Second Coming)
Paul of Tarsus (St.) 25, 76, 80, 93, 95, 100, 111, 118, 120–125, 141, 155–167, 173–198, 204, 207–208, 231
Pauline epistles 21, 24, 243
Pelagius/Pelagianism 160–161, 163, 231
Pentecost 223
Pentecostal-Holiness 211, 213–214, 215
Perennial Philosophy, The 244
Peter (St.) 102, 183, 203, 205, 210
Pharisees 78, 194
polytheism 43, 46
Pope/Papacy 112, 205, 218
praeterist interpretation 223–224
Predestination 184–188
Presbyterians 188, 208, 212, 225, 236

prevenient grace 182
process theology 54–56
prophet, Prophets (The) 18
Protestant/Protestantism 17–18, 111, 114, 146, 156, 163, 192, 210, 236, 239
Providence 45, 51, 116, 232
Pseudepigrapha 31, 238
Puritan/Puritanism 191, 212, 218
Q (Quelle) Source – 26
Quaker/Quakerism 69, 206, 211, 212, 218, 240–241
Qur'an 68, 79, 183
Rabbi 94, 120
rationalism 50, 232
reconciliation 173, 176, 179
redemption 173, 179
Reformation (see Renaissance-Reformation)
Reformed Protestantism 188, 215
relativism 143, 145–146, 148, 193
Religious Science 242
Renaissance-Reformation 110–111, 113–115, 222
Restoration Churches 211, 213, 214
Resurrection (The) 98–100, 132
resurrection of the body/dead 194–197
Revelation (Book of) 19, 24–25, 102, 221–224
righteous/righteousness 173, 178, 188, 189
Roman Catholicism 17–18, 113, 156, 163, 180, 187, 203, 208, 210–212, 215, 220, 236, 239, 240, 249
Russell, Charles Taze
sacrament/sacramental 206, 212–213, 214–215, 240
salvation 171, 173–179, 213
sanctification 171, 189–191
Satan 46–47, 60, 146–148, 150–153
Savior 96
Science of Mind 242
Scientology 241, 245
Second Coming of Christ 205, 221–224 (see also *parousia*)
sect 109, 209–210, 213

Sectarian Christianity 210, 212–213
separation of church and state 219–221
Septuagint 18, 30–31, 79
serpent 150–153
Shema 47–48
Sheol 195
Shahada 47–48
sin 149, 152–167, 173
Son of God 95, 109, 125
Son of Man 94–95, 100
soul 194–197
Spinoza, Baruch (Benedict) 52
Tanakh (see Hebrew Bible)
Tao/Tao Te Ching /Taoism/Taoist 43, 52, 68, 70, 79, 85, 183, 197, 246, 250–251
Teilhard de Chardin, Pierre 242, 243
Teleological ethics 193
Theism/theistic model 43–49, 51, 239, 242, 247
theodicy 57, 60–65, 153
theology 41–70, 112
Theosophy 241
Thomas, Gospel of (see gospel)
Thomas Didymos 83
Thoreau, Henry David 43
Tillich, Paul 242
Torah (see Law)
traducianism 159
transcendence (see immanence and transcendence)
Transcendentalism/Transcendentalists 42, 43, 241
Trent, Council of 111, 114
Trinity/Trinitarian 45, 47, 119, 125, 237
Unitarian-Universalists 186, 237
United Church of Christ 211, 212, 215, 216, 236
United Methodist Church 208, 212, 213, 215, 216, 225, 236
Unity/Unity Scool of practical Christianity 242
universalism 186–187
Virgin Birth, virginal birth 78–81, 132
Wesley, John 164, 231, 236
will, freedom of/free will 65, 159–160
Writings, The (*Khetuvim*) 19–20
Zoroastrianism 148–149, 196

I

Index

The End